INTERMEDIATE

Language LEADER

TEACHER'S BOOK and Test Master CD-ROM

David Albery

CONTENTS

To the teacher: introduction by the authors

We are pleased to welcome you to this new course: *Language Leader.* In this introduction we outline some of our ideas about the course. We have done our very best to write a series of books that teachers (and students!) will enjoy using, and we very much hope that, although we may be physically far apart, we share with you – as teachers – a common set of beliefs and practices, and a common sense of purpose.

Approach

Language Leader is an international course with a global focus, and is aimed at citizens of the 21st century world – people who cross (and communicate across) national borders. We believe that students are curious about the modern world, and that this course engages with it. *Language Leader* enables students to be better informed and helps them understand and express their ideas and feelings about the world.

We believe it is important to offer students stimulating topics that engage their interest and increase their motivation for learning. We have made use of our diverse backgrounds, personalities and interests as authors, in the hope of providing students with a rich variety of different topics. Each unit contains an 'umbrella topic' with a different subtopic in each lesson, allowing us to explore a range of issues within a single topic and also to recycle vocabulary. We think that the approach to the topics in the course will challenge students and allow them to develop their powers of expression and analysis and their critical thinking skills. *Language Leader* reflects our belief that language learning is not merely a form of training, but should be situated in a broader educational context. We hope that students who use the series will not only learn English, but – through English – will also learn interesting things about the world and about themselves. Perhaps, sometimes, they may not even be aware that they are actually learning English!

Language Leader is not based on one particular teaching 'philosophy' or methodology, but is informed by sound pedagogical principles, plus an intuitive sense – the result of many years' experience – of what works in the classroom. Having said this, we use a broadly communicative methodology and a text and task-based approach. Pair and group work is an important part of the learning process. The Common European Framework has informed many of the speaking activities.

Language development

Throughout the units, there is careful development and logical staging of new language, as well as substantial recycling of previous language, enabling students to move forward rapidly. The Review, Language Reference and Extra Practice sections consolidate and extend students' learning.

The texts in *Language Leader* not only provide context for grammar and vocabulary but systematically develop students' reading and listening skills. The reading texts are authentic or semi-authentic, or at lower levels based on real sources, and are taken from a variety of genres (for example, newspapers, magazines, literature and publicity materials). Listening skills are also developed throughout the course. Each unit has a number of listening activities and there is a wide variety of different listening texts (for example, radio programmes, conversations, interviews, talks and lectures), as well as a varied range of activity types.

There is considerable variety in the length of these reading and listening texts: some are relatively short, but *Language Leader* also offers students an opportunity to deal – in a supported way – with some longer texts. Students who suddenly find themselves in an English-speaking environment – whether in their home country or abroad – often have difficulty with the large quantities of spoken and written English that they are exposed to. This course helps them to build up their confidence in handling extended amounts of English. In addition, many of the reading and listening exercises are based on exam-type questions.

There are constant opportunities throughout the course for students to improve their speaking skills, with speaking exercises in every unit. Students can comment on the topics and discuss the issues that arise, as well as talk about more personal experiences and knowledge, through a variety of exercises, such as information gaps, personalised question and answer activities, role plays and debates.

The Scenario lessons are, we believe, an important communicative feature of *Language Leader.* Every unit includes a Scenario lesson, devoted to extended speaking practice in a real-life situation. Information has to be processed – and decisions made – leading to a specific outcome. Students are given language support to carry out the task.

The course covers all the key grammar points. These points are all contextualised and students are generally encouraged to analyse and understand grammar through an inductive approach with reference to examples in the texts. The grammar is practised in motivating and interesting activities. The Language reference and Extra practice section at the back of the book extends students' knowledge of grammar and provides essential further practice. It can be used in the class or for independent study at home.

Lack of vocabulary is one of the main problems many students face. Consequently, students struggle to make sense of texts and express themselves. They need more words. To address this, *Language Leader* has a wide range of vocabulary, and students are able to acquire and use this vocabulary through contextualisation and recycling.

Writing skills and study skills

Writing in English has become increasingly important, but is often students' weakest skill and something that they don't really enjoy. Even with very able students, it often drags down their scores in examinations in which they would otherwise do well. We consider, however, that writing is also a skill in which – with a little help – students can make significant progress. *Language*

Leader has a page in every unit that is devoted to the development of writing skills, and there are also further writing activities throughout the course. Because of the systematic approach to the development of writing skills in the course, students should be able to make real progress in their writing, and derive great satisfaction from this. Again, there is wide variety in the length and type of tasks. We place considerable emphasis, even at the lower levels, on discourse features of written English, with frequent analysis of text models and plenty of writing practice at both paragraph and text level. In addition, we have included activities designed to encourage students to be rigorous in checking their own writing.

Each unit also includes a Study skills page, which aims to encourage students to be independent learners with a high level of self-awareness. The skills that we cover in this section are not just for students who are on educational courses in schools, colleges and universities; they are also transferable skills which will be useful to students in many different contexts, including their careers and personal lives.

Flexibility

Of course, we hope that you will use every page in the book! But the *Language Leader* format deliberately lends itself to different teaching situations and can be adapted easily depending on the length and type of course you are teaching.

To conclude, we trust that you and your students will find *Language Leader* interesting, motivating and enjoyable. We also hope that it will meet your students' needs as well as providing something new. We welcome your comments on the course and hope to have the pleasure of meeting you in the future!

David Cotton, David Falvey, Simon Kent (Intermediate and Upper Intermediate)
Gareth Rees, Ian Lebeau (Elementary and Pre-intermediate)

Language Leader: course description

Language Leader is a general English series for adults and young adults. The course has a topic-based multi-strand syllabus which includes comprehensive work on grammar, vocabulary, pronunciation and integrated skills, where strong emphasis is placed on reading, writing and study skills as well as speaking and listening. With its purposeful approach *Language Leader* is particularly suitable for general English students working towards exams, and those learners who may go on to, or are already in, further education.

Language Leader has four levels and takes learners from Elementary to Upper Intermediate; each level offers 90 – 120 hours of work.

Coursebook

The twelve Coursebook units are divided into double-page lessons, each with a clear aim, which are designed to make the course flexible and easy-to-use.

- **Introduction lesson:** in *Language Leader Intermediate* the first spread is where the unit topic is presented with core vocabulary and lexis through reading and listening texts, and where students discuss some of the themes of the unit and activate any previous knowledge and vocabulary.
- **Input lessons:** there are two input lessons in each unit. Here, new language is presented through informative texts with a balanced mix of grammar, vocabulary, pronunciation and skills work.
- **Scenario:** in the fourth lesson, learners integrate and practise the language presented in the previous lessons through a communicative task. This major speaking activity is carefully staged; the Key language section gives extra support by developing functional exponents and the Other useful phrases boxes provide helpful fixed phrases.
- **Study and Writing Skills:** the fifth lesson consists of a Study skills section, followed by Writing skills, which helps students to write a particular text type.

Language Leader Coursebook also features the following:

- **Review:** the Review spreads occur after every three units; these provide mixed practice for ongoing revision. The Language check section is a quick self-edit exercise and Look back encourages reflection on the previous units.
- **Language reference/ Extra practice:** this section consists of one cross-referenced spread for each unit. The left-hand page includes a grammar summary for the unit, plus reference lists for Key language and Vocabulary. The right-hand page provides extra practice for consolidation.

CD-ROM

- This component is attached to the back of the Coursebook.
- It provides extra practice and self-assessment for the learners with a variety of exercises, including listening. With the help of the Language Reference and the Dictionary, the CD-ROM helps learners develop their learning skills. The unique Writing section includes models for different writing tasks from everyday notes to academic essays.

Class CDs

- These provide all the recorded material from the Coursebook.

Workbook

- This contains further practice of areas covered in the corresponding units of the Coursebook and introduces Extra vocabulary to build lexis in the topic area.
- To help the development of language skills, useful strategies are introduced through Read better and Listen better boxes.
- In each unit there is a Translation exercise for students to compare English with their L1, and Dictation exercises provide more listening and writing.

Workbook CD

- Attached to the back of the Workbook, the CD contains all the recorded material for extra practice.

Teacher's Book

- This provides all the support teachers need from detailed teaching notes to extra photocopiable activities.
- There are **warning points** to alert teachers about possible problem areas as well as **teaching tips** to help them. Taking into account teachers' busy schedules, the Teacher's Book notes are designed as lesson plans, with ideas for **extension** and **adjustment**, which are especially useful for mixed ability groups.

warning points **extension**

teaching tips **adjustment**

Test Master CD-ROM

- Attached to the back of the Teacher's Book, the Test Master CD-ROM is an invaluable resource to accompany *Language Leader*. The tests are based strictly on the content of the Coursebooks, providing a fair measure of students' progress.
- The audio files for the listening tests are conveniently located on the same CD-ROM.
- The tests can be printed out and used as they are, or can be adapted using Microsoft® Word to edit them to suit different teaching situations.
- The Test Master CD-ROM contains the following:
  - Placement Test (to identify levels)
  - Unit Tests (one 'A' and one 'B' test for each unit)
  - Progress Tests (one 'A' and one 'B' test for every three units plus additional optional speaking and writing tests)
  - Final Test (one 'A' and one 'B' version)

Syllabus areas

- **Topics:** to motivate learners the units are based on up-to-date topics of international interest or new angles on familiar subjects. Themes have been carefully chosen to engage the learners and to provide a springboard for their own ideas and communicative needs.
- **Grammar:** *Language Leader* follows an established syllabus progression and learners are actively involved in developing their knowledge of grammar. The Grammar sections in the input lessons focus on the main language points presented through the texts and learners are encouraged to work out the rules for themselves. They are supported by the Grammar tip boxes and cross-referred to the corresponding Language reference and Extra practice pages at the back of the book for reinforcement.
- **Vocabulary**: vocabulary input is derived from the unit topics and texts, allowing the teacher to build on words and phrases the students already know to create lexical sets. Additional attention is paid to word building and lexical patterns. The vocabulary is recycled through the speaking activities in each unit, revised in the Review lesson and Extra practice and practised further in the Workbook.
- **Pronunciation**: regular pronunciation sections are integrated with the presentation of new language or included on the Scenario spread as part of the communicative task. The pronunciation syllabus covers word and sentence stress, difficult sounds, contractions and intonation.
- **Reading**: there is a wide range of reading material in *Language Leader* and a variety of exercise types developing the reading skills. The informative texts have been chosen for their interest and to provide a context for the grammar and vocabulary items being studied. The texts are based on real-life sources (magazines, websites, etc) and related activities include comprehension, vocabulary and reading sub-skills work.
- **Listening**: students are given many opportunities to develop a wide range of listening skills in *Language Leader,* both in terms of text types and activity types (e.g. checking predictions, table and note-completion). There is more listening practice in the Workbooks and CD-ROMs to further build the learners' confidence.
- **Speaking**: opportunities for oral practice of language and freer discussion appear regularly in every lesson. There is at least one explicit speaking activity per lesson and a major communicative task in the Scenario lesson.
- **Writing**: the writing syllabus introduces students to different genres and develops students' writing through analysis of models and practice in producing different text styles.
- **Study skills**: a systematic approach to developing study skills fosters independent dictionary use, encourages students to take notes effectively and gives them help in approaching exams and learning outside the classroom.

External organisations and link to examinations

- **Common European Framework of Reference:** the ethos of the CEFR is reflected throughout *Language Leader* in a variety of ways. For example, the outcomes of the Scenario lessons reflect the 'Can do' descriptors and help students use the language they have learnt effectively. Also, great emphasis is placed on the development of independent learning across the course including the extensive work on study skills, good study habits and self-assessment. For more information on *Language Leader* and the CEFR see the website www.pearsonlongman.com/languageleader.
- **Bologna Process**: as part of this initiative to harmonise tertiary education, many institutions now offer credit-bearing English language programmes. *Language Leader* reflects the values of the Bologna Process with its emphasis on individual responsibility for learning.
- **Link to examinations**: ELT examination exercise-types occur regularly throughout *Language Leader* to help prepare students for a range of common exams (IELTS in particular). The website provides grids correlating *Language Leader* to international ELT exams.

How a unit works (Intermediate)

Introduction lesson

The contents of each unit are clearly labelled at the top of the opening page.

Stimulating topic-related quotation to engage learners.

Vocabulary exercises present and practise topic-specific lexis.

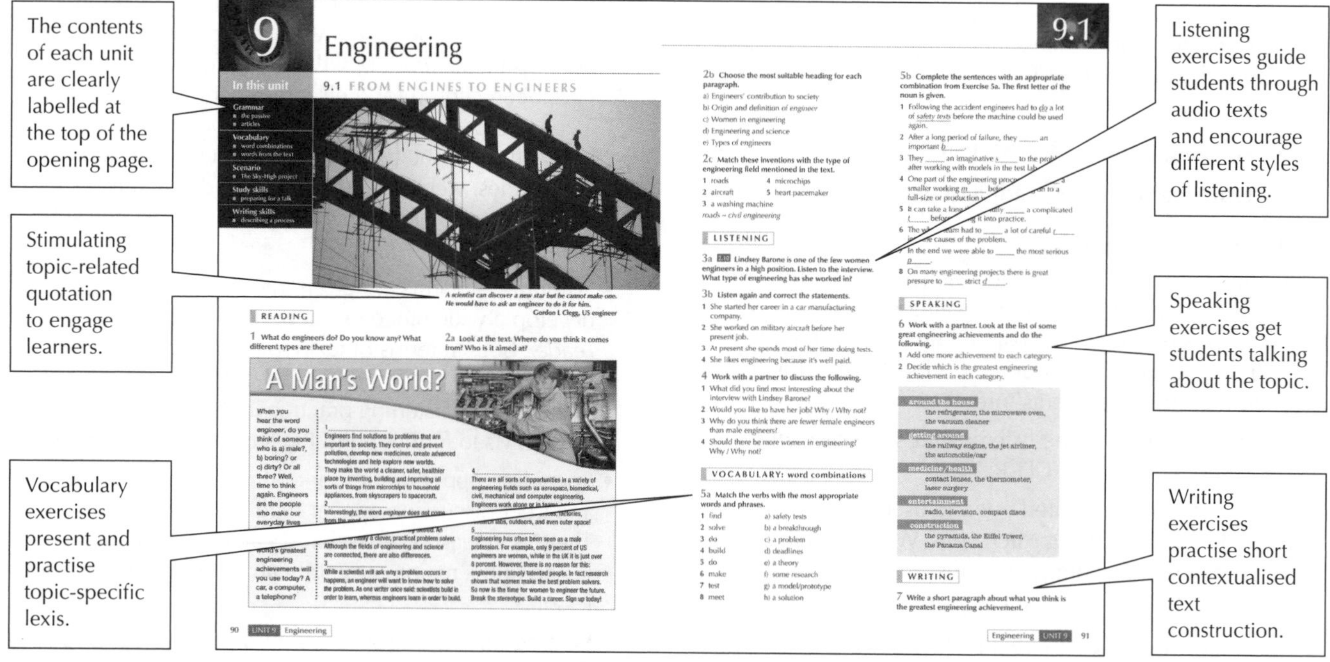

Listening exercises guide students through audio texts and encourage different styles of listening.

Speaking exercises get students talking about the topic.

Writing exercises practise short contextualised text construction.

Input lesson (1)

The informative reading text provides a context for the language and vocabulary being studied.

Reading exercises aid comprehension of the text and develop skills.

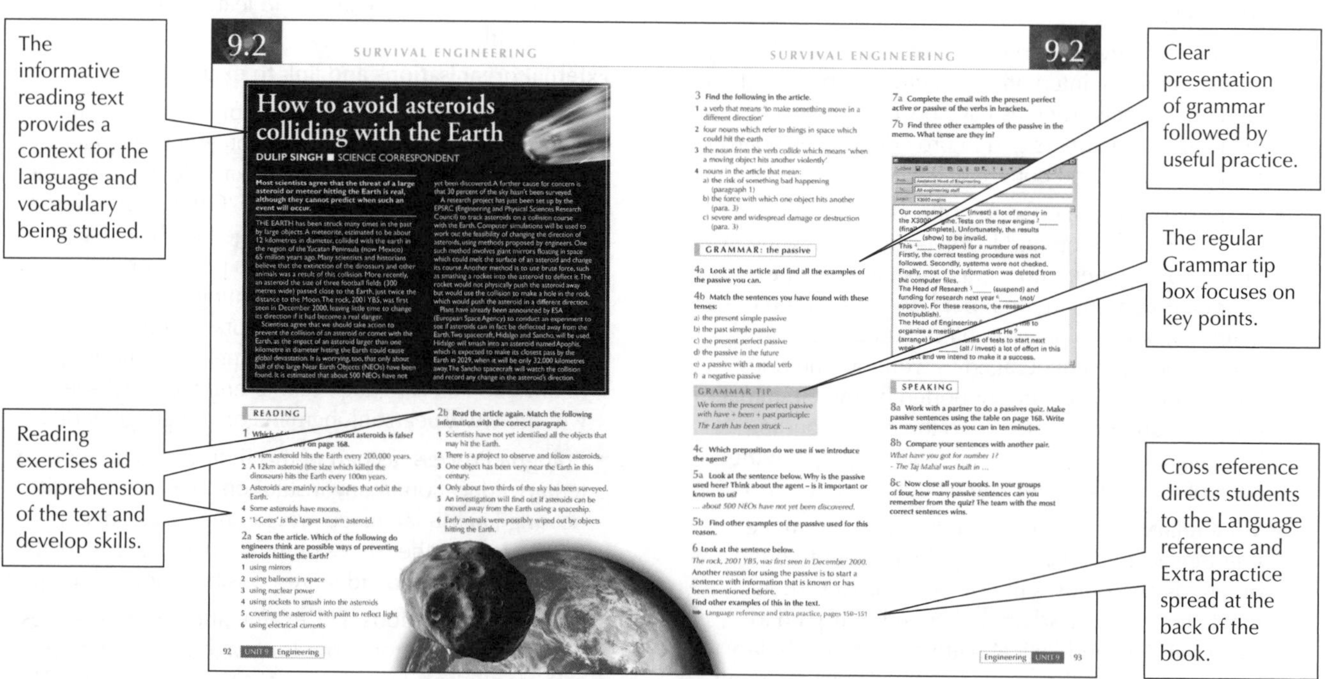

Clear presentation of grammar followed by useful practice.

The regular Grammar tip box focuses on key points.

Cross reference directs students to the Language reference and Extra practice spread at the back of the book.

Input lesson (2)

Concept-check questions encourage students to work out the grammar rules themselves.

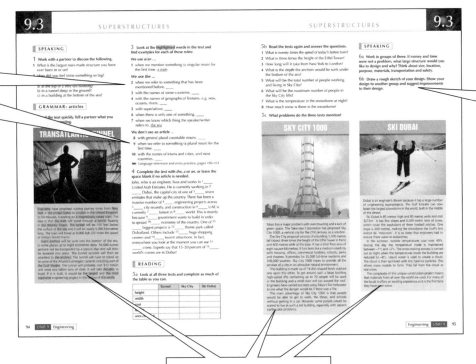

Speaking exercises personalise the language and encourage communication.

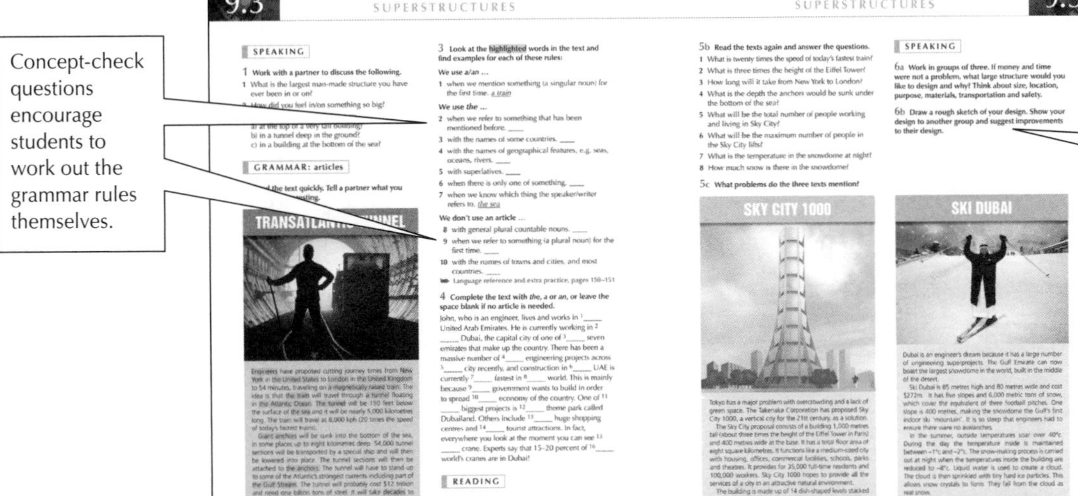

Interesting, real-life texts provide models for the new structure.

Scenario

Scenario lessons practise Key language from the unit through a meaningful final task.

The situation sets up the background information.

Students are given preparation for the task through different activities.

The Key language of the lesson is presented and practised.

The clear, well-structured communicative Task enables students to practise language in a meaningful context.

The regular Other useful phrases boxes provide extra help for students to carry out the task.

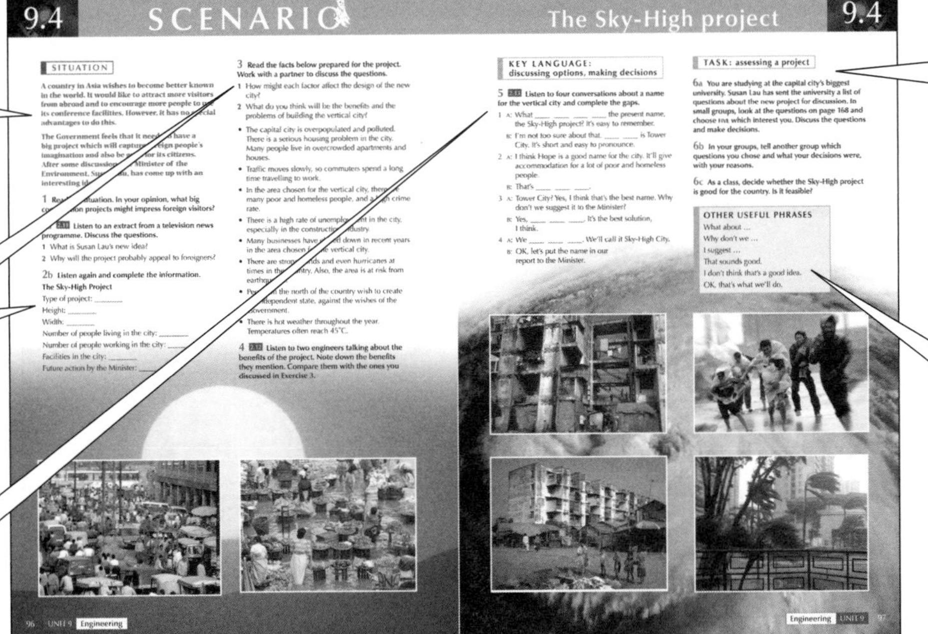

Study and writing skills

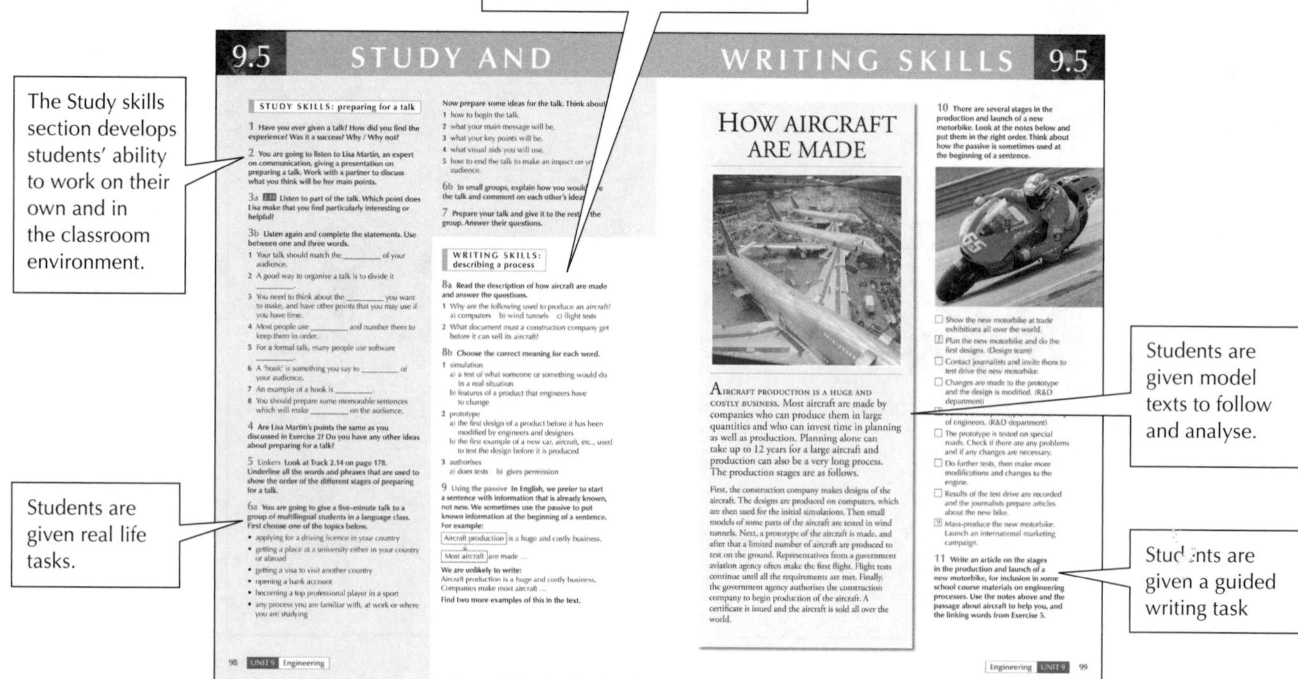
Writing Skills focus on a different genre of writing in each unit.
The Study skills section develops students' ability to work on their own and in the classroom environment.
Students are given real life tasks.
Students are given model texts to follow and analyse.
Students are given a guided writing task
9.5 STUDY AND WRITING SKILLS 9.5
STUDY SKILLS: preparing for a talk
WRITING SKILLS: describing a process
HOW AIRCRAFT ARE MADE

Other sections

Review

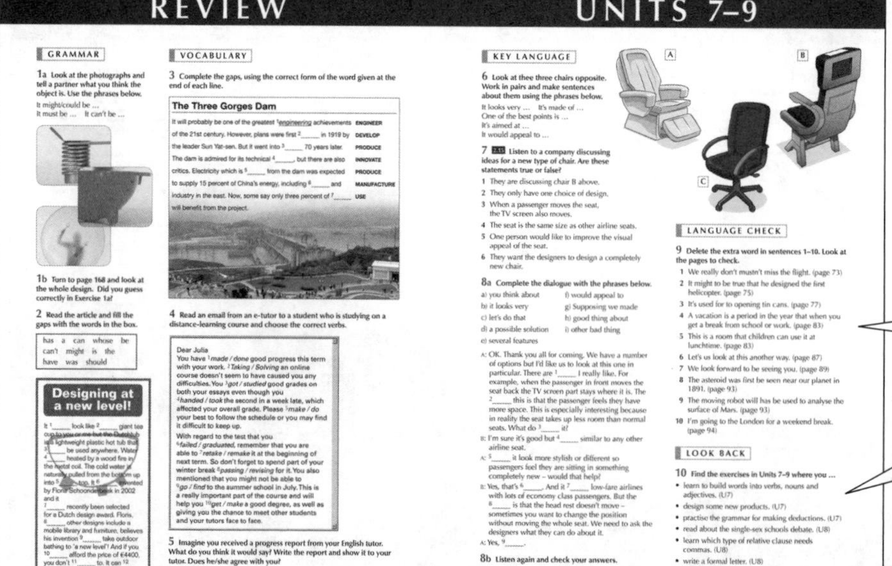
Review lessons occur after every three units; they revise and consolidate the Grammar, Vocabulary and Key language from the previous units.
Students are encouraged to check and comment on their own learning, and reflect on what they have learned.
REVIEW UNITS 7–9
GRAMMAR
VOCABULARY
The Three Gorges Dam
Designing at a new level!
KEY LANGUAGE
LANGUAGE CHECK
LOOK BACK

Language reference / Extra practice

There is one Language reference and Extra practice spread for each unit at the back of the book.

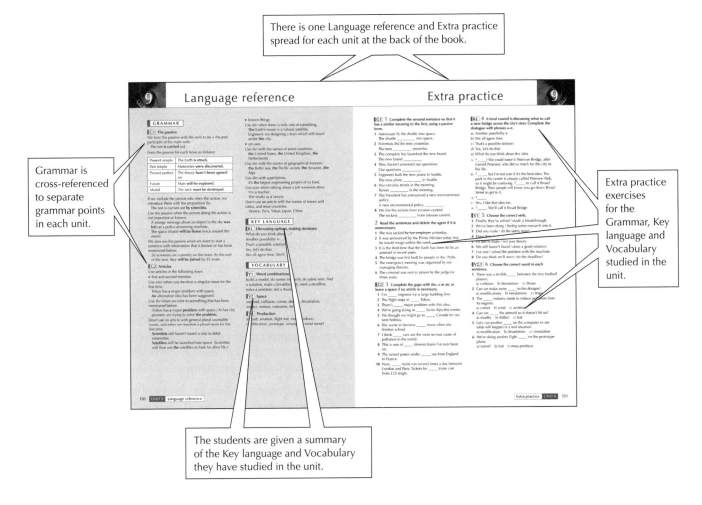

Grammar is cross-referenced to separate grammar points in each unit.

9 Language reference

Extra practice 9

Extra practice exercises for the Grammar, Key language and Vocabulary studied in the unit.

The students are given a summary of the Key language and Vocabulary they have studied in the unit.

Workbook spread

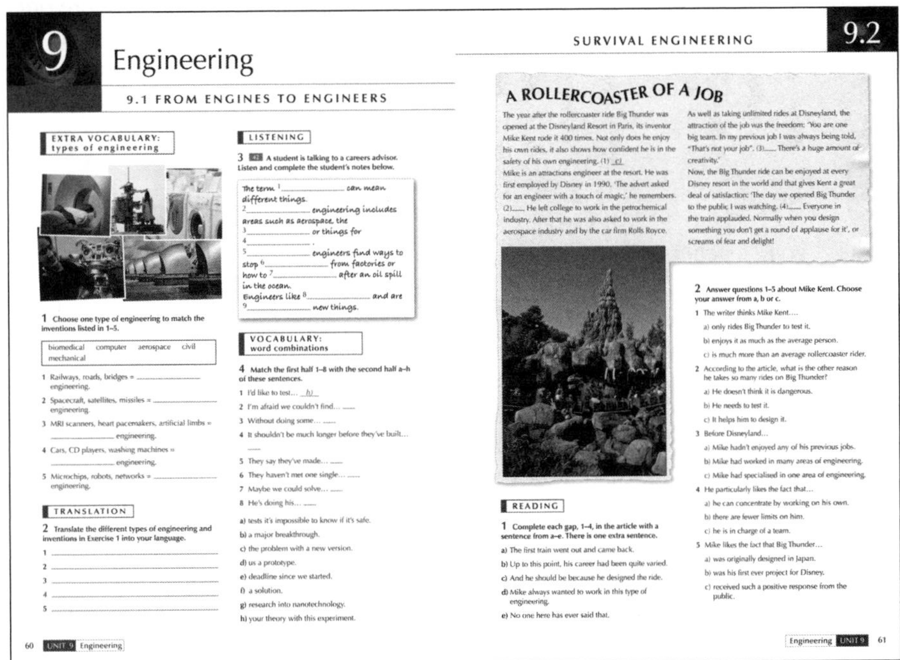
9 Engineering

9.1 FROM ENGINES TO ENGINEERS

SURVIVAL ENGINEERING 9.2

A ROLLERCOASTER OF A JOB

1 Personality

1.1 PERSONALITY TYPES

IN THIS LESSON

Lesson topic and staging

This lesson focuses on different personality types. Students are introduced to adjectives to describe different personalities (e.g. *creative, energetic, generous*). This vocabulary is then contextualised in a listening, about appearance versus type of personality. The lesson continues with a reading text about Carl Jung and his ideas on personality. This text contextualises the vocabulary and gives students practice in reading for specific information. The lesson finishes with a discussion on the benefits of having a particular personality and how you can guess someone's personality.

Objectives

By the end of the lesson students should have:

- increased their range of vocabulary to describe personality types
- practised extracting specific information from a listening and a reading text
- expressed their opinions and listened to others' opinions on different aspects of personality

Timings

If time is short, you could leave exercise 9 on page 7 until the beginning of the next lesson and use it as warmer/revision of vocabulary before continuing with the theme of personality.

A possible lesson break would be after the listening exercises on page 6.

WARM-UP

- On the board, write *A good teacher is …, A good doctor is …*, and *A good taxi driver is …* or another job your students know. Elicit a personality adjective to finish the first sentence, for example *A good teacher is patient.*
- Put students in pairs or small groups and ask them to finish the sentences with as many different personality adjectives as possible in five minutes. The winner is the pair/group with the most ideas.

Japanese proverb:
The meaning of this proverb is 'you can find out a person's personality if you look at the kind of people who are attracted to them'. For example, if their friends are lively and happy, then the person is also likely to be lively and happy. Or if their friends like to talk a lot, then the person is probably a good listener.

VOCABULARY: personality adjectives

1a Use the warm-up as a lead in to this exercise. Put students into pairs and ask them to think of as many other personality adjectives as they can in three minutes. Ask each pair for a few ideas.

1b Give students a minute to decide which three adjectives describe their own personality. Then put them in pairs or small groups to exchange information and say why they chose these adjectives.

2 Before students do this activity, check they understand *neutral* (neither positive nor negative).

- For feedback, draw three columns on the board and write *positive, negative* or *neutral* at the top of each.
- Ask the class for their answers, write the adjectives in the correct column on the board and correct any pronunciation problems.

Ask if students want to use these adjectives instead of the answers they gave in exercise 1b to describe their own personality and to discuss why they have now chosen these.

(!) *Sensitive* and *sensible* are often confused by speakers of Latin languages (Spanish, French, etc.).

Students' answers may vary in different cultures, contexts and depending on the point of view of the speaker. For example, *sensitive* can be negative if the speaker believes that *sensitivity* is a bad characteristic to have in a particular culture or context. The answers given below reflect perhaps the most normal use of these adjectives. *Bossy* and *moody* are very rarely used with a positive meaning.

> Positive: adventurous; ambitious; creative; energetic; generous; organised; reliable; sensible; sensitive; sociable; thoughtful
> Negative: bossy; moody
> Neutral: assertive; cautious; quiet; serious; talkative

3a Do the example with the whole class. Students then do the activity as per the Coursebook.

- Ask students not to use dictionaries at this stage because they will discover meaning in exercise 3c.
- Ask students to compare with a partner before you check the answers with the whole class.

> **1** a easy going; **2** d open-minded; **3** e even-tempered; **4** f hard-working; **5** b self-confident; **6** a strong-willed

pronunciation

3b Word stress

- Say one of the compound adjectives from exercise 3a and ask students where the main stress is.
- Write this adjective on the board and mark the stress with a box above the stressed syllable.
- Put students in pairs to mark where the stress is on the other adjectives.
- Play the audio track and pause after each adjective so that students can check their answers.
- If necessary, play the track again to check or say the adjectives yourself.

Audioscript and answers:
Track 1.2
1 a easy-**go**ing; 2 d open-**mind**ed; 3 e even-**tem**pered; 4 f **hard-work**ing; 5 b **self-con**fident; 6 a **strong-willed**

3c Tell students to read the first example before doing this activity.

- Put them in pairs/small groups to compare their answers before checking with the whole class.

1 even-tempered **2** strong-willed **3** easy-going **4** open-minded **5** hard-working **6** self-confident

Ask if students want to use these adjectives instead of the answers they gave in exercise 1b to describe their own personality and to discuss why they have now chosen these.

4 Give students a short time to think of adjectives to describe people they know. Encourage them to use adjectives from exercises 2 and 3a.

- Put students into pairs and ask them to swap ideas and give reasons for their choice of adjectives.
- Finally, ask students if any of the people they talked about have similar personalities.

LISTENING

5a Ask students to read the example and give them a short time to decide on their ideas.

- Put students into pairs or small groups to discuss their ideas and to agree/disagree with each other.

5b Check that students understand *accurate* (correct).

- Play the track without pausing.
- Give students two minutes to discuss if their ideas from exercise 5a were accurate.
- If students found the track difficult, play it again and give them another minute to discuss their answers.
- To follow up, ask students to decide which photo is probably Helen and which is Christina. Then ask students if they know someone whose personality is different from their appearance.

Track 1.3
Christina, Helen, George

C: Oh, Helen, come on! You can tell a lot from a person's appearance. I mean, when people meet me for the first time, they can see I'm quite a sociable person – I love parties, going out, enjoying myself, that sort of thing. I always try and have a good time and not take life too seriously.

H: I don't know, Christina. It's certainly not the same for me. Look, I've got quite a lot of friends, but most of them say they thought I was really quiet and serious when they first met me. Maybe it's the way I dress. But you know me, I think I'm quite energetic. And I'm interested in everything.

G: Mmm.

H: Maybe people think I'm strange because of my sense of humour, I don't know, or because I don't care what people think. I like to do things my way. Anyway, you always laugh at my jokes, George.

G: Yes, I think you're really funny.

H: What about you, George? You're very different from how you look.

G: How do you mean?

H: Well ...you've got a really good job, running your Internet company. You're hard working, very focused on your career. You seem to know exactly what your aims are. People would never guess, just looking at you – they'd probably think you're an out-of-work actor or something.

G: Yeah, you're right, Helen. I suppose I am a bit strange because I don't dress like a typical manager or businessman. I think I'm a pretty serious person, and people don't always realise that when they first meet me. I like to be in control, I plan everything very carefully, and I don't like too much change in my life. That's the way I am.

C: I suppose you are very different from your appearance, George, and you are a bit strange ...

H: Christina!

C: *[laughing]* ... you're a good friend, that's the important thing.

H: She's right. You're very reliable and you have high standards. I think you're a person with real principles, and there aren't too many people like that these days.

G: Thanks, Helen. I think that's a good description of me, you know me well, don't you?

READING

i Myers-Briggs and David Keirsey tests: used by some clinical psychologists and psychoanalysts to help people identify their significant personality traits.

Federico Fellini (1920–1993): one of the most influential and admired Italian film-makers of the 20th century. His best-known film is probably *La Dolce Vita* (*The Sweet Life*).

Stanley Kubrick (1928–1999): an extremely famous and influential American film director. His best-known films are probably *2001: A Space Odyssey*, *A Clockwork Orange* and *The Shining*.

6 Put students into pairs/groups for this activity and encourage them to discuss the different possibilities.

> Answers will depend on students' opinions. Answers, according to Jung, are given in exercise 7a.

7a Give students two minutes to read the text. Tell them not to worry about unknown vocabulary.

- Put students in the same pairs/groups as exercise 6 to discuss if their answers were correct.

> Extroverts: self-confident; talkative; adventurous
> Introverts: thoughtful, quiet, cautious

7b Give students two to three minutes to read the text again and answer the questions.

- Ask students to compare their answers with a partner and then check answers with the whole class.

> **1** False (Jung studied medicine in Basel); **2** False (he identified extroverts and introverts but not balanced personality); **3** True; **4** True; **5** True

7c Ask students to close their Coursebooks before doing this activity.

To add a competitive element:

- Put students into pairs and give them three minutes to list as many qualities of introverts and extroverts as they can remember.
- Ask each pair how many they remembered. The pair with the most (correct) qualities wins.

> Extroverts: find meaning outside themselves; they like other people; form close relationships, enjoy excitement of crowds; assertive; self-confident; they are leaders; energetic; busy lives; talkative; adventurous; sociable
> Introverts: introspective; find meaning in themselves; feel comfortable alone; don't like crowds; relaxed; thoughtful; reflect before they do things; quiet; cautious; good concentration; creative

8 Students do the activity as per the Coursebook.

- To lead in, remind students of the warm-up activity and the personality adjectives they listed for *teacher* and the reasons for their choices. If you didn't do the warm-up, write *teacher* on the board and ask students what kind of personality a good teacher should have (e.g. patient, good with people, etc.)
- Then ask students to choose four from the remaining jobs in the exercise.
- Give them about eight minutes to make notes about each job and to ask you if they need additional vocabulary.
- Ask students to compare their answers with a partner, to give reasons for their choices and to agree/disagree with each other if necessary.
- For feedback, choose two of the jobs students talked about and get ideas from the whole class.

To make this activity more personal:

- Ask students to choose a job (not necessarily from the exercise) that they would like to do, *or* they think someone else in the class would be good at.
- Give them a few minutes to list the qualities that make them (or another person) good for this job.
- Choose two or three students to tell the class the job they chose and the qualities they listed.

SPEAKING

9 If time is short, choose one or two questions only.

- Give students a few minutes to think about their answers to the questions.
- Put them into pairs to discuss their ideas and monitor to make sure that all the students understand *personality clash* (when two people's personalities are so different that they don't like each other).
- Encourage students to give as much detail as possible in their answers and to ask each other questions.

Extend exercise 9 by asking pairs of students to discuss their ideas with other pairs.

HOMEWORK OPTIONS

Students do the exercises on page 4 of the Workbook.

Students write a personality description of someone they know. They must give examples to support the qualities they describe.

1.2 MEASURING PERSONALITY

IN THIS LESSON

Lesson topic and staging

This lesson continues the topic of personality and focuses on different personality tests and the people who use them. Students discuss different ways of measuring personality and then listen to an interview on measuring intelligence and personal qualities. This listening contextualises the grammar focus of the lesson: question forms. Students study question forms in different tenses and practise the different structures before using the questions in an information-gap activity. Students then read a text about the Japanese director of two popular horror movies and the lesson ends with further practice of question forms.

Objectives

By the end of the lesson students should have:

- been introduced to/revised the structure and use of question forms in different tenses
- used different question forms to find out and swap information
- practised listening to a text in order to notice grammatical structure
- practised extracting specific information from a reading text

Timings

If time is short and students are making few mistakes in using question forms, you could drop exercise 8 on page 8. Alternatively, you could drop exercise 10 on page 9 and use it as a warmer for the next lesson.

A possible lesson break would be after exercise 8 on page 8.

WARM-UP

If you cut exercise 9 from lesson 1.1, you could use it as a warmer here. Alternatively, to lead in to this lesson and to revise vocabulary from lesson 1.1:

- Write the names of two or three famous people (known to your students) on the board.
- Put students into pairs or small groups and give them three minutes to list as many adjectives as possible to describe these people's personalities. The team with the most adjectives wins.

LISTENING AND SPEAKING

1 Check students understand the verb *judge* (to decide something based on evidence).

- Ask students to give you different ways of judging someone's personality.
- Tell students to read the ideas in exercise 1 and check they understand *star signs/horoscopes* (by showing an example from a newspaper or a magazine) and *handwriting analysis* (studying someone's handwriting to decide what it can tell about the person's character).
- When students have finished the discussion, ask which 'test' they think is the most/least useful.

2 Put students into pairs or small groups to discuss this question.

3a Tell students to read the topics (1–5) before you play the audio track.

- Play the track without pausing and tell students not to worry about unknown vocabulary.
- Give students one or two minutes to compare their answers and, if necessary, play the track again.

1, 2 and 4 should be ticked.

Track 1.4

Anchor, Presenter, Frank Partridge

A: And now at 11 o'clock it's over to Jenny Mason and today's edition of 'Changing World'.

P: Good evening everyone. Our guest tonight is Dr Frank Partridge, an expert on personality. Dr Partridge, our listeners are very interested in personality tests, so can I ask a few questions about those before we talk about your current research?

F: Yes, certainly, and good evening, everyone.

P: OK, my first question. What exactly does psychometrics mean?

F: Well, psychometrics is really related to the measurement of intelligence and personal qualities. It measures four things: [PAUSE] the measurement of knowledge, [PAUSE] the measurement of abilities, [PAUSE] the measurement of attitudes [PAUSE] and personality traits. It's really about the differences between individuals.

P: I see. How did psychometric testing start? I mean, who designed the early tests?

F: Well, the first psychometric tests were designed to measure intelligence. I think the first usable intelligence test was the Stanford-Binet [*bee-'ney*] test. The test was developed originally by a French psychologist called Alfred Binet [*bee-'ney*].

P: Mmm, interesting. So, how useful are the tests? Are they reliable? That's what most people want to know.

F: Well, that's a good question. All tests must have reliability and validity. Let me explain what I mean. When you use a reliable test, you get the same results each time. If the test is valid, it measures what it's supposed to measure ... and not something else.

P: Mmm. I wonder if you could you give us an example of what exactly you mean by validity?

F: An example? Well ... if you test a teacher on how many books they can carry, that's not a valid measure of their ability as a teacher.

continued...

P: Right, I see. Well, what can personality tests tell you about a person?
F: Well, there's one test, called the Myers-Briggs test, which is widely used all over the world. It's based on an Internet study of more than 20,000 people. Organisations think it's useful when you want to work out people's roles in a team. Some people say it's useful to decide your personality type. You can, for example, find out how organised, reliable and sociable you are. I think the questions are quite interesting and people seem to enjoy doing them. There are questions like: 'Can you stay calm under pressure?' 'Are you a good team player?' 'How motivated are you?' And so on.
P: Have you taken any of these tests yourself?
F: Yes, I have. The results were very interesting. *[laughs]*
P: OK, thanks for that. Now, let's get on to your research. What are you working on at the moment, Dr Partridge?
F: I'm currently carrying out research into personalities of identical twins. I'm looking at the similarities and differences of their personalities and, I can tell you, it's ... *[fade]*

3b This activity is to focus students on the question forms in the listening and not to test their understanding.

- Give students about five minutes to try to complete the questions (1–7) individually. Make sure all students have written down the complete questions because they will need to refer to them in exercises 4 and 5 below.
- Put them into pairs to compare their answers and then play the track to check.
- If your class found the listening difficult the first time, pause the track after each question to give students time to complete the gaps.

1 What exactly does psychometrics mean?; **2** How did psychometric testing start?; **3** How useful are the tests?; **4** Are they reliable?; **5** What *can* personality tests tell you about a person?; **6** Have you taken any of these tests yourself?; **7** What are you working on at the moment?

GRAMMAR: question forms

4 Students should work individually before comparing their answers with a partner.

- Get answers from the class. but don't elicit or give information on the structure of these questions. Students will focus on the structure in exercise 5 below.

1 present simple; **2** past simple; **3** present simple (using the verb *be*); **4** present simple (using the verb *be*); **5** present simple (using a modal auxiliary *can*); **6** present perfect; **7** present continuous

5 Do the first question as a whole class and show students they can use the questions in exercise 3b to help them with the answers in this activity.

- When you check the answers with the class, ask students to give as much information as possible, e.g. number 3 is false because we use the auxiliary *did* in past simple questions.

1 True (see exercise 3b questions **3** and 4)
2 False – we use *do/does*, but we can also use modal auxiliary verbs (see exercise 3b questions **1** and 5)
3 False – we use the auxiliary verb *did* (i.e. *do* in the past simple) (see exercise 3b question 2)
4 False – we put *is/are* before the subject (see exercise 3b question 7)
5 True (see exercise 3b question 6)

For a full explanation and further practice, ask students to look at the Language reference on page 134.

6 Give students five minutes to read the sentences and answer the questions before comparing with a partner.

1 a; **2** b; **3** Object questions (for example, sentence b). *Do/does* is used here in the past simple *did* because this is a past simple question.

For a full explanation and further practice, ask students to look at the Language reference on page 134.

7a Students can do this activity individually before comparing with a partner.

- Monitor the class while they are working to point out any mistakes they make and encourage them to self-correct by referring to the Language reference on page 134.
- Go through the answers, and check students understand *influenced* (had an important effect on you).

1 Do you ever get worried?; **2** Are you a confident person?; **3** Do you make friends easily? (Note the position of the adverb *easily* in this question.);
4 Were you happy when you were a child?; **5** Did you have many friends at your first school?;
6 What has influenced you most in your life?; **7** Have you ever taken a personality test?; **8** Are you succeeding in achieving your aims?

7b Before students ask/answer the questions, check their pronunciation of *worried* and *influenced*, the contracted pronunciations of *do you* and *did you*, and the weak forms of *were* and *are*.

- Some of these questions are quite personal. If your students don't like talking about such personal topics, you could teach them the phrase 'I'd rather not say' and tell them to answer only answer the questions they're comfortable with.
- Encourage them to ask follow-up questions (e.g. 'What makes you worried? What do you worry about?').
- For feedback, ask two or three students to tell the class something interesting they found out.

SPEAKING

8 This is an information gap activity where two students have to exchange information to complete the text.

- Explain the activity using the example (or ask a stronger pair to demonstrate).
- Give students about five minutes to plan the questions they need to ask.
- Put students into A/B pairs to ask and answer the questions. Make sure Student A asks the first question and that A/B then take it in turns.
- Monitor students and note errors while they are doing the activity. At the end of the activity, correct some of the more common mistakes.

If you have a weaker class, divide the students into two groups initially (group A and group B). Ask the students in each group to help each other decide which questions they need to ask to find the information. Then put them into A/B pairs to ask/ answer the questions and complete the gaps.

Student B question 4 is in the passive voice. Monitor to check that students are able to use this form before they ask/answer the questions

Student A
1 Who was born on 6th May 1856?
2 Where did he study medicine? *Or* Which university did he study medicine at?
3 When did he graduate?
4 Who was the first president of the International Psychoanalytical Association?
5 Who lost all his property when he left Vienna?
6 When did he (Freud) die?
Student B
1 Where was Sigmund Freud born?
2 What did he study at the university of Vienna?
3 How long did he live in Vienna? *Or* How many years did he live in Vienna?
4 Who was introduced to Freud in 1907?
5 Who emigrated to London?
6 Where was the house Freud lived in? *Or* Where did Freud live?

READING

Hideo Nakata is a Japanese film director. He was born July 19, 1961, in Okayama. He is most famous outside Japan for his horror movies.

9a Write 'Hideo Nakata' on the board and ask students if they know anything about him. (Don't read the Background information to the class at this stage because students will find out who he is when they do the exercise.)

- Ask students to read the four items in exercise 9a before they read the introduction. (Note: the introduction to the article ends with '... that focus on female personalities'.)
- To follow up, ask the class if anyone has seen the films, if they liked them and why.

1 Hideo Nakata: a Japanese film director (see Background information above)
2 *Ring* and *Ring 2*: the films that made him internationally famous
3 Reiko Asakawa: the actress who plays the main character (a reporter) in *Ring*
4 Suzuki Koji: the man who wrote the book that *Ring* was based on. (Note: in Japanese, it is normal for the family name to precede the first name i.e. in the text it says Koji Suzuki.)

9b Check students understand *reviews, overrated, underrated.*

- Ask students to read all the questions before they read the text and decide where they go.
- Tell students to compare with a partner before you check with the whole class.

1 7; **2** 3; **3** 1; **4** 8; **5** 6; **6** 2; **7** 5; **8** 4

9c Put students in pairs or small groups for this activity.

- Tell them to discuss possible reasons other than the one given in the text. The answer in the text is: Nakata likes to make movies that focus on female personalities. Other answers will depend on students' own opinions.
- Finally, get a few ideas from the class and ask if any students would like to see *Ring* or *Ring 2* and why.

WRITING

10 Give students a minute to think of a famous person. If they have problems thinking of someone, write a few examples on the board (choosing people known to all your students).

- While they are writing their questions, monitor to help with any vocabulary they need. Encourage students to write interesting questions like the ones in the text in exercise 9.

- When they have compared their questions with a partner, ask two or three students to tell the class the best questions they heard and why they think these are good.

Choose two famous people who all your students know and write the names on the board.

- Divide the class into two groups, A and B, and give one famous person to each group.
- Give students about ten minutes to write five questions to ask the other group's famous person.
- Put the students into pairs (A/B in each group) and tell student A to ask all their questions. Then ask student B to ask all their questions.
- When they have finished, ask the class which was the best question and the most interesting answer.

If students don't know the real answers to some of the questions, tell them to invent some interesting information.

HOMEWORK OPTIONS

Students do the exercises on pages 5–6 of the Workbook.

Students write a brief profile of a famous person (either the person they wrote the interview questions for in exercise 10, Task adjustment or anyone else who particularly interests them). Refer them to the texts on Sigmund Freud and/or Hideo Nakata for ideas.

1.3 CHARISMA

IN THIS LESSON

Lesson topic and staging

This lesson begins with a reading text on the concept of charisma and students read the text for specific information. The reading provides a context for the vocabulary work that follows in which students extend both their vocabulary and knowledge of prefixes. Next, students discuss people who are charismatic and decide how important charisma is for a person's career. Students then focus on the uses of the two grammatical forms, present simple and present continuous, before using the language to write questions. The lesson ends with a speaking activity in which students ask each other the questions.

Objectives

By the end of the lesson, students should have:

- increased their range of vocabulary to describe personality types
- practised extracting specific information from a reading text
- practised extracting vocabulary and grammatical structure from a reading text
- extended their knowledge and ability to use prefixes and present simple and present continuous forms

Timings

If short of time, you could drop exercise 5 and/or set exercise 8a on page 11 for homework. In the next lesson, you could check the answers for exercise 8a and then follow the procedure on page 18 of this book for exercise 8b.

A possible lesson break would be after exercise 5 on page 11.

WARM-UP

- Write *charisma* on the board and ask students what it means (a quality of personality that makes people attracted to you – it is *not* physical attractiveness). As an example, ask students to give you the names of charismatic people or provide some examples yourself.
- Write the following words on the board: *friendly, assertive, serious, intelligent, funny, sensitive, self-confident, generous*.
- Elicit and write on the board a few other adjectives that students believe describe a charismatic person.
- Put student in pairs and tell them they have to agree on three of the adjectives on the board that best describe a charismatic person.
- When they have finished, ask the pairs for their ideas and encourage the other students to agree/disagree.

READING

1 Students do the activity as per the Coursebook.

- If your students don't know some/any of the people in the photos, read them the information below.

> **1** Photo A: Marilyn Monroe: famous American movie actress in 1950s and 1960s; Photo B: Kemal Ataturk (1881–1938): Turkish nationalist leader, and founder and first president of the Republic of Turkey; Photo C: Oprah Winfrey: famous present-day American TV talk-show presenter and actress; Photo D: David Beckham: famous present-day British football player
> **2** Answers will depend on students' own opinions and what they know about the person.

2a Tell students not to worry about vocabulary at this stage because they will look at new words later.

- Ask students to compare their ideas with a partner before you go through the answers below.

> **1** Bill Clinton; Oprah Winfrey; Marilyn Monroe; Joe DiMaggio (married to Marilyn Monroe); Arthur Miller (married to Marilyn Monroe)
> **2** Bill Clinton: was President of the USA; is now a popular speaker. Oprah Winfrey: is a business woman, a TV presenter, runs a book club, and publishes magazines. Marilyn Monroe: was an actress. Joe DiMaggio: was a baseball player. Arthur Miller: was a famous writer.

2b Give students a longer time to read the article than in exercise 2a above.

- Ask them to read the questions before they reread the article and compare their answers with a partner.

(!) Students may not understand *overshadowed* in the answer to question 5. When you go through the answers, give students the meaning but, note, this is also one of the vocabulary items in exercise 3a.

> **1** Because he has a special quality: charisma.; **2** They think it's the same as 'fame'.; **3** She is probably best-known as the presenter of a very popular talk show.; **4** She relates well to people who attend her shows and they respond well to her. She gives a sense of 'togetherness'.; **5** He felt overshadowed by her, i.e. people thought she was more important, attractive and successful.

VOCABULARY: prefixes

3a Use number 6 as an example because this was mentioned in exercise 2b above.

- Give students about five minutes to find and underline the other words in the article, and then compare with a partner.

> **1** ex-President (Note: *ex-* is normally hyphenated.); **2** redefine; **3** misunderstand; **4** underrated; **5** ex-baseball player; **6** overshadowed

3b Write *overrated* on the board and underline *over*.

- Elicit that *over* is a prefix. Ask students to underline the prefixes in the other words and match them to the meanings.

> ex: before; re: again; mis: incorrect; under: not enough; over: too much

4a Ask students to do this activity in pairs to encourage discussion of the different possibilities.

- If necessary, tell students to use their dictionaries to find the words and then decide what the prefix means.

> **a** bi: two (two wheels on a bicycle); **b** anti: against, opposite to, not (against society, not sociable, opposite to the accepted ideas of society); **c** mono: single, one (one rail for a train to run along); **d** out: more than, better than, exceed (perform better than someone else or better than expected); **e** semi: half (half a circle); **f** dis: not (not comfortable)

4b Do the first example with the whole class and tell them that they should be able to work out the answers by looking again at exercises 3a, 3b and 4a above.

> **1** overconfident; **2** outran; **3** ex-boss; **4** bilingual (Note: students may have written *bilanguage*. *Lingual* is the adjective of *language*.); **5** redo; **6** underused; **7** misbehave; **8** dislike

For further practice, ask students to do V2 exercises 6, 7 and 8 on page 135 in the Language reference.

SPEAKING

5 Encourage students to give reasons for their answers to the two questions. If you are short of time, tell students to discuss one question only.

Set the first question and tell pairs to choose three charismatic people for the article.

- Then put two pairs together (groups of four) and tell them to choose three charismatic people from the suggestions they now have in their group of four.
- While they discuss the people to choose, they should give reasons for their choice and agree/disagree with one another.
- If you have enough students, put the students into groups of eight and ask them to choose three people from the suggestions they now have,
- Students then do exercise 5, question 2 as per the Coursebook.

GRAMMAR: present simple and present continuous

At this level, the grammar should not be a problem and you can probably treat these exercises as revision. However, the idea of present continuous for changing situations *may* be new to students.

6a Students do the activity as per the Coursebook.

> **1** … regularly gives talks all over the world – PS; **2** She owns several houses and publishes her own magazines – PS; **3** Currently, she is presenting a new series – PC; **4** … people are reading more these days in the USA – PC

6b Check students understand *trend* in sentence d.

- Tell students to do this activity individually and then compare their answers with a partner to encourage student–student teaching.

> **a 3** Currently, she is presenting a new series – present continuous (Note: *currently* means *at or around the present time* and often implies the action is temporary.); **b 1** … regularly gives talks all over the world – present simple; **c 2** She owns several houses and publishes her own magazines – present simple; **d 4** People are reading more these days in the USA – present continuous (Note: the word *more* adds to the idea that the situation is changing.)

GRAMMAR TIP

Ask students to read the grammar tip and look at the photo on page 10 to reinforce the example.

For a full explanation and further practice, ask students to look at the Language reference on pages 134–135.

7a Check students understand *carrying out* (doing) in sentence 4.

- Ask students to do this activity individually before comparing with a partner.
- Monitor the class and point out any mistakes they make. Refer them to the Language reference on page 134 if they need extra help.

7b Go through the answers to 7a before students do this activity.

> **1** Dr Partridge regularly gives talks about personality: a regular or habitual action.; **2** The professor is interviewing a candidate at the moment and can't come to the phone: an action happening around now.; **3** The number of companies using personality tests is growing: a trend or a changing situation.; **4** I do lots of different research but today I'm carrying out research into the personalities of twins: an action happening around now.; **5** He drives to work every day: a regular or habitual action.; **6** People are becoming very interested in how personalities develop over time: a trend or a changing situation.; **7** A psychologist studies the way people's minds work: a fact or general truth.; **8** The doctor's practice is in Harley Street: a fact.

Harley Street is in London (UK) and is famous for the large number of private and expensive medical practices and clinics situated there.

8a Monitor while students do this activity and encourage students to self-correct by referring to the Language reference on page 134.

> **1** Do you make friends easily?; **2** What do you usually do at the weekend?; **3** What are you reading at the moment?; **4** Do you enjoy art and music?; **5** Do you prefer extroverts or introverts?; **6** Are you working on any new projects now?; **7** Are you doing anything interesting at the moment? (Note: *at the moment* does not refer here to *at this precise moment*, it means *around the present time*, e.g. in your life outside school.); **8** Do you lose your temper easily?

8b Give students a few minutes to think of personal answers to the questions before you put them into pairs.

- Focus students on the contraction of *I am* in the answers they will give and explain that this will make their answers sound more natural.
- Tell students to ask follow-up questions to get as much information as possible.

Students write the numbers of the questions down the left-hand side of a large piece of paper and then draw three further columns.

- Follow the procedure in 8b above, but then ask students to move around the rooms asking three different students the questions and noting the answers in the columns.
- Put students into pairs to compare their notes and decide on the most interesting piece of information.

HOMEWORK OPTIONS

Students do the exercises on pages 7–8 of the Workbook.

Students use some of the information they gathered in exercise 8b to write a short paragraph about another student in the class. They need to pay attention to the grammar they used.

Students choose one of the charismatic people from the reading text (or other charismatic person, perhaps one they discussed in exercise 5) to find out more about, using the Internet if they wish. They then write a paragraph about this person. If possible, this should be a living person, so that students can practise the present simple and present continuous.

1.4 SCENARIO: PERSONALITY CLASH

IN THIS LESSON

Lesson topic and staging

Students are introduced to the scenario and discuss the possible problems a new employee might have working for two bosses. They then listen to two people discussing the same problem and extract specific information about the two people from the listening text. This is followed by a focus on the KEY LANGUAGE of giving opinions, agreeing and disagreeing and on important qualities for the job. This preparation leads to the main TASK in which students use the language they have learned in this unit to choose a suitable candidate for the job.

Objectives

By the end of the lesson, students should have:

- extracted specific information and language from a listening and a reading text
- learned useful phrases for giving opinions, agreeing and disagreeing
- used this language in a 'real-life' situation to solve a problem
- participated effectively in extended speaking practice

Common European Framework

Students can use language effectively to give opinions, agree and disagree with other speakers.

Timings

If short of time, you could cut the number of candidates discussed in exercises 5a–c, and 6. In exercise 5a, give student A the candidate May Lin and Student B the candidate Celine (ignore the profiles on Richard and Anil on page 160).

A possible lesson break would be after exercise 4 on page 12.

SITUATION

1 Ask students the name of the city in the photo (Vancouver, Canada).

- Give students 30 seconds to read the situation and check they understand *broadcasting station* (the place from where TV and radio programmes are transmitted to the audience) and *hire* (employ).
- Put students into pairs or small groups to discuss and write down the possible problems.

Answers will depend on students' own ideas.

Students will probably say that one problem is people not liking each other. Take this opportunity to teach *get on with somebody* because this is key in the listening text for exercises 2a and b.

2a Play the audio track without pausing and tell students to listen for the general (not individual) problem.

Ben and Sylvia have different personalities and the assistants preferred one boss to the other. They complained to one boss about the other. There were personality clashes between the assistants and the two bosses. It's also possible that the two bosses don't like each other.

Track 1.5

Ben, Sylvia

B: I can't understand it, Sylvia, two assistants leaving us in the last three months. It's not our fault, is it?

S: I don't know, Ben, maybe it is. Let's face it, we're not easy people to work with. You're very intelligent and ambitious, but you seem to forget other people don't have those qualities. I think you probably expect too much from them. And then you get angry if they don't do their job properly.

B: Hmm, I suppose I am a bit bad-tempered sometimes. I shout if things go wrong. But Barbara didn't seem to mind.

S: I don't know, I think it really upset her. What did she say about you? That you were bossy, and, erm … insensitive. [PAUSE]

B: OK, but maybe she said that because I wouldn't give her time off to do her shopping. I pay people to work 9.00 to 5.00, Sylvia, not to leave the office whenever they feel like it.

S: Come on, Ben, an hour off, just before Christmas? Not asking for much.

B: OK, maybe Barbara asked at a bad moment, I don't know. Anyway it wasn't just that. She didn't like me smoking in the office – it really bothered her. You know, I like open-minded people, so I was really quite pleased when she left. Anyway, I got on alright with Louise, but she didn't like you or your secretary much, did she?

S: Well, it's true, Louise and I didn't get on. I reckon she didn't like me because I'm very sociable and I'm a bit noisy when I'm enjoying myself. Louise was a very quiet person. Another thing – she was really jealous because Susan and I have a good relationship. *[laughs]* Louise didn't like it when Susan made fun of her. She just couldn't take a joke – she was far too serious. [PAUSE]

B: I don't agree, Sylvia. Actually I thought Louise was quite nice, but she was a little sensitive, I agree. She told me you were really moody, one minute nice to her, the next unpleasant. I think she was afraid of you in the end.

continued…

S: Really? You surprise me. I know I've got a strong personality – some people don't like that. But moody? I don't think so … Look, Ben, why don't we try and get a man as our assistant this time? To be honest, I think we'd both work better with a man. [PAUSE]
B: I don't know – male or female, does it really matter, as long as they have the right personality? We've got to get someone who'll fit in here. The skills are less important – most people seem to have the basic skills we're looking for. It's not a problem. What we need is someone who'll be a good match for us. I suggest we contact the agency again. Let's see what they can come up with this time. We'll give them a good briefing so they know exactly what we want.
S: Great idea. Let's do it.

2b If your class found the listening difficult in 2a, pause the track as indicated in the audioscript.

- For feedback, draw the grid on the board and write in the answers.
- To follow up, ask students if they would like to work for these two bosses or not, giving their reasons.

(!) There are a lot of personality adjectives in the text, but many of them are about the two assistants. Tell your students to focus *only* on the adjectives to describe Ben and Sylvia. In addition, the adjective *intelligent* is used to describe Ben, but this is not a personality adjective and is not included in the answers below.

Ben		**Sylvia**	
+	–	+	–
ambitious	bad-tempered bossy insensitive	sociable strong personality	moody noisy

KEY LANGUAGE: giving opinions, agreeing and disagreeing

3a Give students three minutes to fill the gaps before they listen again. Then play the track, pausing after each answer to give students time to fill the gaps.

3b Students do the activity as per the Coursebook.

1 Sylvia: I don't know, Ben, maybe it is: DISAGREEING; **2** Sylvia: I don't know, I think it really upset her: GIVING AN OPINION; **3** Sylvia: Come on Ben, an hour off, just before Christmas?: DISAGREEING; **4** Sylvia: Well it's true, Louise and I didn't get on: AGREEING; **5** Ben: I don't agree, Sylvia. Actually I thought Louise was quite nice: DISAGREEING; **6** Sylvia: Great idea. Let's do it: AGREEING

4 To lead in to this activity, ask students what they think Ben and Sylvia do next.

- Ask students to read the situation and the questions before they read the email.
- Emphasise that they are only reading for the most important qualities.
- Put students into pairs to discuss their answers to the questions, then ask one or two pairs for their ideas. Students may argue that some other qualities in the email are more important. Be prepared to accept other answers because the exact answers are not important to the next activities.

1 the right personality (e.g. lively, tolerant, hard-working, calm, able to work under pressure); strong personality (not sensitive to criticism); a good sense of humour
2 Answers depend on students' own opinions but some examples might be: able to make suggestions and make decisions (if Ben and Sylvia disagree on something), able to work independently, confident, etc.

TASK: choosing a new team member

5a Lead in by asking students what happens next in this situation and then read through the rubric.

- Emphasise that students are noting good and bad points in relation to the job (e.g. in the May Lin text, 'doesn't smoke and thinks smoking should be banned in public places' may be a bad point because Ben smokes in the office). Tell students they will need to say why they think these qualities are 'good' or 'bad' for this job.
- Monitor to help students with vocabulary or ask them to use their dictionaries.
- When they have finished, put all the As into one group and the Bs into another to compare their answers.
- Monitor to check that students have found all the relevant points but do not do an open feedback at this stage.

Some qualities are obviously either 'good' or 'bad', but some depend on the students' own opinion in relation to the candidate's suitability for the job.

5b Look together at the OTHER USEFUL PHRASES on page 13. Give or elicit an example of the phrases for making suggestions to demonstrate what an infinitive/*-ing* is (e.g. 'I suggest we choose', 'How about choosing …').

- Put students into A/B pairs and give them about ten minutes to discuss their ideas.

- Monitor and make notes of any important or common mistakes when using the KEY LANGUAGE and OTHER USEFUL PHRASES.
- When they have finished, elicit or give corrections to some of the mistakes you noted.

5c Keep students in their pairs and give them about five minutes to rank the candidates.

- Encourage them to use the KEY LANGUAGE and OTHER USEFUL PHRASES and to pay attention to the mistakes you corrected in exercise 5b.
- Don't elicit students' answers at this stage because this will happen automatically in exercise 6.

6 If you have a large class, divide the students into two groups making sure that the A/B pairs from exercise 5 stay together.

- Give students 10–15 minutes for their discussion and encourage them to use the KEY LANGUAGE and OTHER USEFUL PHRASES.
- When they have finished, ask one student in the class (or group) which candidate they chose and why.

HOMEWORK OPTIONS

Students do the exercises on page 9 of the Workbook.

As a follow up to exercises 5 and 6, students write short notes on two of the candidates to send to Ben and Sylvia at Pacific Television. These should summarise the good and bad points for each candidate. They need to state clearly why this person was/wasn't chosen for the job interview and make recommendations for questions that should be asked during the interview itself.

1.5 STUDY AND WRITING SKILLS

IN THIS LESSON

Lesson topic and staging

This lesson focuses on the skills of note-taking and writing a comparative essay. Students do a reading on women and men drivers and use this text to experiment with two different ways of taking notes. Students are then introduced to common symbols and abbreviations in note-taking and use these to make their notes. The activities which follow prepare students for writing a comparative essay, focusing on essay structure, linking phrases and the process of planning what to write. Students write their essay, then finally read and comment on another student's essay to gain further practice of taking notes.

Objectives

By the end of the lesson, students should have:

- experimented with different methods of note-taking and decided which works best for them
- been introduced to common symbols and abbreviations in note-taking and used these to make notes
- been introduced to essay structure and useful linking phrases for writing a comparative essay
- written a comparative essay, and commented on another student's essay

Common European Framework

Students can take notes efficiently and write a comparative essay.

Timings

If time is short and your students are fairly confident using the linkers in exercise 5b, cut either exercise 6a or 6b.

A possible lesson break would be after exercise 3b on page 15.

WARM-UP

This activity introduces the topic of differences between the sexes and the skill of note-taking.

- On the board, write 'At school, girls/boys are better because …'
- Put students into small groups (perhaps all-female and all-male groups if you have enough of both in the class).

- Tell each group to make notes on *either* girls or boys. Tell them which to write about so that half the groups write about girls and half about boys. Students can write about studies, behaviour, socialising or any other topics they want.
- Emphasise that all the students in each group must keep notes and should not write full sentences.
- When they have finished, mix the groups up so that there are equal numbers of 'girls' and 'boys' in each new group.
- Tell students to compare their ideas using their notes and try to persuade each other that their opinions are correct. After the discussion, get a few ideas from the class.
- Finally, lead in to exercise 1 by asking students why they needed to take notes in this warm-up and what techniques they used (e.g. abbreviations, symbols). If students didn't use any techniques beyond simply shortening sentences, this is a good opportunity to tell them that this lesson will give them more options.

STUDY SKILLS: note-taking while reading

1 Students do the activity as per the Coursebook.

- Elicit ideas from two or three pairs and ask the rest of the class if their ideas were similar.

Answers will depend on students' own experience.

2a To lead in, tell students to read the title of the text and decide if they think men or women are better drivers.

- Elicit opinions from two or three students and ask them to say why they have this opinion.
- Give students two minutes to read the text and say if it agrees or disagrees with their own opinion.
- Check students understand *road rage* (become extremely angry and violent with other drivers), *risk* (a possibly dangerous action), *overtake* (drive past another moving car) *tend not to* (don't usually), *spatial* (adjective of *space*, relating to the position and size of things), *minor accident* (not serious).
- Set the activity as per the Coursebook and tell students they need to write one word in each space (1–20).
- Ask students to compare their answers with a partner before you elicit answers from the class.

(!) Other vocabulary that might worry students is: *stereotype, controversial, behind the wheel*. However, students do not need this to understand the text.

1 polite; **2** pedestrians; **3** cyclists; **4** calm; **5** stressful; **6** rage; **7** risks; **8** overtaking; **9** responsible; **10** drive; **11** tired; **12** slowly; **13** confidence; **14** easily; **15** children in the car; **16** reading; **17** problems; **18** right; **19** awareness; **20** minor

2b Students discuss the question in pairs. Ask a few students for their ideas in open class.

3a Lead in by asking students what the benefit is of using symbols and abbreviations in note-taking.

- Students do the activity individually and then compare answers in pairs.

1 h **2** k **3** c **4** e **5** j **6** b **7** d **8** a **9** i **10** l **11** g **12** f

3b Before students do this activity, give an example by writing the following on the board: *patient and polite to others on the road*. Then elicit the following change from the class: & (and).

- Students then work individually to change the remaining sentences before comparing their ideas with a partner.
- Finally, go through the sentences with the class and elicit possible changes. Students may have made different changes from those given below. Accept any reasonable answers.

Suggested changes: e.g. ;& (and); (like); ∴ (use this before *road rage* and *less*); < (fewer, less); > (more).

To give students more practice in using the symbols and abbreviations, ask them to look again at the notes they made in the warm-up and change them using the ideas in exercise 3a. Ask them to compare with a partner before getting a few ideas from the class.

WRITING SKILLS: a comparative essay

4 Students should not need to reread the text in order to do this activity. Set a very short time limit.

a paragraph 4; **b** paragraph 2; **c** paragraph 1; **d** paragraph 3

5a Tell students to read through the options (1–4) before they find examples in the text.

- Go through answers with the class. If students are unsure, refer them to the sentences with the highlighted examples to demonstrate their use.

1 In addition, Firstly, Secondly, Thirdly; **2** such as, for instance, for example, in particular; **3** However, although, On the other hand, Despite the fact that, In contrast; **4** To sum up; on balance (Note: *on balance* is used to introduce a conclusion when there are two or more options being discussed.)

5b Ask students to discuss the questions with a partner.

- Go through answers with the class.

However, In contrast, On the other hand – need a new sentence; although, despite the fact that – need two clauses.

6a Read through the example with the class and point out the comma after *However*. Tell students to use the examples in the text on page 14 to check the punctuation of the other sentences they write.

- Students work individually to complete the other sentences and then compare their answers with a partner.
- Elicit answers from students and write them on the board so that the whole class can see the correct sentences and punctuation.

> He is patient and careful at work. On the other hand, he is impatient and aggressive when he drives.
> He is patient and careful at work. In contrast, he is impatient and aggressive when he drives.
> Although he is patient and careful at work, he is impatient and aggressive when he drives. *Or* He is patient and careful at work, although he is impatient and aggressive when he drives.
> Despite the fact that he is patient and careful at work, he is impatient and aggressive when he drives. *Or* He is patient and careful at work, despite the fact that he is impatient and aggressive when he drives.

6b Students work individually while you monitor to prompt and correct if necessary. Students compare their answers with a partner. Ask one or two stronger students for examples.

- The answers to this activity will vary, monitor students to make sure they are producing accurate sentences.

> These are suggested answers. Students' answers will vary. **1** ... However, he worked very hard when he got there.; **2** ..., their personalities were very different.; **3** ... he always went to parties when he was invited.; **4** ... find them very difficult to learn.

7a & **b** For these activities, the groups should have a maximum of four students. You may need to prompt with a few ideas of your own.

- When brainstorming their ideas, all students should note down the ideas so that they can use them to write an essay in exercise 8. Tell students not to write sentences at this stage.

7c Give students about 15 minutes to work individually and then put them back into a group to compare ideas. Monitor to check that the two statements students write (task 2) are accurate.

> Answers will depend on students' own ideas and opinions.

8 Before students start writing their essay, remind them of the structure of the comparative essay discussed in exercise 4, and the linking phrases in exercise 5a and b on page 15.

- Monitor students to prompt and correct if necessary.

9a If possible, make sure that students are not in a pair with a student from the groupings in exercises 7a and b. Ask them to look again at the two systems of note-taking on page 14 and the abbreviations they studied in exercise 3a on page 15. Give them about 15 minutes to make notes.

9b Tell students to return the full version of the essay to the original writer (so that they can't refer to it and have to rely on their notes alone).

- Put students into new pairs and give them about five minutes to tell their partner about the essay they read.
- Tell them to ask each other questions about the essay if necessary.
- Finally, ask the class which was the most interesting essay they read or heard about.

It's a good idea to read and mark the full versions of the essays yourself; this gives students further motivation. When marking the essays, pay particular attention to the structure, the use of linking phrases and the balance/range of ideas expressed.

HOMEWORK OPTIONS

Students do the relevant exercise on page 10 of the Workbook.

Students can write a second essay using the notes they took in exercise 9a. This will give a real outcome to the note-taking activity.

Travel

2.1 TOURISM AND TRAVELLING

IN THIS LESSON

Lesson topic and staging

This lesson looks at travel and tourism. Students work on vocabulary connected to travel and tourism which is contextualised in a listening text. This is followed by a discussion on different reasons for travelling. Students then read a text on travel and tourism and answer questions to build up a detailed understanding of the content. Finally, students talk about and write a list of travel tips for someone visiting their country.

Objectives

By the end of the lesson students should have:

- extended their vocabulary within the topic of travel and tourism
- practised extracting specific information from the listening and a reading text
- focused on fluency and accuracy in speaking

Timings

If short of time, students could do exercise 8 individually after the lesson. Begin the next lesson by asking students to compare their travel tips with others in the class and decide on the best general tips.

A possible lesson break would be either after exercise 3b on page 16 or after exercise 5b on page 17.

WARM-UP

This activity introduces the topic of travel and *why* people travel.

- Focus students on the photo on page 16 and ask them where the men are and what they're doing.
- Ask students if they have seen *Easy Rider* (see Background information below) or a similar movie. Get students either to tell a partner about the movie or ask a few students to tell the rest of the class.
- Ask students individually to think of two reasons why people might go on long journeys (as in the movie *Easy Rider*).
- Put students into pairs to compare their ideas and decide which of the reasons is most likely.
- Finally, get a few ideas from the class.

(i) The photo shows a scene from the influential movie *Easy Rider* (1969). This is one of the most famous examples of a 'road movie', a story based on travelling by road across the USA. The main characters ride their motorcycles across the country to look for the 'real America'.

George Moore quote:

This quote is a very common idea and it is quite likely that your students have something similar in their own language. In summary, everything a person needs can be found at home and it's not necessary to travel to find it.

LISTENING AND VOCABULARY: travel expressions

1a Students do the activity as per the Coursebook. Ask students to compare their answers with a partner before you get answers from the class.

> **1** home; **2** abroad; **3** trip; **4** package; **5** journey; **6** travel; **7** destinations

1b Put students into pairs or small groups to ask/answer the questions. Encourage them to ask each other follow-up questions.

- For feedback, ask students what was the most interesting piece of information they heard.

Make this activity into a class survey by telling students to talk to as many different people as possible.

- When they have finished, put students into pairs to compare the information they found and prepare to report to the class on the following:
  - the student who has travelled the furthest from home
  - the number of students who have been abroad
  - the reasons people don't like package holidays
  - the most popular destinations for people from two different countries (if all your students are from the same country, leave this out).
- Finally, ask each pair to report their findings to the class.

2a Tell students there are four people asking Nadia questions, including some of the questions from 1a. Play the track without pausing.

> The following questions should be ticked: **1, 5, 7, 6.**

2b Before you play the track again, put students into pairs to discuss if they can remember any of the answers Nadia gives.

- Play the track, pausing at the points indicated in the audioscript to give students time to write.

- Tell students to write notes, not full sentences.
- Put students back into pairs to compare their answers before getting some ideas from the class.
- If there is a map in your room, point to the different places or ask students to find them. Ask if any of the students have been to these places.

Audioscript and answers (bold) to exercise 2b: Track 1.6

Nadia, Lisa, Armando, Jacques, Tom

N: OK, so that's my experience. Have you got any questions?
L: Hi, Nadia, my name's Lisa.
N: Hi, Lisa.
L: Nadia, what's the furthest you've travelled from home?
N: Mmm, let me think … well, I suppose the answer is **Indonesia**.
L: Indonesia? Did you enjoy it?
N: Yeah, it was fascinating, I went with a friend and we got on really well. And she's still a good friend, I'm pleased to tell you. The country's got thousands of islands and we visited quite a few of them. I must say, I'll never forget Komodo – they have the largest lizards in the world there, Komodo Dragons, and one of them chased us across the beach. It was absolutely terrifying, I can tell you! [PAUSE]
L: Wow! What an experience!
N: Mmm, not to be forgotten. Who's next?
A: Hi, I'm Armando.
N: Hi, Armando.
A: What's the longest journey you've been on?
N: You mean, in time?
A: Yeah, in time.
N: Well, **I've travelled for four months, three times.** During those trips, I visited … er … Mexico, Indonesia, India and many other south-east Asian countries, like Thailand and Vietnam. I loved Vietnam – the people were so friendly, and the food was wonderful. But it was a bit noisy in the streets – you know, a lot of people travel on motorbikes, and you hear them everywhere. [PAUSE]
J: Hi, I'm Jacques. Erm, what are the most popular destinations for people from your country?
N: Depends a lot on the group, Jacques, but **I'd say older people, say the over-fifties, they like to go to the Canary Islands, and young people prefer Thailand**, to really get away from it all. Next question? [PAUSE]
T: Hello Nadia, I'm Tom. People say that travel broadens the mind. What are the reasons why people travel, in your opinion?
N: Hmm, interesting question, Tom. I suppose there are lots of reasons. Some want to see new sights and explore new places, erm, meet new people and experience different cultures. I certainly wanted to do all those things. But I also wanted to learn new skills, especially social skills. I wanted to become more self-confident. Oh, yes, and I was also interested in learning a new language, or at least getting some knowledge of an Asian language. NOW my friend, Joanne, she just wanted to earn some money while she was abroad, to finance her studies. But there are lots of other reasons why people travel.
T: How do you mean, exactly?
N: Well, how can I put it, erm, some people travel to … erm, find themselves, I mean, to learn more about themselves, and perhaps become more independent, and just generally to broaden their horizons. One thing's for sure, Tom, if you travel a long way from home, for a long time, you're a different person when you return. It makes you into a …

3a Give students three minutes to try to complete the gaps before asking them to read the audioscript to check.

- When students have found all the answers, check they understand *find themselves* (discover more about your own personality), *get away from it all* (completely relax away from the problems of modern life), and *broaden their horizons* (get more understanding of life and different cultures).

1 see; **2** experience; **3** learn; **4** find; **5** become; **6** get; **7** meet; **8** explore; **9** learn; **10** broaden

3b Tell students to explain their reasons and to agree/disagree with each other if necessary.

- Ask two or three pairs to tell the class their three choices.

READING

4 Give students about five minutes to discuss the questions.

- Students may not understand question 3. It means: 'Can you experience different countries and cultures when you stay at home?'

(i) Thomas Cook (British, 1808–1892) started the travel agency with the same name. This agency is now internationally famous.

5a Give students three minutes to read the text and choose the headings. Tell them not to worry about unknown vocabulary.

a 3, b 1, d 2
Students may disagree on some of the answers. Encourage discussion and accept other reasonable ideas.

5b Check students understand *holiday resort* (a place specially designed for holidays), *tourist trap* (a place with a lot of tourists), *go off the beaten track* (go to places most other people don't go).

- Give students a maximum of ten minutes for this activity.

- Ask them to compare their answers with a partner. Then check with the whole class.

> **1** A traveller doesn't stay in holiday resorts, or go to tourist traps; a traveller goes for experience, longer and more challenging journeys, goes off the beaten track, discovers new places. A tourist goes on holiday to relax for a short time.; **2** Probably started by Thomas Cook who arranged first package tour in 1841. A 19 km trip for 500 people.; **3** Many may have only visited a small part of their own country. In the US, many people don't leave their own country.; **4** Someone who 'visits' different countries by watching TV at home.; **5** People can 'visit' different countries or parts of their own countries by watching documentaries on TV. So, some people argue there's no need to travel.; **6** Maybe people will use interactive computer programmes for 'virtual travel' instead of physically leaving their own homes.

SPEAKING AND WRITING

6 Give students a few minutes to think about the questions. Put them in pairs to discuss their answers.

7 Check students understand *travel tip* (advice to help people when travelling). Students then do the activity as per the Coursebook. Tell students to use their dictionaries if necessary.

> **1** read; **2** be; **3** insurance; **4** inoculations; **5** documents; **6** take; **7** find out; **8** customs; **9** respect; **10** accommodation

8 If your students are mostly from different countries, make sure they work with someone from the same country. Alternatively, tell them to write their travel tips individually and then compare with a partner.

HOMEWORK OPTIONS

Students do the exercises on page 11 of the Workbook.

Students write their travel tips after the lesson and compare their ideas at the start of the next lesson.

2.2 EXPLORERS

IN THIS LESSON

Lesson topic and staging

The topic of travel continues in this lesson with a focus on famous explorers. Students read a text on one of three explorers and then share the information with other students. This is followed by a focus on phrasal verbs and grammar (the past simple), both of which are contained in the texts students have read. Students work on the meaning, pronunciation and form of different verbs in the past simple tense before finally asking and answering personalised questions about each other's lives using the grammar from the lesson.

Objectives

By the end of the lesson students should have:

- learned a set of phrasal verbs connected to travel
- revised the form and use of the past simple tense
- revised/learned the pronunciation of *-ed* endings in regular past simple verbs
- practised reading a text to extract specific information and language items

Timings

If short of time, you could drop exercise 7 on page 19 and ask students to do it at home. If very short of time, you could also drop exercise 2b on page 18, but only if you feel students have learned enough about the texts from doing exercise 2a.

A possible lesson break would be after exercise 3b on page 19.

WARM-UP

This activity gives you the opportunity to assess students' knowledge/use of the past simple.

- Explain that students are going to find out about other students' last holiday.
- Ask students to draw two columns on a sheet of paper or in their notebooks.
- Write the following on the board and ask students to copy the list into the left-hand column:
  - stayed in this country
  - went to a different country
  - stayed in a hotel
  - travelled by plane
  - travelled by car
  - lay by the pool
  - went sightseeing
  - had a bad time

- Ask students what questions they need to ask (e.g. 'Did you stay in this country? Did you travel by plane?') and check they understand *went sightseeing* (visiting famous or interesting places).
- Tell students to move around the room asking as many people as possible and if the answer is 'yes', to write that student's name in the second column and ask follow-up questions ('Why did you stay in this country? Was the hotel nice?').
- Finally, ask students for the name of someone who did each of the things in the list.

READING

1 If students don't know or can't guess what these people did, explain they are all explorers and ask students to predict from the pictures and titles if they explored similar places or very different ones.

2a Make sure students only read their chosen text, and not the texts of the others in their group.

- Give students five minutes to read their text and complete their section of the chart.
- In their groups of three, students share information and complete the chart by telling each other information.
- Encourage students to help each other with problem vocabulary or ask them to use their dictionaries.

	Marco Polo	Cousteau	Tereshkova
Nationality	Italian	French	Russian
When born	1254	1910	1937
Job/work	Traveller and merchant	Film maker, undersea explorer, environmentalist, inventor	Textile plant worker, cosmonaut
Where travelled to	Across Asia and into China	The world's oceans	Space
Length of journey	24 years	No information	3 to 4 days
Greatest achievement	No information	Invented the aqualung	First woman in space
What they were called	Man of a million lies	No information	Chaika (seagull)
When died	1324	1997	No information

2b Students will probably not need to read their texts again to answer these questions.

- Put students back into their groups to share the information they found.
- As follow up, ask students to discuss who they think is the most interesting, brave or important explorer.

1 Jacques Cousteau; **2** Marco Polo; **3** Marco Polo; **4** Valentina Tereshkova; **5** Jacques Cousteau; **6** Valentina Tereskova (Note: *have a relationship* here means married/boyfriend/girlfriend, etc.); **7** Marco Polo; **8** Jacques Cousteau

VOCABULARY: phrasal verbs (1)

3a Ask or tell students what a phrasal verb is (verb + preposition with a meaning not obvious from its form) and give a few examples. Students then do the activity as per the Coursebook.

(!) The verbs in the text are in the past simple (except *look around*) while the meanings are in infinitives. Don't give or ask students for spelling changes at this stage because these are focused on in exercise 4b.

Set out: leave; Stop off: break a journey; Get back: return; Get to: arrive; (Note: *get back* means *arrive at where you started from*, not *return journey*.) Look around: explore; Carry on: continue.

3b Students do this individually and then compare with a partner.

Students have to decide if *get back* is infinitive or past simple. Tell students to look at the grammar around the verb (i.e. *didn't* + infinitive).

1 set out; **2** stopped off; **3** carried on; **4** got to; **5** looked around; **6** get back

GRAMMAR: past simple

4a Make sure students have found six verbs before starting exercise 4b and, if necessary, ask them to compare with another student who read the same text.

- Point out to students that in the Marco Polo and Jacques Cousteau texts there are more than six regular past simples.

4b Give students about five minutes to think about the spelling changes.

- Put them into the same groups of three as in exercise 2a and ask them to share the information they have.
- Ask them to think of rules to say what changes there are to spelling of these infinitives in the past simple.
- Write all the infinitives and past simples on the board to clearly show the spelling changes.

For a full explanation, ask students to look at the Language reference on page 136.

Marco Polo text
lasted: last + ed; sailed: sail + ed; stopped off: stop + ped; carried on: carry - y + ied; used: use + d; talked: talk + ed; believed: believe + d; died: die + d

(!) *Advanced* is an adjective in this text, not a verb.

Jacques Cousteau text
worked: work + ed; allowed: allow + ed; invented: invent + ed; produce: produce + d; introduced: introduce + d; started: start + ed; received: receive + d; died: die + d

(!) *fascinated* and *varied* are adjectives in this text, not verbs.

Valentina Tereshkova text
parachuted: parachute + d; jumped: jump + ed; worked: work + ed; lifted off: lift + ed; re-entered: re-enter + ed; married: marry - y + ied

(!) *selected* and *based on* are regular past participles. They are used in the passive voice here.

4c Students may know these verbs already. Give them a few minutes to write the past simple forms and check their answers in the texts.

become: became; begin: began; write: wrote; lead: led; take: took (Note: the verb is *take off – took off.*); go: went

5 Students think about the statements individually and then compare with a partner.

Statement **2** is not true (see Warning! below)

(!) Statement 2: *all my life* isn't generally used with the past simple. *Never* and *ever* are quite commonly used with the past simple (e.g. 'Did you ever get to Paris? No, I never got there.'). *Yet* can be used with the past simple, but this is more common in North American and Australian English.

With students at intermediate level, it may be better to restrict the information you give and simply tell them that statement 2 is not true.

For a full explanation and further practice, tell students to look at the Language reference on page 136 and Extra practice on page 137.

pronunciation

6a *-ed* endings. Before you play the audio track, ask students if they know how these endings are pronounced.

- Play the track and pause after each sentence so that students can compare what they heard with a partner.
- If necessary, play the track through once more without stopping.

Audioscript and answers:
Track 1.7

1. In 1943, Cousteau and engineer Emile Gagnan invented /ɪd/ the aqualung.
2. Cousteau produced /t/ many films and books ...
3. His journey lasted /ɪd/ 24 years ...
4. They sailed /d/ south from Venice ...
5. Marco Polo talked /t/ about his experiences in China ...
6. As a teenager she worked /t/ in a textile plant ...
7. The craft lifted /ɪd/ off from Tyuratam Launch Centre ...

Notes

- In verbs ending in *-ted* or *-ded*, the final *-ed* is pronounced /**Id**/.
- In verbs ending in a voiced consonant, the final *-d* or *-ed* is pronounced /**d**/, which is also voiced.
- In verbs ending in an unvoiced consonant, the final *-d* or *-ed* is pronounced /**t**/ which is also unvoiced.

(Tip) To demonstrate voiced/unvoiced to students, ask them to put their hands to their throats and make the sound /**s**/ and then the sound /**b**/. With /b/ they should feel vibration, with /s/ they should feel no vibration. Students can use this rule to decide how the *-ed* or *-d* ending should be pronounced.

6b Play the track again pausing after each sentence for students to repeat the *past simple verb* only.

- Listen carefully to what students produce and correct if necessary.

(!) Other words in these sentences will distract students. For this reason, ask them to only repeat the verb.

7 Students have seen most of these verbs so only set a short time limit. Check that students understand *pilot* (fly) before they begin.

1 explored/photographed/flew; **2** led / sailed; **3** brought; **4** found or discovered; **5** died/found or discovered. (Note: refer students to the preposition *in* to explain why the answer is *died*.); **6** piloted/ flew/hit

SPEAKING

8 Before students do this activity, ask them how to form past simple questions (this has not been covered in the lesson previously). If students have problems, write the form on the board i.e. *did* + *you* + infinitive (without *to*).

- As an example, write the year you started teaching at your school on the board and get students to ask you questions (e.g. 'Did you start university in ...?').

- Give students about five minutes to think of six dates or years. If they have problems thinking of any, prompt them with examples (e.g. when you started school/got your first job/left school/got your degree).
- Elicit the pronunciation of *did you* /dɪd jə/ and ask students to repeat.
- Then put students into pairs to ask/answer questions. Encourage them to ask follow-up questions.
- Monitor while students are speaking and note any common errors with the use of the past simple.
- At the end of the lesson, ask two or three students to tell the class something interesting they found out.
- Finally, correct a selection of the errors you noted earlier.

HOMEWORK OPTIONS

Students do the exercises on pages 12–13 of the Workbook.

Students review the past simple in the Language reference on page 136.

Students write sentences to explain the dates and years they wrote in exercise 8.

Students imagine they have a chance to interview one of the three explorers in the READING exercises. Ask them to write the questions they would like to ask, using the past simple and some of the phrasal verbs they learned in this lesson.

2.3 THE EMPTY QUARTER

IN THIS LESSON

Lesson topic and staging

This lesson begins with a text about Wilfred Thesiger, the famous explorer. Students do activities to help them focus on specific information and expressions/words contained in the text. This is followed by a listening activity and activities to focus students on specific information in the text and then on the pronunciation of weak forms. Next, students revise the present perfect and past simple, and contrast the uses of forms of these tenses. Finally, students do a speaking activity to decide if they are suitable for four travel-related jobs.

Objectives

By the end of the lesson students should have:

- extended their vocabulary
- revised and/or extended their knowledge of the form and use of the present perfect and past simple
- practised the pronunciation of weak forms in the present perfect and past simple
- practised reading an authentic text to extract specific information and language items

Timings

If short of time, you could drop exercises 9b, 10a and 10b on page 21 and ask students to do them after the lesson. In the following lesson, check the answers to these exercises and ask students to do the question/answer pairwork in exercise 10b.

A possible lesson break would be after exercise 5 on page 20.

WARM-UP

- Write the following words on the board: a compass; water; salt tablets; a good book; warm clothes; cool clothes; food; a satellite navigator; sunglasses; boots; a friend; a radio; a camel; a sun-hat. Check that students understand *compass, satellite navigator* and *camel.*
- Ask students to look at the photo on page 20. Tell students they have been left in the middle of a desert and they have to escape to safety. They only have three of the items from the list and they need to choose which ones they think would be the most important to keep. They need to think of reasons for their choices.
- Put students in pairs to compare their choices and to agree on three items. The pairs then form groups of four and repeat the procedure.
- Repeat the procedure until the whole class has decided the three things they would choose.

READING

1 Ask students to look at the photo, the author's name and the title on page 20. Ask why they think this text is called the 'Empty Quarter'.

- Put students into pairs to discuss the two questions, then share their ideas with the class.

> 1 &2 Students give their own ideas.

2a Give students a maximum of one minute to read the first text at the top of the page. Tell them not to worry about unknown vocabulary at this stage (for example, they may want to know the meanings of *urge* and *fierce*), as they will cover this later, in exercise 4.

> Wilfred Thesiger was attracted to the desert because he wanted to go somewhere other people had not been. He enjoyed the 'sense of space, the silence, and the crisp clearness of the sand'. He loved the Bedu.

2b Give students a maximum of three minutes to do this activity.

> **1** one of the greatest; **2** have won many literary prizes; his best known book; **3** a vast, waterless desert; **4** tribespeople living in the area; **5** he learned to love the Bedu and they learned to respect him

3 To lead in, ask students the name of Thesiger's best known book (they read this information in exercises 2a & b).

- Pre-teach *sunset* (when the sun goes down), *over* (finished), *ahead* (in front of/in the future).
- Students then do the activity as per the Coursebook.
- Finally, ask students if the Uruq al Shaiba are somewhere they'd like to visit.

> **1** False ('we would go on again at sunset'); **2** True ('the worst should be over now'); **3** True ('the worst of the journey which I had thought was behind us was still ahead'); **4** False (when they stopped the *second* time, they were near the Uruq al Shaiba); **5** False (Thesiger dreamed they were bigger than the Himalayas)

4 Students do the activity as per the Coursebook.

> **1** praised; **2** vast; **3** fierce; **4** respect; **5** urge; **6** bordered; **7** dune

5 Put students into pairs or small groups to discuss this question. Ask them to give reasons. Whey they have finished, ask how many students want to read the book.

LISTENING

6a This listening contextualises the present perfect and past simple which students then look at in exercises 8, 9 and 10.

- Explain that students are going to listen to Alicia Harker being interviewed for a place on an expedition (a journey involving a group of people to explore somewhere unknown or far away).
- Ask students what kind of places people normally go on expeditions to – this will check that they don't think this is normal travelling or a holiday.

> Suggested answers: a mountain range; a desert; a jungle

- Play the audio track without pausing and then elicit the answer from the class.

> An expedition to climb to the summit (top) of Mount Everest.

6b Play the track a second time without pausing and then put students into pairs to check their answers before getting answers from the class.

- Finally, ask students if this kind of expedition is something they'd like to do and why.

> The following should be ticked: 1, 3, 4, 6

i Mount Everest: the highest mountain in the world at 8856m and part of the Himalaya range on the border between Nepal and Tibet.

Sherpa Tensing: Tenzing Norgay: a very famous sherpa (Nepalese climbing guide) who was the first (or second) man to reach the summit of Mount Everest in 1953 along with Edmund Hillary the famous New Zealand climber. There is still debate about which man was the first to stand on the summit.

The Alps: the highest mountain range in Europe.

Audioscript and answers (bold) to exercise 8a: Track 1.8

Interviewer, Alice

I: Alice Harker? Come in. Have a seat.

A: Thank you.

I: Thanks for coming in today. Can I get you a coffee?

A: No thanks. **I've had two cups this morning.**

I: OK. Did you have a good journey here?

A: Yes, thanks. **I travelled up by train yesterday** and **I stayed in a hotel last night.** I'm catching a train back at half past eleven.

I: Oh, right, we'd better begin then. You've applied for a place on the 'Sherpa Tensing' expedition. Why do you want to go on this expedition?

A: Well, I've visited nearly every continent in the world, and I've done a lot of climbing, but **I've never done anything for charity before.**

continued…

I: I see. **Have you ever been on an expedition like this before?** I mean, this challenging?
A: Oh, yes, I've climbed extensively in the Alps and **I've already taken part in six Himalayan expeditions**, but **I haven't climbed to the summit of Everest yet.**
I: Well, you've had the right mountaineering experience, Ms Harker. So that's not a problem at all. Now, tell me something about your last job.
A: Mmm, well. **I worked as a consultant last year**, for a management consultancy firm, running team-building courses.
I: So why did you leave that job?
A: That isn't really what I want to do. I thought I'd try it, but really, I want to spend more time climbing. **I've been on two expeditions so far this year.**
I: OK, that's all very useful. Now, ... *[fade]*

pronunciation

7a Weak forms: The aim of this activity is to show students that it's often difficult to hear the difference between *I* and *I've* because their weak forms sound very similar.

- Play the audio track without pausing and then ask students to compare their answers before checking with the class.
- Explain that students may not be able to hear the difference between *I* and *I've* because they are both weak forms (the stress in on the verb).
- Write *I travelled* and *I've travelled* on the board and mark the stressed syllable (**tra**velled). Then write a schwa and schwa + /v/ (aɪ and aɪv) above *I* and *I've*. Say the sounds for students and ask them to repeat a few times.

If students cannot hear the difference between the weak forms at all, tell them that one way of deciding is to listen to the rest of the sentence. For example, if they hear *yesterday* or *last year*, the speaker will have used the past simple with *I* and not the present perfect with *I've*. (Don't give too much explanation at this stage because students will look at the past simple and the present perfect in exercises 8–10.)

Audioscript and answers:
Track 1.9
1 I travelled up by train yesterday.
2 I stayed in a hotel last night.
3 I've visited nearly every continent in the world.
4 I've climbed extensively in the Alps.
5 You've had the right mountaineering experience.
6 I worked as a consultant last year.

7b Pause the track after each sentence and ask students to repeat. Correct their pronunciation of weak forms *I* and *I've* if necessary.

GRAMMAR: present perfect and past simple

8a Before students begin this activity, check they know what a time adverb is by asking for or giving an example (e.g. *ever*).

- Point out to students that there are more than three examples of present perfect + time adverb in number 2. Tell students to find at least three in the audioscript.
- Ask students to compare their answers with a partner before you check with the whole class.
- As you go through the answers, ask students to underline the time expressions and adverbs.

The time expressions and adverbs are underlined in the answers below.
1 I travelled up by train <u>yesterday</u> / I stayed in a hotel <u>last night</u> / I worked as a consultant <u>last year.</u>
2 I've <u>already</u> taken part in six Himalayan expeditions / I haven't climbed to the summit of Everest <u>yet</u> / I've <u>never</u> done anything for charity <u>before</u> / Have you <u>ever</u> been on an expedition like this <u>before</u>?
3 I've had two cups <u>this morning</u> / I've been on two expeditions <u>so far this year</u>

8b Tell students to look at the example sentences they found in exercise 8a to help them with this activity.

- When you elicit the answers, ask students to give examples from exercise 8a.

1 present perfect: e.g. 'I've been on two expeditions so far this year.'; **2** past simple: e.g. 'I travelled up by train yesterday.'; **3** present perfect: e.g. 'I've never done anything for charity before.'

This is a good opportunity to revise the form of the present perfect. Ask students to look again at the example sentences in exercise 8a and then elicit the form to the board as follows:

Have or *has* + past participle; *haven't* or *hasn't* + past participle/*have* or *has* + subject + past participle (questions)

9a Students do the activity as per the Coursebook.

Sentences in track 1.8 with *already* and *yet*:
I've <u>already</u> taken part in six Himalayan expeditions / I haven't climbed to the summit of Everest <u>yet.</u>
1 yet; **2** before the main verb; **3** at the end

9b Monitor students to prompt them and correct if necessary. Ask students to compare with a partner before you go through the answers.

1 already; **2** this week; **3** never; **4** yet; **5** before

For a full explanation and further practice activities, ask students to go to pages 136–137 in the Language reference.

10a Students do this activity individually and then compare their answers with a partner.

- In feedback, ask students to say why the answers below are correct by referring to the information in exercise 8b.

1 I've never been; **2** left; **3** have already visited; **4** haven't finished; **5** I've known; **6** I've never been

10b Go through the example as a whole class.

- Give students about ten minutes to change the sentences to questions. Monitor to prompt and correct.
- Go through the answers before putting students in pairs to ask/answer the questions.
- Encourage students to ask follow-up questions (e.g. 'Why did you go to hospital?').
- Monitor while students are asking/answering questions and note errors with grammar form and the pronunciation of weak *I* and *I've*.
- For feedback, ask a few students to tell the class something interesting they found out.

1 Have you ever been in hospital?; **2** When did you leave school?; **3** Have you ever visited a foreign country?; **4** Have you finished your university studies yet?; **5** How long have you known your best friend?; **6** Have you ever been on a plane?

SPEAKING

11a Check students understand *field trip* (a scientific expedition to get information and examples, e.g. plants), and *volunteer* (someone who is not paid for doing this work).

- Give students five minutes to make notes about the four jobs. Monitor to check that they are writing appropriate ideas and to help with vocabulary they need.
- In feedback, write the jobs on the board and list some of the students' ideas under each one.

Answers will depend on students' ideas.

11b Give students two minutes to read about their jobs and check they understand *enthusiastic* (very willing and happy to do things) and that *voluntary* is the adjective of *volunteer*.

- Put students into A/B pairs and ask them to summarise the jobs for each other. (Note: students should not simply read the job descriptions out loud.)
- Ask students to read the example questions provided and then give them about five minutes individually to think about the questions they want to ask.
- Monitor students to help with vocabulary and correct the use of the past simple and present perfect.
- Put them back into A/B pairs to ask/answer the questions. Monitor to note errors with form and the pronunciation of weak *I* and *I've*.
- For feedback, ask students which job they think they (or their partner) are suitable for.
- Finally, correct some of the errors you noted earlier.

HOMEWORK OPTIONS

Students do the exercises on pages 14–15 of the Workbook.

Students review the past simple and present perfect on page 136 and do exercises G2 3 and G3 4 on page 137 of the Language reference.

Students write a summary of why they think their partner in exercise 11 (or they) wouldn't/wouldn't be suitable for the job(s). They need to use the third person singular and both the past simple and present perfect.

2.4 SCENARIO: A STUDY TRIP

IN THIS LESSON

Lesson topic and staging

This lesson looks at overseas study trips. Students are introduced to the scenario and discuss what could go wrong on a university trip to a foreign country. They then read a report summarising the mistakes made on such a trip, compare the ideas they had and categorise the mistakes. Students then listen to two organisers discussing specific problems mentioned in the report and focus on the KEY LANGUAGE of discussing advantages and disadvantages. This preparation leads to the main task in which students use the language they have learned to discuss the advantages and disadvantages of suggestions made for the next trip.

Objectives

By the end of the lesson, students should have:

- extracted specific information and language from a listening and a reading text
- learned useful phrases for discussing advantages and disadvantages
- used this language in a 'real-life' situation to discuss different suggestions
- participated effectively in extended speaking practice

Common European Framework

Students can use language effectively to discuss the advantages and disadvantages of different suggestions.

Timings

If short of time, you could drop exercises 3 and 4 b on page 22 as these are not essential to students' understanding of the reading and listening texts.

A possible lesson break would be after exercise 5 on page 23.

WARM-UP

- Ask students to look at the photos on pages 22 and 23 and ask if anyone has been to these places/ countries.
- Then ask students to think about trips they went on when they were at university or school (either with the university/school or with their family/friends), where they went and why.
- Put students into pairs to tell each other about one of these trips and any particularly memorable or amusing incidents, or something that went wrong.
- Finally, ask students to tell the class the most amusing or interesting thing they heard about.

SITUATION

1 Give students 30 seconds to read the situation and then put them in pairs to discuss the question.

Answers will depend on students' own ideas.

2a Give students two minutes to read the text and compare the mistakes with the ones they discussed in exercise 1.

2b Check students understand *theft* (stealing something). Give students three minutes to reread the text and then compare their answers with a partner.

1 language; **2** organisation; **3** violence; **4** money; **5** theft; **6** organisation; **7** transport; **8** language

3 Students do the activity as per the Coursebook. Groups should have a maximum of three students.

1 & 2 Answers will depend on students' own opinions and discussion.

4a Introduce the context and then play the track without pausing.

Theft: their cameras were stolen; language: students were afraid to go to the police because of the language problem.

Audioscript and answers (bold) to exercise 5: Track 1.10

Harry, Ingrid

H: We need to think about the problems on the last trip so we don't have the same ones this year.

I: I agree with you, Harry, a lot went wrong. The group never became a team, did it? They just didn't get on with each other at all.

H: Yeah, some of them ended up hating each other. The problem was that they didn't know each other well enough before they left.

I: Yeah, I agree, it was a big problem throughout the trip.

H: Definitely. You know, another thing, they didn't know what to do if anything went wrong, like, erm ... remember when they lost their cameras?

I: Oh, hold on, Harry, they didn't lose their cameras, they were robbed. But why didn't they go immediately to the police and report the matter? We only heard about it a couple of days later, when it was too late. So, they got no money from the insurance company because they didn't report the matter.

H: Well, they said they were afraid to go to the police – they didn't think the police would speak English.

continued...

I: That was pretty stupid, surely. Lots of people speak English there now. You know, the students got on my nerves at times – they were always complaining. The accommodation was no good, the hotels were for business people, not students. I mean, it was rubbish. The hotels were fine, in my opinion. And you know what really upset me, Harry?
H: Yeah?
I: They said we tried to do too much during the trip. They didn't have enough free time.
H: Well, we talked about that before we went, how much free time to give them. There are **arguments for** and **against**, aren't there? On the one hand, giving them a lot of free time is good – they have a chance to explore places they visit. **On the other hand**, if they have too much time, they say we haven't organised enough trips. You can't win, can you?
I: True, and don't forget Harry, **another disadvantage** of giving them a lot of free time is that they get into trouble. You know, they do stupid things. Look what happened last time – remember those students who slept all night in the park?
H: Don't remind me! Actually I've got a few suggestions for this next trip.
I: Me too.
H: Good. Well I think **we should** have more meetings with the students before they leave. An advantage of this is they get to know each other a lot better.
I: Yeah. That's true. Also, it'd be **a good idea** to give the students maps of the cities they visit. I suggest **we write** to the tourist boards and ask them to send us some.
H: Yeah, why not? And **how about** asking the students where they want to stay? Do they want to share a room in a cheap hotel, or stay in a youth hostel? There are lots of possibilities.
I: Yeah, let's do that, Harry, let's ask them and then they won't be able to complain later.

4b Play the track again and ask students to make notes on the other problems the organisers talk about, comparing their notes with a partner. In feedback, check students understand *got on my nerves* (irritated me).

Relations with students: students didn't get on with each other – they didn't know each other before the trip; students complained to organisers; students got on Ingrid's nerves.
Hotels: students said accommodation was no good – hotels were for business people, not students.
Free time: students said they didn't get enough free time – but it's a difficult balance between too much and too little free time.

KEY LANGUAGE: discussing advantages and disadvantages; making suggestions

5 Play the track again, pausing after each extract to give students time to write. If students find the listening difficult, pause the track after each answer. In feedback, go through the notes in brackets below.

1 arguments for (tell students that 1&2 make a single phrase); **2** against (see note above); **3** On the other hand (the first part of this phrase is *On the one hand*. Used to balance opinions); **4** another disadvantage (followed by *of* + verb-*ing*); **5** we should (*should* + infinitive. Used to give advice or suggestion); **6** good idea (followed by *to* infinitive); **7** we write (*suggest* + subject + verb); **8** how about (*how about* + verb-*ing*. Used to give a suggestion)

6 Give students two minutes to think about their answers. Put them in small groups to discuss their ideas.

TASK: organising a study trip

7a Read through the situation with students and look together at the OTHER USEFUL PHRASES on page 23.

- Give students three minutes to think about their ideas individually and then put them in small groups for the discussion.
- Monitor students during the discussion and note common or important mistakes, but don't interrupt them.
- In feedback, go through some of the mistakes you noted above and tell them they will get a chance to practise the KEY LANGUAGE in exercise 7b and c.

7b Give the groups about five minutes for this activity and make sure they all write the suggestions down.

7c Put the groups together to form larger groups or, to avoid groups becoming too large, put one student from each group from exercise 7b into new groups of about the same number.

- For each suggestion, the group should discuss the advantages and disadvantages.
- Monitor and note common or important mistakes and provide corrections after the activity.

HOMEWORK OPTIONS

Students do the exercises on page 16 of the Workbook.

Students write an email to the Head of the History Department at Arcadia University summarising the five best suggestions from exercise 7, and using some of the KEY and USEFUL LANGUAGE from page 23.

2.5 STUDY AND WRITING SKILLS

IN THIS LESSON

Lesson topic and staging

This lesson focuses on the skills of note-taking while listening and writing a biographical profile. Students discuss different ways of taking notes and then listen to a talk about the famous explorer, Thor Heyerdahl, to put these ideas into practice. The students then read a short biography of the famous aviator, Amelia Earhart. The accompanying activities prepare students for writing a similar profile by focusing them on text structure and time linkers (*before*, *when*, *while*, etc.). Finally, students write a profile of Thor Heyerdahl using the notes they made at the beginning of the lesson.

Objectives

By the end of the lesson, students should have:

- experimented with different ways of note-taking while listening and decided which works best for them
- been introduced to the structure and use of time linkers (*before*, *while*, *during*, etc.)
- written a short biographical profile

Common European Framework

Students can take notes efficiently and write a biographical profile.

Timings

If time is short, ask students to do exercise 4 on page 25 and/or the writing exercise 7 for homework.

A possible lesson break would be after exercise 2d on page 24.

WARM-UP

- To lead in to the activities on note-taking, ask students if they find taking notes while listening difficult (the answer will be 'yes'!).
- Put students into pairs and ask them to list as many reasons as possible why they find this difficult.

STUDY SKILLS: note-taking while listening

1a Explain that students are going to read and discuss different ways of making notes while listening.

- Ask students to read through the bullet points individually before putting them in pairs to discuss.
- Walk round the room to help students with vocabulary (e.g. *structuring language, mind maps*).

Students will probably agree with bullet points: 1; 2; 3; 5; 7; 8; 10 – but be prepared to accept other answers.

1b When students have finished this activity, put the pairs together in groups of four to share their ideas.

2a Go through the introduction and explain that we focus on nouns, verbs and sometimes adjectives because they carry the most meaning in a text.

- Put students into pairs to discuss the extract and notes, then elicit ideas and examples.
- Finally, ask students if they think the notes are clear and if they can use this method.

The notes use the important nouns, verbs and adjectives. There are no prepositions, subject pronouns or articles. They also use abbreviations (e.g. trav., 20C, Mid. East) and symbols (e.g. –).

2b Focus students on the photo on page 24 and ask if anyone knows about the Kon-Tiki raft (boat).

- Ask students to read the first sentence of the rubric and then look at the notes on page 24.
- Check students understand the Roman numerals (i.e. i = 1, ii = 2, iii = 3, iv = 4, v = 5).
- Tell students not to fill the gaps but only to predict the kind of information (e.g. gaps 1 and 2 will probably be places and dates, gap 4 will probably be where he studied).

2c Play the track without pausing. After students have compared their answers, play the track again.

To make this activity as realistic as possible, it's better not to pause the track. However, the text is very long and if your students find it difficult, pause the track where indicated in the audioscript, then ask students to read the audioscript on page 170 to check their answers.

1 Southern Norway; **2** 1914; **3** studied; **4** Oslo; **5** expedition; **6** 1938; **7** islands; **8** 1947; **9** 101; **10** sailors; **11** oceans; **12** organised; **13** 1952; **14** Island expedition; **15** sailed; **16** Atlantic; **17** America; **18** believe; **19** expeditions; **20** ideas; **21** 1948; **22** 1980; **23** awards; **24** Sciences; **25** American; **26** 1960; **27** film; **28** won; **29** documentary; **30** Italy

Track 1.11

Good morning. The subject of today's talk is the explorer Thor Heyerdahl. First of all I'll give you some background information before going on to look at his career, achievements and finally his main publications and awards.

Heyerdahl was born in Larvik in Southern Norway in 1914. He studied Zoology and Geography at the University of Oslo and then made his first expedition to Polynesia from 1937 to 1938. While he was staying in Polynesia, Heyerdahl became interested in how the islands were first inhabited. He had the idea that humans

continued...

came with the ocean currents from the west. [PAUSE]
Now I'd like to look at his career. After giving up his study of geography he set out to prove his theories. How did he attempt to test his theories? Well, to begin with, in 1947 he built a raft named the *Kon-Tiki*, and then with five companions crossed from Peru to Polynesia in 101 days. The main idea he wanted to prove was that the cultures of the ancient world were linked by sailors who could cross oceans. [PAUSE] After the success of the Kon-Tiki expedition, Heyerdahl continued to travel. He organised the Norwegian Archaeological Expedition to the Galapagos Islands in 1952, before leading an expedition to Easter Island from 1955 to 1956. In addition to this, during 1969 and 1970 he sailed two more rafts, *Ra 1* and *Ra 2*, across the Atlantic, to show that ancient Egyptians had contact with South America. [PAUSE]
What will Heyerdahl be remembered for? Well, most people believe his greatest achievement was the Kon-Tiki Expedition. However, all his expeditions and ideas had a great influence on anthropology and archaeology. Moving on to his publications, the most famous were *The Kon-Tiki Expedition*, in 1948, *The Ra Expeditions*, in 1970 and *The Tigris Expedition* in 1980.
Finally, I'd like to turn to his awards. He received many awards during his lifetime – two of the most important were his election to the Norwegian Academy of Sciences in 1958, and then the American Academy of Science in 1960. Furthermore, his film of the *Kon-Tiki* expedition won an Oscar in 1951 for best documentary feature.
Thor Heyerdahl died in 2002 at his home in Italy.

2d Students do the activity as per the Coursebook.

a ii); c iv); d v); e iii); f i); headings b and g are extra.

WRITING SKILLS: a biographical profile

3 Focus students on the photo and title on page 25 and elicit or tell them that Amelia Earhart is a famous aviator/pilot (who died in the 1930s).

- Give students three minutes to do the activity and tell them not to worry about vocabulary because they will look at this in exercise 4.

a paragraph 4; **b** paragraph 1; **c** paragraph 2; **d** paragraph 5; **e** paragraph 3

4 Students have seen some of this vocabulary before, so give them two minutes to suggest any verbs they can *before* reading the text.

(!) The verbs in the text are in the past simple, but the definitions in exercise 4 use infinitives. Accept either form as answers. Number 8 (*be awarded*) is in the passive voice in the text, but this is not clear from the definition.

1 fired; **2** graduate; **3** train; **4** attend; **5** give up; **6** move; **7** publish; **8** be awarded

5a Time linkers: Students work individually and then compare their answers with a partner. Go through the notes below with the class.

Before: + noun + past simple, e.g. *before her third book was published* (past simple passive voice)
After: + verb-*ing*, e.g. *after graduating, after stopping* OR + time phrase (noun) e.g. *after a year*
When: + noun + past simple, e.g. *when her father was fired* (past simple passive voice)
During: + time phrase (noun) + past simple, e.g. *during that time, she also wrote*
While: + past continuous e.g. *while she was crossing*
(Note: the nouns following *after* and *during* are time phrases [*a year; that time*] in these examples. Other nouns can also be used, e.g. *after dinner; during summer*.)

(!) Tell students that *before* + verb-*ing* is a possible structure because they will need this in exercise 6.

5b Give students a short time to discuss the question in pairs before you elicit the answer.

During is followed by a time phrase (e.g. *during that time*), *while* is followed by a verb/an action (*while she was crossing*).

6 This is a challenging activity, so ask students to work in pairs. Monitor to help students if necessary.

1 Heyerdahl received a number of awards <u>during</u> b) his lifetime.; **2** Heyerdahl went to the Galapagos Islands <u>before</u> a) leading an expedition to Easter Island ; **3** Heyerdahl became curious about how the islands were inhabited <u>while</u> c) he was staying in Polynesia.; **4** He set out to prove his theories <u>after</u> d) giving up his study of geography.

7 Give students plenty of time to write their biographical profiles.

- Tell students to ask if they need help with vocabulary and walk round the room to spot mistakes in using time linkers. Encourage students to self-correct by looking again at exercises 5 and 6.
- Ask students to read each other's profiles and try to correct mistakes.
- Take the profiles in for marking, paying particular attention to how well they have used the notes in exercises 2c and 2d, and their use of time linkers.

HOMEWORK OPTIONS

Students do the exercises on page 17 of the Workbook.

Students listen to a text in English after the lesson (e.g. a podcast, a radio report, a television report) and practise taking notes. In the next lesson, students use their notes to tell a partner what they heard about.

Work

3

3.1 JOBS

IN THIS LESSON

Lesson topic and staging

This lesson looks at different jobs and work situations. Students discuss a selection of jobs and then listen to five people talking about their jobs. Next, students look at adjectives to describe jobs (e.g. *stressful*) Students then read four job advertisements and focus on vocabulary from the texts and dependent prepositions (e.g. *responsible for*). Next, students write job advertisements and practise using the vocabulary introduced earlier. Finally, students discuss important factors in a job and their own 'dream job'.

Objectives

By the end of the lesson, students should have:

- discussed the pros and cons of different jobs and decided on what kind of work they would like and why
- revised and extended their vocabulary and dependent prepositions in the context of jobs
- extracted specific information and language items from a listening and reading texts
- written a job advertisement

Timings

If short of time, you could drop exercise 7 on page 27 and set it for homework.

A possible lesson break would be after exercise 6 on page 27.

WARM-UP

- Tell students to think of a job (e.g. teacher, doctor, etc.) but not to tell anyone what it is,
- Put students into groups of three or four and tell them to ask each other five questions to find out what the job is.
- They can only ask 'yes/no' questions (e.g. 'Do you work with people?').

Groucho Marx quote:

This quote uses the fairly common English phrase 'I worked myself up from nothing to become the richest/most successful/top business person/actor, etc'. Marx has used the phrase but ended it in an unexpected way to say that he was originally unsuccessful and it still unsuccessful now. The humour depends on our knowledge of the original phrase and how it is normally used.

(i) Groucho Marx (1890–1977). A famous American comedian and film star who normally worked with his brothers Harpo, Chico and Zeppo. They made many well-known films including *Duck Soup* (1933) and *A Night at the Opera* (1935).

SPEAKING

1 Check students understand *status* in question 2.

- Then put them in pairs or small groups to discuss the jobs and questions.
- Help students with vocabulary or ask them to use their dictionaries.
- Finally, ask a few students to tell the class about two jobs they talked about.

If time is short, tell students to discuss only five jobs from the list.

LISTENING

2a Pause the track after each speaker to give students time to choose the job.

- Ask students to compare with a partner before you check answers with the class.
- Don't focus on problem vocabulary at this stage because students will learn this in exercise 2b.

1 nurse; **2** lawyer; **3** model; **4** shop assistant; **5** journalist

2b Put students in pairs to list the key words they heard and can remember.

- Then, if necessary, ask students to look at the audioscript on page 171 to check.
- Go through answers with the class.
- Finally, check they understand the key words by asking for examples (e.g. *shifts* – working from 24.00–08.00, or 04.00–12.00) or giving definitions.

Key words are: **1** shifts, patients; **2** (routine) paperwork, cases (i.e. legal cases), clients (i.e. a more formal word for *customers*), court (i.e. a court of law); **3** glamorous, photographers, stylists; **4** filling shelves, window displays, customers, refunds, big chain (i.e. a company with a lot of shops), branch (i.e. one of the shops in the chain); **5** interviewing people, article (i.e. a text written for a newspaper or magazine), published, monthly magazine, (tight) deadlines

2c Set the activity and tell students the speakers don't always say they dislike something but it is implied.

- Play the track and pause after each speaker to give students time to make notes.
- Ask students to compare with a partner before you check answers with the class.

1 Likes: colleagues; variety of the work; contact with patients; helping people. Dislikes: long hours; work shifts; the pay; **2** Likes: meeting clients; going to court; good opportunities for promotion; travel. Dislikes: paperwork; a lot of meetings; **3** Likes: the pay; the travel. Dislikes: not much job security; doesn't always work (i.e. has to break for a few weeks); waiting around for photographers and stylists; **4** Likes: dealing with people; boss is a lovely person. Dislikes: [some parts of the job are] not very interesting e.g. filling shelves, changing the window displays; disorganised boss; problem customers. **5** Likes: very flexible; work from home sometimes; meeting and interviewing different people; finishing a long article which is published; writing a book. Dislikes: tight deadlines

Track 1.12

1

Well, the hours are very long and I have to work shifts, but I like my colleagues and I enjoy the variety of the work. You know, every day's different. I suppose the main reason I like the job is the contact with patients. I like to feel that I'm helping people, and my colleagues are great, so that makes the job very rewarding. It's certainly not the pay – that's terrible!

2

I really enjoy my job, although there can be a lot of routine paperwork and I have to attend a lot of meetings. Preparing cases takes up a lot of my time, and can be very challenging. The best parts of the job are meeting clients and going to court. I work for a big international firm so there are good opportunities for promotion and I get to travel quite a lot, which is nice.

3

Some people would say it's a glamorous job, and I suppose it is sometimes, but actually it's very hard work as well. There's also not much job security. The pay's good, but sometimes I don't work for a few weeks so that can be a worry. I suppose I enjoy the travel – there's a lot of that – but sometimes there's a lot of waiting around for photographers and stylists, which can be really boring.

4

Some parts of the job are not very interesting, like filling shelves. Also, changing the window displays gets a bit repetitive. Really, it's dealing with people I like, on the phone and face to face. My boss is a lovely person but he's so badly organised. He usually gets me to deal with problem customers who want refunds, that kind of thing. Some people think I'm a workaholic, and it's true I do a lot of overtime, but I like to do a job well and I'm proud of my work. It's a big chain so I hope I'll become assistant manager next year if I move to another branch.

continued…

5

What I particularly like is that it's a very flexible job. I can work from home some of the time. I find it exciting, meeting and interviewing different people. It's also satisfying when you finish a long article and it's published. I've got a book coming out next year as well. One thing about working on a monthly magazine is that I have a lot of tight deadlines. That makes the job very stressful.

VOCABULARY: work adjectives

3a Do number 9 with the class an example (*flexible* was included in exercise 2 above).

- Give students five minutes to complete the other words.
- Check answers with the class.
- Then, put students into pairs or small groups to answer the question.
- Finally, ask a few students to tell the class their answers and to give reasons.

1 rewarding; **2** challenging; **3** glamorous; **4** stressful; **5** boring; **6** repetitive; **7** satisfying; **8** exciting; **9** flexible

You can use students' answers and ideas to check the meaning of the adjectives (1–9 above). For example, if students don't believe a firefighter's job is stressful, or say that a teacher's job is glamorous, it might mean they don't understand the adjective.

3b Give students a few minutes to tick the jobs they would like to do and cross the ones they wouldn't.

- Then, put them into pairs or small groups to compare their answers.
- Tell them to give reasons and to ask each other follow-up questions.
- Finally, choose three or four of the jobs from exercise 1 and ask students if they'd like to do them and why.

To extend this activity, ask students to talk to as many others as possible to find someone who wants to do the same jobs as them. Alternatively, they could do a class survey to find the most/least popular jobs.

READING

4 Focus students on the four job advertisements and ask where they might see these (e.g. in a newspaper).

- Tell students to read the eight statements and check they understand *anti-social hours* (working hours outside the normal working day, e.g. after 6 p.m., before 8 a.m. or at weekends) and *in charge of* (the boss of someone).

- Give students five minutes to do the activity and tell them not to worry about unknown vocabulary at this stage. (Note: Don't pre-teach vocabulary from the four texts because this will give students the answers to this activity.)
- Go through answers with the class and check students understand the vocabulary shown in bold below. (Note: there are two possible answers for statement four. Students are likely to answer A [Marketing Executive], but some may also suggest C [Assistant to Finance Director].)

1 A Marketing Executive (the country's leading sports shoe manufacturer); **2** D Chief Administrator; **3** C Assistant to Finance Director (and the Chief Executive when she travels abroad); **4** A Marketing Executive (spend time at our **overseas** branches in Rome and Berlin); C Assistant to Finance Director (and the Chief Executive when she travels abroad) ; **5** D Chief Administrator (some evening and weekend work); **6** B Sales Manager (**Annual Bonus**); **7** C Assistant to Finance Director (**prospects** for rapid **career progress**); **8** B Sales Manager (**leading** and **motivating** a large sales team)

5 Check students understand *fluency* (number 6).

- Give them one minute to match the prepositions to the words without reading the advertisements again.
- Then give students two minutes to find and underline the words plus prepositions in the advertisements.
- Go through answers with the class.

1 looking for; **2** experience of; **3** depend on; **4** responsible for; **5** knowledge of; **6** fluency in; **7** report to; **8** prospects for

6 Give students one minute to think about their answer and reasons.

- Put them into pairs and ask them to tell each other the reasons they chose a particular job.
- For feedback, ask for a show of hands for each job and decide which is the most popular and why.

WRITING

7 Give pairs one minute to decide what job to advertise and if they can't decide, provide a few examples.

- Monitor to make sure they are using the adjectives plus prepositions from exercise 6 and to provide additional vocabulary if necessary.
- When they have finished, ask students to swap their advertisements with another pair and decide if they want to apply for this job and why.

While monitoring, you could focus students' attention on other useful language patterns, e.g. the use of the future simple is very common in job advertisements.

To extend this activity, post the advertisements around the room. Tell students to read them all and decide which job they would like to apply for. Finally, vote on the most popular job advertisement.

SPEAKING

8 Read through the list with the class and check students understand *pension* (money paid after you stop work at 60–65, for example), *prestigious* (high status), and *competitive salary* (a salary that is at least as good as those offered by similar jobs in similar companies).

- Give students one minute to think about their answers individually before discussing with a partner.
- Encourage them to use their own ideas as well as those in the list provided.

To extend this activity, ask students to speak to as many others as possible to find out which ideas in the list are the most/least important to the class as a whole. Then put them into pairs to compare their findings. To follow up, ask the pairs to discuss some of the questions below:

Did the others in the class find the same things important as you?

Did students from the same country find the same things important? Why/why not?

Do you think people 50 years ago would find the same things important?

8b Keep students in the same pairs as exercise 8a.

- Give them one minute to think about their answer individually.
- If your students don't have the experience to think of their own 'dream jobs', give them a few suggestions first.
- For feedback, ask a few students to tell the whole group their ideas.

HOMEWORK OPTIONS

Students do the exercises on page 18 of the Workbook.

Students look at some job advertisements in a newspaper or on the Internet and choose one they would like to do. In the next lesson, ask students to tell each other about the job they chose and why they chose it. Students should use the vocabulary learned in this lesson when reporting back.

3.2 HOMEWORKING

IN THIS LESSON

Lesson topic and staging

This lesson looks at the benefits and difficulties of working from home. Students read an article on homeworking, focus on expressions connected with time and work and then discuss the pros and cons of homeworking. Students then study the meaning and form of the present perfect continuous and practise using it. Next, students listen to five people talking about homeworking and complete sentences using the grammar studied earlier. They then do an activity on sentence stress to correct misinformation. Finally, students use the grammar to talk about their own experiences.

Objectives

By the end of the lesson, students should have:

- considered the advantages and disadvantages of working from home (homeworking)
- extracted specific information and language items from a reading and listening text
- learned a set of collocations connected with time and work
- revised and extended their knowledge and use of the present perfect simple and continuous to talk about time-frames beginning in the past and continuing in the present
- discussed their opinions on homeworking and used the present perfect simple and continuous in a personalised speaking activity

Timings

If short of time, and your students are confident with the grammar focus, set exercise 7 for homework.

A possible lesson break would be after exercise 4 or 5c on page 29.

WARM-UP

This activity introduces/tests the present perfect continuous with *How long?*

- Write *How long?*, *house*, and one of the following: *city*, *country*, *town* (which you write will depend on the class you have).
- Ask students to ask as many other students as possible 'How long have you been living in your house/this city?'
- At the end of the activity, ask who has been living there the longest.

READING

1a Focus students on the photo. Ask what the man is doing and where he is (doing 'office work' but he's at home, not in an office).

- Set the questions and elicit answers from the class.

While getting answers from the class, also elicit/give the word *homeworking*.

1b Give students one minute to think about their answers and then put them in pairs to compare.

- Get answers from the class and write them on the board so students can refer to them in exercise 2a.

> Answers will depend on students' own ideas.

2a Remind students their ideas from exercise 1b are written on the board.

- Give students two minutes to read the article and tell them not to worry about vocabulary at this stage.
- Ask students to compare with a partner before you check answers with the class.

2b Set a longer time limit than in exercise 2a.

- Ask students to compare with a partner before you check answers with the class. (Note: Don't follow up by asking if students would like to work from home because this is discussed in exercise 4.)

> **1** since he was five; **2** for three years; **3** 2.1 million (another eight million spend some time working from home); **4** office space is costly; reduce workstations; move to a smaller site; employees often work better at home; employees can start the day fresher and therefore work more efficiently; **5** employees miss the social side of work; **6** phone, email and video conferences

VOCABULARY: expressions connected with time and work

3a Tell students that all the expressions (1–5) come from the article in exercise 2.

- Give students one minute for this activity.

> **1** b; **2** a; **3** e; **4** c; **5** d

3b Students work individually and then compare answers with a partner

- Go through answers with the class.

> **1** time management; **2** spend (a lot of) time; **3** time-consuming; **4** workstations; **5** work-life balance

SPEAKING

4 Give students a maximum of five minutes to think about their answers individually.

- Put them into pairs and allow plenty of time for the discussion.
- Monitor to note mistakes with 'time' and 'work' expressions.
- When they have finished, ask a few students to summarise their discussion.
- Finally, correct some of the most common mistakes you noted earlier.

An alternative procedure is: Divide the class into two groups: employers and employees. Tell the 'employers' to discuss question 1 and the employees to discuss question 2. Both groups should discuss question 3 from the perspective of either 'employers' or 'employees'. Then put the class into pairs, one employer and one employee in each pair, and give them five minutes to persuade the other that homeworking is a bad (or a good) thing. When they have finished, ask each pair what they decided.

GRAMMAR: present perfect continuous

Students at this level will probably have been introduced to the present perfect continuous before. Often, they can recognise it but are unsure about using it.

5a Students answer the question individually and then compare with a partner.

- Check answers with the class.

Students might think *last* in *For the last three years* is being used in the same way as *last week* or *last year* and therefore think that this sentence refers to an activity that is finished. Tell them that *For the last three years* means a period beginning three years ago and continuing now.

> Statements 1, 3 and 4 are all true about the present perfect continuous.

5b Give students 30 seconds to complete the rule.

- Check answers with the class.
- Finally, read through the GRAMMAR TIP with the class and give a full example (e.g. 'We can't use: I've been knowing him since I was at school.'). Elicit/tell students that we have to use the present perfect simple ('I've known him since I was at school.') instead.

> We use *since* + a point in time (when the activity started) and *for* + a period of time.

There is a useful timeline in the Language reference on page 138 that clearly demonstrates *for/since*.

For exercise 5c, students need to know the question form, but this is not included in the Language reference. Make sure you either introduce *how long* + *has/have* + subject + *been* + verb-*ing* before students do the next exercise, OR monitor to correct them if they make a mistake.

5c Read through the instructions and the example with the class.

- Give students five to ten minutes to complete the sentences.
- Monitor to point out mistakes, but encourage students to self-correct by using the Language reference and exercises 5a, 5b and the GRAMMAR TIP.
- Ask students to compare with a partner before you check answers with the class.

To make feedback as clear as possible, write the sentences on the board as you elicit them from the class.

> **1** Cristina has been working as a designer since she graduated.; **2** I've known Yukiyo for six months.; **3** How long has Mohamed been studying engineering at university?; **4** Fuat has been living in Istanbul since he got a job there.; **5** Marianna has been working at home for two years.; **6** I haven't been living here for very long.; **7** Ji Hyun has understood the problem since yesterday morning.; **8** Have Mark and Julie been teaching at the same college for a year?

LISTENING

6a Ask students some of the reasons Sunjit Patel gave for working from home (exercise 2).

- Then set the activity and play the track without pausing.
- Elicit answers from the class.

> **1** translator; **2** writer; **3** website designer; **4** designer; **5** marketing

6b Give students one minute to write any answers they can remember before you play the track again.

- Pause the track after each speaker to give students time to note their answers.
- Ask students to compare with a partner before you check answers with the class.

> **1** 12 years; likes working from home, work-life balance easier to manage (this is necessary because of the children); **2** 18 months; doesn't like working from home, paying a lot more for heating, misses the office gossip, it's lonely; **3** since 2004; likes working from home, being his own boss, has more time, taking guitar lessons; **4** since January; likes working from home, doesn't have to commute on crowded trains, has lots more time, learning Spanish; **5** since January; likes working from home, can get up late and work late in the evenings, not a morning person (doesn't like getting up/can't work well in the morning)

To extend this activity, ask students if any of the reasons given above are reasons that they would/ wouldn't like to work from home. Put them in pairs to discuss their answers and ask each other for more information, e.g. 'Why do you want more time?'

7 Give students a maximum of five minutes to complete the extracts.

- Ask them to compare with a partner before you check answers with the class.
- Alternatively, play the recording again so that students can check their answers or ask them to look at the audioscript on page 171.

1 I've been translating; **2** I've been working; **3** I've been paying; **4** I've been working; **5** I've been taking; **6** I've been learning; **7** I've been living; **8** I've (never) been. (Answers are in bold in audioscript below.)

Audioscript and answers to exercise 7:
Track 1.13

1
I'm a language graduate and **1 I've been translating** from Italian to English for most of my career. We've been in Milan for nearly 20 years and **2 I've been working** from home for 12 years, since my first child was born. I've found that my work-life balance has been easier to manage since I started working from home – and it needs to be easy to manage when you've got children!

2
I'm a writer and I've been working from home for the last 18 months. I must say it's been pretty tough. For one thing **3 I've been paying** a lot more for heating. And I've missed the office gossip. To be honest, it's quite lonely … I almost wish I could go back to my old job.

3
Working from home has really changed my life. I love it. I love being my own boss. **4 I've been working** from home as a website designer since I left my last job in 2004. I have a bit more time these days … I've bought myself a new guitar and **5 I've been taking** guitar lessons for the last six months.

4
It's not for everybody, but I like working from home. I do contract work in design. The best thing is that I don't have to commute to work on crowded trains. I've had lots more time and **6 I've been learning** a new language since I started working at home in January. I've always wanted to learn Spanish.

5
I'm German but **7 I've been living** abroad for five years. I've been working in marketing for a pharmaceutical company near London and I've been working from home part of the time since January. I work from home three days a week and commute in to the office twice a week. I was very lucky to get this opportunity. When I work from home I get up late and work late in the evenings. **8 I've never been** a morning person.

pronunciation

8 Correcting politely

- Ask students to read the dialogue and tell them that speaker B is politely correcting speaker A.
- Play the track and then ask students to compare their answers with a partner.
- Elicit answers from the class and reinforce this by playing the track again and repeating the dialogue yourself.

Track 1.14
A: So you've been working in Shanghai for six months?
B: No, actually, I've been working in Shanghai for two months.

8b Pause the track after sentence A and ask students to repeat.

- Play sentence B, and ask students to repeat and correct the stress if necessary.
- Put students into pairs and ask them to repeat the dialogue taking it in turns to be A and B.
- Then label students A and B and ask them to turn to the correct page in the Coursebook.
- Ask a stronger pair to demonstrate the first dialogue.
- While students are practising the dialogues, monitor to correct mistakes with stress.

SPEAKING

9 Give students a few minutes to think about what they will say, but tell them not to write any sentences.

- Provide help with vocabulary if necessary.
- Focus students on the example and check they understand *revising* (looking again at study notes to prepare for an exam).
- Students then follow the instructions in the Coursebook.
- Tell students to ask questions to get as much information as possible.
- Monitor and note mistakes with the present perfect continuous.
- When they have finished, ask a few students the most interesting/surprising things they heard.
- Finally, correct some of the most common mistakes you noted earlier.

HOMEWORK OPTIONS

Students do the exercises on pages 19–20 of the Workbook.

Students do exercise G1 1 and 2, V1 6, V2 7 and V3 8 on page 139 in the Language reference.

Students write a letter or an email to a friend/family member to tell them their news. Students should include information about the activities they described in exercise 9 on page 29.

3.3 KILLER QUESTIONS

IN THIS LESSON

Lesson topic and staging

This lesson looks at job interviews and killer questions (questions that are difficult to answer). Students read a leaflet giving advice on preparing for interviews and killer questions. They then study vocabulary to describe people's roles at work and in interviews. Next, students do activities to look at the present perfect simple and continuous before practising this grammar and the pronunciation of contractions and weak forms. Finally, students practise asking and answering killer questions.

Objectives

By the end of the lesson, students should have:

- explored the topic of job interviews and killer questions, and practised asking and answering them
- extracted specific information and language items from a reading text
- learned a set of nouns to describe people in job interviews and work
- revised and extended their knowledge of the present perfect simple and continuous

Timings

If short of time, you could drop exercise 8b and set it for homework.

A possible lesson break would be after exercise 4 on page 30.

WARM-UP

- This activity introduces the topic of difficult questions to answer.
- Write the following on the board:
  - Do you love me?
  - How old are you?
  - Can I borrow $50,000?
  - Do you like my new shoes?
  - Do you think I'm attractive?
- Tell students to order the questions from most (1) to least (5) difficult to answer.
- Put students in pairs to discuss their order and give reasons for their choice.

READING

(!) In some cultures, it is not as usual to ask killer questions as it is in, for example, Europe and North America. Ask students if killer questions are asked at job interviews in their countries.

1a Remind students of the questions in the Warm-up and explain that they are going to look at difficult questions in job interviews.

- Put students in pairs to talk about the questions.
- Elicit answers from a few students.

If some students have never had a job interview, pair them with a student who has. If no students have had a job interview, you could ask them to talk about other interviews (university, exams, etc.) or drop this exercise and go to 1b below.

1b Lead in by focusing students on the title of this lesson (Killer Questions) and elicit/tell students what it means (questions that are surprising and/or difficult to answer).

- Do the first question in this activity as a whole class.
- Then give students two minutes to rank the questions in the list (a–e).
- Ask students to compare with a partner before you check answers with the class.

If no students have had a job interview or if killer questions aren't used in their cultures, ask them to *predict* difficult kinds of questions.

To extend this activity, when students compare their ranking with a partner, tell them they must agree on an order. Then put the pairs in larger groups (two or three pairs in each group). Ask them to compare their answers and tell them the whole group has to agree on a final ranking. They must give reasons for their decisions.

Answers depend on students' opinions.

2a Read through the instructions with the class and check students understand *recruitment agency*.

- Ask the class what kind of advice the leaflet might give (e.g. appropriate style of dress for an interview).
- Read through the headings and check students understand *contact details* (address, phone number, etc.), *shock tactics* (methods to surprise and/or upset someone); and *hypothetical* (not real, imaginary).
- Give them a maximum of five minutes to match the headings to the paragraphs.
- Ask students to compare with a partner before you check answers with the class.

1 E; **2** B; **6** C; **7** A; **8** D

2b Tell students to read the sentences (1–6) before they read the text again. (Note: students may find answer 1 difficult because it is not absolutely transparent in the leaflet. If they do, tell them to go on to question 2 and then spend time in feedback explaining where and how this idea is mentioned [see notes in brackets in answers below]).

- Ask them to compare with a partner before you check answers with the class.

1 Mentioned in Paragraph D (The *way* you answer killer questions is very important, rather than your actual answer: '...the interviewer isn't interested in your response as much as the way you respond'. Also, the whole leaflet implies that your answers to killer questions are extremely important.); **2** Mentioned in paragraph A; **3** Not mentioned; **4** Not mentioned (Paragraph C says 'Killer questions often come *early in the interview* ...'); **5** Mentioned in paragraph C; **6** Not mentioned (Paragraph D says 'buy some time', i.e. give general opening answers to allow yourself time to think.)

3 Students do the activity as per the Coursebook.

- Ask students to underline the words in the leaflet when they find them.
- Tell students to compare with a partner before you check answers with the class.
- In feedback, check students' pronunciation of *employee* and *interviewee* (with the stress on the final syllable).

1 a candidate (paragraphs A, B, C); **2** an interviewer (paragraphs A, B, C, D); **3** an employer (paragraph B); **4** an interviewee (paragraph A); **5** an employee (paragraph C); **6** an expert (paragraph C)

4 Give students one minute to think about their answers to these questions.

- Put them in groups and allow about five minutes for the discussion.
- While they are speaking, monitor to spot mistakes using the vocabulary from exercise 3.
- Get a few ideas from two or three groups and then correct some of the more common mistakes you noted earlier.

GRAMMAR: present perfect simple and present perfect continuous

(!) Students at this level will probably have been introduced to the present perfect before and have revised some areas in lesson 3.2. Often, they are able to recognise it but are still unsure about the uses of the different forms.

5 Lead in by reminding students they looked at the present perfect continuous in lesson 3.2 and elicit an example.

- Ask students to decide which examples (1–4) are present perfect simple or present perfect continuous.
- Then, ask students to underline the examples in the leaflet (to give the full context).
- Give students one minute to complete the rules on page 31.
- Ask students to compare with a partner before you check the answers with the class.
- In feedback, ask students which sentences (1–4) gave them the answers.
- Finally, read through the GRAMMAR TIP and elicit which example is simple and which continuous.

a present perfect continuous; **b** present perfect simple

For a full explanation, ask students to read G2 on page 138 of the Language reference

6 Do the first example with the class and then give students five to ten minutes to complete this activity.

- Monitor to point out mistakes, but encourage students to self-correct by using exercise 5 and the Language reference.
- Ask students to compare with a partner.
- Go through the answers and notes in brackets with the class.

In feedback, check whether students have used contractions (*I've*, *He's*, etc.), and if necessary elicit the form of these. This will help lead in to exercise 7.

1 I've (have) been writing emails all day.; **2** I've (have) written 20 emails today.; **3** He's (has) been learning Polish for six months.; **4** He's (has) learned six new words today.; **5** I've (have) asked dozens of killer question over the years. (Note: *dozens* = a great many; *one dozen* = 12); **6** Interviewers have been asking killer questions for years. (Note: *have* is not contracted here.); **7** Shizuka's (has) been watching TV all afternoon.; **8** Shizuka's (has) watched five TV programmes this afternoon.

For further practice, ask students to do Extra practice activity G2 3 on page 139 in the Coursebook.

pronunciation

7 Elicit the pronunciation of each word/phrase from the group.

- Students will probably give the fully stressed form, i.e. /aiv/, /bi:n/, etc.
- Play the track and focus student on the unstressed sounds of these words/phrases.
- Play the track again, pausing after each sentence for students to repeat.
- Correct as necessary.

Track 1.15

1 We've ... We've employed people from your university.
2 We've been ... We've been interviewing candidates all morning.
3 I've been ... I've been waiting in this office for more than two hours.
4 He's ... He's interviewed 14 candidates.

8a Go through the examples with students.

- Emphasis they don't need to write full sentences and that the 'when' column should say when the activity started.

- Given them two minutes to think of as many ideas as possible.

8b Focus students on the two examples and show them how the notes in 8a have been expanded.

- Give students five minutes to write their sentences.
- Monitor to point out mistakes, but encourage students to refer to exercises 5 and 6 and the Language reference if they need help.
- When students compare their answers with a partner, encourage them to ask follow-up questions, e.g. 'Do you like living here? Are you good (at playing the piano)? Why did you choose the piano?'
- While students are speaking, monitor and note mistakes they use with the form and pronunciation (contractions) of the present perfect simple and continuous.
- For feedback, ask one or two students to tell you the most interesting/surprising thing they found out.
- Finally, correct some of the more common mistakes you noted earlier.

SPEAKING

9a Divide the class into at least two groups, making sure there are no more than three or four students in each group.

- Give students a maximum of ten minutes to think of their killer questions.
- Monitor the groups and help with additional vocabulary and to point out mistakes.
- Tell students to form a pair with a student from another group and give them ten minutes to ask their questions.
- Encourage them to ask follow-up questions for more information.
- Monitor to note mistakes with the present perfect simple and continuous
- In feedback, ask a few students what was the best answer they heard.
- Finally, correct some of the more common mistakes you noted earlier.

HOMEWORK OPTIONS

Students do the exercises on pages 21–22 of the Workbook.

Students do exercise G2 3 on page 139 of the Language reference.

Students think of another situation where they might be interviewed and write a list of their own tips for doing a good interview in the context they have chosen.

3.4 SCENARIO: SITUATION VACANT

IN THIS LESSON

Lesson topic and staging

This lesson looks at organising job interviews. Students are introduced to the situation of a health club looking for a manager of a new branch. Next, students look at responsibilities and tasks in this job and listen to two managers talking about the skills and qualities needed. Students then do a listening which introduces the KEY LANGUAGE of framing and asking questions, and giving answers. They write, ask and answer questions to practise framing expressions. Finally, students do the TASK to prepare for and conduct a job interview.

Objectives

By the end of the lesson, students should have:

- learned a set of fixed framing phrases and expressions
- learned a set of vocabulary connected to job skills and personal qualities
- practised using these in a 'real-life' situation to conduct a job interview
- extracted language items from a listening text

Common European Framework

Students can use framing expressions when asking questions and answering questions in a job interview.

Timings

If short of time, you could drop exercise 6 on page 33 and use exercise 7 and the TASK to practise framing expressions.

A possible lesson break would be after exercise 4b on page 32 or exercise 6 on page 33.

WARM-UP

This activity revises ideas and language from lesson 3.3.

- Remind students of the leaflet in lesson 3.3.
- Put students in pairs and give them two minutes to list advice from the leaflet without looking at it again.
- Tell them you want to find out which pair can write the most ideas.
- After two minutes, ask each pair how many pieces of advice they have and elicit ideas from the students.

(Note: if students haven't included *buying time, avoiding silence, not hesitating* or something similar, provide it for them.)

SITUATION

1 Explain that students are going to read about a health club chain that needs a manager for their new branch.

- Check students understand *chain* and *branch* (i.e. each branch is a separate club, there a number of branches in the chain).
- Ask students to read the question before they read the situation.
- Get answers from the class.

2 Check students understand *strategy* (a plan of how a company will develop) and *personnel* (the people who work for a company).

- Ask students to compare with a partner before you check answers with the class.

1 b; 2 e; 3 d; 4 a; 5 c

3 Elicit one example from the students (e.g. 'good at preparing budgets', 'motivating').

- Give students two minutes to list their ideas.
- In feedback, write students' ideas on the board so they can refer to them in exercise 4b below.

4a Read through the introduction with the class.

- Play the track twice if necessary.
- Ask students to compare with a partner before you check answers with the class.
- In feedback, help students with the meaning of unknown vocabulary (e.g. *dynamic, enthusiastic*).

Skills: able to work long hours, lots of ideas, work with people from different cultures, an interest in health and fitness, good communication skills, fluent in another language, able to build up the club.
Personal qualities: flexible, dynamic, energetic, enthusiastic, desire to succeed, outgoing, extrovert

Track 1.16
Harry, Marta

H: I think you're right, Marta, educational qualifications and experience are not really so important – we've got to find someone with the right skills and personal qualities.

M: Exactly. The person we choose will get six months' training in New York, so that'll prepare them well for the job. As you say, it's the personal qualities which are so important. It'll be pretty stressful, building up the club here. They'll have to work long hours and be very flexible. OK, we're offering a competitive salary, good perks, a nice working environment – that should attract some good candidates. But the job's not as glamorous as it sounds. We'll need someone who's very dynamic, energetic, erm enthusiastic, and with lots of ideas.

continued...

H: Absolutely. And I think the best candidate will be very determined, someone who has a real desire to succeed – because it won't be easy. We need an outgoing person, I'd say, who can work with people from different cultures. Don't forget – a lot of our customers won't be English. All the candidates must also have an interest in health and fitness, don't you think?

M: Definitely. And I agree, we need a fairly extroverted person, with really good communication skills. If possible, they'll be fluent in another language – French, German, Japanese, whatever.

H: Yeah, I like the sound of that. But most important of all, we want someone who's looking for a long term career with us, someone who'll stay with us and build up the club. There's tremendous potential here for a health club, we know that, and the right manager can make a lot of money for us.

M: OK, I've made a note of the points we mentioned. Now let's write the advertisement.

4b Remind students their ideas from exercise 3 are on the board.

- Ask students if they think any of their ideas should be added to those in the listening.

KEY LANGUAGE: asking questions, giving answers

Read through the introduction with the class and if possible elicit/give an example ('I was wondering what you …', 'Let me just think about that …').

5a Tell students they will be using framing expressions in an interview later.

- Emphasise that students should only listen for the interviewer's questions.
- Tell them to read sentences 1–8 before you play the track.
- Ask students to compare with a partner but don't give the answers (these will be given in exercise 5c).

5b Emphasise that students should only listen for the candidate's answers.

- Tell them to read sentences 1–8 before you play the track.
- Ask students to compare with a partner but don't give the answers (these will be given in exercise 5c).
- If necessary, play the recording a third time so that students can complete gaps in 5a and 5b.

5c Give students a maximum of five minutes to check their answers by looking at the audioscript on page 171 of the Coursebook.

- Tell them the KEY LANGUAGE is listed on page 138 of the Language reference.

5a 1 I'd; **2** in; **3** candidates; **4** was; **5** question; **6** follow; **7** could; **8** final
5b 1 glad; **2** good; **3** detail; **4** think; **5** ask; **6** thought; **7** expert; afraid
(Answers are in bold [5a] or underlined [5b] in the audioscript below.)

Audioscript and answers to exercise 5c:
Track 1.17
Interviewer, Candidate

1
I: Now, looking at your C.V. **I'd** like to know what you feel you learned in your last job.
C: I'm glad you asked me that because I developed some important skills while I was there.

2
I: I'm also interested **in** knowing your reasons for leaving the job.
C: That's a very good question. Basically, it was no longer challenging enough.

3
I: Now, a question we like to ask all our **candidates**. What are your strong points?
C: Well, without going into too much detail, I have very good people skills.

4
I: I **was** wondering what you feel you can bring to this job?
C: Let me just think about that for a moment. Well, my sales and marketing experience should be very useful to you.

5
I: OK. thank you. A **question** now about your computer skills. What software are you familiar with?
C: I thought you might ask me something about that. Well, what I can say is, I have a good knowledge of Excel and Word, and can prepare excellent Powerpoint presentations.

6
I: Let me **follow** that up with another question. How do you feel about working abroad?
C: I haven't really thought about that, to be honest, but I think it'd be really interesting.

7
I: Right, thank you. Moving on, **could** you tell me what you think the growth areas in the leisure industry are?
C: Well, I'm not an expert, but I think the boom in fitness centres will continue in the next few years.

8
I: OK. Just one **final** question. Where do you think you'll be in five years' time?
C: I'm afraid I don't know the answer to that, but I hope to be working for your company in a senior position.

6 Students do the activity as per the Coursebook.

- Monitor to correct pronunciation if necessary.

7 Give students five minutes to write their questions.

- Monitor to give ideas if necessary and to point out mistakes they make.
- Put students into pairs and allow five to ten minutes for them to ask/answer.
- While students are speaking, note mistakes they make with the KEY LANGUAGE.
- When they have finished, ask one or two pairs to demonstrate a few questions and answers for the class.
- Finally, correct some of the mistakes you noted earlier.

TASK: taking part in a job interview

8a Remind students of the Shape-Shifters situation on page 32 and the responsibilities, tasks, skills and personal qualities from exercises 2, 3 and 4.

- Give students about five minutes to write their questions and tell them to use framing expressions for questions from exercises 5a.

8b Go through the OTHER USEFUL PHRASES box with the class and elicit when each phrase is used.

- Put the students into pairs and give them ten minutes to ask and answer the questions.
- Monitor to note mistakes with the KEY LANGUAGE (for correction in exercise 9).

9 Students do the activity as per the Coursebook.

- Monitor to help with vocabulary or ask students to use their dictionaries.
- When they have finished, ask students what their greatest strengths were and what they need to work on.
- Finally, correct some of the mistakes you noted in exercise 8b above.

If the students *all* need practice at being candidates, ask students to swap roles (i.e. candidates become interviewers and vice versa). For exercise 8b, ask them to think about how they can improve the interview (based on the evaluations of candidates/interviewers they did in exercise 9).

HOMEWORK OPTIONS

Students do the exercises on page 23 of the Workbook.

Students do exercises KL 4 and 5 on page 139 of the Coursebook.

Students write a paragraph explaining why they would/wouldn't offer the job to the person they interviewed in exercise 8b, *or* why they wouldn't/wouldn't accept the job. Take work in for marking, with particular attention to vocabulary learned in this lesson.

3.5 STUDY AND WRITING SKILLS

IN THIS LESSON

Lesson topic and staging

This lesson focuses on organising ideas in paragraphs and then writing a covering letter and curriculum vitae (CV). Students complete a text on paragraphing and discuss why we use paragraphs. Then, students analyse a paragraph for important features before ordering information for another paragraph. Next, students write paragraphs for a covering letter. Students then listen to a careers counsellor discussing covering letters and read a sample letter. Next, students listen to people talking about CVs and read a sample CV. Finally, students write a covering letter and CV for the job in lesson 3.4.

Objectives

By the end of the lesson, students should have:

- learned useful phrases to use in covering letters and CVs
- learned about the organisation, style and content of a typical covering letter and CV
- extracted specific information from listening and reading texts
- written a covering letter and CV

Common European Framework

Students can organise ideas in paragraphs and write a covering letter and CV.

Timings

If short of time, you could drop exercise 4 but make sure that students write draft paragraphs in exercise 10 in order to practise writing paragraphs. Alternatively, set exercise 10 for homework.

A possible lesson break would be after exercise 4b or exercise 6 on page 34.

WARM-UP

This activity revises vocabulary from lesson 3.4. The vocabulary will be useful when students write covering letters later in this lesson.

- Remind students of the context of job interviews in lesson 3.4.
- Write the following headings on the board: areas of responsibility; skills; personal qualities.
- Put students in pairs and give them three minutes to write as many words as they can under each heading.
- Students then check their answers by looking at exercises 2, 3 and 4 in lesson 3.4 on page 32.
- The pair with the most correct items wins.

STUDY SKILLS: organising ideas

1a Paragraphs

- Lead in by asking students to tell you what a paragraph is and some features of paragraphs.
- Give students 15 seconds to read the text and compare their ideas from above.
- Then give students one minute to complete the gaps.
- Go through answers with the class.

If you have time before the lesson, prepare a text without paragraphing. Show students the text and ask what they notice about it. Elicit 'no paragraphs' and/or use the text to pre-teach *paragraph*. Avoid too much discussion on the advantages of paragraphing because this is done in exercise 1b below.

> **1** link; **2** main; **3** information; **4** texts; **5** logically

1b Elicit answers to this question from the class.

> Accept any reasonable answers or provide them if students don't know.

2 Organising a paragraph

- Elicit or remind students of the Shape-Shifters situation in Lesson 3.4.
- Read through the introduction with the class and then give students five minutes to read the paragraph and discuss the questions in pairs.
- Check answers with the class.

> **1** I have been interested in healthy living and fitness for many years; **2** This is why I chose to study for a degree in Sports Management at my local university. I had excellent grades throughout my studies and expect to graduate in a few weeks' time. After this, I am thinking of going on to do a part-time Masters degree in Business Administration; **3** Because it isn't directly related to sports, fitness or management.

3 Tell students to write 1–4 next to the appropriate sentence (a–d) to show the order.

- Ask students to compare with a partner before you check answers with the class.

> **1** b = the topic sentence; **2** d; **3** a **4** c

4a Give students one minute to think of a position and an organisation.

- If individual students don't have any ideas, elicit possibilities from the whole class.
- Give students five minutes to note their answers to the questions.
- If necessary, tell students to look again at the skills and personal qualities they listed in the Warm-up activity above or in exercises 2, 3 and 4 on page 32 in lesson 3.4.

If students have found it difficult to think of skills and qualities, ask them to compare with a partner. This might give them some ideas for exercise 4b.

4b Students only need to write the title of the job in the paragraph provided before writing their own paragraphs.

- Tell students to look at exercises 2 and 3 on page 34 for ideas on organisation.
- Give them 15 minutes to write the two paragraphs.
- Monitor to help with vocabulary and organisation.
- When the students have finished writing, ask them to swap with a partner and comment on the organisation of each other's paragraphs.
- Then ask the class if they would invite their partner for an interview for the job.

It isn't necessary to take students' work in for marking because they write a full covering letter in exercise 10. However, if your students want your comments, take the paragraphs in and mark for organisation.

WRITING SKILLS: covering letter and curriculum vitae (CV)

5a Covering letter

- Set the activity and then play the track without pausing.
- Go through answers with the class.

1 What is it [a covering letter] exactly?; **2** How long should it be?; **3** Could you give me a little more detail about what to put in each paragraph?

5b Emphasise that students should only write notes and not whole sentences.

- Play the track again and, if necessary, pause at the points shown in the audioscript below to give students time to write.
- Ask students to compare with a partner and then read the audioscript on page 172 to check.
- Ask students to underline any advice they think is useful (they will need this when they write a covering letter in exercise 10).

Audioscript and answers (bold) to exercise 5b: Track 1.18

Student, Counsellor

S: I know you usually send a covering letter with a CV. But, what is it exactly?

C: Well, really **it's a letter telling an employer why you're interested in their company or organisation. You can tell them about your special skills and qualities and why you want to work with them. It gives you an opportunity to sell yourself to the employer**. [PAUSE]

S: I see. Erm, how long should it be?

continued...

C: It depends. But generally I'd say a **covering letter should be short, perhaps one side of an A4 sheet of paper**. And the tone should be enthusiastic and professional. [PAUSE]

S: Right. Could you give me a little more detail about what to put in each paragraph?

C: OK, I'll suggest a structure, a way to organise the paragraphs, if you like.

S: Thank you.

C: Right. **The first paragraph is your introduction. You say who you are, why you're writing, and where you saw the position advertised**. [PAUSE]

S: OK, I've got that.

C: **In paragraph two, tell the employer why you want the job** – in other words, say what attracted you to the organisation. **Show that you're enthusiastic and motivated.** [PAUSE]

S: Right.

C: **The third paragraph** is really important. This is where you sell yourself. **Here you mention your qualities, erm, skills and experience that match what they are probably looking for. You tell them what you can contribute to their organisation.** Okay? [PAUSE] Now we come to the **final paragraph. Say when you're available for interview. And end on a positive note**. For example, say you look forward to hearing from them soon, or something like that. OK, that's about it.

S: Thanks, that's really helpful.

6 First, ask students to read the letter quickly and tell you if Denise Martin has followed the advice in exercise 5 above (yes, she has).

- Students then do the activity as per the Coursebook.

1 position; **2** degree; **3** delighted; **4** skills; **5** work placement; **6** available for interview; **7** look forward

7 Curriculum Vitae (CV)

- Focus students on the CV on page 35 and ask them what it is.
- Then put students into pairs to discuss the questions.

1 A CV gives employers information on you, your career, and your skills.; **2** No, however, many industries or cultures have generally accepted formats.; **3** Answers depend on students' opinions – accept any reasonable answers.; **4** Profile, Personal information, Education, Work Experience, Interests, and any other reasonable suggestions from students.; **5** Answers depend on students' opinions but it is normally accepted that you should always tell the truth when writing your CV.

8a If necessary, pause the track after each speaker to give students time to write.

- Don't check answers with the class because students will compare with a partner in exercise 8b.

8b Give students five minutes to discuss their notes and ideas.

- Ask a few pairs to tell the class which speakers they agreed/disagreed with and why.

Track 1.19

1
I think you should put as much as possible in a CV so the employer gets a complete picture of your qualities and skills and qualifications. If you don't do that, they may not call you for an interview.

2
It's essential to write a personal profile at the beginning of your CV. Everyone's doing it these days. It helps to focus your reader's attention on what you really have to offer their organisation. It's where you can sell yourself as a candidate.

3
If you're sending out CVs to lots of companies at one time, I mean if you're just seeing if there's any interest, not replying to an ad for a job, then I think your CV should be really short, just one side of an A4 sheet.

4
I try to write as much as possible in the Work Experience section. I start with my first job then put my most recent job last – that's the order I prefer. I had a period of six months when I was unemployed, but I never show that on my CV.

5
I have just one CV which I send out whenever I'm looking for a new job. Of course, I always bring it up to date. That's the advantage of keeping it on my computer – it's easy to bring my employment history up to date.

6
To be honest, I think the covering letter's much more important than your CV. If they like what they read in your letter, they'll look at your CV. But if your letter's no good, they'll throw your CV in the bin right away.

9 Give students three minutes to complete the gaps.

- Check answers with the class.

1 e; **2** b; **3** d; **4** c; **5** f; **6** a

10 First, give students one minute to decide which vacancy to apply for.

- Allow about one hour for students to write their CVs and covering letters.
- Suggest that students write the CV first (because the covering letter will use some of this information).
- Tell them to make notes about the information to include in their CVs/covering letters. For ideas, they could look at exercises 6, 8 and 9.
- Then, students write a draft CV/covering letter while you monitor to help with organisation and language.
- Put students in pairs to compare their CVs/covering letters and give each other corrections and advice.
- Students write a final draft CV/covering letter.
- Take the work in for marking, paying particular attention to organisation.

Post the CVs and letters around the classroom walls. Ask students to read all the texts and decide who should be given an interview.

HOMEWORK OPTIONS

Students do the exercises on page 24 of the Workbook.

Students choose another job from a newspaper and write a covering letter.

REVIEW

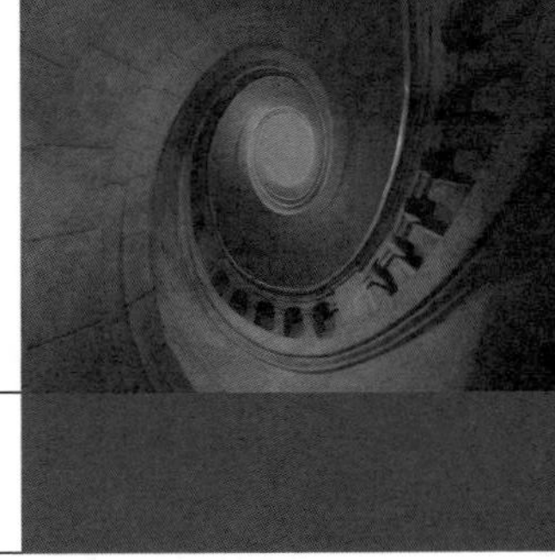

UNITS 1–3

GRAMMAR

1 Focus students on the titles of the profiles and ask what they think each person does.

- Than ask them to quickly read the profiles and check their predictions.
- Students then do the activity as per the Coursebook.

> **1** think; **2** spend; **3** 're filming; **4** was; **5** took; **6** doesn't have; **7** known; **8** 'm learning; **9** graduated; **10** sent; **11** has been working; **12** became; **13** take

2

> **1** do you; **2** do you; **3** have you been; **4** are you; **5** Have, wanted

In feedback, check students' pronunciation of the questions to prepare for exercise 3a below.

3a & **3b** When students answer the questions, tell them to give as much information as possible.

- Tell the 'journalists' to ask follow-up questions if necessary.
- Monitor while students are speaking and note mistakes with the tenses and pronunciation.
- When students have finished exercise 3b, correct some of the mistakes you noted.
- Tell students they will get another chance to practise the tenses in exercise 4.

4 If students don't have a job, give them 30 seconds to think of a job they would like to do.

- The students asking questions should ask them all before students swap roles and repeat the exercise.
- Tell students to take notes about their partner's answers to use when writing the article.
- Give students 15 minutes to write their article.
- Monitor to point out mistakes with the grammar from exercise 1, but encourage students to self-correct by referring to the Language reference for Units 1–3 on pages 134–138 in the Coursebook.
- Take the articles in for marking, paying attention to their use of different tenses.

VOCABULARY

5a Tell students to read the advertisement through once before they complete the gaps.

- When students have finished, ask them if they think they have the personality to apply for this job.

> **1** self; **2** easy; **3** hard; **4** even

5b Tell students to read the advertisement through once before they complete the gaps.

- When students have finished, ask them if they would like to apply for this job.

> **1** ambitious; **2** assertive; **3** organised; **4** creative; **5** bossy

5c Tell students to read the advertisement through once before they complete the gaps.

- When students have finished, ask them if they would like to apply for this job.

> **1** for; **2** of; **3** for; **4** to; **5** of

KEY LANGUAGE

6 Ask students if they can remember what KEY LANGUAGE was taught in Units 1–3 and to quickly check in the Coursebook (either in each Unit or in the Language reference on pages 134–138).

- Tell students to read the statements before you play the track.
- Ask students to compare with a partner before you check answers with the class.

> **1** not given; **2** true; **3** false ('But we're going to want to have some time doing nothing after our exams, aren't we?'); **4** false ('Don't get me wrong. Pavel's fine as a person …'); **5** false ('I did it last year and it's a really good way to meet other travellers.'); **6** not given

Track 1.20
Kris, Piotr

K: I think we should head for Greece, Piotr. For one thing it's cheap to fly there.
P: I don't know. It's a bit too hot for me. Besides, what will we do?
K: Well, on the one hand you've got loads of historical sites so that's interesting and on the other hand you can always spend a few days by the sea relaxing.
P: Yes, well it's true about the history and broadening the mind but sitting on the beach isn't my idea of real travelling!
K: What does that mean?
P: Well, we only have four weeks and I can go to a beach any time I want!

continued…

K: But we're going to want to have some time doing nothing after our exams, aren't we?
P: Yes, you're right. OK then. It'd be a good idea to go to an island, get a tan and then after about a week we can go to Athens and travel on the mainland.
K: Great idea. Oh, by the way, I was wondering if Pavel could come with us?
P: What? Err, I don't know about that.
K: Why not?
P: Don't get me wrong. Pavel's fine as a person but it'll be easier to book rooms for two than three.
K: Well, if we stay in hostels we'll share rooms with lots of people anyway. I did it last year and it's a really good way to meet other travellers.
P: That's true, but another disadvantage of Pavel coming is that there'll be three of us, which always makes it harder to come to decisions about what to visit – you know, one person wants to do one thing and someone else doesn't want to.
K: OK. He doesn't have to be with us all the time but how about saying to him that he can meet up with us somewhere?
P: Let me just think about that for a minute.

7a Students do the activity as per the Coursebook. Don't confirm answers until after exercise 7b.

- Ask students to compare with a partner and monitor to see which gaps they found difficult.

1 should **2** know; **3** one; **4** other; **5** true; **6** good; **7** idea; **8** wondering; **9** disadvantage; **10** that; **11** about; **12** minute

7b If students found 7a difficult, pause the track after the problem gaps to give students time to write.

- In feedback, either go through answers with the class or ask them to look at the audioscript on page 172.

8 Give students five minutes to do this activity.

- Ask them to compare with a partner before they check in the Coursebook.

If students find this activity difficult, it might help to tell them where the prepositions or adverbs should go.

1 away; **2** out; **3** off; **4** on; **5** since; **6** for; **7** into; **8** about; **9** for; **10** in

(!) Students may want to answer *around* (i.e. *look around*) in question 3. Tell them it is unusual to use *look around* + *at* in this particular sentence.

LOOK BACK

9 The aim of this activity is to remind students of areas they looked at in Units 1–3. This will help reinforce any language or skills they had difficulties with or were particularly good at.

personality adjectives: 1.1, exercises 2 and 3a; forming questions: 1.2, exercise 7a; article on charisma: 1.3, exercises 2a and 2b; compare being a traveller with being a tourist: 2.1, exercise 4; phrasal verbs for talking about a journey: 2.2, exercise 3a; profile of someone's life: 2.5, exercise 7; what is important when choosing a job: 3.1, exercise 8a; asking killer questions: 3.3, exercise 9

If students have problems remembering these exercises, you could put them into small groups to remind each other (as appropriate) of the vocabulary learned, the content of the text, the topic they talked about.

To extend the activity, ask students to choose one of the exercises and write a test for other students. This could be a list of questions, a true/false, a gapfill, etc.

Language

4

4.1 LEARNING LANGUAGES

IN THIS LESSON

Lesson topic and staging

This lesson looks at language learning. Students are introduced to vocabulary related to language learning, for example, *native*, *bilingual*. They then read a text on one way of learning a foreign language which contextualises the next vocabulary focus: phrasal verbs. Students work on the meaning of these verbs and practise using them. Finally, students do a speaking activity in which they discuss different issues related to language learning.

Objectives

By the end of the lesson, students should have:

- expanded their range of vocabulary related to language learning
- practised extracting specific information and language items from a reading text
- expanded their range and practised the use of a set of phrasal verbs
- participated in a speaking activity to practise accuracy and fluency

Timings

If short of time, you could drop exercise 1 and begin the lesson with exercise 2.

A possible lesson break would be after exercise 4c on page 38.

WARM-UP

This warm-up is a quiz on languages and where they are spoken.

- Write the following languages and countries on the board in the order shown below:

1 English	a) Singapore
2 French	b) Argentina
3 Arabic	c) Algeria
4 Chinese	d) Brazil
5 Spanish	e) Saudi Arabia
6 Portuguese	f) Jamaica

- Students match the languages to the countries. (Explain to students that some countries have more than one language.)
- Check students' answers (1 a and f; 2 c; 3 c and e; 4 a; 5 b; 6 d).

Federico Fellini quote:

This quote means that the language of a particular country or region is inextricably linked with its culture. It's not possible to learn to speak a different language without also learning about/absorbing the culture and world view. For more information on Fellini, see page 11 in this Book.

VOCABULARY: language learning

1 To lead in, focus students on the photo on page 38 and ask what they think it shows.

(i) The photo shows a meeting of the European Union member states. There are currently 27 states in the Union: Belgium; France; Germany; Italy; Luxemburg; Netherlands; Denmark; Republic of Ireland, United Kingdom; Greece; Portugal; Spain; Austria; Finland; Sweden; Cyprus; Czech Republic; Estonia; Hungary; Latvia; Lithuania; Malta; Poland; Slovakia; Slovenia; Bulgaria; and Romania. The present Union was founded in 1992 but the original Union began in 1957.

- Tell students there are many different languages spoken at these meetings. Ask if they think it's easy to learn a foreign language.
- In pairs, students do the activity in the Coursebook. Check students understand *tango* (a difficult Argentinian dance for two people).
- Encourage students to give reasons for their answers and to disagree with each other if necessary.
- Walk round the room to provide extra vocabulary if students need it.

Answers will vary depending on students' opinions.

2 Keep students in their pairs to discuss the question. Ask two or three pairs to share their ideas with the class, giving reasons.

Answers will vary depending on students' opinions.

3 This activity introduces the meaning of the words in the box. (It isn't necessary to pre-teach any of these items.)

- When students have completed the statements, ask them to compare their answers and discuss the question with a partner.
- When you check students' answers, check/correct their pronunciation (particularly *bilingual*), and the meaning of *slang* (very informal, sometimes offensive).

1 grammar; **2** accent; **3** native/foreign; **4** dialects; **5** bilingual; **6** slang

READING

4a Check students understand *purpose* (Why is it written?, What is it trying to do?).

- Then focus students on the photos and headings, but tell them not to read the text yet.

> The text is probably from a magazine/newspaper or a leaflet. It is advertising 'Learn Fast'.

4b When students have read the text, ask them to compare their answers in pairs before you check.

> **b** native English speakers

4c Check students understand *not given* (the information is not in the text), and *fluent* (speak a language like a native speaker).

- Tell students to read the statements before reading the text.
- To follow up, ask students if they have ever used a course like this one and what it was like.

> **1** not given; **2** true; **3** false (the course is for native English speakers; the languages listed do not include English); **4** false ('... within six weeks you will pick up the basics ...'; **5** true

VOCABULARY: phrasal verbs (2)

5a First, ask or remind students what a phrasal verb is (verb + preposition with a meaning not obvious from its form) and give a few examples.

- Encourage students to work out the meaning of the phrasal verbs in the context of the text before they do the exercise.
- Go through the answers and notes below with the class.

> **1** keep up with; **2** pick up; **3** catch on; **4** fall behind; **5** get by **6** let you down; **7** take up (Note: In *keep up with, catch on, fall behind* and *get by* the verb and preposition(s) cannot be separated – we cannot say *catch something on*. In *pick up* and *take up*, you can put a noun or pronoun between the verb and preposition, e.g. *I picked French/it up quickly* but you can only put a noun after the preposition e.g. *I picked up French* NOT *I picked up it*. *Fall behind* is followed by the preposition *in* (see the text for an example). *Get by* is followed by the preposition *in*, e.g. *I can get by in French*. *Let someone down* always has a subject between the verb and the preposition.)

For a full explanation of these verbs, ask students to read the Language reference on pages 140–141.

5b Give students five minutes to complete the gaps individually.

- When they compare their answers, tell them to ask follow-up questions to get as much information as possible.
- In feedback, ask students the most interesting/surprising thing they heard.

While students are completing the gaps, walk round the room to check their answers make sense. This will let you know if they understand the meaning of the phrasal verbs.

> Answers will depend on students' own experience. Accept any reasonable ideas.

SPEAKING

6 Give students, in pairs, five minutes to decide their opinions of the statements.

- Encourage students to give reasons and examples for their ideas, and to agree/disagree with each other if necessary.
- In feedback, ask a few students which statements they agreed/disagreed with and why.

If you are short of time, choose the two or three statements most relevant to your students and ask them to discuss only these.

HOMEWORK OPTIONS

Students do the exercises on page 25 of the Workbook.

Students write a list of tips for learning English. First, in class, ask students to brainstorm a list of ideas but not to write their tips yet. At home, students expand their ideas into a list of tips using some of the vocabulary learned in this lesson. In the next lesson, post the tips around the room and ask students to read them all. Finally, ask students which they think are the best tips. To follow up, write the best tips on a large sheet of paper, post it on the wall and ask students to refer to it in all their lessons.

4.2 LANGUAGE AND TEXTING

IN THIS LESSON

Lesson topic and staging

This lesson extends the topic of language to include the effect that SMS texting has on English. Students do a listening activity which provides the context for examples of text messages and which leads into the main grammar focus: future forms. Students do a series of activities to focus them on the contrasted meanings of *will, going to* and the present continuous. Next, students read a text on the effect of SMS texting on the English language and this provides a context for vocabulary work on *allow, permit* and *let*. Finally, students discuss their opinions on texting and its effect on written English.

Objectives

By the end of the lesson, students should have:

- practised listening to a conversation and reading a text to extract specific information
- learned (more) about the conventions of English in SMS texting
- revised the future meanings of *will, going to* and the present continuous
- extended their knowledge of the meaning and form of *allow, permit* and *let*
- practised their fluency in expressing opinions

Timings

If short of time, set exercise 4 on page 40 or exercise 7 on page 41 as homework and check answers in the next lesson.

A possible lesson break would be after exercise 4 on page 40.

WARM-UP

- Focus students on page 41 and ask what the people in the two photos are doing.
- Write the following on the board – c u tues 4 dinner – and tell students this is typical of a text message in English.
- Put students in pairs to write the full version of the message (See you Tuesday for dinner).
- Elicit/explain that we often abbreviate when writing a text message.
- Elicit/give other examples of abbreviations and write them on the board (e.g. 2 = to, two, too; ur = your; y = why.
- Ask students to write a text message of their own and monitor to provide help if necessary.
- Ask students to swap their message with a partner (or with more than one person) and then to write the message in full.
- Finally, write a few of the students' messages on the board and elicit the full versions.

LISTENING

1 Put students in pairs to briefly discuss the questions before getting answers from the class.

2a Introduce the situation and then play the track without pausing.

- When you check answers, don't elicit or give any further information for the answers to exercise 2a because this is included in exercise 2b.

> Fred is calling Howard to invite him to the cinema.

2b Students listen to the track again to complete the sentences.

- Play the track again without pausing.
- Students compare their answers with a partner before you check with the class.

> **1** tonight; **2** by tomorrow; **3** James; **4** Thursday; **5** Friday; **6** tomorrow

2c This is quite a difficult activity so before you check the answer, give students time to discuss it with a partner. Alternative, ask students to read the three messages and then play the track again.

Remind students that Howard is the first person to speak on the track. Students need to know who is speaking in order to decide which is the right text message.

> Fred sent text 1.

After you have checked the answer, ask students for examples of text-messaging in English and write the examples on the board.

- Explain that numbers and single letters are often used because they sound like words.
- Ask students to give the full versions.

> Txting = texting; will = I will; 2moro = tomorrow; 2 lecture = to the lecture; pres = presentation; Fri = Friday; Found article = I found the article; Can't find article = I can't find the article; Think can remember main points = I think I can remember the main points; Tell u in seminar = I will tell you in the seminar

Audioscript and answers (underlined) to exercise 3a:
Track 1.21
Howard, Fred
H: Hello.
F: Oh, hi, Howard. It's Fred here.
H: Fred, hi. Have you finished the essay on King Lear yet?
F: No, not yet. I'm going to finish it tonight. What about you?
H: I'm finding it quite tough. I'm not very good with Shakespeare … but I'm definitely going to finish it by tomorrow's class. I want it out of the way!
F: Howard, I'm just phoning to ask – James and I are going to the cinema on Thursday evening, do you want to come?
H: No, I can't. I'm giving my presentation to the language seminar group on Friday, …
F: Oh, of course.
H: … so I have to prepare that. I'm doing it on SMS – you know, text messaging. I read something recently that said that text language will be the English of the future – can you believe that?
F: Yeah, I can. We all use it, don't we? I saw an article about it in the paper the other day. I'll find it for you.
H: Thanks, that'd be great. When's your presentation?
F: **It isn't till the end of next week.**
H: Do you know what you're doing?
F: Yeah, I'm doing mine on spelling and how important it is.
H: That's interesting. I saw a film a while ago on spelling competitions in America. They're really popular there. Anyway, I'd better get on with the essay. I'll see you at the lecture tomorrow.
F: Great. I'll text you when I find that paper.
H: Thanks. Bye.
F: Bye.

GRAMMAR: future forms

3a Students do this activity individually and then compare with a partner to make sure they have found all the examples.

(!) Students may not realise that the present continuous is being used as a future form in the audioscript. Tell them to decide what time is being referred to, e.g. *tomorrow*, *Friday* and then underline the future form. There is also an example of present simple with future reference (bold in the audioscript text above). If students notice this, tell them that we can use the present simple to refer to programmed/timetabled actions in the future. However, the main focus here in on *will*, *going to* and the present continuous.

(Tip) If possible, reproduce the audioscript, so that the whole class can see it (maybe using an Interactive Whiteboard or an overhead projector). As you go through the answers, underline the examples in the text.

The examples are underlined in the audioscript above. (Note: 'Do you know what you're doing?' and 'I'm doing mine on spelling' may refer to the future or to the present. The context does not make the time reference completely clear.)

3b Tell students to write 1–4 next to the underlined examples in the text so that they have a clear record for exercise 3c below.

1 will be the English of the future / I'll see you at the lecture tomorrow; **2** I'll find it for you / I'll text you when I find that paper; **3** I'm going to finish it tonight / I'm definitely going to finish it by tomorrow's class; **4** James and I are going to the cinema on Thursday evening / I'm giving my presentation to the language seminar group on Friday. (Note: see the note above in the answers to exercise 3a.)

3c Tell students to look at their answers to exercise 3b and the audioscript to help them complete the rules.

1 will; **2** present continuous; **3** going to

(!) *Going to* and the present continuous are very similar in their use. Native English speakers will sometimes use them interchangeably. To avoid confusion, focus students on the meanings in exercise 3c and the examples in the audioscript. It is better not to introduce examples from other sources.

- Ask students to look at the examples again and tell you the structure of each. Write the structures on the board so that all students are clear.

1 *Will* + infinitive (without *to*); **2** *be* + verb-*ing*; **3** *be* + *going to* + infinitive (without *to*)

(Tip) This is a good opportunity to remind students of the contractions *I'll*, *I won't*, *I'm* because they will see these in exercise 4.

For a full explanation, ask students to read the Language reference on pages 140-141.

4 Tell students, in their pairs, to refer to 3b, 3c and audioscript track 1.21 on page 172 to help them choose the best answers in the conversation.

(Tip) To help students learn the uses of this grammar, don't interrupt the pairs while you monitor them. If you see a mistake, point it out and tell them to discuss the answer again.

- In feedback, ask students for the reason they chose each structure.

1 I'm going to take; **2** will challenge; **3** I'll take; **4** I won't know; **5** I'll probably decide; **6** We're meeting; **7** I'm playing; **8** I'll go

READING

5 Explain that in English many people believe that correct grammar and spelling are important, but not everyone agrees. Students then do the activity as per the Coursebook.

Answers will depend on students' own experience and opinions.

6a Focus students on the photos and title on page 41 and elicit a few ideas as to why SMS might be bad for young people.

- Check students understand *literacy* (reading and writing), and *ban* (a rule to stop someone doing something) before they read the text.

Arguments for:
Texting is just a modern means of communication; teachers who want to ban it are 'old-fashioned'; children need to learn to communicate in a range of ways; text is a new type of language and teachers should learn it
Arguments against:
A negative effect on young people's literacy skills; texting is preventing young people from writing properly; good grammar, spelling and sentence structure is forgotten; SMS users are not able to write correct English; we'll never get a good education if we keep using text language; it will create problems for teachers – most of them don't understand text language; it will affect your spelling when you're older

6b If necessary, students can read the text on page 41 again.

Don't pre-teach any of the vocabulary in the box because this will help students too much with the answers. Instead, go through any difficult vocabulary during feedback.

1 increasing; **2** literacy; **3** affected; **4** allowed; **5** means; **6** teachers

VOCABULARY: *allow, permit, let*

7 A good dictionary for this activity is the *Longman Active Study Dictionary*.

1 Most formal = permit. Most informal = let. (Note: all the words have the same meaning. *Permit* as a verb has a stress on the second syllable, as a noun it is on the first syllable.)
2 c) is incorrect because we do not use *to* after *let*.

For a full explanation of the structure of these verbs, ask students to read the Language reference on pages 140–141.

Ask students to note their answers to the following (checking that they understand *borrow*). They should write the words randomly on a page, not in order:

– two things you aren't permitted to do when driving in your country

– two things your parents wouldn't allow you to do when you were fifteen

– two things you would never let someone borrow from you

- Tell them to swap their page with a partner and ask questions to find out about the words/phrases, e.g. 'Is this something your parents wouldn't allow you to do?'
- Encourage students to ask follow-up questions.
- In feedback, ask students the most interesting/surprising thing they heard.

SPEAKING

8 Give students five minutes to decide their opinions of the statements.

- In their pairs, ask students to give reasons and examples for their ideas. Encourage them to agree/disagree with each other if necessary.
- Move around the room noting any common mistakes (particularly with the use of *will*).
- In feedback, ask a few students which statements they agreed/disagreed with and why.
- Provide correction of the mistakes you noted.

If you are short of time, choose the two statements most relevant to your students and ask them to discuss only these.

When students have finished discussing the statements, students work individually and move around the class speaking to as many people as possible and noting if they agree or disagree.

- Students then tell you how many people agreed/disagreed with each statement.

HOMEWORK OPTIONS

Students do the exercises on pages 26–27 of the Workbook.

Students choose one of the statements from exercise 8, decide if they agree/disagree and why, and then write their own comment for posting on the website.

4.3 DISAPPEARING LANGUAGES

IN THIS LESSON

Lesson topic and staging

This lesson extends the topic of language to include languages around the world that are disappearing. Students read a text on languages that are in danger of disappearing and work on a set of vocabulary from the text. Next, students listen to an interview on promoting Gaelic (spoken in Scotland and Ireland) which contextualises the grammar focus for this lesson: the first conditional. Students then do activities to focus them on the meaning and form of the first conditional. Finally, students prepare for and hold a debate on promoting minority languages.

Objectives

By the end of the lesson, students should have:

- practised listening to an interview and reading a text to extract specific information
- revised or been introduced to the meaning and form of the first conditional
- practised their accuracy and fluency in speaking using the first conditional

Timings

If short of time, you could drop exercise 3 on page 42 and ask students to do it for homework. Students could also do exercise 8a (preparing the debate) at home and then hold the debate at the beginning of the following lesson.

A possible lesson break would be either after exercise 3 on page 42 or exercise 5a on page 43.

WARM-UP

This warm-up is a quiz on minority languages and where they are spoken.

- Write the following languages and countries on the board in the order shown below:

1 Gaelic	a) Belgium
2 Flemish	b) Wales
3 Welsh	c) Scotland and Ireland
4 Basque	d) North west Spain
5 Catalan	e) New Zealand
6 Maori	f) South east Spain

- Students match the languages to the countries. (Note: Catalan is spoken in Catalonia and Basque is spoken in the Basque country. Both are regions of modern Spain but many people want independence. Basque is also spoken in south west France.)
- Put students into pairs to compare their answers and tell them to guess the ones they don't know.
- Check students' answers (1 c; 2 a; 3 b; 4 d; 5 f; 6 e).

READING

1 Get a few ideas from the class before giving the definition below.

> A dead language is one which is no longer spoken by any community. It may be spoken/understood by a few academics.

2a Check students understand *died out* (stopped existing) in question 2.

- Put students in pairs to discuss the questions and then give them 30 seconds to read the first two paragraphs.

(!) The answer to question 3 is not immediately obvious. At least half of 6,000 languages = over 3,000.

> **1** c; **2** c; **3** a

2b Tell students to read all the questions before they read the text.

> **1** people moving from rural to urban communities; people moving because environments are destroyed; natural disasters; governments establishing 'official languages'; **2** because it's part of human evolution and there are great benefits to people speaking one language; **3** because we also lose ways of life, knowledge and identity; **4** a) Steve Sutherland: in the past 500 years, 4.5% of languages have died out; b) The Ethnologue: 417 languages are in the final stages of becoming extinct (dying out); c) Ani Rauhihi: language and identify are linked

3 Ask students the meaning of *died out* from exercise 2b and use this as an example for question 1.

- Ask students to compare their answers with a partner before you check with the class.

> **1** verb = disappear (are disappearing – line 5), phrasal verb = die out (have died out – line 10) ; **2** extinction; **3** disappearance; **4** extinct; **5** devastate; **6** disastrous

LISTENING

4 As a lead in, focus students on the photo of the road sign and ask them if they know what the second language is (i.e. the one that isn't English). Then ask students if there is more than one *official* language in their country.

(i) The photo on page 43 shows a road sign from Ireland. The words in capitals are in English, the others are in Irish Gaelic. Cork and Killarney are towns in the south and south west of Ireland.

- Before students discuss the questions, explain they will listen later to an interview about languages in Scotland.

1 English and Scottish Gaelic are the *official* languages (Gaelic since 2005).; **2** Answers will depend on students' own ideas. Accept any reasonable suggestions (e.g. government documents in majority and minority languages; minority languages taught in schools, etc.).

5a Go through the introduction with the students and ask them to read the list of items (1–6).

- Play the track without stopping and then ask students to compare their answers with a partner.

The following should be ticked: 1; 2; 4; 6

i The Celts were/are a group of European peoples dating from pre-Roman times. The main populations were in Britain, Ireland, Spain and France. Celtic refers to the culture of these peoples, including languages such as Irish Gaelic and Welsh.

5b Give students a few minutes to try to fill the gaps before playing the track again. If necessary, to give students time to write, pause the audio at the points indicated in the audioscript below.

1 have; **2** have; **3** continue; **4** reach; **5** get
(Answers are bold in the audioscript.)

Audioscript and answers to exercise 5b:
Track 1.22
Presenter, Bradana

P: Now, for our 'Language now' slot. My guest today is Bradana MacKinnon, spokesperson for the Society for the Promotion of Gaelic. Thank you for being on our radio programme today and indeed, on our series on different languages.

B: Thank you. It's a pleasure to be here.

P: Bradana, I'd like to begin with your name. It's quite unusual. Is it a Celtic word?

B: Yes, it is, and it's not common. It's a Gaelic word meaning 'salmon'. Just a small point here – Celtic usually refers to the culture; Gaelic is the language.

P: Thank you, Bradana, I'll remember that. If you don't mind, I'll get straight to the point. Should we fight to keep a dying language alive, even if few people will ever use it or hear it?

B: Mmm, that is something to consider, I suppose, but I'm not sure it's a relevant question here. It's true that in the last 100 years or so, the number of Gaelic-only speakers in Scotland, and I mean people speaking just Gaelic and no English, well, that number has fallen from nearly 44,000 to zero. And yes … Gaelic has declined throughout the 20th century. But it's also true to say that since the 1970s there has been a revival in the Celtic culture and Gaelic language.

P: I see. So where do you find that revival – in schools?

B: Yes, definitely in schools, and that's important. **If we have Gaelic-medium education at all levels, more people will speak Gaelic.** There has been a huge increase in the number of young children being educated in Gaelic in primary schools … and nurseries. So, if Gaelic is a dying language, then why are more and more Gaelic schools starting in Scotland? [PAUSE]

continued…

P: Good point, but if it's only schools …

B: Yes, I agree. We need more. **If we have more TV and radio programmes in Gaelic, more people may listen to the language.** Also, if the economy in the Gaelic-speaking heartland improves, then Gaelic will not die out. Opinion polls show that people are more confident in the Gaelic-speaking communities – they feel that the economy is improving. If young people return to live and work in those communities after university, then things will improve. [PAUSE]

P: Well, that all sounds very promising. So, what is the Society for the Promotion of Gaelic doing now?

B: Oh, we have lots going on. **Unless we all continue to promote Gaelic, there might not be a significant increase in speakers** of Gaelic.[PAUSE] But, to answer your question … at the moment we're trying to raise our profile, and we have a new fund-raising campaign. **When we reach our targets, we'll invest in more Gaelic books in public libraries.** [PAUSE] **And as soon as we get more Gaelic speakers involved, we'll run more Gaelic language classes.** But unless we recruit and train more Gaelic-medium teachers, we won't make a big difference in schools. Basically our fund-raising supports all of that.[PAUSE]

P: To go back to my first question, Bradana, why should we fight to keep Gaelic alive?

B: Well, I believe that every language provides us with knowledge about human thinking and behaviour. And every language, like every species of animal, is unique and worth protecting. When we lose a language, we lose a lot of knowledge.

P: Bradana MacKinnon, thank you very much.

GRAMMAR: first conditional

6 Give students five minutes to decide their answers and then discuss with a partner. In feedback, ask students to say which example(s) in exercise 5b shows them the answers and underline the relevant parts (e.g. the present simple).

1 *if* + present simple (examples 1 and 2); **2** *if not* (example 3); **3** the present simple (examples 4 and 5); **4** real possibilities (all examples).

To reinforce the meaning of the first conditional, ask students if they think Bradana MacKinnon believes the examples in exercise 5b are real possibilities or unreal situations.

For a full explanation and extra practice, ask students to look at the Language reference on pages 140–141.

7a Before students do this activity, check they understand *revise* (study something again) and *damage* (make something worse/harm).

- Monitor to help if necessary and refer students to exercises 5b and 6, and the Language reference.

1 d; **2** b; **3** g; **4** c; **5** a; **6** f; **7** e

7b Make sure all students have a note of the correctly matched statements in exercise 7a.

- While they are speaking, walk round the room and note any mistakes they make with the first conditional.
- At the end of the activity, ask two or three pairs to tell the class what they discussed.
- Finally, correct a few of the more important or common mistakes you noted earlier.

If you are short of time, choose only one or two of the statements for discussion.

SPEAKING

8a Lead in to this activity by reminding students of what Bradana MacKinnon said about promoting Gaelic. Elicit that this would mean the government spending more money.

- Check students understand *debate* (a 'formal' discussion giving arguments for and against) and read through the motion with the class.
- Put the class into two groups (A and B) and tell students to prepare the debate with the others in their group. All the students should make notes.
- While they are preparing, monitor the groups to provide prompts, help with vocabulary and the use of the first conditional.

If you have a large class, to give students more chance to speak, divide the class into two x As and two x Bs. Then follow the procedure above. This will mean that there are two simultaneous debates.

8b Tell the groups to decide on a spokesperson or nominate a stronger student yourself.

- Go through the debate procedure as a whole class and give the following timings: 1 three to five minutes; 2 three to five minutes; 3 ten minutes; 4 one minute.
- While students are speaking, note common or important mistakes with the first conditional. When students have voted (stage 4), correct a selection of these.

HOMEWORK OPTIONS

Students do the exercises on pages 28–29 of the Workbook.

Students write a paragraph summarising the arguments they used in the debate (exercise 8).

Students use the Internet to research and write a paragraph about a minority language or write about a minority language they already know of in their own country. In the next lesson, students swap paragraphs and if necessary ask each other follow-up questions.

4.4 SCENARIO: LANGUAGE TRAINING

IN THIS LESSON

Lesson topic and staging

Students are introduced to the scenario of a medical aid charity deciding to provide English language training for its employees. They read an email summarising a survey on the staff's English language ability, and discuss the advantages and disadvantages of the survey's proposals. They then listen to three people talking about these. The listening contextualises the KEY LANGUAGE of accepting and rejecting ideas; and considering consequences. Students then do an activity to focus on this language. This leads to the main task in which students use the language to discuss the different possibilities for the language programme.

Objectives

By the end of the lesson, students should have:

- learned useful phrases for accepting and rejecting ideas, and considering consequences
- used this language in a 'real-life' situation to discuss different options
- extracted specific information and language from a listening and a reading text
- participated effectively in extended speaking and listening practice.

Common European Framework

Students can use language effectively to discuss the advantages and disadvantages of different proposals.

Timings

If short of time, you could drop exercise 2a and/or 3a on page 44 as these are not essential to students' understanding of the reading and listening texts.

A possible lesson break would be after exercise 4 on page 45.

SITUATION

Lead in to the situation by asking students if they have ever worked for a charity, what charities they know about and what these particular charities do.

1 Tell students to read the two questions before they read the SITUATION.

> **1** Because they decided that English will now be the working language in the whole organisation.
> **2** The Human Resources Department

2a Give students a maximum of two minutes to read the email and answer the question.

- When you elicit the answers, check students understand *proposal* (plan or suggestion which is made formally to a person or group).

Problem 1: the budget for language training for the first year is only 150,000 Euros.
Problem 2: they can't agree on the best proposal.

2b Explain that *the agency* refers to the charity (IMA) and check students understand *crash course* (short, intensive course) in Proposal 4.

Students will need to use their notes in exercise 5a. To help make their notes clear, draw the chart below on the board and ask students to copy it.

	Advantages/ disadvantages: staff	Advantages/ disadvantages: agency
Proposal 1	+ near to the office – 20 hours a week for 4 weeks is a lot?	+ can train 150 staff for 150,000 Euros – need to give staff time off?
Proposal 2		
Proposal 3		
Proposal 4		
Proposal 5		

- If necessary, do Proposal 1 with the class and write the ideas on the board. An example is given in the chart above.
- In feedback, write a selection of students' ideas in the chart on the board.

Answers depend on students' own ideas.

To save time, divide the class into five groups, give one proposal to each and tell them to make notes. Elicit the advantages and disadvantages from the groups and write them in the chart on the board. Ask the other students to copy the notes.

3a Read through the introduction with the class and then play the track without pausing.

No, they don't agree on each point.

3b Your students may find this activity challenging. To make it easier for them:

- Draw a chart on the board (see answer chart below, as an example). Ask students to copy it and write notes (not sentences) in the relevant box.
- Pause the track at the points shown in the audioscript below.
- Tell students that Sven is the first man to speak and tell them who speaks first after each pause.
- Give students plenty of time to compare their notes in groups.
- When you elicit the answers, write notes clearly in the relevant box on the board. (Don't ask students to look at the audioscript because it will give them the answers to exercise 4 below.)

	Sven	Don	Delphine
1	Focus first, crash courses in UK, improve English quickly. 1 or 2 directors/few senior staff to UK – others get one-to-one in free time	Problem = bad effect on work – too many senior people away	Doesn't like the idea. Important projects now need senior staff
2	Agrees	Agrees	Some staff may prefer US English. **1** US and **1** UK teacher?
3	Other staff more important than volunteers	Doesn't mention volunteers (only 'other staff')	

KEY LANGUAGE: accepting and rejecting ideas; considering consequences

4 Pause the track after each item to give students time to write. If necessary, tell students to read the audioscript to check their answers.

1 know about; 2 will have; 3 you're; 4 would work; 5 like; 6 idea; 7 good idea; 8 worth considering; 9 sure about (Answers are bold in the audioscript.)

Audioscript and answers to exercise 4: Track 1.23
Sven, Don, Delphine

S: As I see it, we can't do much with such a small budget … so I think we should focus, first of all, on the directors and senior staff. How about sending some of them on crash courses to Britain? It's a quick way to improve their English. What do you think, Don?

DO: Mmm, I don't **know about** that. I can see a problem right away. If we send them to England, it **will have** a bad effect on our work. We don't want to lose half our top people just like that. I mean, who'd run the charity?

S: Yeah, I think **you're** right. That would create problems for us. Well, how about this? Why don't we just send one or two directors and a few senior staff to England and offer the rest one-to-one classes when they have free time?

DO: Yes, I think that **would work**. Good idea, Sven. What do you think, Delphine?

DE: Well, I'm afraid I don't **like** the **idea**. If we do that, what will happen? Just when we need to talk to one of them, they won't be here, they'll be in Britain.

continued…

We've got so many projects going on at the moment, we need everyone here to deal with the work. [PAUSE] You know, I'd like to discuss another problem if that's OK with you.

DO, S: OK.

DE: I wonder, should we teach British or American English? Some of our staff might prefer to learn American English, you know.

S: I think you're right, Delphine – some staff will want to learn American English. What do you suggest?

DE: Well, we could hire two teachers to run courses at our head office. One could be British and the other American. I think that would solve the problem.

S: Mmm, **good idea**, Delphine.

DO: Yeah, I like that idea. It's definitely **worth considering**. [PAUSE] Another thing I'd like to talk about Sven ...

S: Oh, yes?

DO: We've talked mostly about the directors and senior staff. What about the other staff? They'll need to improve their English too. And we'll need to set up a programme very soon.

S: I'm not **sure about** that, Don. The volunteers will need to improve their English, it's true, but other staff will have to have priority. Don't forget, our budget for language training is limited this year and we can't afford to ... *[fade]*

TASK: selecting an English language programme

5a Put students into groups of four (A, B, C, D). Give students five minutes to read their information and the notes they made in exercise 2b, and decide on their arguments.

- Go through the OTHER USEFUL PHRASES as a whole class.
- Read through the procedure with the class and then give students 20 minutes for their discussion.
- Tell students to say why they want to accept or reject others' suggestions.
- While they are speaking, walk round the room and note any common or important mistakes with the first conditional, and phrases for accepting and rejecting ideas, considering consequences.
- In stage 3 of the procedure, tell students to decide on a spokesperson. Tell the spokeperson to present only the suggestions their whole group has accepted and to give reasons for the choice.

5b At the end of this activity, correct a selection of the mistakes you noted in exercise 5a above.

HOMEWORK OPTIONS

Students do the exercises on page 30 of the Workbook.

Students write an email to the Director of the IMA head office giving the suggestions their group decided on in exercise 5a. They can use the email on page 44 as a model.

4.5 STUDY AND WRITING SKILLS

IN THIS LESSON

Lesson topic and staging

This lesson focuses on the skills of describing tables and charts, and writing a report based on a chart. Students are first introduced to language for expressing fractions, percentages, and changes in numbers. They then use this language to practise interpreting a table of numbers and then a bar chart. Students then interpret a second bar chart and order sentences based on the information in the chart. Finally, students use the language and the example sentences to write their own report based on a bar chart.

Objectives

By the end of the lesson, students should have:

- been introduced to a set of vocabulary to describe fractions, percentages, changes in numbers and trends
- revised the use of linkers (e.g. *However*) in written texts
- had extensive practice in interpreting charts based on models provided
- written a short report to interpret information given in a bar chart

Common European Framework

Students can write a report to interpret information given in a bar chart.

Timings

If time is short, ask students to do writing exercise 9 for homework.

A possible lesson break would be either after exercise 4 or exercise 5 on page 46.

WARM-UP

This activity introduces the topic of surveys and tests students' knowledge of phrases to express numbers.

- Tell students they are going to do a survey to find out how many, and which languages people in their class speak
- Tell students to move around the room asking all the other students 'How many languages do you speak?' and noting their answers. It is not important if you have a small class (e.g. three to five students).
- When they have finished, ask students to use their notes to count the number of students who speak one, two, three, etc. languages.

- Write the total number of students in the class on the board.
- Then put students into pairs to decide how to express the numbers they counted above (e.g. class = ten, four students speak three languages; phrases = almost half, four out of ten, 40%, etc.) (Note: if students have only a limited range of phrases, tell them they will be studying more in this lesson.)
- Finally, ask students if they found any of the survey results surprising.

STUDY SKILLS: describing tables and charts

Some students may not be comfortable with numbers. Tell them that these exercises are looking at language and they won't need to do any Maths.

1 Before students do this activity, tell them that numbers 1–8 are percentages and letters a)–h) are fractions.

- When you check the answers, focus on the pronunciation of *percent* (stress on the second syllable), *quarter*, and *approximately* (five syllables, not six).

To check that students understand the phrases in a)–h), ask for synonyms for *just under* (a little less than), *just over* (a little more than), and *slightly* (a little).

1 b; **2** c; **3** e; **4** a; **5** d; **6** h; **7** f; **8** g

2 Students do the activity as per the Coursebook.

1 c; **2** a

3 Read through the introduction with the class and stress that there were 100 people questioned (this will make percentages easy for students to work out).

- Focus students on the table and check they understand *satisfied* (happy, content).
- Ask students if they have ever completed a questionnaire to find this kind of information. If so, which organisation gave them the questionnaire? Do they think these questionnaires are useful?
- Set the true/false task and make sure students only look at the results for last year (the first column).
- Monitor to help students who have little confidence in Maths.
- Ask students to compare their answers with a partner before you check with the class.
- Go through the notes below as you check students' answers.

1 True; **2** False (20% of the students were quite satisfied with the facilities); **3** False (just under a third were very satisfied with the facilities); **4** False (more than a third were satisfied with the facilities); **5** False (a majority was very satisfied, a minority was satisfied with the teaching: a minority [approximately a third] was very satisfied or satisfied with the facilities) (Note: it's not necessary to use 'the majority of students' if the noun [students] is already known.); **6** True (Note: it's not necessary to use 'minority of students' if the noun is already known.); **7** False (12% weren't satisfied with the teaching and 8% weren't satisfied with the facilities)

! You can't mathematically add the two numbers (12% and 8%) together to get a percentage including both teaching and facilities.

4 Give pairs ten minutes to write their sentences.

- Monitor while students are working. Point out mistakes, but ask students to help each other rather than correct them yourself.
- Give students a maximum of ten minutes to compare their sentences with another pair and encourage them to correct each other if necessary.

It's a good idea to tell students how many sentences you want them to write, depending on how much time you have or how much practice you think students need. The most they should write is six sentences.

Ask the pairs to write true/false statements similar to those in exercise 3.

- Tell them to swap their statements with another pair, decide if they're true/false and correct them if false.

5 Focus students on the chart and show them that *50 years ago* is in red and *today* is in blue because they refer to the same two colours in the chart. The numbers on the vertical line are in millions. 1 billion = 1000 million.

To make students feel more comfortable interpreting the chart, elicit or give the following example: 50 years ago there were approximately 100 million Spanish speakers; today there are approximately 350 million. Ask students or show them how this is demonstrated by the chart.

- Check students understand *significant increase* (large increase); *figures* (numbers), and *over* (during).

! *Over* has a different meaning here from exercise 1.

- When they have finished the activity, ask students to compare answers with a partner before you check with the class.

1 a; **2** g; **3** b; **4** c; **5** f; **6** d; **7** e (Note: *however* shows a contrast with the previous sentence where no figures were given.)

WRITING SKILLS: a report

6a Lead in by asking students if they've ever written a report, what it was about, and who it was for.

- Focus students on the chart and show them the colour key to the bars in the bar chart.
- Read through the introduction and the three questions with the class. Check they understand *highest* (biggest) in question 2 and *entirely* (only) in question 3.
- Put students into pairs or groups for the discussion.
- Go through answers with the class and ask if they found any of the information surprising.

> **1** approximately or just over 85%; **2** Malaysia (approximately 30%); **3** Barbados

6b Give students a few minutes individually to think about their statements before putting them into pairs or small groups to discuss.

> Answers will depend on students' own ideas.

For a more competitive activity:

- Ask students to individually write four true or false statements about the countries in the chart. Encourage them to use the language they studied in exercises 1–5.
- Put students into groups of three or four and tell one student to read out his or her first statement.
- The other students look at the chart and say if the statement is true or false. The first one to say this correctly wins the statement.
- Students then take it in turns to read out a statement while the others guess.
- The overall winner is the student with the most statements.

7a Tell students not to worry at this stage about the boxes at the beginning of each sentence.

- If necessary, do the first example with the whole class before asking students to do the rest.
- Monitor the class to point out mistakes in language use, but encourage students to self-correct.
- Go through the answers with the class.

There may be alternative answers. Accept any reasonable and accurate ideas from students. (Note: the grammar varies depending on whether students use *people* or the *population*; this is shown in the answers below.)

> **4** In Malaysia almost a third of the population speaks English as a second language.
> **7** There were no figures given for (the percentage of) speakers of English as a first or second language in Nigeria.
> *continued...*
> **2** Overall, the chart demonstrates that four countries in the chart have a majority of people/the population who speak English as a first language.
> **1** This chart shows the percentage of people from a number of countries who speak English as a first or second language.
> **6** The country with the lowest percentage of speakers of English as a first language is Malaysia.
> **5** In South Africa, just under a quarter of people use/the population uses English as a second language.
> **3** It is also interesting that in Barbados 100% of the population speaks/people speak English as a first language.

7b Students do the activity as per the Coursebook.

> See above for answers. Students may have decided on a different order. Accept any answers that are logical.

8 Give students two minutes to underline the linkers before asking them to compare with a partner.

- Ask students to discuss what the linkers are used to introduce.
- Go through the answers and notes below with the class.

> In addition (Note: this adds information to a previous idea.)
> Similarly (Note: this introduces another piece of information that is similar in some way to the previous idea.)
> On the contrary (Note: this introduces information that is the opposite or different in some way to the previous idea.)

9 Give students plenty of time to write their reports.

- Tell students to ask if they need help with vocabulary and walk round the room to spot mistakes in using the phrases from exercises 1–5, linkers and logical ordering of ideas.
- Encourage students to self-correct by looking again at exercises 1–5 and 7.
- Ask students to read each other's reports and try to correct mistakes.
- Take the profiles in for marking, paying particular attention to logical ordering of ideas, use of phrases to describe charts, and linkers.

HOMEWORK OPTIONS

Students do the exercises on page 31 of the Workbook.

Advertising

5.1 WHAT MAKES A GOOD ADVERT?

IN THIS LESSON

Lesson topic and staging

This lesson looks at ways of making a good advert. Students read a text to introduce them to different opinions on what makes a good advert. They then do a series of activities to focus on vocabulary from the text connected to advertising. Next, students listen to three people discussing different adverts and focus on the adjectives used to describe them. Finally, students use the vocabulary in a speaking activity where they discuss photos for use in advertising a particular product.

Objectives

By the end of the lesson, students should have:

- expanded their range of vocabulary in the context of adverts and advertising
- practised extracting specific information and language items from a reading and a listening text
- focused on accuracy and fluency in speaking

Timings

If short of time, you could drop exercise 1 and begin the lesson with exercise 2. Instead of using exercise 1 as a lead in, use the photo to prompt a brief discussion before doing exercise 2.

A possible lesson break would be either after exercise 2b or exercise 4 on page 49.

WARM-UP

This activity introduces the topic of advertising by focusing on famous logos.

- Reproduce about five famous logos and remove the name of the company.
- Place the logos around the room and give students five minutes to look at each one and guess the company.
- The first student to guess all five correctly wins.

SPEAKING

1 As a lead in, focus students on the photo on page 48 and ask them if they have advertising like this in their countries. Then focus students on the Mark Twain quote and ask if they think this is true and to give examples.

Mark Twain quote:

This quote means that if you advertise something well, even unimportant things can seem important and attractive.

(i) Samuel Langhorne Clemens (1835–1910) is known by the pen name Mark Twain. He was an American writer most famous for his novels *Adventures of Huckleberry Finn* and *The Adventures of Tom Sawyer*.

- Tell students the advert they describe can be on television, in a magazine, on the radio, etc.
- Give students a minute to think about their answers to the questions before discussing with a partner.
- When they have finished, ask two or three students for their ideas.

This is a good opportunity to teach the pronunciation of *advert*. Tell students the stress is on the first syllable.

READING

2a Focus students on the jobs of the people quoted in the three texts and check they understand *advertising executive* (responsible for advertising contracts and new business), *head of* (director, most senior manager), and *illustrator* (draws the pictures and logos).

- Tell students to read the true/false statements before they read the opinions and not to worry about vocabulary because they will study this in exercises 3 and 4. (Note: *slogan* in statement 5 is explained by referring to 'the real thing' [Coca-Cola] in the text.)
- Ask students to compare their answers with a partner before you check with the whole class.

> **1** True; **2** True; **3** True; **4** False (people want adverts that 'take away the ordinariness of everyday life'); **5** True; **6** False ('But for me, an instantly recognisable logo is really important')

2b Check students understand *illustrate* in number 3 (give an example of) and *car chase* in 3a (one car following another, very fast).

- Give students five minutes to discuss the questions and tell them to give reasons for their answers and agree/disagree if necessary.

> **1** Answer depends on student's own opinion; **2** Text 3: Coca-Cola; **3** Answers depend on students' own opinions but logical answers are: a) Text 1; b)Text 3; c) Text 2

Ask students to discuss examples they have seen of the three types of adverts, a), b) and c).

VOCABULARY: adjectives, advertising

3 To help students with this activity, tell them to first find the word/phrase they think is the answer, then read the sentence around the word to help them work out the meaning, and if necessary, check in their dictionaries.

- When you go through the answers, focus on the pronunciation of *catchy*, *persuasive* and *exotic* (phonemic script needed here) and ask students to repeat the words. This will help students recognise the words in the listening exercise 5b below.

1 attention-grabbing; **2** eye-catching; **3** catchy; **4** shocking; **5** effective; **6** persuasive; **7** witty; **8** dull; **9** original/creative; **10** exotic

Some vocabulary from the texts on page 48 (but not focused on in this activity) is useful for students in exercise 6b on page 49 (*recognisable*, *inspirational*, *irritating* and *informative*). You could take this opportunity to elicit the meanings or ask students to check in their dictionaries.

4 Check students understand *say publicly* (for all the people to hear).

- When you go through the answers, focus on the pronunciation of *sponsorship*, *slogan* and *logo* (phonemic script needed here). This will help students recognise the words in the listening exercise 5b below.

1 commercial; **2** sponsorship; slogan; **4** endorse; **5** misleading; **6** logo; **7** promote

To further help students understand the meanings, elicit or give them examples (e.g. a company that gives sponsorship to a football team; the Coca-Cola slogan in Text 3, exercise 2a on page 48).

Ask students to discuss some of the following:

- Their favourite TV commercial
- How many slogans they can remember (in their language or in English)
- How many famous people they can remember who endorse products
- An advert or a commercial they think is misleading

5a The aim of this activity is to check students' understanding of vocabulary from exercises 3 and 4, not to extract *content* information from the text.

- Give students 30 seconds to read the dialogue once without choosing the answer.
- Then give them longer to read the dialogue again and do the activity.

5b Play the track without pausing and then ask students to compare with a partner before you check answers with the class.

Audioscript and answers (bold) to Exercise 5b: Track 1.24

A: OK, let's brainstorm how we're going to **1 promote** this product.

B: Well, we could get a famous celebrity like David Beckham to endorse it.

A: I think that would be much too expensive. **2 Sponsorship** of a TV programme would also cost a lot. And a TV **3 commercial** is out for the same reason. I've seen some great TV shots which are visually beautiful and really **4 eye-catching**, often set in romantic or **5 exotic** locations. But I don't think they've been very **6 effective** as people can't remember the product they're advertising.

B: I agree, but we don't want something **7 dull** and boring. How about advertising on the radio – would the budget run to that?

A: Yes, we could stretch to that.

B: And would you like something witty and **8 catchy**?

A: Maybe. I want something new and **9 original**. But most importantly, it must be **10 persuasive**. It must get people to buy the product.

You could also ask students to do Extra practice exercise V1 6 on page 143 of the Language reference.

LISTENING

6a Introduce the context, set the activity, and then play the track without pausing.

- When you go through the answers, ask students for the name of a soft drink (e.g. Coca-Cola), and what washing powder is used for (washing clothes). This will check that they understand the vocabulary.

1 a car; **2** a soft drink; **3** washing powder

If students tell you the car in 1 is a Ford, take this opportunity to teach *brand*.

6b Students should read all the questions before you play the track again. (Note: for question 1, only one brand is mentioned by name.)

- Your students may find Question 3 difficult because there is a lot to write. If necessary, play the track a third time and pause after each speaker.
- Ask students to compare their answers with a partner before you check with the class. Alternatively, ask students to read the audioscript on page 173 to check their answers.
- Some adjectives in question 3 were included in the texts for exercise 2a but not focused on in the activities. When you go through the answers, you could focus on *recognisable*, *inspirational*, *irritating* and *informative*. Elicit the meanings from students and/or ask them to check in their dictionaries.

1 Text 1: Ford; Text 2: no brand ('I can't remember which one it was'); Text 3: no brand ('I can't even remember what the brand was')
2 Text 1: Yes; Text 2: Yes; Text 3: No
3 Text 1: eye-catching; attention-grabbing; original; creative; catchy; recognisable; effective; persuasive; Text 2: humorous; inspirational; lively; exotic; creative; Text 3: dull; catchy; irritating; informative.

Track 1.25
1
I remember a really eye-catching advert for a Ford car. It showed the car starting, then being driven out of the car park and through the city. And it started all the lights in the surrounding buildings. In the country it powered the overhead power lines and the electricity seemed to follow the car along the road. It really was an attention-grabbing ad. It is difficult to be original with car adverts but I thought this was quite creative. It also had a catchy slogan: 'Feel the power. Ford. We have ignition.' You could also see the recognisable Ford 'blue oval' logo. It must have been an effective ad because I've actually remembered that it was a Ford car. It was also quite persuasive as I would consider buying a Ford next time.
2
I normally like humorous ads. But the ad that sticks in my mind was really inspirational. The music was really lively and it was set in different exotic locations. Everyone was drinking this soft drink, but I can't remember which one it was, and the camerawork was really creative. It made you want to be there, drinking that soft drink, having fun.
3
I saw this really dull advert for washing powder on the television recently that I'd really like to forget. But it had this really catchy tune that I can't get out of my head. It's so irritating. It was informative – it gave you lots of information about the product but I can't even remember what the brand was.

6c Put student into pairs or small groups to discuss this question and tell them to give reasons.

Probably the most effective advert was the one for the Ford car, but students may have their own opinions.

SPEAKING

7a Give students three minutes to look at their photos and think about how to describe them.

- Tell them to ask you for vocabulary if necessary.
- Then put them into A/B pairs to do the activity as per the Coursebook.

7b While students are discussing the questions, monitor and note mistakes when using the vocabulary introduced in this lesson.

- When students have finished, ask two or three pairs for their ideas.
- Finally, correct a selection of the mistakes you noted earlier.

HOMEWORK OPTIONS

Students do the exercises on page 32 of the Workbook.

Students ask friends, family or their classmates to name an advert they really like or hate, and to say why. Students take notes. At the beginning of the next lesson, put students into pairs or small groups to tell each other what they found out, using vocabulary learned in lesson 5.1.

5.2 WAYS OF ADVERTISING

IN THIS LESSON

Lesson topic and staging

This lesson looks at different ways of advertising. Students read an article about different advertising methods in the past and today, and do activities to ensure they understand the text. Next, students work on vocabulary contextualised in the reading. This is followed by a listening and activities which focus on the second conditional, as it appears in the listening. Students then do two activities to explore the meaning and form of the second conditional, and finally use the grammar in a speaking and a writing activity.

Objectives

By the end of the lesson, students should have:

- practised listening to a conversation and reading a text to extract specific information and language items
- learned (more) about different methods for advertising
- extended their vocabulary in the context of ways of advertising
- revised/been introduced to the second conditional for unreal situations in the present or future

Timings

If short of time, you could drop exercise 2c on page 50 or set it for homework. You could also leave out exercise 8 and set it for homework.

A possible lesson break would be after exercise 3 on page 50.

WARM-UP

This activity introduces the lesson topic by focusing students on the images on pages 50 and 51. It also tells you if students remember vocabulary from lesson 5.1 and if they already know vocabulary introduced in this lesson.

- Put students into pairs, ask them to look at the two images and give them four minutes to write down as many similarities and differences between them as possible.
- Ask students to compare the similarities and differences they noted with another pair.
- Finally, get a few ideas about each image from the class.

READING

1 While students are discussing these questions, listen for the vocabulary they use. This will help you decide how many items in exercise 3 will be new.

2a Tell students to underline items they think may be ways of advertising even if they're not sure. Ask them not to use their dictionaries because they will look at vocabulary in exercise 3.

> Ways of advertising: word of mouth; inscriptions on walls; (papyrus) posters; wall or rock painting; handbills; advertisements in weekly newspapers; classified adverts; mail order catalogues; product placement; TV commercials; endorsements

2b Check students understand *ancient times* (a long time ago, e.g. Roman times).

- Tell students to read the questions before they read the three paragraphs.
- Put them in pairs to compare answers before you check with the class.
- When you check answers, teach or elicit the meaning of *household goods* (products used in the home, e.g. furniture, cleaning products).

> **1** political campaigns; household goods for sale; things people had lost or found; goods; **2** it increased the forms of advertising; **3** a True; b False (they gave more *specific* information); c True; **4** USP = Unique Selling Point (the qualities that make a product different from other products)

2c Tell students to try to fill the gaps without looking at the text.

- Put them in pairs to compare their answers and then tell them to read paragraphs 4–7 to check.
- Students may have alternative answers to those below. Accept any answers that are reasonable and grammatically correct.

(!) Students can use no more than three words in each gap. This means that they cannot copy from the text and may make mistakes with grammar. Monitor to point out mistakes and encourage students to self-correct. Alternatively, when students compare their answers with a partner, tell them to check for grammar.

> **1** endorse/promote goods/products/sales; **2** companies; **3** 30-second TV commercial (Note: *30-second* is one word); **4** increase sales

VOCABULARY: advertising methods

3 Students will already have seen a lot of this vocabulary in exercise 2a above. Give them a few minutes to see if they remember any of the words before they reread the text to find the rest.

1 word-of-mouth; **2** poster; **3** wall or rock painting. (Note: *inscriptions on walls* refer to writing not images.); **4** handbills; **5** classified adverts; **6** mail order (Note: the catalogue is the book with descriptions of the products.); **7** product placement; **8** endorsement (Note: the noun is needed here.)

To further check that students understand this vocabulary, ask the following questions:

- Do advertisers give a handbill or a poster to people on the street? (a handbill because it is small)
- What kind of things are advertised in the classified adverts? (personal belongings, e.g. an old car, unused sports equipment)
- What do people often buy from mail order catalogues? (clothes, furniture)

You could also ask students to do Extra practice exercise 7 on page 143 of the Language reference.

LISTENING

4a Read through the introduction and questions with students and check they understand *consumers* (people who buy products).

- Play the track without pausing and then elicit answers from the class.

The product is watches; the consumer group is young people.

4b Before you play the track again, ask students to try to complete the gaps they can.

- Play the track without pausing and then go through the answers.

1 had; **2** were; **3** could; **4** might; **5** wouldn't. (Answers are bold in the audioscript.)

Audioscript and answers to exercise 4b: Track 1.26

JP, Roberta

JP: We both know it won't be easy to advertise the Raymond Jacquet Classique range. Our problem is money. If we **1 had** a bigger budget, we'd get someone well-known to endorse the product. There are plenty of performers in the movie industry who'd do it, but they're very expensive. We couldn't afford it.

R: OK. Well, if I **2 were** you, I'd look for a cheaper way of doing it. You don't always have to pay a fortune to get good publicity. An endorsement by someone famous isn't the only solution …

JP: Mmm, what exactly do you mean?

continued…

R: Well, you want to reach younger people with the Classique range, right? If you did that, you'd achieve your objective, to sell to a new group of consumers.

JP: Yes. That's true.

R: How about this then? If you ran a series of short TV commercials, you **3 could** reach a younger audience and it'd be a lot cheaper than using a film star or whatever.

JP: OK, but what sort of commercials should we run? We haven't really thought about that.

R: Well, I have. Why don't you contact some people who are really good at their job, let's say, at the top of their profession, and use them in your commercials? I don't mean stars or famous people, who cost the earth, I mean, for example, a young concert pianist, erm, a young lawyer or professional tennis player – no-one famous, but they'd all be young, attractive and good at their job. The sort of successful people a young person would identify with. A role model, if you like.

JP: Mmm, interesting. Yes, if we got the right people, it **4 might** be a lot cheaper than using a film star. We'd be able to afford them, probably.

R: Exactly. In each commercial, you could show them briefly at work, with no mention of Raymond Jacquet, and then in the final shot, the camera could zoom in and focus for a few seconds on their wrist. They'd be wearing the Classique model, of course. Some nice modern music would play in the background.

JP: Mmm, good idea. It's clever, very subtle, in fact. Just right for a stylish range of watches aimed at young people.

R: Yeah, and if you got a young director to do the films, you **5 wouldn't** have to pay them too much. I'd say that's the solution to your problem.

JP: Mmm, it's worth considering. Definitely. I'll put it to everyone at our next meeting, and let you know what they think.

GRAMMAR: second conditional

5 Explain that the sentences in exercise 4b are all examples of the second conditional.

- Give students five minutes to do this activity while you move round the room prompting if necessary.
- When you go through the answers, ask students to give you an example of each from exercise 4b. Focus students on the contraction of *I would* (*I'd*) in sentence 2 and *would not* (*wouldn't*) in sentence 5.

1 past simple; *would* + infinitive without *to*; **2** the main clause; **3** unreal; **4** *If I were you*

For a full explanation, ask students to look at pages 142–143 in the Language reference.

6 Monitor while students do this activity to point out any errors. Advise students to look at exercises 4b and 5, and the Language reference on pages 142–143 if they need help.

(!) Number 4 has the *if* and main clauses in a different order from the examples students have seen. Be prepared to help if necessary.

1 knew, 'd/would phone; **2** had, 'd/would advertise; **3** were, would you do? **4** would happen, advertised; **5** applied, wouldn't/would not get

You could also ask students to do Extra practice exercise 1 on page 143 of the Language reference.

SPEAKING AND WRITING

7 Give students a minute to read the different possibilities and check they understand *media/ medium* (use the items in the box as examples and tell students *media* is plural and *medium* singular); *radio spots* (short periods of time to advertise); *billboards* (places for putting posters – see the image on page 50); *leaflets* (similar to handbills but perhaps with more pages); *raising money* (getting money); *antique* (very old).

- Give students 20 minutes for the discussion and remind them when they have five minutes remaining.
- While students are speaking, note mistakes they make in using the second conditional.
- In feedback, ask a few groups to tell the class two or three of their decisions and reasons.
- Provide correction of the most important mistakes you noted.

To make sure that all students get a chance to speak, the groups should not be bigger than three or four.

If you are short of time, choose five of the products from the bulleted list. Alternatively, to extend this activity, put groups together and tell them to persuade each other that their decisions are better.

8 If you are short of time, set this activity for homework. When you mark the descriptions, pay particular attention to the use of the second conditional and vocabulary from this lesson.

HOMEWORK OPTIONS

Students do the exercises on pages 33–34 of the Workbook.

5.3 ADVERTISING AND CHILDREN

IN THIS LESSON

Lesson topic and staging

This lesson looks at the kind of products aimed at children and how these are advertised. Students do a series of activities to help them read an article about targeting children in adverts. They then focus on adjective/noun + noun collocations from the reading text and use the combinations in personalised activities. Next, students focus on the grammar of comparison contained in the text and do activities to revise the structure of comparative and superlative forms. Finally, students use the comparisons in a group speaking activity.

Objectives

By the end of the lesson, students should have:

- practised reading a text to extract specific information and language items
- learned (more) about the arguments for and against advertising to children
- extended their range of adjective/noun + noun combinations
- revised and used the grammar of comparatives and superlatives

Timings

If short of time and your students are confident using comparisons, you could drop exercise 7 on page 53 and set it for homework. Alternatively, you could drop exercise 4 on page 53.

A possible lesson break would be after exercise 5 on page 53.

WARM-UP

This activity introduces products and ways of advertising aimed at children.

- Write the following on the board:
  - Watched a lot of TV
  - Went to fast food restaurants
  - Had a mobile phone
  - Ate a lot of chocolate
- Explain that students have to find someone who did these things when they were a child.
- Give or elicit the questions they need to ask (past simple e.g 'Did you watch a lot of TV?')

- Ask students to move round the room and when someone says 'yes', to write their name and ask follow-up questions (e.g. 'How many hours of TV did you watch a week?')
- For feedback, ask students to tell you the most surprising thing they found out.

READING

1 Focus students on the title of the article on page 52 and give or elicit the meaning (advertisers are directing their adverts specifically at young people).

- Students discuss the questions in pairs before you get a few ideas from the class.

Answers depend on students' own ideas.

2a Tell students to read the topics (1–5) before they read the article.

- Go through the answers with the class.
- Finally, ask if any of the students' ideas from exercise 1 were mentioned in the article.

Topic 1 is not mentioned in the article.

2b Before students do this activity, check they understand *impose* (force).

- Give students a longer time to read the article than in exercise 2a and tell them to note their answers.
- Ask students to compare with a partner before you check answers with the class.
- In feedback, check students understand *gimmicky packaging* (packaging with a superficial or deceptive design used to catch attention) and *ban* (to not allow).
- To follow up, ask students if they liked adverts when they were children, were they persuaded by them? Did they ask their parents to buy things they saw in adverts?

1 show an ad many times during school holidays; make TV commercials louder than programmes; sponsor programmes and show commercials before the programme starts (Paragraph 2); children's advert are short, imaginative and often cartoons (Paragraph 3); offers of free toys, models of cartoon characters, gimmicky packaging and interactive websites (Paragraph 5); **2** children love adverts and watch them like entertainment programmes (Paragraph 3); children are less critical than adults and don't realise the advert has a persuasive message (Paragraph 4); many adverts promote unhealthy food (Paragraph 5); **3** Sweden; Greece; Denmark; the Netherlands (Paragraph 6); **4** France; Britain; Germany; **5** Sweden bans advertising to children under 12; Greece bans TV adverts for children's toys between 7a.m. and 10 p.m.; France, Britain and Germany use self-regulation

VOCABULARY: word combinations

3 Go through the instructions with students and do the first example as a whole class.

- Tell students only to look for words immediately *before* the nouns in this activity e.g. *advertising* + *managers* (see Warning! below).
- Tell students to use their dictionaries for vocabulary in any combinations that they don't know.
- When you go through the answers, tell students to underline the combinations in the article.

(!) In paragraph 5, there are three combinations with *food (junk food, fast food* and *food products*). Students should only look for words immediately *before* the noun in this activity (i.e. *junk* and *fast*).

a advertising managers: noun + noun; b attractive target: adjective + noun; c TV commercial: noun + noun; d persuasive message: adjective + noun; e vast sums: adjective + noun; f junk food: noun + noun/fast food: adjective + noun; g interactive websites: adjective + noun; h television advertisements: noun + noun

4 Do the first example with the class, e.g. they could say 'I think advertising managers should be more careful when advertising to children.'

- Monitor while students are working to give vocabulary they need and to point out mistakes.
- Finally, ask a few students to tell the class one or two of their sentences.

Answers will depend on students' own ideas.

To extend this activity:

- When students have written their sentences, ask them to compare with a partner.
- Encourage students to give reasons for their opinions and to agree/disagree if necessary.

5 Give students a few minute to think about their opinions before you put them into pairs to discuss.

- Tell students to give reasons for their opinions and to agree/disagree with each other if necessary.
- In feedback, ask two or three pairs to tell the class something they discussed.

Answers will depend on students' opinions.

GRAMMAR: comparison

6a First, tell students to find the highlighted adjectives and check they understand *strict* (an order or rule that must be obeyed). Students then do the activity as per the Coursebook.

> **1** *-er* (louder – paragraph 2)/more (more aware – paragraph 7)
> **2** *-est* (strictest – paragraph 6)/most (most worrying – paragraph 4)

If this activity is revision for your students, ask them to complete the rules and *then* find highlighted examples in the text.

6b Tell students to find *all* the examples in the article before completing the rules.

> **1** a lot (higher)/much more (relaxed); **2** a little (louder); **3** as/as (as sure as); **4** less (less critical)

For a full explanation, see the Language reference on pages 142–143.

7 While students are working, monitor to prompt if necessary.

- If they need help, ask them to look at the examples and rules in exercises 6a and 6b, and the Language reference on pages 142–143.
- In feedback, ask students to give reasons for their answers and go through the notes below.

(!) Number 2 uses the irregular adjective *bad*. Either tell students before they begin or encourage them to use the Language reference on pages 142–143.

> **1** ~~most~~ biggest; **2** ~~a~~ much ~~more bad~~ worse (Note: *bad* is an irregular adjective, with one syllable it doesn't use *more*.); **3** ~~so~~ as expensive as (Note: *so* is used in negative sentences, e.g. not so expensive as that one.); **4** much ~~more~~ better (Note: *better* is the irregular comparative of *good*, it doesn't use *more*.); **5** a lot faster than; **6** as ~~tastier~~ tasty as (Note: *as/as* uses the base form adjective and not the comparative form.); **7** the ~~more~~ most (Note: the clause *in the world* shows this is a superlative sentence.)

You could also ask students to do Extra practice exercise G2 3 on page 143 of the Language reference.

SPEAKING

8a Read through the situation and make sure students know that a motorbike has an engine (unlike a pedal bike).

- Ask students what a young person would want and what parents would not want in a quad bike (e.g. speed, size).
- Tell students to read their information and then put them into groups of three.

If you have a lot of male students in your class and they don't want a female role, change the *mother* to *uncle*. If you can't form groups of three, make a group of four with two children.

8b Give students a few minutes to read the table on page 167 and check they understand that a bigger engine (e.g. 300cc) makes the motorbike more powerful.

- Give the groups 20 minutes to discuss the different bikes and tell students to remember their role when deciding which one to buy.
- While students are speaking, monitor and note common mistakes when using comparisons.
- When they have finished, ask each group which bike they chose and why.
- Correct a selection of the mistakes you noted earlier.

HOMEWORK OPTIONS

Students do the exercises on pages 35–36 of the Workbook.

Students think of two places to take a friend or a family member on holiday. They then write a paragraph describing and comparing the places and saying why they would choose one over the other for their friend/family member.

5.4 SCENARIO: B-KOOL SOFT DRINKS

IN THIS LESSON

Lesson topic and staging

Students are introduced to the scenario of a new soft drink being launched onto the market. They then listen to an advertising agency talking to the company about the product and write notes on how to promote it. Next students listen to three presentations that the agency gives to the company and focus on some KEY LANGUAGE for giving presentations. This leads to the main task in which students prepare and give a presentation on advertising the new drink.

Objectives

By the end of the lesson, students should have:

- learned useful phrases for giving presentations
- used this language in a 'real-life' situation to give a presentation on advertising a new drink
- extracted specific information and language items from listening texts
- participated effectively in extended speaking practice

Common European Framework

Students can use language effectively to give (formal) presentations in a business context.

Timings

If short of time, you could drop the presentation stage (exercise 5b) and do it in the next lesson.

A possible lesson break would be after exercise 3 or 4c on page 55.

SITUATION

To lead in to exercise 1:

- Ask students to look at the photo on page 54: have they ever tried any of these exotic fruits?
- Focus students on the title of this lesson (B-Kool soft drinks). Ask what they think B-Kool is and how the photo and the title might relate .
- Give students 30 seconds to read the SITUATION text to see if their ideas were correct.
- Finally, ask students if they liked this kind of drink when they were children (or now).

> B-Kool is a company making soft drinks; the fruit is a mixture of exotic fruits to be used in a new soft drink.

ⓘ The name B-Kool is used because in English it sounds the same as *be cool* (fashionable, interesting, attractive). Children of 8–14 really want to be cool.

1 Tell students to read the questions and check they understand *carton* (a paper or card container for liquid, e.g. milk) and *can* (a metal container for liquid, e.g. Coca-Cola).

- When discussing the questions, tell students to give reasons for their answers.
- Ask one or two pairs to tell the class what they decided.

> Answers depend on students' own ideas.

2a Go through the introduction with the class and then play the track without pausing.

- Tell students to compare with a partner before you check answers with the class.

🔧 If you have a strong class, set exercises 2a and 2b at the same time. Students will then have two tasks to do while listening to the track.

> The five points are: new ideas for names; a good slogan; ideas for the design of the packaging; kind of advertising to use; (interesting) ideas for special promotions

2b Give students a few minutes to see if they can remember the information without listening to the track again.

- If they can remember the information, go through the answers and then do exercise 2c.
- If they can't remember the information, play the track again without pausing and then go through the answers.

> Two ways not mentioned are: posters and newspapers

2c Tell students to read through the notes and see if they can complete any gaps before you play the track.

- If necessary, to give students time to write, pause the track as shown in the audioscript below.
- Ask students to compare with a partner before you go through the answers with the class.

> **1** colour; **2** shape; **3** TV commercial; **4** Internet; **5** different commercials; **6** radio; **7** sponsor; **8** free cans; **9** cheap T-shirts

Track 1.27

Amy, Larissa

A: There are several points I'd like your team to cover in their presentation.

L: OK.

A: Well, for a start, we can't agree on a name for the drink. We've had lots of suggestions but none of them have been very exciting, so could you come up with some new ideas for names, please?

L: Certainly, no problem.

A: We need a good slogan too, something that's easy to remember and original. One of our staff wanted to call the drink 'Krakkle' – she came up with the slogan 'Kool kids drink Krakkle', but no-one really liked that one. We'd also like your ideas for the design of the packaging. Should it be a can or bottle, or something different? Nothing too detailed, just … oh I don't know, design, colour, shape – that sort of thing. [PAUSE]

continued…

L: OK, what else do you want us to look at?
A: Well, we've talked quite a lot about the kind of advertising we should use. Should we have a TV commercial during children's TV in the afternoon? Or maybe early in the evening? [PAUSE] How about advertising in children's magazines? Should we use the Internet as well? Another question is, do we want just one TV commercial, with different languages for the various markets, or should we have a different TV commercial for each country? [PAUSE]
L: Interesting. What about radio spots?
A: Ah yes, I forgot to mention that. Do you think we should advertise on radio? If you do, what time of the day should we choose for a radio spot, and what sort of programmes could we sponsor? [PAUSE]
L: Is that everything?
A: I think so … Oh yes, one other thing, if your team have any interesting ideas for special promotions, let us have them. I mean, would it be a good idea to give out free cans in schools? Or offer cheap T-shirts with the logo on them? That sort of thing.
L: Fine. I'm sure we can come up with some good ideas for you. We'd certainly like to be your agency for the campaign.
A: Well, if we like your presentation, you'll have a good chance of winning the contract.
L: That's good enough for me.

3 Give students about ten minutes for this activity and make sure that all of them make notes.

- Tell students to ask you if they need help with extra vocabulary.

The groups should have a maximum of four students to make sure that they all get a chance to speak. In exercise 5b, they will divide the presentation between them. If there are more than four in a group, each student will have very little to say.

KEY LANGUAGE: the language of presentations

4a Remind students that Larissa Klein is the head of the advertising agency they heard in exercise 2 and then go through the introduction with the whole class.

- Tell students to read sentences 1–4 and try to guess what goes in each gap.
- Play the track without pausing and then ask students to compare their answers with a partner.
- If necessary, play the track again.
- In feedback, check students understand *purpose* (reason, objective, aim) and model its pronunciation.

When you go through the answers for exercises 4a, b and c, write the phrases on the board so that students can refer to them when they give their presentations in exercise 5.

1 introduce my colleagues; **2** purpose today; **3** is divided into; **4** have any questions (Answers are bold in the audioscript.)

Audioscript and answers to exercise 4a:
Track 1.28
Good morning, I'm Larissa Klein, head of Klein Benson Advertising. I'd like to **1 introduce my colleagues**, Emilio Sanchez on my left, and next to him, Karl Reiner.
Our **2 purpose today** is to present some ideas for your new product. We'll also suggest how to advertise and promote it. Our presentation **3 is divided** into three parts. First, I'll talk to you about our ideas for the name of the soft drink and a suitable slogan. After that, Emilio will give you our ideas about the can – he's an expert on packaging – and finally Karl will tell you our ideas about how to advertise and promote the drink. If you **4 have any questions**, we'll be pleased to answer them at the end of our presentation. *[fade]*

4b Ask students who Emilio is (one of Larissa's colleagues) and tell them to read sentences 1–2.

- Check students understand *refer to an illustration* (to give a visual example).
- Play the track without pausing and then ask students to compare their answers with a partner.
- If necessary, play the track again.
- In feedback, check students understand *screen* (the white area for showing computer images or slides).

1 moving on now; **2** Please look at the screen

Audioscript and answers to exercise 4b:
Track 1.29
1 Moving on now to the design of the can. We asked a group of young people about this. We showed them ten different designs. **2 Please look at the screen.** As you see, we've numbered the designs one to ten …
If we now look at the table of results, it's very clear. Over 80 percent of the group preferred design six, the blue can with the yellow stripe … *[fade]*

4c Ask students who they think ends the presentation (probably Karl – another colleague), and tell them to read sentences 1–3.

- Play the track without pausing.
- Ask students to compare their answers with a partner and if necessary, play the track again.

1 summarise our main; **2** for your attention; **3** any questions (Answers are bold in the audioscript.)

Audioscript and answers to exercise 4c:
Track 1.30
Well I've given you our ideas for advertising and promoting the drink. I hope you've found them interesting. Now, let me **1 summarise our main points**. Larissa gave you three possible names and mentioned the one we prefer. She told you what slogan we liked, with her reasons.
Emilio showed you the design for the can that we recommend. Finally, I talked about ways of advertising the drink and told you about our ideas for special promotions.
Thank you very much, everyone, **2 for your attention**. Are there **3 any questions**?

TASK: giving a formal presentation

5a Give students about 30 minutes to prepare their presentation and decide who will give which part.

- Tell students to look at the notes they made in exercise 3 and the organisation of the presentation in exercises 4a–c.
- While students are working, move round the class helping with vocabulary if necessary.

5b Before students give their presentation, tell them to look at the answers to exercises 4a–c for examples of phrases they can use.

- Then go through the OTHER USEFUL PHRASES with students and elicit/tell them when each phrase could be used (e.g. 'I'm going to talk to you about …' = at the beginning of each section of the presentation; 'Now, I'll sum up …' = at the end of each section or at the end of the whole presentation).
- Tell students to give their presentations and ask the students listening to make notes on how interesting/creative/persuasive they are.
- While students are talking, make notes on common mistakes when using the language from exercises 4a–c, and advertising vocabulary. Correct these after exercise 6.

If you have more than four groups, divide the class in two so that two groups are giving presentations to different audiences at the same time. This will save time and prevent students becoming bored when listening.

6 Give students five minutes to discuss the presentations they heard.

- When they have decided, vote on the presentation they thought was most interesting/creative/persuasive.
- Finally, correct a selection of the mistakes you noted in exercise 5b.

Rather than have the whole class discussing this question, put students back into their groups to discuss the presentations they heard. This will save time and allow more students to give their opinion.

HOMEWORK OPTIONS

Students do the exercises on page 37 of the Workbook.

Students write the presentation (either all of it, or just their section). When you mark these, pay particular attention to the language for giving a formal presentation, and advertising vocabulary.

5.5 STUDY AND WRITING SKILLS

IN THIS LESSON

Lesson topic and staging

This lesson first focuses on the skill of using a dictionary. Students read a short text and then do an activity to practise guessing meaning from context. Next, students explore the information they can find in a dictionary and practise finding information themselves. The lesson then focuses on formal letter writing. Students read a text and listen to a conversation about a controversial TV advert to provide ideas for the letter they will write later. They then read a letter complaining about the advert and focus on dependent prepositions. Finally, students write a formal letter in reply to the complaint.

Objectives

By the end of the lesson, students should have:

- used a dictionary to find a variety of information about words
- revised/learned a set of verbs/adjectives/nouns + dependent prepositions
- extracted content and language items from a reading and a listening text
- written a formal letter in defence of a controversial topic

Common European Framework

Students can write a formal letter of reply in defence of a topic.

Timings

If time is short, you could drop exercises 6b and 7. These focus on dependent prepositions, but students will be able to write their letters without doing them. However, if you drop exercise 7, ask students to read the letter as a model for their own writing.

A possible lesson break would be after exercise 4b on page 56.

WARM-UP

This activity introduces the idea of controversial television commercials.

- Write the following on the board and check students understand *fast food chains* (e.g. Macdonalds), and *sugary drinks with additives* (substances added to make drinks taste better).
  - Cigarettes
  - Fast food chains
  - Political parties
  - Credit cards
  - Sugary drinks with additives

- Tell students all these items are advertised on the television in some countries, but many people think they shouldn't be.
- Put students into pairs or small groups and tell them they have five minutes to decide which three items should definitely NOT be advertised on television and why.
- Finally, ask a few pairs/small groups for their three items and the reasons for their choices. Ask the rest of the class if they agree and why/why not.

STUDY SKILLS: using your dictionary

Lead in to these activities by asking students the following:

- Who regularly uses a dictionary in their English studies?
- Who uses an English/English dictionary. Why/why not?
- Who finds it difficult to use a dictionary? Why?

1 Focus students on the photos and the title of the short text on page 56 and elicit what they think it's about.

- Check students understand *teen* (teenager – 13–19 years old) and *campaign* (planned actions for a specific purpose).
- Then ask students to do the activity as per the Coursebook.
- Follow up by asking students if this is a problem in their country and if they have similar campaigns.

> The aim is to reduce the number of teenagers killed or seriously injured on London's roads.

2a Ask students if there are any words they don't know in the text.

- Tell them a good way to guess the meaning is to look at the context (the information around the words).
- When they have finished the activity, ask what information from the text they used to guess the meaning of the words.

> **1** b; **2** c

2b Students can use English/English or translation dictionaries for this activity. However, if possible, give them a copy of the same English/English dictionary.

(Tip) Students may not understand what all the other information in the dictionary is (pronunciation, grammar, etc.). Tell them not to worry at this stage because they will find out in exercise 3a.

> Answers will depend on the dictionary and whether students understand the information. Accept any correct answers but don't insist that students tell you *all* the extra information they can find. Extra information may include: pronunciation; dependent prepositions, singular/plural; formal/informal; combinations of words; example sentences to show how the word is used, etc.

3a Read through the rubric with the class and elicit the answer.

> You find information on how to use the symbols, abbreviations, etc. in the dictionary entries.

3b Tell students to read the questions before they look at the dictionary entries for *advertisement* and *advertising*.

- Tell them not to worry if they can't answer all the questions.
- When you check answers with the class, tell students they can find out what the abbreviations mean and how to use the dictionary by looking at the *Guide to the dictionary* mentioned in exercise 3a.

(!) Students may not know the phonetic symbols. It is enough in this lesson for you to show them that the stress is shown by an apostrophe (') before the stressed syllable. Copy the phonetics for *advertisement* on to the board and show them the stress apostrophe. Then elicit the pronunciation from the class.

> **1** *advertisement* = stress on second syllable; *advertising* = stress on first syllable; **2** noun; **3** British English; **4** American English; **5** *for*: it includes + *for*, and the example sentence shows us this; **6** [U] = uncountable; **7** a phrase and a noun + noun combination

3c Check students understand *rhymes* (sounds the same).

- Tell students to read the statements before they read the entry.
- When you check with the class, ask what information they used in the entry to decide their answers.

(Tip) Statement 1: If students don't know the phonetic symbols, tell them to ignore the symbols but use the stress apostrophe. This will give them enough information to decide if the words rhyme.

> **1** False (*foreign* = 1st syllable stressed); *campaign* = 2nd syllable stressed; **2** True ([C] = countable and therefore can take plural *s*); **3** False (It can also be followed with *against*: + *for/against*.); **4** True (bold numbers **1** and **2**)

4a and **4b** Give students ten minutes to find the words and note the information, and then ten minutes to ask/answer questions with their partner.

(Tip) To save time, tell students to find their three words in the dictionary but NOT to take notes. When their partner asks about the words, they can use the dictionary entry to answer.

WRITING SKILLS: a formal letter

5 Tell students to discuss their answer to this question in pairs.

Because it shows a teenager being knocked down and killed/injured by a car. It's very hard-hitting.

6a Tell students to read the questions before you play the track without pausing.

1 Lisa: You have to shock drivers to change their behaviour and drive more slowly so accidents will decrease.
2 Eric: He thinks they shouldn't show such shocking things on TV. He couldn't sleep afterwards; is worried by this advertising trend.
4 Rebecca: She thinks more research is needed into the effects of shock advertisements: do they really work?

6b Tell students to read the extracts and see if they can complete any gaps before you play the track again.

- Ask them to compare with a partner before you check the answers.

1 on; **2** about; **3** about; **4** by; **5** with; **6** into; **7** in
(Answers are bold in the audioscript below.)

Audioscript and answers to exercise 6: Track 1.31

Presenter, Eric, Lisa, Rebecca

P: Tonight we're focusing **1 on** road safety. Before we talk to the experts, we've invited three members of the public to give their opinion about a new television advert. Good evening, Eric, Lisa and Rebecca.

E/L/R: Good evening …

P: Let me start with you, Eric – I know you have strong feelings. You've seen the television advertisement. A teenager is knocked down in the street because the driver is going too fast. You see the boy lying on the road. Dead. How do you feel **2 about** this?

E: I think it's awful and it shouldn't be on our screens. You see the boy lying there with blood coming from his ears. It's a terrible commercial. I saw it last night and couldn't sleep all night thinking **3 about** it. I'm really worried **4 by** this advertising trend. Why on earth do they show such shocking things? It's just not right!

P: Thank you, Eric. Lisa, what's your opinion? Do you agree **5 with** Eric that the advert shouldn't be on our screens?

L: No. I agree that it's shocking, but that's the point, isn't it? Too many teenagers are killed or injured on our roads. We've got to do something about it. It's true, the advertisement is hard-hitting, but it has to be. You've got to shock drivers, so that they change their behaviour and drive more slowly. That way, accidents will decrease. And that's what we all want, isn't it?

P: Thanks, Lisa. Now Rebecca, how do you feel about this?

continued…

R: It's difficult really. I think the adverts are really shocking and that's not good for some people, like people who are sensitive, or people who have heart problems. On the other hand, if the advertisements reduce the number of deaths of teenagers, it's worth showing them, isn't it? Actually, I think we need more research **6 into** the effects of this type of advertising. I mean, will shock advertisements result **7 in** fewer deaths of young people? I'm not sure about that.

P: Thanks Rebecca. I agree – more data about the effects would be very useful. Now let's turn to the experts … *[fade]*

7 Before students do this activity, ask them to read the text quickly and decide if the following statements are true or false:

1 Marina Warner says a lot of other people think the commercial is in bad taste. (True)
2 She thinks the advertisement will stop people driving too fast. (False)
3 She asks people to phone her if they want to join her campaign. (False)

- Tell students that in exercise 6b they looked at dependent prepositions and elicit an example.
- Students then do the activity as per the Coursebook.

(!) Some verbs are separated from their prepositions by a noun (e.g. *prevent any advertiser from*); the preposition connects to the verb not to the noun. Some verbs are in the passive voice which may confuse students (e.g. *being shown on*).

1 complain about; [being] shown on (passive voice); [be] banned from (passive voice); lying on; pouring from; discourage [people] from; prevent [any advertiser] from; succeed in; **2** horrified by; interested in; **3** advertisement for; law against; a campaign against

8 Give students two minutes to read through the instructions and ask you for help if necessary.

- Remind students they can use some of the ideas from exercise 6a on page 57.
- While students are writing, walk round the room to spot mistakes in using dependent prepositions and presentation of ideas.
- Ask students to read each other's reports and try to correct mistakes. Then take the letters in for marking.

HOMEWORK OPTIONS

Students do the exercises on page 38 of the Workbook.

Give students a list of words you know they have had trouble with in this Unit. Ask them to find out about the words by using their dictionaries. In the next lesson, ask them to compare what they found out.

Business

6.1 IN BUSINESS

IN THIS LESSON

Lesson topic and staging

This lesson looks at different roles in the business world and setting up a business successfully. Students are introduced to a set of vocabulary in the context of business terms and roles. They then read a leaflet about business plans and listen to an interview giving advice on starting a business. A second listening in which two people talk about setting up a new business prepares students for a final speaking activity in which they discuss plans for a business in their own town.

Objectives

By the end of the lesson, students should have:

- expanded their range of vocabulary in the context of business and roles in the business world
- practised extracting specific information from a reading text and listening activities
- used the vocabulary they have learned to plan a new business in their own town
- focused on accuracy and fluency in speaking

Timings

If short of time and you feel students are already well-prepared for the speaking exercise 8, you could drop exercise 7 on page 59.

A possible lesson break would be after exercise 5 on page 59.

WARM-UP

This activity introduces the topic of roles in business with a focus on staff members and employers.

- Divide the class into small groups making sure you have an even number of groups.
- Tell half the groups they are employers and the other half they are staff members.
- On the board, write *1 to succeed in business, your staff should …*, and *2 to succeed in business, your employer should …* .
- Tell students to finish the sentence in three different ways (the staff members should do sentence 2, the employers sentence 1.)
- When they have finished, put students into new groups with staff members and employers in each to compare their sentences.
- If the sentences are different, students need to persuade each other that their perspective is right.
- Finally, get a few ideas from the staff members and the employers, and ask the class to vote on which perspective they think is the right one.

Greek proverb:

This proverb means that it's much better to do business with people you don't know well because personal relationships will distract you from good business decisions.

VOCABULARY: business terms and roles

1a As a lead in, focus students on the photo on page 58 and ask them where they think the men are and what they're doing.

- Explain that the first part of this lesson will look at vocabulary connected to business and set the activity.
- When you go through the answers, check the pronunciation of *competitors* (stress on the second syllable).
- Finally, to lead in to exercise 1b, ask if students agree with any/all these statements.

1 staff; **2** profit; **3** wages; **4** prices; **5** law; **6** taxes; **7** customer; **8** community; **9** competitors; **10** loss

1b Give students ten minutes to discuss the statements and encourage them to agree/disagree with each other if necessary.

If you are short of time, choose only five of the statements for students to discuss.

To extend this activity, when pairs have finished their discussion, put them into groups of four and ask them to compare what they talked about. Encourage them to agree/disagree if necessary.

2 Check that students understand *job role* (what someone does in their job).

- Ask students to compare with a partner before you go through answers with the class.

Some of the definitions will seem very similar to students. Monitor while they are working to spot mistakes and ask students to think again. If necessary, tell students to use their dictionaries.

1 retailer; **2** manufacturer; **3** entrepreneur; **4** partner; **5** wholesaler; **6** customer; **7** supplier

To prepare students to use these words in exercise 3, elicit/give the stress on the following words and ask students to repeat: *manufacturer* (third syllable);

retailer (first syllable); *supplier* (second syllable); *wholesaler* (first syllable). Elicit/give the pronunciation of *entrepreneur* /ˌɒntrəprəˈnɜː/.

3 Give students three minutes to read through the questions and think about their answers before you put them into pairs.

- Move around the room to help with additional vocabulary if necessary.
- While you monitor students, listen carefully to their answers to check they have understood the vocabulary.

Answers depend on students' own ideas.

If you are short of time, you could cut question 4.

READING

4 Focus students on the leaflet on page 59, tell them to read the title and ask them when you need to write a business plan (when you are setting up a new business).

- Tell students to read the four headings before they read the leaflet.
- Tell students not to worry about unknown vocabulary because they will study this in exercise 5.

Students will find this activity easier if they read the whole leaflet before they match headings to sections.

1 c; **2** d; **5** b; **6** a

5 Ask students to read the definitions and check they understand *long and short term* (for a long or short period of time) and *reduction* (decrease).

- Ask students to compare with a partner before you check answers with the class.
- Finally, ask students if there are other words they need help with or tell them to use dictionaries.

1 business premises; **2** business objectives/aims; **3** funding; **4** market leaders; **5** discount; **6** profit and loss forecast

LISTENING

6a Read through the introduction with the class and check they understand *tip* (a piece of advice).

- Students have a lot to write in this activity. If they need extra time, pause the track where indicated in the audioscript below.

The activity mentions *promotion* but in the text, Allan says *promote*. In feedback, make sure students know that *promote* is the verb and *promotion* is the noun. The meaning of *promote* should be clear from the context.

1 finance, tax, selling, marketing; **2** price, costs, promotion, competitors; **3** market [the product] in a different way to different people / good marketing

Track 1.32
Interviewer, Allan

I: Tonight, we're focusing on starting your own business. I have with me Allan Smith, an accountant and business adviser. Good evening, Allan – thanks for joining us.
A: Good evening, John – it's a pleasure.
I: Allan, could I start by asking you to give us the most important tips for someone setting up a business?
A: Certainly. First of all, I'd say you must understand you'll never know everything there is to running a business – it's as simple as that. So, you'll need help in certain areas – maybe with finances and tax or perhaps with selling and marketing. Once you know the areas where you need help, you can train yourself, or bring in an employee who has the skill you need. Another way is to get advice from an expert or a friend who has their own business. OK? [PAUSE]
I: Right, very useful. Anything else?
A: Yes, my second tip is all about marketing. You need to be sure that your product will sell in sufficient numbers, at a price that covers your costs. In other words, it must give you a return on your money; it's got to make a profit. To do this you must be clear about how you price your product – for example, are you going to price it above, the same as or below your competitors? Then, you must also think about how you'll promote it. I mean, how are you going to let people know about the product, so they become aware of it? That's important. And, you know, you may have to market it in a different way to different people. That could be the key to success.
I: OK, so good marketing is essential when you start your own business.
A: Exactly.

6b Tell students the text in the question is not exactly the same as the listening because it is a summary.

- When you check answers with the class, ask if there is vocabulary they want to know e.g. cash flow.

1 moved on; **2** main customer; **3** planning; **4** tax. (Answers are bold in the audioscript.)

Audioscript and answers to exercise 6b:
Track 1.33
Interviewer, Allan

I: You spent many years, Allan, working in accountancy firms with businesses that failed, that went bankrupt. Why did most of them fail?

A: Erm, I think there were three reasons really. Firstly, some failed because the market had **1 moved on**, and the business was left behind. It was using old equipment that just wasn't up-to-date, wasn't efficient – the printing trade is a good example of that. Another reason was that some of them depended too much on one **2 main customer**, and then if the customer decides they don't need you any more … And the third reason, well … it could be a number of things, poor **3 planning**, cash flow problems, bad debts, erm, not dealing with **4 tax** properly, that sort of thing – just not managing the business properly.

6c Tell students to read the statements before you play the track.

- Don't pre-teach *vital* or *straight away* before students listen even though they need these to answer statements 1 and 4. If necessary, elicit/give the meaning when you go through the answers.

1 True; **2** False (sales may still be lower); **3** False (people can't deal with unexpected things when the plan is in their head); **4** True (Answers are bold in the audioscript.)

Audioscript and answers to exercise 6c:
Track 1.34
Interviewer, Allan

I: A final question – what do you think about business plans?

A: Oh, **1 they're vital**. You should think of them as a map which'll take you from today to how the business will be in a few years' time. The business plan will set out your objectives, how you are going to get there, to achieve them, and how you are going to measure your progress. **3 Too many people say their plan is in their head. But when that happens, they often can't deal with unexpected things**, like, erm, **2 sales that are lower than they hoped**, or rising costs. You should get your forecasts down in writing.
Check how you are getting on and use your plan to help you succeed in the business. Oh, yes, one other thing – **4 don't expect to get the forecasts right straight away**. You'll improve later when you have more experience.

I: Thanks very much, Allan. Some good advice there for people starting up a business.

SPEAKING

7 Tell students to read the statements before you play the track.

- Students compare their answers with a partner and, if necessary, play the track again.

(i) It is fairly common in English for businesses to use a 'K' instead of a 'C' in their names. It is believed that this makes the name a bit more catchy and easy to remember.

1 car washing; **2** Kar Klean; **3** don't need much equipment; won't cost too much to set up; could make quite a lot of money; **4** Answer depends on students' opinions.

Track 1.35

A: I think a car washing business is a good idea. We'll need to research the market a bit first. Maybe the supermarkets will allow us to wash customers' cars in the car park?

B: Yes, good idea.

A: Also, how about contacting a local taxi firm? They have a lot of cars which always seem to be dirty. There could be a cleaning service for the inside of the cars as well. We wouldn't need much equipment, but we should have a good name – how about something like Kar Klean, with a K – you know, K–A–R K–L–E–A–N?

B: Yeah, good idea. We could give people a discount to start with and print a few leaflets to advertise the business.

A: Yes, I don't think it'd cost much to set up the business and we could make quite a lot of money.

8 Explain that students are going to have a similar discussion to the one they heard in exercise 7.

- While they are speaking, monitor and note common mistakes when using the vocabulary from this lesson.
- Ask a few pairs to present their ideas to the rest of the class.
- Finally, correct some of the mistakes you noted earlier.

If your students all live in different towns, ask them to decide on a business for the town where your school is. If none of the business ideas in this activity is appropriate to the local environment, choose a list of ideas that are more suitable or ask students to think of their own ideas.

HOMEWORK OPTIONS

Students do the exercises on page 39 of the Workbook.

Students write a brief business plan summarising the ideas they had in exercise 8. In the next lesson, post the business plans around the walls and ask students to read them all. (Note: there will be two plans for each idea because students were in pairs for exercise 8. Make sure each pair's plans are posted next to each other.) Finally, ask the class to decide which business idea is most likely to succeed.

6.2 BUSINESS DILEMMAS

IN THIS LESSON

Lesson topic and staging

This lesson looks at dilemmas people might face in business. Students read three short texts describing different ethical dilemmas and focus on the use of pronoun referencing (e.g. *their, this, it, those*). Students then do a speaking activity to discuss what they would do in these situations. The readings contextualise the grammar focus for this lesson and students do a series of activities to explore the meaning, form and pronunciation of the past continuous before using it in a group speaking activity. Finally, students write a paragraph describing one of the situations they discussed in the group speaking activity.

Objectives

By the end of the lesson, students should have:

- practised extracting specific information and language items from three reading texts
- focused on the use of pronoun referencing in a the texts (e.g. *their, this, it, those*)
- revised/extended their knowledge of the meaning, form and pronunciation of the past continuous
- used the past continuous in a speaking and a writing activity

Timings

If short of time, you could drop exercise 4b on page 61 because this does not add to students' understanding of the texts.

A good lesson break would be after after exercise 4b on page 61.

WARM-UP

This activity introduces the topic of ethical dilemmas.

- Write the following on the board: What would you do if:
    - a classmate had cheated in an exam, got a higher grade than you and won the school prize for their results?
    - you found out your friend's girl/boyfriend was married but your friend didn't know and was completely in love?
    - your colleague had stolen some money from the office, told you they'd done it and then offered to buy you dinner with the money?
- Check students understand *cheat* (e.g. copy another person's work).
- Put them into pairs to discuss the questions *honestly* and tell them to give reasons for their answers.
- Get a few ideas from two or three pairs.

READING

1a Check students understand *dilemma* (a difficult choice), *ethical* (morally right or wrong) and *job centre* (the government office where jobs are advertised and you get money to help you).

- Give pairs a maximum of ten minutes to discuss the dilemmas before getting a few ideas from the class.

> Answers will depend on students' own ideas.

If you are short of time, tell students to discuss only one question.

1b Students do this activity in the same pairs as exercise 1a.

- Give them five minutes to discuss before getting a few ideas from the class.
- Write students' ideas on the board.

2a Focus students on the three texts on pages 60–61 and ask them to use the pictures and titles to predict what the dilemma is in each text.

- Then tell students to read the three options (a–c) before giving them two minutes to read the texts.
- Check answers with the class.
- Finally, ask students if any of the dilemmas written on the board in exercise 1b were mentioned here.

> Text 1: c; Text 2: a; Text 3: b

2b Tell students to read the statements for Text 1, then reread the text and answer.

- Repeat this procedure for Texts 2 and 3.
- Before students begin, check they understand *decent* (good), *rotten* (bad), *bonus* (extra money paid for good performance or because of good profits), *illegally* (against the law), *go bankrupt* (be without enough money to pay what you owe).
- To follow up, ask students which dilemma they think presents the most difficult decision.

> Text 1: **1** False (he said you weren't paying enough attention to your *work*); **2** True; Text 2: **3** False (waste is within legal limits); **4** False (the company could go bankrupt); Test 3: **5** True; **6** False (you were given a watch and an antique clock)

3 Explain that we use these pronouns to refer to things already mentioned or things mentioned later in texts. This is to avoid repeating the previous noun or phrase.

- When you go through the answers, ask students if the pronoun refers to something already mentioned or mentioned later. See below for answers.

1 the shirts (already mentioned); 2 the company (already mentioned); 3 equipment (already mentioned); 4 the polluted waste (already mentioned); 5 everyone, including yourself (already mentioned); 6 overseas supplier (already mentioned); 7 another present (already mentioned); 8 another supplier's radios (mentioned later)

To provide extra practice, tell students to look at a text they read in one of the earlier lessons in the Coursebook. Choose a text they found interesting. Tell them to find similar reference pronouns and note which nouns or phrases they refer to.

SPEAKING

4a Give students five minutes to think about their answers to the questions and look up *gift*, *bribe* and *punishment* in their dictionaries. (Don't pre-teach *gift* and *bribe* because this will make it unnecessary to discuss question 3.)

- Students then do the activity as per the Coursebook.

Groups should have no more than four students to allow everyone the chance to speak.

1&2: Answers depend on students' own ideas and opinions; **3** If you are given a *bribe*, the giver expects a favour from you. A bribe is often illegal in business in business and politics.

4b Tell students to give as much information as possible and to ask follow-up questions.

- While students are working, move around the class to provide help with additional vocabulary.
- In feedback, ask a few students to tell the class the most interesting or surprising thing they heard.

GRAMMAR: past continuous

5 To lead in, ask students if they can give you an example of the past continuous.

- Before students do this activity, ask them to underline all the examples (1–4) in the texts.
- Tell them to compare their answers with a partner, before you check with the class.
- In feedback, refer to the context(s) when checking students' answers.
- Write one example from 1–4 on the board, elicit and underline *was/were* and verb + *-ing*.

To encourage students to think about meaning, refer them to the context and the Language reference rather than correct them while they are doing this activity.

1 b; **2** c **3** d **4** a

For a full explanation and extra practice, see pages 144–145 in the Language reference.

6 Check students understand *lucrative* (it will make a lot of money) in sentence e).

- Make sure students have matched the sentences correctly before they write them in full.
- In feedback, write the answers on the board so that students can see the form and the use of commas. (Note: all the sentences can be written with the *when/while* clause first or second. If it is first, the clause must be followed by a comma.)

To encourage students to think about meaning and form, refer them to the context and the Language reference rather than correct them while they are doing this activity.

1 c) I met my old boss while I was travelling to Warsaw for a conference.; **2** d) IBM offered me a job while I was studying at Harvard.; **3** e) The company was having financial problems when a lucrative new contract was agreed.; **4** b) The sun was shining brightly when I left home at 7 o'clock this morning.; **5** f) She found the missing file while she was looking for some other documents.; **6** a) We were talking about our future strategy in a meeting when the President suddenly announced her resignation.

i Warsaw is the capital city of Poland. Harvard is a very famous university near Boston in the USA.

pronunciation

7a Weak forms

- Say the weak and strong forms for students a couple of times before you play the track.
- Pause the track after each sentence to give students time to decide their answer.
- Check answers and if necessary, play the track again.
- In feedback, ask students why the *was/were* is strong (because it is a contrast to the first weak use).

7b Pause the track after each sentence for students to repeat and correct their pronunciation.

Audioscript and answers to exercise 7:
Track 1.36

1 We (were) having a meeting when the fire alarm went off.
2 When the phone rang, I (was) talking to a customer.
3 '(Was) he working for you then?', 'No, he wasn't.'
4 '(Were) they planning to buy another shop?', 'Well, they said they were.'

8 Read the example with the class (*Last month I ...*) before giving students three minutes to think about their answers.

- Students then do the activity as per the Coursebook.

If you are short of time, focus students only on the third bullet (important world events) and give or get two examples known to everyone in the class. Then put students into small groups to discuss these.

WRITING

9 Tell students to pay particular attention to the past continuous/past simple when writing.

- When they have finished, ask students to swap with a partner and try to correct any mistakes.
- Take the paragraphs in for marking with a particular focus on the past continuous/past simple.

To encourage students to think about meaning and form, refer them to exercises 5 and 6 and the Language reference rather than correct them yourself. If they have a lot of difficulty, prompt them with corrections.

Before or after taking the paragraphs in for marking, post them around the walls or your classroom. Ask students to read the paragraphs and then vote on the best/most interesting/funniest/serious.

HOMEWORK OPTIONS

Students do the exercises on pages 40–41 of the Workbook.

Students write the paragraph in exercise 9 at home.

Students write a short paragraph to describe the situation and difficult ethical decision in exercise 4b.

6.3 BUSINESS ICONS

IN THIS LESSON

Lesson topic and staging

This lesson looks at famous business people. Students read different texts about business people and then share the information with a partner in a follow-up discussion. They then work on business word combinations, for example, *make a profit*. The texts they read at the beginning of the lesson contextualise the grammar focus (past perfect): students do a series of activities to explore the meaning and form before practising this grammar in a speaking activity. Finally, students discuss a topic related to the texts they read.

Objectives

By the end of the lesson, students should have:

- practised reading texts to extract specific information and language items
- extended their range of word combinations in the context of business
- revised/learned more about and used the past perfect
- engaged in a group discussion

Timings

If short of time, you could drop exercise 3b on page 63 and set it for homework.

A possible lesson break would be after exercise 3 on page 63.

WARM-UP

- This activity is a quiz on famous business people and their nationalities.
- Write the following on the board:

1 Ratan Tata	a) American	i) manufacturing, communications and services
2 Richard Branson	b) Italian	ii) media
3 Oprah Winfrey	c) British	iii) transport and music
4 Donatella Versace	d) Indian	iv) fashion

- Explain that the names are of famous business people and the other two columns are their nationalities and main areas of business.
- Students match a person with a nationality and an area of business as quickly as possible.
- The first to finish wins. (Answers are: 1d i; 2 c iii; 3 a ii; 4 b iv.)

READING

1 You could use the WARM-UP above as a lead in and ask students which of these people they know.

- Students then do the activity as per the Coursebook, but think of different people from the WARM-UP.
- When they have finished, get ideas from one or two groups, ask the other students if they've heard of these people and if they can add more information.

If students can't think of any famous business people, write 'Bill Gates' on the board and ask students to talk about him. At least some of the class will know some information.

Answers will depend on the people students choose.

2a Check students understand *obituaries* (short newspaper biographies written after a person's death).

- Tell students that they won't be able to answer all the questions but will find out more information from other students later.
- Tell them to ask you or use their dictionary for problem vocabulary.
- When they have answered as many questions as possible, put As and Bs in pairs.
- Tell them to share information by speaking but NOT to read each other's texts.
- Finally, go through answers with the class.

For question 7, students need to *compare* the information they have to find the correct answers.

1 Freddie Laker: air travel; Coco Chanel: fashion; Mark McCormack: sports marketing; Akio Morita: electronics; **2** Freddie Laker: low-cost air travel; Coco Chanel: [probably] perfumes; Mark McCormack: he started the sports marketing industry / he was first to realise that sports personalities could earn money from endorsements and sponsorship; Akio Morita: Sony, one of the first truly global companies; **3** Freddie Laker; **4** a Coco Chanel; b Mark McCormack; c Akio Morita; d Freddie Laker; **5** a Akio Morita; b Akio Morita; **6** a Freddie Laker and Coco Chanel; b Mark McCormack and Akio Morita; c Mark McCormack and Akio Morita; d Mark McCormack and Akio Morita; e Freddie Laker and Coco Chanel; **7** a Freddie Laker (four times); b Coco Chanel; c Coco Chanel; d Mark McCormack

2b Give students five minutes to do this activity.

- In feedback, ask students who they think had the happiest/poorest/unhappiest/interesting childhood.

VOCABULARY: business word combinations

3a Check students understand *negotiate* (discuss to reach agreement), *found* (start), *launch* (start publicly).

(!) Students may confuse *found* with the past simple/participle of *find*. *Found* here is a completely separate regular verb.

All the words are from the texts in exercise 2 but it may be very time-consuming to find them. Tell students to make the combinations they know and then go through the answers below.

1 negotiate a contract; **2** make a profit; **3** found/run/launch a company; **4** make/introduce/launch a product; **5** go bankrupt; **6** go into business

3b While students are writing, move round the room to point out mistakes they make with the vocabulary.

- Ask one or two stronger students to read their sentences to the class.

GRAMMAR: past perfect

4a Students do the activity as per the Coursebook.

Underlined verbs: launched; had noticed; celebrated; had started

(!) *Love* is not a verb here, it is a noun.

4b Tell students to compare with a partner before you check answers with the class.

- While students are working, write the two sentences from exercise 4a on the board.
- In feedback, underline and number the relevant parts of the sentences on the board.

To encourage students to think about meaning and form themselves, refer them to the sentences in exercise 4a and the Language reference rather than correct them while they are doing this activity.

1 launched; celebrated; **2** had noticed young people's love of music; had started his own company; **3** launched the Walkman; celebrated his 26th birthday; **4** Past perfect = action that happened first
We form the past perfect with *had* + *(not)* + the past participle.

Take this opportunity to remind students of the contractions of *had* (*I'd*, *he'd*, etc.) and *had not* (*hadn't*).

5 Tell students both sentences are in the texts on page 62 (1 = Coco Chanel paragraph 3; 2 = Freddie Laker paragraph 1).

- In feedback, emphasise that *by* means *at some time in the period up to …*

We use the past perfect to talk about events that happened by a certain time.

For a full explanation and extra practice see the Language reference on pages 144–145.

6 Students do this activity individually and then discuss difficult items with a partner.

- Move round the room to point out mistakes and encourage students to use the Language reference and exercises 4 and 5 if they need help.

(!) Both past simple and past perfect are possible in answer 5.

1 had bought; **2** was; **3** was; **4** had made; **5** completed/had completed; **6** began; **7** died; **8** had not lived; **9** had made; **10** set up; **11** was; **12** had given

SPEAKING

7a & **b** The aim of these activities is to practise the past perfect, NOT to test students' general knowledge.

- While students are speaking in pairs, note mistakes they make with the past perfect.
- In 7b, encourage them to use contracted forms.
- At the end of the activity, go through answers and ask students if they found out any new information.(Do not give students the answers until they have finished exercise 7b.)
- Finally, correct a selection of the mistakes you noted earlier.

Apart from the first four, students may not know these people. To help, you could do some or all of the following:

1 Tell students to guess and then check their answers in exercise 7b.
2 Teach them the phrase *I think* + past perfect, *but I'm not sure*.
3 Tell them to check their answers with different students until they find a definite answer.
4 Emphasise the aim of the activity (given above) and simply tell students the correct answers when you do feedback.
5 Ask students to use the Internet to find the correct information for homework.

1 had started his own company; **2** had gone bankrupt; **3** had expanded her business; **4** had become the most powerful person in sport; **5** had composed his first piece of music; **6** had won an Oscar; **7** had climbed Mount Everest; **8** had won the World Cup; **9** had flown to Australia

(i) Mozart: 1756–1791, Austrian classical composer

Orson Welles: 1915–1985, American film director and actor

Edmund Hillary: born 1919, New Zealand mountaineer and explorer

Pelé: born 1940, Brazilian (soccer) football player

Amy Johnson: 1903–1941, British aviator

Oscar: awards (gold statuettes of a man) of the American Academy of Motion Picture Arts and Sciences

8 Give students a few minutes to think about their ideas before putting them into pairs or small groups for the discussion.

- While they are speaking, move round the class noting common or important mistakes.
- For feedback, ask groups if they agreed or disagreed with the title of the discussion.
- Finally, correct a selection of the mistakes you noted earlier.

HOMEWORK OPTIONS

Students do the exercises on pages 42–43 of the Workbook.

Students research one of the people they learned about in exercise 7 and write a short biography using the past perfect and past simple.

6.4 SCENARIO: SUNGLASSES AFTER DARK

IN THIS LESSON

Lesson topic and staging

This lesson focuses on effective negotiations. Students discuss the value of some tips for negotiating and are then introduced to the scenario of an Italian wholesaler who wants to import sunglasses from overseas. Students then listen to two people negotiating the import of this product before focusing on KEY LANGUAGE taken from the listening text and a further list of useful phrases. Finally, students use this language in the main Task: to negotiate a deal.

Objectives

By the end of the lesson, students should have:

- learned useful phrases for negotiating (making offers, stating a position and bargaining)
- used this language in a 'real-life' situation to negotiate a deal for the import of sunglasses
- extracted specific information and language items from a listening text
- participated effectively in extended speaking practice

Common European Framework

Students can use language effectively to negotiate in a business context.

Timings

If short of time, you could drop exercise 1 and begin the lesson with exercise 2. However, make sure you tell students that negotiating is not only useful in the business world.

A possible lesson break would be after exercise 5b on page 65.

WARM-UP

- Tell students to look at the photos of sunglasses on pages 64 and 65.
- Students choose a pair they like, but don't tell the other students which it is.
- Put students in pairs and tell one to describe their sunglasses to the other. The second student tries to guess which pair.
- Repeat the procedure with the second student describing their sunglasses.

SITUATION

1 The aim of this activity is to lead in to the lesson but also to show students that negotiation isn't just important in the business world.

- Give students a maximum of five minutes to discuss the questions.
- Get a few ideas from two or three pairs.

Negotiate was taught in lesson 6.3, but you may need to remind students of the meaning here.

> Answers depend on students' own ideas and opinions.

2 Give students five minutes to discuss the list and give a time check after three minutes.

> Answers will depend on students' opinions.

To extend this activity, when students have chosen four tips, put the pairs together to form groups of four. Tell the new groups they have to agree on four tips and set a time limit. Repeat the procedure until the whole class agrees on four tips.

3 Tell students that Domino s.p.r.l is a wholesaler involved in fashion.

- Students then do the activity as per the Coursebook.
- In feedback, check students understand *peak season* (the time of year when the largest number of people do the same thing).
- Follow up by asking students if they wear sunglasses in winter and/or in the evening. Why?

> Because people are wearing sunglasses all year round, and also in the evening as fashion accessories.

4a Read through the situation and the question with the class, and then play the track without pausing.

- When you check the answer, don't elicit reasons for the negotiation being unsuccessful because this will give students the answers to exercise 4b.

> The negotiation is not successful.

4b Tell students to read the questions before you play the track without pausing.

- Tell students to compare with a partner before you check answers with the class.

> **1** about 50,000; **2** Vanessa wants them in August, but Bob can't deliver until maybe September; Bob wants payment on delivery, Vanessa says she'll pay after 60 days, Bob asks for payment after 30 days but Vanessa isn't sure about this.

KEY LANGUAGE: making offers, stating a position, bargaining

5a Before students do this activity, check they understand *stating a position* and *bargaining* by telling you when these happened in the listening (stating a position: Vanessa says she wants the sunglasses in August, Bob says they're very busy; bargaining: they discuss the payment date – on delivery, 60 days, 30 days).

- Ask students to try to complete as many gaps as possible before you play the track again.
- Play the track without pausing and ask students to compare with a partner.
- Check answers with the class and tell students *placing* means the same as *making* here.
- Ask students if Vanessa and Bob sounded polite or rude (impolite) and emphasise that it's important to use a fairly high tone to sound polite in this context.

1 order; **2** placing; **3** afraid; **4** pay; Will; **5** understand; **6** feel; **7** fine (Answers are bold in audioscript below.)

Audioscript and answers to exercise 5a: Track 1.37

Vanessa, Bob

V: Could I speak to Bob, please?

B: Yes, speaking, how can I help you?

V: Hi Bob, it's Vanessa from Domino in Italy here.

B: Hi Vanessa. How are things?

V: Fine. Did you get my email?

B: Yes, I did, but I've been really busy – sorry I haven't replied. You want to order some sunglasses from us.

V: Well yes ... maybe. Thanks for the samples you sent us, Bob, they certainly look good.

B: They sure are Vanessa, they're selling really well. OK, how many would you like to **1 order**?

V: Mmm, well, We're thinking of **2 placing** quite a large order, about 50,000, at the price you gave us in the email.

B: Great!

V: Yeah, but it's really important that you can deliver to us in August.

B: Oh, I'm **3 afraid** that would be a bit difficult, Vanessa, we've already still got quite a few summer orders to deal with. Maybe in September – that should be OK.

V: What about if we **4 pay** earlier? **4 Will** you be able to deliver in August?

B: Vanessa, let me check if I **5 understand** you, do you mean payment on delivery, in August? Well, that would be good ...

V: No, we couldn't pay that soon. I was thinking of paying after 60 days. How do you **6 feel** about that?

B: Sorry Vanessa, I don't think we can wait that long. How about 30?

continued...

V: I'm not sure about that. OK, Bob, look ... I'll think it over and maybe get back to you.

B: That sounds **7 fine**. Well ... I hope to hear from you soon.

V: Right, Bob, thanks a lot. Bye for now.

B: Bye.

When you go through the answers, write the phrases (as below) on the board so that students can refer to them when they negotiate in exercise 6b.

- We're thinking of + verb-*ing*
- I'm afraid that would be a bit difficult
- What about if we +infinitive?
- Will you be able to +infinitive?
- Let me check if I understand you ...
- How do you feel about that?
- That sounds fine

5b Give students three minutes to do this activity individually.

- When you elicit the answers, check students' pronunciation.

a 5; **b** 2; **c** 1; **d** 7; **e** 4; **f** 6; **g** 3

You could add these phrases to the board next to those from exercise 5a:

- Let's see if I've got this right
- We're considering +verb-*ing*
- What sort of +noun do you have in mind?
- That seems ok
- If we +infinitive, can you ...
- What do you think of the +noun?
- I'm sorry. That could be a problem

TASK: negotiating a deal

6a To lead in to this activity, remind students that the negotiation wasn't successful and ask them what they think Domino s.p.r.l should do next.

- Divide the class into two groups (As and Bs). If you have a large class, you could have two groups of As and two of Bs.
- Give students a maximum of five minutes to read and think about their answers before they discuss with the group.
- Gives the groups ten minutes to discuss the questions and take notes that they can use in the negotiation later.
- While they are working, move round the room to help with any extra vocabulary they need.
- Give the class regular time checks so that all the groups finish at the same time.

6b Before students begin the negotiation, remind them of the phrases from exercises 5a and 5b, the tips in exercise 2, and go through the OTHER USEFUL PHRASES box on page 65.

- If you have an odd number in your class, form a group of three with two As or two Bs.
- Give a maximum of ten minutes for students to finish their negotiation.
- While students are negotiating in pairs, monitor and note common mistakes when using the KEY LANGUAGE from exercises 5a and 5b.
- At the end of the activity, ask each pair if both A and B students got a good deal. Why? Why not?
- Finally, correct some of the most common mistakes you noted earlier.

When A/B pairs have finished their negotiation, put students back into their groups from exercise 6a. Tell them to present the deal they made to the others in their group and to discuss who got the best deal for the company.

HOMEWORK OPTIONS

Students do the exercises on page 44 of the Workbook.

6.5 STUDY AND WRITING SKILLS

IN THIS LESSON

Lesson topic and staging

This lesson focuses on the skills of recognising formal and informal language and then writing emails. Students study the differences between formal and informal use of language in different written texts. They then decide on the procedure for writing emails and revise/learn phrases to use when writing an email of their own. Next, students practise changing register from formal to neutral and from informal to formal. Finally, students write their own emails using situations provided.

Objectives

By the end of the lesson, students should have:

- learned/revised the differences between formal, informal and neutral register in writing
- revised/learned a set of useful phrases for use when writing emails
- extracted language items from extracts from different types of correspondence
- written emails in both formal and informal business contexts

Common European Framework

Students can write emails in formal and informal contexts.

Timings

If time is short, you could drop one or two of the situations from exercise 7 and set these for homework.

A possible lesson break would be either after exercises 3 or 4 on page 66.

WARM-UP

This activity introduces the topic of formality and informality.

- Write the following phrases on the board:
  - Hi
  - Could you help me with this, please?
  - How's it going?
  - That really gets on my nerves
  - Nice meeting you
  - How do you do?
  - It's been a pleasure meeting you
  - Good afternoon
  - Give me a hand, will you?
  - I'm afraid that makes me feel rather angry

- Tell students to put the phrases into two groups: more/less formal, and then to compare their answers with a partner.
- Finally, elicit from students in what situation you could use each phrase.

(Answers: More formal: Could you help with this, please?; How do you do?; It's been a pleasure meeting you; Good afternoon; I'm afraid that makes me feel rather angry

Less formal: Hi; How's it going?; That really gets on my nerves; Nice meeting you; Give me a hand, will you?)

STUDY SKILLS: recognising formal and informal language

1a Check students understand *correspondence* (pieces of writing – often sent – to communicate between people).

- Ask students to try to label the different types of writing before they look at the list given.
- Then tell them to look at the list to check their answers and label the pieces they didn't know.
- When you go through the answers, check students understand *minutes* (a record of a formal meeting).
- To follow up, ask students which of these types they have written/write regularly in English and in their own language.

1 report; **2** note; **3** letter; **4** email; **5** minutes

1b Tell students to compare their answers with a partner before you check with the class.

Students may just say that a piece is informal *because* of the language used. Prompt them by asking 'But why does the writer *want* the piece to sound more/less formal?'

1 Formal, because it's for an unknown and/or public audience.; **2** Informal, because Dan and Jane have a friendly relationship. Also, Dan is possibly superior to Jane in the company.; **3** Formal, because the two people don't know each other and have a business, not a personal relationship. Also, this is a letter which often has a more formal register than an email or a note, for example.; **4** Informal, because the two people know each other and have a friendly relationship. (Note: it is not true that emails are normally less formal than letters; it depends on the context and the audience.); **5** Formal, because it's the minutes from a meeting, which is a more formal context.

2a Students do the activity as per the Coursebook.

- In feedback, tell students that the answers are generally true but there are exceptions. For example, informal writing will use full forms instead of contractions to emphasise a point.

1 informal; **2** formal; **3** formal; **4** informal; **5** formal; **6** informal; **7** informal (and formal, if the text is written in note form e.g, text 5); **8** informal and formal (depending on the type of text)

2b Before students do this activity, go through the list of features and elicit how the passive is formed (*be* + past participle), what a phrasal verb is (verb + preposition with a meaning not obvious from the words themselves), and the imperative (no subject pronoun).

- Give students five to ten minutes to find the examples. Tell them to underline these and note the text number next to the relevant feature in the list.
- Students compare with a partner before you check answers with the class.
- In feedback, go through the notes provided in brackets with the answers below.

(!) Students may ask why some informal words in the examples for feature 5 are just as long as the formal ones. Tell them it is how common they are that is more important.

Tell students when they learn a new word (e.g. the examples for feature 5), it is always a good idea to learn how formal/informal or neutral they are. They can find this information in a good dictionary.

1 Contractions: Text 2: I'll; Text 4: I'll.; **2** No contractions: Text 1: it is; Text 3: I will, I would; Text 5: Martin Schwartz will prepare (Note: we don't normally contract a person's name and *will* in either informal or formal texts.); **3** Passive constructions: Text 1: It is recommended, are contacted, informed, should be arranged; Text 5: was approved; **4** Phrasal verbs: Text 2: get back (meaning = reply), find out (meaning = discover); Text 4: firm up (meaning = make more definite); **5** Longer words instead of shorter, more common ones: Text 1: therefore (so), option (choice, idea), improve (make/get better), morale (happiness), recommended (it's a good idea), informed (told), requirements (what we need); Text 3: unfortunately (sorry, but), unable (can't), attend (come to), due to (because of), previous (earlier), engagement (meeting, plan), however (but), grateful (pleased); **6** Direct questions: Text 2: can you find out what …?; **7** missing out words: Text 1: March/April (March *or* April); Text 4: got (I/we got), Text 5: for next meeting (for *the* next meeting), prepare detailed budget (prepare *a* detailed budget). (The formal texts are missing words because they are written in note form – this does not make them less formal.)

3 Students do the activity as per the Coursebook.

- If feedback, elicit a few other examples of formal and informal endings (e.g. Formal: Regards, Yours faithfully. Informal: Lots of love, All the best).

Letter: Dear …; Yours sincerely. Email: Hi … Best wishes

WRITING SKILLS: writing emails

4 To lead in, ask students if they write emails or other texts in English and if they make mistakes or find this type of writing difficult.

- Tell them you are going to look at a procedure that might help them when writing.
- Go through the instructions and list with students and check they understand *draft* (a first copy that can be improved), *edit* (correct spelling mistakes, change the order, choose a different word, etc.), *brainstorm* (think about all the possible content without thinking about the order), and *functions* (the purpose of the email – to complain, to recommend, etc.).
- Emphasise it is the bold letters that will spell a word if the order is correct.
- Ask students to compare with a partner before you check answers with the class.
- To follow up, ask students if they think this is a useful procedure and why.

> **1** Who; **2** Register; **3** Information; **4** Type; **5** Edit; **6** Send. (The word is WRITES.)

Tell students that this procedure is useful for all the writing they do in English and in their own language. They will need to change the focus of some points (e.g. 'Who is the email to?' becomes 'Who is going to read this essay?'), but the procedure stays the same.

5 Focus students on the table on page 67 and go through the layout (register across the top, functions on the left, language examples in the main part).

- Give them a minute or two to read the examples in the table and note where the gaps are.
- Then ask them to read all the phrases in exercise 5 before they decide where they should go.
- Ask students to compare with a partner before you check answers with the class and go through the notes in brackets below.

Some of the notes in brackets will help students with the grammar they need to use in exercise 6a.

> **1** Got your message on … (+ day); **2** I have some good news (about …) (+ noun OR + verb-*ing*; **3** I regret to inform you … (regret = sorry); **4** I would be grateful if you could … (+ infinitive verb); **5** I can't make it as … (make it = come to the arranged meeting; as = because); **6** Speak to you/See you soon.; **7** Please find attached …; **8** If I can help in any way, please contact me again.

6a Before students do this activity, ask them to quickly read Text 1 and tell you its function (to give information about online shopping).

- Tell students to look at the words around the bold phrases before they decide their answer.
- While they are working, monitor to point out mistakes students make.

> I am writing to advise you of = I am writing to tell you about a new development …
> I am delighted to inform you that = I have some good news about shopping at Shoes 4U (or any reasonable and accurate answer)
> I would be grateful if you could take = Could you possibly take …
> I look forward to hearing from you soon = Looking forward to hearing from you soon

6b Before students do this activity, ask them to quickly read Text 2 and tell you its function (to refuse an invitation and make a request).

- Tell students to look at the words around the bold phrases before they decide their answer.
- While they are working, monitor to point out mistakes students make.

> Got your email on Friday = With reference to your email of last Friday
> Sorry, but I can't make it = I would like to apologise for not being able to attend but …
> Please let Mark know = I would be grateful if you could let Mark know
> Please feel free to call/mail me again if you need any more help = If you need any further help, please do not hesitate to contact me again
> Speak to you soon = I look forward to hearing from you in the near future

7 Before students begin to write, ask them to read the procedure in exercise 4 again.

- Tell students to ask you if they need extra vocabulary.
- In the editing stage, tell students to ask you if they are not sure if a word or piece of grammar is correct.
- When they have finished each email, tell students to swap with a partner to comment on each other's content, language and point out any mistakes.
- Take the emails in for marking with particular attention to features of formal/informal writing and use of phrases from exercise 5.

If you are short of time, choose one or two situations to do in class and set the other for homework.

HOMEWORK OPTIONS

Students do the exercises on page 45 of the Workbook.

If students have access to an email account and if you are willing to give them your email address, ask them to write you an email about their day/week/weekend and send it to your address. You can mark the email and then return it to them electronically.

REVIEW

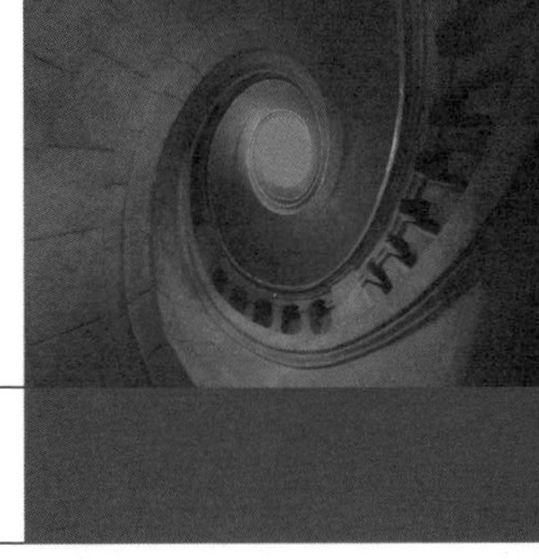

UNITS 4 – 6

GRAMMAR

1 Ask students to discuss these questions in pairs, or have a whole class discussion.

2 Focus students on the title of the article and elicit ideas on what 'neuromarketing' might be.

- Ask students to read the article quickly to check their predictions.

Neuromarketing is using brain tests to find out which adverts and brands are attractive to customers.

- Students then complete the gaps in the article.
- Check answers with the class.

1 c; **2** c; **3** a; **4** c; **5** b; **6** b; **7** b; **8** c; **9** b; **10** a; **11** a

3 Put students into pairs or small groups for this activity.

- When they have finished their discussion, get a few ideas from the class.

Answers depend on students' own opinions.

VOCABULARY

4 Give students three minutes to write as many answers as they can, then put them in pairs to compare and complete the other answers.

- Check answers with the class.

If possible, reproduce the crossword so that the whole class can see it (perhaps on an Interactive Whiteboard or an overhead projector). As you go through answers, fill them in on the crossword.

1 bilingual; **2** grammar; **3** texting; **4** slogan; **5** persuasive; **6** accent; **7** logo; **8** commercial; **9** slang; **10** languages

5a Give students one minute to complete the questions with the words from the box.

- Check answers with the class.

1 contracts; **2** products; **3** profit; **4** business; **5** bankrupt

5b Give students one minute to answer the questions for themselves.

- Then put them in pairs to ask/answer the questions and encourage them to give reasons and ask follow-up questions.
- Finally, check students understand *entrepreneur* and then tell them to count the 'yes' and 'no' answers to decide if they are one.

Answers depend on students' own experience.

KEY LANGUAGE

6 Set the situation and tell students to read the notes.

- Play the track without pausing.
- Ask students to compare with a partner and, if necessary, play the track again.
- Ask students to read the dialogue in exercise 7a to check their answers (but not to fill the gaps at this stage).

1 twenty; **2** five; **3** next week OR in one week; **4** month; **5** calls; **6** overseas calls

7a Monitor while students do this activity to make sure they have made all the necessary additions to the sentences.

- Ask them to compare answers with a partner and monitor to see which items students found difficult.
- Don't confirm answers until after exercise 7b.

7b Play the track and if students found some answers difficult in exercise 7a, pause after those items to give them time to write.

- Go through answers with the class or ask them to look at the audioscript on page 175.

1 thinking, placing; **2** would, order; **3** afraid, difficult; **4** sounds fine **5** check, understand; **6** afraid, idea; **7** What, if; **8** think, work

Track 1.38

A: Hello. Can I help?

B: Yes, we're thinking of placing quite a large order of mobile phones. I run a company and some of my staff need them.

A: Right. How many would you like to order?

B: Well, about twenty I think. Five of them are going to a conference this weekend so we'd need them straight away.

A: I'm afraid that would be a bit difficult for us. We don't have a lot in stock. But I could probably get you five today and the rest in one week. It depends a bit on the model.

B: That sounds fine.

continued…

A: So when you say you want the phones, are you saying you also want an account with us? We have some good company rates. For example, you can pay a flat monthly fee for all phones.
B: Let me check if I understand you. We'd pay one fee every month. But how much would the phones be?
A: You don't pay for the phones. Just the calls.
B: So that's even if my sales people are on the phone all the time, is it?
A: Well, it doesn't include overseas calls of course.
B: Oh. I'm afraid I don't like that idea. What about if we included that as well? What would it cost?
A: You mean include the overseas calls in a flat monthly fee?
B: That's right.
A: Yes, I think that would work. Look, let's go through some of the options …

LANGUAGE CHECK

8 Tell students they might need to add extra punctuation in some sentences.

- Tell students to try all the sentences before they look at the page in the Coursebook to check.

1 I can't keep up with my friend; **2** I won't let you down; **3** If we leave early, I'll call; **4** If you can save a language, then you should OR then should you?; **5** What would happen if we paid late?; **6** The new advert isn't as successful as the old one; **7** My computer is a little more powerful than yours [is]; **8** This brings me to my next point; **9** Thank you very much for your attention; **10** By the end of the year, the company had launched five new products.

LOOK BACK

9 The aim of this activity is to remind students of areas they looked at in units 4–6. This will help reinforce any language or skills they had difficulties with or were particularly good at.

seven new phrasal verbs: 4.1, exercise 5a; read about whether texting can cause problems: 4.2, exercises 6a and 6b; article about disappearing languages: 4.3, exercises 2a, 2b and 3; listen to views about adverts: 5.1, exercise 6a and 6b; compare which bike to buy: 5.3, exercise 8a and 8b; give a marketing presentation: 5.4, exercise 5a and 5b; make a business plan: 6.1, exercise 8; practise business word combinations: 6.3, exercise 3a and 3b

If students have problems remembering these exercises, you could put them into small groups to remind each other (as appropriate) of the vocabulary learned, the content of the text, the topic they talked about.

To extend the activity, ask students to choose one of the exercises and write a test for other students. This could be a list of questions, a true/false, a gapfill, etc.

Design

7.1 DESIGN IS EVERYWHERE

IN THIS LESSON

Lesson topic and staging

This lesson looks at design and what designs students like. Students read extracts from a design book which contextualises the language focus for this lesson: word building and adjectives. Students then do an activity to explore patterns in word building (e.g. verb/noun: *design/designer*, etc.) and practise the pronunciation of these words before using them to create sentences of their own. Next, students are introduced to a set of adjectives (e.g. *elegant*, *simple*) and finally use the vocabulary to describe designs they prefer.

Objectives

By the end of the lesson, students should have:

- expanded their range of vocabulary in the context of design
- revised/learned patterns in word building (verb/noun/adjective)
- practised extracting specific information and language items from a reading
- used the vocabulary they have learned to describe designs they prefer

Timings

If short of time and students have a good understanding of the text extracts, you could drop exercise 2b on page 70. Alternatively, drop exercise 7a on page 71.

A possible lesson break would be after exercise 5b on page 71 .

WARM-UP

This activity introduces the idea of designs people prefer and why.

- Focus students on the title of this lesson 'DESIGN IS EVERYWHERE' and write prompt words on the board e.g. *cars*, *computers*, *mobile phones*.
- Put students in pairs or small groups to discuss what kind of design they prefer for the prompts listed on the board (you could use the photo of the VW Beetle on page 70 as an example).
- When they have finished, ask the class which were the most popular kinds of design and why.

Raymond Loewy quote: (Note: there is a reading about Raymond Loewy on page 74 of the Coursebook.)

What Raymond Loewy is implying is that a well-designed product will last for a very long time, therefore manufacturers will not need a new design for a long time – so they will not give you (the designer) more work. It may also mean that it will be difficult for you to design something equally good in the future.

(i) The photo shows the Volkswagen (VW) Beetle. It was first made in Germany in 1938. VW introduced a new design in 2003 (see the red car in the photo on page 71). The Beetle has been produced for longer than any other car, and is the most produced car in the world. Originally called the Type 1, VW starting using the name 'Beetle' because this is what the public called it (it reminded them of an insect). It is also called the Bug.

READING AND SPEAKING

1 As a lead in, ask students to read the quote on page 70 and tell you what it means (see Raymond Loewy quote above).

- Then ask students to look at the photo and tell you the name of this car (see background information above). What is special about the design? Do they like the design (why/why not)?
- Get answers from a few students and elicit/teach *well-designed* and *badly-designed*.
- Students then do the activity as per the Coursebook.

> Answers depend on students' own ideas and opinions.

2a Tell students to read the list (1–5) and check they understand *essential* (extremely important) and *restrictions* (things that stop you doing something well).

- Give students three minutes to read the extracts and answer the question.
- In feedback, check students understand *misconceptions* (wrong idea/belief) in Extract 4.

> **1** Extract 4 (misconceptions); **2** Extract 3; **3** Extract 1; **4** Extract 5; **5** Extract 2

2b Tell students to read the statements first and emphasise these aren't True/False statements, but students need to correct them.

- If necessary, do the first statement as a whole class.
- Give students five minutes to reread the extracts and correct the statements.
- Tell them to compare with a partner and then check answers with the class.

- To follow up, ask students if their understanding of design is now different.

> 1 Scientists can invent technologies, ... engineers can make them work ... only designers can combine all these things. (Extract 2)
> 2 Magazines make mistakes. They use *design* when they mean *style* or *fashion* (Extract 4).
> 3 Design is *also about* how things work (Extract 4).
> 4 A design *doesn't have to be* new and different, but it must fulfil a need (Extract 3).
> 5 Designers *don't have* freedom like artists do. They can't just follow their creative feelings (Extract 5).

VOCABULARY: word building, adjectives

3 Ask students what *word building* is (e.g. making nouns from verbs) and elicit or give an example (e.g. *teach – teacher*).

- Check students understand *concept* (idea) in the third column of the table.
- Tell students to fill all the boxes in the table they can, before they look at the extracts to check.
- Tell students to guess the meaning of words they don't know by looking at the context (e.g. *innovative* is clear in Extract 3).
- When you go though the answers, elicit them from students and listen to their pronunciation. But don't correct problems with stress at this stage.
- For extra practice, ask students to do exercise V1,2 5 on page 147 of the Language reference.

The answers are in bold below.

verb	noun (person)	noun (thing, concept)	adjective
design	**designer**	**design**	**well- designed**
	scientist	science	scientific
manufacture	**manufacturer**	manufacturing	
produce	producer	**product/ production**	productive
engineer	**engineer**	engineering	
use	**user**	use	useable
develop	developer	**development**	developing
innovate	innovator	innovation	**innovative**
invent	inventor	invention	inventive
	artist	art	artistic

pronunciation

4 Word stress

- Remind students that in a dictionary stress is marked by an apostrophe (') in the phonemic script.
- Give an example by asking students to find *design* in their dictionaries. Then write the phonemic script on the board and ask students where the apostrophe is. Say or elicit the pronunciation of the word to demonstrate the stress.
- Tell students to mark the stress on all the words they can without looking in the dictionary.
- Students then find the stresses they don't know, using their dictionaries (this will save time).
- Play the track without pausing for student to check their answers.
- Play the track again, pausing after each set of words, and ask students to repeat.
- Correct their pronunciation.
- If necessary, play the track again so that students have another chance to practise the words.

Check that students' dictionaries have phonemic script entries. Using a dictionary was covered in Unit 5 STUDY AND WRITING SKILLS on pages 56–57. As an alternative lead in to this activity, you could ask students to look again at these pages and tell you how pronunciation is shown.

TRACK 1.39
'science, 'scientist, scien'tific
pro'duce, pro'ducer, 'product, pro'ductive
'innovate, 'innovator, inno'vation, 'innovative
'artist, art, ar'tistic

5a Give students a few minutes to think about their answers to the questions before you put them into pairs.

- If students can't think of answers to some questions (e.g. number 1 and number 8), tell them to listen to their partner's ideas and ask him/her for more information in the next stage of this activity.
- Allow at least ten minutes for the discussion and tell students to ask each other follow-up questions.
- While they are discussing, note mistakes with the use/pronunciation of words from exercises 3 and 4.
- When they have finished, ask a few students to tell you the most interesting/surprising thing they heard.
- Finally, correct some of the mistakes you noted earlier.

If you are short of time, ask students to discuss only three or four of the questions. You could ask them to discuss questions 3, 7 and 8 because these are all linked by 'product'.

Answers depend on students' own ideas.

5b Tell students the number of questions you want them to write (three or four should be enough).

- While they are writing, move round the room to help with extra vocabulary if necessary.
- When they have written their questions, give them ten minutes to speak to as many different students as possible and to note the answers.

- Listen to note if students are making the same mistakes as in exercise 5a.
- When they have finished, ask a few students to tell you the most interesting/surprising thing they heard.
- Finally, correct some of the mistakes you noted.

Tell students that this activity is another chance to use the vocabulary correctly and encourage them to write questions with words from exercise 3 that they find difficult.

6a Tell students to work individually to circle the words they don't know.

- Put them into pairs to compare and teach each other unknown words.
- Students then use a dictionary to find the words neither of them know.
- Don't go through answers at this stage because meaning is checked by exercises 6b and 6c below.

To save time, tell students in each pair to divide the unknown words between them, find them in their dictionaries, and then tell each other the meaning.

6b & **c** The aim of these two activities is to check that students understand the words in exercise 6a correctly.

- Students work in the same pairs as exercise 6a.
- Go through the answers with the class and correct students' pronunciation of the words in preparation for exercise 7a and 7b. Alternatively, ask students to check the word stress by using their dictionaries as they did in exercise 4.

> **6b 1** retro, traditional; **2** handmade, mass-produced; **3** futuristic, innovative
> **6c 1** stylish; **2** up to date; **3** streamlined; **4** elegant; **5** simple; **6** functional

If students are still confused by some words, elicit/give examples of products that can be described in this way.

SPEAKING AND WRITING

7a Give an example by telling students what qualities you look for in a car.

- Give students two minutes to think about their answers before forming groups for the discussion. The groups should have three or four students so that everyone gets a chance to speak.
- In feedback, ask students if their group thought the same qualities were important and get a few ideas.

7b Tell students to ask you if they need help with extra vocabulary.

- While they are speaking, monitor to note mistakes they make with the vocabulary from exercise 6a.
- For feedback, ask each group which was the most popular car/telephone and why.
- Finally, correct some of most common mistakes you noted earlier.

To extend this activity, tell the groups to agree on the best designed car and telephone. Encourage them to argue, but tell them they have to choose only one of each. Then ask them to talk to students from other groups and compare their ideas, giving reasons and asking each other follow-up questions. Finally, ask students which were the most popular designs in the class and why.

8 Give students 20 minutes for this activity.

- Tell them to ask you for help with extra vocabulary or to use their dictionaries.
- Take the paragraphs in for marking, paying attention to use of the vocabulary taught in this lesson.

HOMEWORK OPTIONS

Students do the exercises on page 46 of the Workbook.

Students write a paragraph to describe a product they use at home or in school/college/at work. They should explain why they think it is well-designed, and how 'it fulfils a need'. Students could include a sketch of the product with annotated notes if they wish.

7.2 DESIGN THROUGH THE AGES

IN THIS LESSON

Lesson topic and staging

This lesson looks at design in different decades of the 20th century. Students read three texts on design in three decades and discuss which period was most interesting. They then learn a set of abstract nouns from the texts (e.g. *consumerism, modernity*). This is followed by a listening activity which contextualises the main grammar focus: modals. Students do two activities to practise/ revise the use of modal verbs (e.g. *have to, must*) and finally use these in a speaking activity to design a new product.

Objectives

By the end of the lesson, students should have:

- practised extracting specific information and language items from three reading texts
- extended their range of abstract nouns
- extended/revised their knowledge of the meaning and form of modal verbs
- used modal verbs in a speaking activity

Timings

If short of time, you could drop exercise 4 on page 72 and set it for homework. A possible lesson break would be after exercise 4 on page 72.

WARM-UP

This activity revises adjectives from lesson 7.1 and gives students a chance to discuss the three photos on page 72 in preparation for exercise 1.

- Put students into small groups.
- Tell them to look at the photos and decide which design they like most and why.
- Finally, ask a few students which design they liked most and if the other students agreed.

READING

1 Read through the introduction with the class.

- Elicit the answers to question 1 before you put students into small groups to discuss question 2.
- In question 2, encourage students to give reasons for their answers.
- Don't give the answers for question 2 at this stage because they will read the texts to check in exercise 2b.

1 A = 1990s (a wind-up radio – it doesn't need a battery); B = 1960s (the Ball Chair – this is a design *always* associated with the 1960s); C = 1930s (a typical design for an expensive car); **2** Answers depend on students' opinions.

2a Check students understand *recycling* (using the materials from products again, e.g. paper).

- Give students three minutes to read the texts and tell them not to worry about unknown vocabulary.
- Ask them to compare their answers in the same groups as exercise 1.
- Go through the answers and ask if students guessed correctly in exercise 1. Tell students not to worry if their answers are different from those below because some items might fit into different decades. Accept any reasonable answers from the class, but encourage them to give reasons.

1930–1939: streamlining; ergonomic design; 1960–1969: young consumers; short-lived products; 1990–1999: advances in communication; recycling

2b Give students a longer time to read the texts and make notes.

- Go though answers with the class and check students understand *domestic appliances* (e.g. washing machine, fridge, etc.), *throwaway products* (something you use for a short time, throw away, and then buy a new product), *durability* (strong, can continue working a long time).
- To follow up, ask students if they like 1930s design, 1960s furniture, and if they think recycled materials are a good idea.

(!) Students may think that the 'Products' box refers only to the products of the named designers. Tell them to list *all* the products mentioned in the texts.

(🔧) To make this activity more communicative, put students into groups of three and tell each student to read a different text. Then tell them to swap information and ask each other questions.

	1930s	1960s	1990s
Ideas	streamlining, ergonomics	short-lived products, 'throwaway' society	recycling, energy-saving, product durability
Designers	Henry Dreyfuss	Verner Panton, Eero Aarnio, Courreges	Jane Atfield, Trevor Baylis
Products	boats, aircraft, cars, domestic appliances, telephone	furniture, plastic chair, Ball Chair (see photo B page 72), clothes, 'silver foil' suits	solar cars, electric cars, shelving unit, mobile telephones, wind-up radio
Materials	Bakelite (an early plastic)	plastic, futuristic materials	recycled materials: paper, plastic

3 Students discuss the question in pairs.

Answers depend on students' own opinions.

VOCABULARY: abstract nouns

4 The nouns in this activity come from the texts in exercise 2.

- Ask students to compare their answers with a partner before you check with the class.
- For extra practice, ask students to exercise V3 on page 147 of the Language reference.

1 c; **2** a; **3** d; **4** f; **5** e; **6** b

LISTENING

5 Tell students to read the questions before you play the track.

- Ask students to compare with a partner before you go through the answers with the class and check they understand new items of vocabulary (e.g. *folding*, *canvas*).
- To follow up, ask students if they have a similar chair to this and why.

1 folding chair; **2** people going camping or fishing or to outdoor concerts, anyone who sits outside for a long time; **3** steel, aluminium, canvas; **4** just before the summer

Track 1.40

A: Let's brainstorm some ideas for our new project, the folding chair. So, first, who exactly is our target consumer?

B: Well, the chair could be useful for all kinds of people, you know, people going camping or fishing, or even going to outdoor concerts. In fact, it could be suitable for anyone who has to sit outside for a long time.

A: OK, what about the materials for making it?

B: Well, it must be light and easy to carry if we want to gain market share. We can't use steel – that's too heavy. We can use aluminium for the frame, and canvas for the seat. And to keep down costs, maybe we should make it in just three colours.

A: Yes, that's important. Also, it must be cheap if we want to be competitive. There are one or two chairs on the market that sell at under 50 euros. We can produce something similar – it doesn't have to be very different for this market. But we can have a second, more expensive model too, if that's what people want.

B: Mmm. Good point. OK, another thing, and this is very important, it has to be safe because the regulations are very strict now. The rules also say it has to be strong enough to support a heavy person.

continued…

A: Absolutely. OK, in terms of timing, we could launch it just before the summer – there'll be a big demand for it then. In fact, we really mustn't miss this opportunity.

B: You're right, but we shouldn't launch it until we're really ready. Look, I think we should wait for the results of our market research before making any decisions. But I can do some designs before we meet again, so we can continue with the development.

A: Right, and I can get more information about our competitors' products. I mustn't forget to do that.

GRAMMAR: modals

6 The aim of this activity is to find out if students already know the meaning of these modals.

- To lead in, elicit or give a few examples of modal verbs.
- Tell students that meanings c) and d) have more than one example.
- While students do the activity, monitor so you know how much time to spend going through answers.

(!) Most students will have seen modals before, but the similarity in meanings makes them difficult to use. Ask *all* students to read the Language reference on pages 146–147 and note the additional examples of use.

(Tip) Remind students of the form of modals (modal + infinitive without *to*). Tell students to underline the forms in sentences 1–10 and tell them *have to* is the verb (not *have*), *doesn't have to* is the negative (*not haven't to*), and all the other modals form negatives by adding *not*, often contracted (e.g. *mustn't*, *can't*).

1 c; **2** a; **3** d; **4** f; **5** g; **6** e; **7** c; **8** h; **9** d; **10** b

For a full explanation and extra practice, tell students to look at the Language reference on pages 146–147.

7 Tell students to read each sentence carefully because the context will help them choose the answer.

1 mustn't; **2** could; **3** could; **4** doesn't have to; **5** must; **6** have to; **7** must

(!) In number 4, the answer could also be *shouldn't* but it would have a different meaning (i.e. prediction) from that given in exercise 6 (i.e. not advisable). It's better not to draw students' attention to this and only use the meanings listed in exercise 6.

SPEAKING

8 Read through the instructions with the class and check students understand *sketch* (a quick, not too detailed drawing).

- Explain that *rules and regulations* here means things you need to know about using the product safely (e.g. 'Don't use an electrical household appliance outside') or possible regulations for use (e.g. 'Wash the shirt in cold water'). Ask students for examples of *sports equipment* (a ball, running shoes), *item of clothing* (shirt, shoes), *household item* (TV, washing machine), *product for a car* (seat covers, CD player).
- Put students into groups of three or four and suggest only one person does the sketch.
- While students are speaking, monitor and note mistakes they making when using modal verbs.
- When they have finished, tell students to show their sketch to another group and explain their decisions.
- Finally, correct some of the mistakes with modals you noted earlier.

To make the sketches as clear as possible, advise students to write information about colour, size, materials and rules and regulations on the same piece of paper.

To extend this activity: When students have drawn their sketches, post them round the room and tell one student from each group to stand next to their sketch (this person can change during the activity). Tell the other students to look at all the sketches and ask questions about the design. When students have seen all the sketches, vote on the best design.

HOMEWORK OPTIONS

Students do the exercises on pages 47–48 of the Workbook.

Students write a paragraph to describe the product they designed in exercise 8.

7.3 A LIFE OF DESIGN

IN THIS LESSON

Lesson topic and staging

This lesson looks at famous designers and some of the things they designed. Students read a text about a famous American designer. This is followed by a listening on different designs and designers which contextualises the grammar focus for this lesson: modals for present deduction (*can't, must, might/could*). Students then do a series of activities to explore the meaning and form of these modals before using them in a speaking activity. Finally, students do a further speaking exercise to discuss what they would like to design.

Objectives

By the end of the lesson, students should have:

- practised reading a text to extract specific information
- practised listening to a text to extract specific information and language items
- learned more about and practised using modals for present deduction (*can't, must, might/could*)
- engaged in a group discussion

Timings

If short of time, you could drop exercise 2a on page 74. Alternatively, if your students can already use modals for present deduction, you could drop either (but not both) exercise 5 or 6 on page 75. If you are very short of time, you could set the READING exercises 1–2 on page 74 for homework.

A possible lesson break would be after exercise 2c on page 74 or 3b on page 75.

WARM-UP

This activity focuses students on famous companies and their logos.

- Ask students to think of a famous international or local company but not tell other students what it is.
- Check students understand logo by showing them the examples in exercise 1 on page 74.
- Put them into pairs and tell them to describe their company using information about its products, customers, logo, size, etc.
- Their partner has to guess the name of the company.

READING

1 Give students 30 seconds to think about the logos.

- Put them into pairs to discuss the answers and then check with the class.

BP = British Petroleum (international oil company); Exxon = international oil company; yellow shell = Shell Oil (international oil company); Lucky Strike = American/international tobacco company; animal is a greyhound = Greyhound (American transport company famous for its inter-city buses)

Take this opportunity to see if students use *it might/could/must/can't be*. This could help you decide if they can use the modals for present deduction.

2a To lead in, focus students on the lesson title (A life of design), the text title (Heroes of design) and the photo of Raymond Loewy.

- Ask students what they think the text is about (his life, designs, products, etc.) and remind them they read a quote by him in lesson 7.1 on page 70.
- Give them a maximum of two minutes to read the text and tell them not to worry about unknown vocabulary.

Products mentioned are: Greyhound; Lucky Strike; Shell Oil; Exxon

2b Give students two minutes to read the text again.

- Put them into pairs to briefly compare their answers.
- Go through answers with the class and check students understand *consultant* (someone who gives professional advice), *interior* (inside); *bet* (to gamble/game with money, e.g. horse racing).

a 200: the number of companies Loewy was a consultant for; **b** 1929: start of his career, redesigned a copying machine; **c** 40: the design of the copying machine lasted 40 years; **d** 50: the time spent streamlining many products, e.g. stamps, company logos, interior of stores; **e** $50,000: the money the President of Lucky Strike bet Loewy he couldn't improve the cigarette packets; **f** 1940: the year the bet was made

2c Ask students to read the sentence halves and check they understand *impact* (effect, influence) and *revolutionary* (completely new, different and original).

- Ask students to try to match the sentence halves before they read the text again.
- Then give them four minutes to read and match the sentences.
- Put students into pairs to compare answers and then go through answers with the class.

1 d; **2** c; **3** e; **4** a; **5** b

LISTENING

3a Ask students to look at the three images and say or guess what they are.

- Elicit a few ideas from the class, but don't give students the answers at this stage because they will find out when they listen.
- Set the question and play the three extracts without pausing.
- Go through the answers with the class and then ask if they correctly guessed what the pictures are.

Pictures are talked about in the following order: A, C, B; (A is a flying machine; B is a racing car; C is a lemon squeezer for making juice.)

If students don't understand l*emon squeezer*, demonstrate the action of using one.

3b Tell students to read the sentences and try to answer as many as they can from memory.

- Play the track again, pausing after each extract to give students time to think.
- Ask students to compare with a partner before you check answers with the class.

1 True (Anna reads the evidence.); **2** True (Barbara reads the evidence.); **3** Not given (Freddie and Elias are *personally* sure because they recognise the design but we don't know for certain.); **4** False (It was made in the 1940s.); **5** False (It is the designer's *best-known* design.); **6** False (No – it doesn't look practical.) (Answers are bold in the audioscript below.)

Audioscript and answers to Exercise 3b and 4a: Track 1.41

Anna, Barbara

1

A: Wow, look at that. What is it?
B: It's a drawing. I think it's a sort of flying machine.
A: Yes, it could be that. Who do you think it's by?
B: Mmm, it might be by da Vinci, I believe he did that sort of thing. Have a look at the sign. What does it say?
A: Er ... **1 yes, you're right, it is da Vinci.**
B: Goodness! It's in very good condition ... **2 it says here he was born in 1452 so it must be over five hundred years old.**
A: Yes, and it's an amazing drawing.
B: Yeah, I read somewhere he was fascinated by birds and flying. Perhaps that's where he got his ideas for the drawing.
A: Yeah, you're probably right.

2

Elias, Freddie

E: Freddie, I want to see the racing cars. Where are they?
F: I haven't got a guide, but I'm sure they're in that large space at the back. Let's go there first.
E: Here they are. Look at that one over there. **3 It must be a Ferrari, surely**.
F: **3 Yes, it can't be anything else.** It's so red and stylish. But it's a pretty old one – look, it's quite high off the ground. What year do you think it is?
E: It could date back to the 1930s.
F: That's impossible. It can't be that old. **4 Look, here it says it was made in the 1940s.**
E: You're right ... It's amazing they were able to go so fast at that time.

continued...

3
George, Sally
G: What's that?
S: I've no idea. What <u>could</u> it be?
G: It <u>might</u> be a spaceship. Well, a toy spaceship. It's the right shape.
S: No, I'm certain that it's not that. It wouldn't really be in a museum of design.
G: Mmm, I see what you mean. And maybe it's too heavy to be a toy. What else <u>could</u> it be?
S: Mmm, I don't know really. What does it say on the notice?
G: It says it's a lemon squeezer. Apparently it's the designer Philippe Starck's **5 best-known design**.
S: OK I see it now. Would you like something like that?
G: **6 No way! It just doesn't look practical.**

GRAMMAR: modals (present deduction)

4a Lead in by asking students for a few examples of modal verbs.

- Check students understand *deduction* by asking them what made the speakers sure or less sure in the listening extracts. (Answer = The information they could read or the things they already knew.)
- Students then do the activity as per the Coursebook.

See audioscript above for underlined answers.

If possible, reproduce the audioscript so that the whole class can see it (maybe using an Interactive Whiteboard or an overhead projector). As you go through the answers, underline the modals.

4b Give students one minute to match the verbs and meanings and encourage them to read the audioscript for the context.

- Go through answers with the class and emphasise that all the verbs mean 'I personally believe this because of something I know or can see'.

1 c; 2 a; 3 b

Elicit or remind students of the form of modals (modal + [*not*] + infinitive without *to*). *Not* is contracted in *can't*. We don't usually contract *might not* when we mean something is possible not true. We don't use *couldn't* to mean something is possibly not true; *couldn't* means the same as *can't* for deduction.

4c Students read the question. Then elicit the answer from the class.

Can't is the opposite of *must* when we are talking about deduction.

Go through the GRAMMAR TIP with the class and ask them to read the Language reference (G2) on pages 146–147.

5 Tell students they will need to change the grammar of these sentences when they rewrite them.

- While students are working, monitor to spot mistakes and refer them to exercises 4a, 4b, 4c and the Language reference (G2) for help.
- Students compare with a partner before you go through answers with the class.

1 Raymond Loewy *must be* one of the most influential designers of all time.; **2** This design *must be* by Armani.; **3** This painting *can't be* by Leonardo.; **4** This painting *might/could be* by Picasso.; **5** They *can't be* promoting it very well.; **6** This product *might/could be* dangerous.; **7** People think it *might/could be* a Loewy design.; **8** That designer *must be* working very hard.

For extra practice, ask students to do exercise G2 2 on page 147 of the Language reference.

i Armani: Georgio Armani, famous Italian fashion designer (born 1934)

Picasso: Pablo Picasso, famous Spanish abstract artist (1881–1973)

6 Remind students of the form of these modals (*must/ might/could/can't* + infinitive without *to*) and elicit or give one example (e.g. 'It might be a …').

- Elicit the form of the other phrases (e.g. 'I'm sure/ certain it's a …'). All phrases use the same form.
- Then put students into pairs to discuss the photos.
- Encourage them to give reasons for their ideas.
- While they are speaking, note common mistakes when using modals or the other phrases.
- Finally, get ideas from the class and correct some of the mistakes you noted earlier.

SPEAKING

7 Give students two minutes to think about their answer and tell them to ask you for vocabulary if necessary.

- Put students into pairs or small groups and tell them to give reasons and ask each other questions.
- Get ideas from three or four students and ask the class if they agree with the ideas and why.

HOMEWORK OPTIONS

Students do the exercises on pages 49–50 of the Workbook.

Students do practice exercise G2 2 on page 147 of the Language reference.

7.4 SCENARIO: MARTELLI DESIGN COMPETITION

IN THIS LESSON

Lesson topic and staging

This lesson focuses on describing and evaluating things. Students are introduced to the scenario of judging a design competition and then read information about it. Students then look at four designs and choose adjectives to describe them. Next, students do two listening activities: the first introduces criteria used to decide the winner (e.g. *durable*), the second contextualises the KEY LANGUAGE for describing qualities. Students then describe the designs they looked at earlier. Finally, the TASK asks students to describe and evaluate designs for the competition.

Objectives

By the end of the lesson, students should have:

- learned useful phrases for describing and evaluating things
- used this language in a 'real-life' situation to describe and evaluate designs for a competition
- extracted specific information and language items from a reading and a listening text
- participated effectively in extended speaking practice

Common European Framework

Students can use language effectively to describe and evaluate things.

Timings

If short of time, you could drop exercise 2 on page 76. The pictures are used again in exercise 4c so students will get a chance to use them.

A possible lesson break would be either after exercise 3 on page 76 or exercise 4c on page 77.

WARM-UP

This activity focuses on describing things.

- Ask students to think of a building, a landmark (e.g. a monument or a statue) or a place in the town/city where you're teaching but not to tell other students what it is.
- Put students into groups of three. Tell two students to ask the third student ten questions to guess the building, landmark or place.
- The third students can only answer 'yes' or 'no' (e.g. the first question should be 'Is it a building?' NOT 'Is it a building or a place?').
- After ten questions, they must try to guess.
- Change the student who answers the questions and repeat the procedure.

SITUATION

Read through the introduction and check students understand *jury* (in this context, a *group* of people who decide the winner in a competition). Take this opportunity to check students understand *a judge* in this context (*person* deciding the winner) to use later.

- Tell students not to read the advertisement at this stage.

1 Tell students to read the questions before they read the advertisement.

- Go through answers with the class.

> **1** young designers – graduated in the last five years or studying now; **2** through the website, or from their design school, university department or studio; **3** $30,000; **4** $10,000

2a Focus students on the four pictures and check they understand *built in* (part of the jacket), *blow-up pillow* (you could mime this) and *commuter* (a person who travels a fairly long distance to their work).

- Ask students for a few suggestions about what these items might be used for.
- Give students five minutes to think of adjectives. If they need more ideas for adjectives, tell them to look at exercise 6a in Lesson 7.1 (page 71).
- When they have compared with a partner, get a few adjectives for each design from the class.

2b Students work in the same pairs as exercise 2a.

- Give them five minutes to answer the questions and then get ideas from two or three pairs.

> Answers depend on students' own opinions.

You could ask students to use modal verbs from lessons 7.2 and 7.3 when discussing the questions.

3 Students have seen most of these words in previous lessons or they can be easily guessed.

- Set the activity and check students understand *timeless* (a popular design in any period of fashion).
- When you go through the answers, correct students' pronunciation of the words if necessary.

> The following should be ticked: durable; easy to use; functional; innovative; stylish; value for money. (Answers are bold in the audioscript below.)

> **Audioscript and answers to Exercise 3:**
> **Track 2.2**
> OK, everyone, I think we agree now on the qualities we'll be considering when we choose the winning design. Let me summarise.
> The winning design will be **innovative**, and will look different from other products in its category. It'll be **stylish** too – in other words, attractive and fashionable. But it'll also be **functional** and **easy to use**. It'll be really useful and also good **value for money**. It shouldn't be too expensive for what the designer is offering. One last thing, we expect the winning design to be well-made, so it's got to be **durable**.

KEY LANGUAGE: describing qualities

4a Go through the introduction and tell students to read the questions before you play the track.

- Ask them to compare answers with a partner and play the track again if necessary.
- Go through answers with the class and teach vocabulary students don't understand (e.g. *a stand*).
- To follow up, ask students if they would buy this desk and why.

1 a stand for a keyboard, a secure section for a laptop, a drinks holder, big file drawers; **2** a business person working from home; **3** She thinks it's excellent value for money – 'not a lot for a desk of this quality'.

4b Ask students to read the sentences to see if they can fill any of the gaps.

- Play the track without pausing.
- Go through the answers and check they understand *appeal to* (business people would like the desk).
- Tell students they can find these phrases on page 146 of the Language reference.

For extra practice, ask students to do exercise KL 4 on page 147 of the Language reference.

Audioscript and answers (bold) to Exercise 4b: Track 2.3
I think this is by far the best entry. It's a desk designed by Vanessa Pironi. She's working in a studio in Milan. As you can see, the desk **1 looks** very stylish. It's got a very modern design; we haven't seen anything quite like it before. It's **2 made** of solid oak, so it's obviously very durable. There are several **3 features** I really like. For example, there's a well-designed stand for your keyboard. There's also a secure section for a laptop. You can hide the computer when you're not using it. I like that design feature. And there's a drink holder – you pull it out – and you can put your cup of coffee, soft drink or whatever in it. I also like the big file drawers – there are two and they have good locks on them. One of the best **4 points** is that the desk's functional. I'd say it's **5 aimed** at home computer use. It would **6 appeal** especially to a business person, working from home. It's really got everything we're looking for. It's excellent **7 value** for money too. The designer thinks the price will be about $1,200. Not a lot for a desk of this quality. In my opinion, we have a winner here.

4c Give students a maximum of ten minutes to write their sentences.

- Monitor to spot mistakes in using the sentences from exercise 4b.
- Finally ask one or two students to read their sentences to the class.

When students have written five sentences, put them into groups of three or four. Ask each student to read their sentences aloud. The others have to guess which picture the sentences are about.

TASK: evaluating designs

5a Tell students to *only* read the description you give them.

- Move round the room to help with vocabulary or tell students to use their dictionaries.

5b Give students five minutes to think about any information they want to add to the description of the product designs in exercise 5a.

- Go through the OTHER USEFUL PHRASES box on page 77 and remind students the KEY LANGUAGE is on page 146 in the Language reference.
- Give students another five minutes to think about what language they will use to describe their product.
- Tell students to write the number of the designs they hear about at the top of each column in the evaluation form. When evaluating, 1 = very bad and 10 = excellent.
- Allow 15 minutes for the group to describe their products and fill in the evaluation forms.
- Tell students to fill in the total at the bottom of the column after each description.
- While students are speaking, note common mistakes they make with the KEY LANGUAGE and OTHER USEFUL PHRASES from page 77, and vocabulary from exercise 3 on page 76.

5c Ask one student to add up the marks for each product and tell you the winner in their group.

- Finally, go through a selection of the mistakes you noted in exercise 5b.

When each student has finished describing their product, tell the others in the group to ask questions. When all the students have finished describing their products, tell the group to discuss the designs and say what they liked about them. (Note: students can only comment on the designs they heard about, not their own.) Finally, add up the marks to find the winner.

HOMEWORK OPTIONS

Students do the exercises on page 51 of the Workbook.

Students do extra practice activities on page 147 of the Language reference.

Students write a short letter to the winner in their group in exercise 5c. They should say what they liked about the design and why it won. When you mark the letter, pay particular attention to students' use of the KEY LANGUAGE and OTHER USEFUL PHRASES from page 77. (Note: some of the language is *not* appropriate to a written description and you may want to point out which language students can use before they do this homework activity.)

7.5 STUDY AND WRITING SKILLS

IN THIS LESSON

Lesson topic and staging

This lesson focuses on the skills of editing, proofreading, and writing a report. Students listen to a teacher giving advice on checking written work and then think about the main problems they have when writing in English. Next, students read a report on mobile phones and practise proofreading and editing. Students then do a series of activities on linkers (e.g. *as a result*). Finally, students write a report themselves using the linkers they studied and practising their proofreading and editing skills.

Objectives

By the end of the lesson, students should have:

- learned/revised the main points to consider when editing and proofreading written work
- proofread and edited both a text provided and their own written work
- extracted specific information and language items from a listening and a reading text
- extended their range of linking words and phrases
- written a report in the context of design

Common European Framework

Students can write a report and successfully proofread and edit written work.

Timings

If time is short, set exercise 7 for homework. Alternatively, ask students to write about one camera in class time and the other at home.

A possible lesson break would be after exercise 5 on page 78 or exercise 6c on page 79.

WARM-UP

This activity introduces the topic of proofreading and editing, and some of the mistakes students might make when writing.

- Copy the following two sentences exactly as they are onto the board
  - I go to home early on Wensday evening because i was tired.
  - when he come at university each day, he studys very hardly.
- Tell students to find all the mistakes and correct them. Point out that there are both spelling and grammatical errors in the sentences.
- The first student to finish wins (but check that all the mistakes are corrected).

Answers: I went ~~to~~ home early on Wednesday evening because I was tired. When he comes ~~at~~ to university each day, he studies very hard~~ly.~~

STUDY SKILLS: editing and proofreading

1 Focus students on the title of this activity and ask them what *proofreading* and *editing* mean (proofreading: reading to find mistakes; editing: correcting mistakes and changing other features to improve the text).

- Read through the introduction with the class and give students three minutes to answer the question.
- Tell them to note their answers down.

Answers depend on students' own ideas.

2a When students compare the teacher's ideas with their own, tell them look at the notes they made in exercise 1.

The points she mentions: check your spelling and punctuation; check for grammatical errors (verb tenses, prepositions, word order); ask yourself 'Is my meaning clear?', 'Will someone reading my work understand what I'm trying to say?'

2b Tell students to read the questions and to answer any they can before you play the track again.

- Ask students to compare with a partner before you check answers.

1 a accommodation, receive, writing; **b** gone/went, catched/caught; **c** depend of/depend on;
2 clear, reading, understand. (Answers are bold in the audioscript below.)

Take this opportunity to check students understand *punctuate* and *full stop* (give them examples).

Audioscript and answers to Exercise 2b:
Track 2.4
Teacher, Erika

T: So you'd like me to give you some advice on editing your work, Erika?
E: Yes, if you could give me a few tips, it would be very helpful. I know I need to check my written work more carefully.
T: OK, I'll try to keep it simple. What are the most common mistakes students make when they write? These are the sort of things you should be looking for. And everyone should think about them when they check their written work.
E: Exactly.
T: OK. I'll give you five or six points to think about. First of all, check your spelling and punctuation carefully. If you've typed your work, don't forget to use a spellchecker.

continued…

E: Oh, yes. Good idea.
T: Of course, you'll make mistakes with difficult words, like, oh, erm **1a) 'accommodation'** or **1a) 'receive'**, but students often make mistakes with simple words, like spelling **1a) 'writing' with two Ts!** And of course you need to punctuate your work correctly. Many students seem to forget that we use full stops when we write English!
E: *[laughs]* I know what you mean. My teacher is always telling me to use a full stop instead of a comma!
T: Right. And don't forget about capitals. Check your written work to make sure that you have used capital letters where they're appropriate.
E: OK. Got that.
T: My next tip is to check your work for grammatical errors. In particular, check your verb tenses and verb forms. Make sure you've used the right tense or form. You have problems using the present perfect tense. Think carefully before you use the tense. It's easy to make a mistake with a verb form, especially with the past tenses of irregular verbs. Don't use **1b) 'gone' when you mean 'went' and don't use 'catched' when it should be 'caught'**. OK?
E: Right, I often make mistakes with irregular verbs – they're very difficult to learn and then I write the wrong form in an essay.
T: Yes, they're difficult and so are prepositions. Check that you've written the correct preposition after an adjective or verb. For example, don't write **1c) 'depend of' when it should be 'depend on'**. So many students make that error, you wouldn't believe it.
E: OK, be careful with prepositions. I'll check them in a dictionary if I'm not sure.
T: Good. Word order is important too. Check that you've used the right word order in your sentences. That's especially important for you.
E: Yes, it's true – I often make mistakes with word order. It's a real problem for me.
T: My final piece of advice is, after you've written something, always ask yourself the questions **2 'Is my meaning clear?'**, and **'Will someone reading my work understand what I'm trying to say?'** That's it, really, I hope my tips will help you.
E: I'm sure they will. I'll put them into practice when I write my next essay.

3 Give students three minutes to answer the questions and tell them to make notes.

Ask students to compare notes to help them remember other problems and mistakes they have.

4 Focus students on the title of the report on page 78 and ask them what it's about (mobile phones).

- Tell them to read the questions before they read the report.
- Ask them to compare with a partner before you go through answers with the class.

1 a Samsung D500; **b** probably the Samsung D500 (because it says the Nokia is small and light); **c** probably the Samsung (one of the most popular phones on the market) – but we don't know the sales for the Nokia; **d** either the Samsung D500 because it's very stylish or the Nokia because it's very functional (but the text doesn't say which is *better* designed) **e** Samsung; **f** Nokia **2** 1.3 Mp camera **3** Nokia is better than Samsung but both are good 'buys' (value for money).

5 To lead in, ask student if they noticed any mistakes in the report and to give two or three examples.

- Give students plenty of time to find mistakes a) –i).
- Go through the answers with the class (corrections are in brackets).
- Finally, ask students if these are similar to the mistakes they make.

If possible, reproduce the text so that the whole class can see it (maybe using an Interactive Whiteboard or an overhead projector). As you go through the answers, underline the errors. Alternatively, ask students to write line numbers in each paragraph (e.g. the first bullet has seven lines) to make it easier to refer to.

a mobil (mobile), stilish (stylish), amont (amount), fotos (photos), diferent (different); **b** nokia (Nokia), we found (We); **c** a full stop is missing after '... functional'; **d** D500s (D500's – possessive); **e** It's (its – possessive); **f** Covers are in five different colours available (Covers are available in five different colours); **g** it also have (has); **h**) It is weighing (It weighs); **i** disappointed for (disappointed in), good in (good at)

WRITING SKILLS: a report

6a Linkers

- Lead in by asking students to give examples of linkers they studied in previous units.
- When you check answers, point out the commas after the three linkers.

1 therefore: show a result; **2** in addition: to add something; **3** However: a contrast

6b Students do the activity as per the Coursebook.

- In feedback, tell students that the words have the same meaning and a comma is used after them.

As a result, consequently

Tell students that *moreover* can be used in the same way as *in addition* but it is not as common. Students should know the other linkers in this activity.

6c Read through the example with the class.

- Tell them they can use all the linkers in exercises 6a and 6b.
- Students work individually while you monitor to point out any mistakes.
- Ask students to compare with a partner before you check answers with the class.

2 The Nokia has more technical features. *In addition,/Moreover,* it is lighter and cheaper.
3 The Samsung Z320i has a new Internet service. *In addition,/Moreover,* it's battery life is excellent.
4 It is one of the smallest and lightest mobile phones. *Therefore,/As a result,/Consequently,* it is very easy to carry.
5 This phone has the best call reception. *In addition,/Moreover,* it is the cheapest of all the phones.
6 The phone worked perfectly after we poured water on it. *Therefore,/As a result,/Consequently,* we recommend it for people who work outside in all weathers.
7 Pay as you go (PAYG) offers good value if you don't use your phone a lot. *However,/On the other hand* a pay-monthly contract is better for heavy users.
8 Our first impressions of the new phone are good. *However,* we will have to test it more thoroughly.

7 Give students five minutes to read the notes and ask you for help with vocabulary or use their dictionaries.

- Then give them 20 minutes to write a first draft.
- Tell them to look at the notes they made on their main problems and mistakes in exercise 3, the teacher's advice in exercise 2, and the mistakes in exercise 5.
- Then ask them to proofread and edit their first draft.
- Ask them to write a second draft.
- Take the reports in for marking, paying particular attention to the use of linkers and common mistakes.

HOMEWORK OPTIONS

Students do the exercises on page 52 of the Workbook.

Students write a paragraph on a product (or comparing two products) they own in order to recommend it (or one of them) to another student in the class. It's not necessary for them to have all the technical information provided in exercise 7. In the next lesson, ask students to swap their paragraphs with another student and decide if they would buy the product described. Then take the paragraphs in for marking, paying particular attention to the use of linking words and phrases.

Education

8.1 EDUCATION ISSUES

IN THIS LESSON

Lesson topic and staging

This lesson looks at current issues in education. Students learn a set of verb/noun combinations and dependent prepositions. They then read a text on single-sex versus mixed schools, study a set of nouns from the text, and then give their own opinion on this issue. Next, students discuss a variety of other issues such as the pros and cons of private education. Finally, students write a message for a chatroom, giving their opinions on one of the issues they discussed.

Objectives

By the end of the lesson, students should have:

- expanded their range of verb/noun combinations and dependent prepositions in the context of education
- practised extracting specific information and language items from a reading text
- discussed a variety of current and important issues in education
- written about their opinions on one issue in education

Timings

If short of time and students have a good understanding of the vocabulary in exercise 2a, you could drop exercise 2b on page 80. Alternatively, drop the number of issues students discuss in exercise 5 and/or set the writing exercise 6 on page 81 for homework.

A possible lesson break would be after exercise 2b on page 70 or exercise 4 on page 71.

WARM-UP

This activity introduces the topic of school and education.

- Write the following on the board:
  - Loved school
  - Was good at Maths
  - Hated school
  - Was good at sport
- Tell students they have to find someone for whom the statements are true.
- Elicit the questions students need to ask (e.g. 'Did you like school?', 'Were you good at Maths?').
- Tell students to talk to as many students as possible and ask follow-up questions (e.g. 'Why did you hate school?').
- When they have finished, ask the class for a few answers by asking 'Who loved school?', etc. and ask students for any interesting information they heard when asking the follow-up questions.

Albert Einstein quote:

This quote means that real education is more than just learning at school. It is the sum of everything you study and experience.

(i) Albert Einstein 1879–1955: A very influential German physicist, most famous for his theory of relativity. He won the Nobel Prize in Physics in 1921.

VOCABULARY: education and studying

1 To lead in, focus students on the photo and ask if it reminds them of their time at school. Why/why not?

- Tell students to read the questions and use their dictionaries to find the words in italics if necessary.
- Go through the meanings with the class.
- Put students into pairs and give them a maximum of ten minutes to discuss the questions.
- Finally, ask a few pairs to give you their answers.

> Answers depend on students' own opinions and experiences.

2a Write the first example on the board and work through it with the class.

- Give students five to ten minutes to do the other phrases and tell them to use their dictionaries for help.
- Check answers with the class and go through the notes in brackets.
- In feedback, check students understand *good grade* (ask them to give an example), *hand in* (give to the teacher), *seminar* (small group of students discussing with a tutor), and *do your best* (try very hard and do something as well as you possibly can).

> **1** go to school / ~~to~~ get a place at university / go to college **2** revise for an exam / revise a subject / study for a test **3** graduate from university / ~~from~~ leave primary school / graduate from high school (US/Australian English. In UK English, we say *leave secondary school*) **4** get a degree / get a good grade / take or sit an exam **5** do homework / take/retake an exam / take/retake a course **6** pass/fail an exam / pass/fail a course / get a good result **7** hand in an essay / go to a seminar / hand in an assignment **8** make progress / do coursework / do your best **9** make mistakes / make progress / do homework **10** do/sit/ study for an exam / study a subject / study a language

2b Ask students to work individually to write four or five questions.

- Move round the class to point out mistakes using the verb/noun combinations.
- Put students into groups of three or four and give them ten minutes to ask/answer each other their questions.
- Tell them to ask follow-up questions to get as much information as possible.
- While they are speaking, note common mistakes when using the verb/noun combinations.
- In feedback, ask students the most interesting/ surprising thing they heard.
- Finally, correct some of the most common mistakes you noted earlier.

Answers depend on students' own questions.

READING

3a Focus students on the title of the text and the photo on page 81 and ask them where it comes from.

- Elicit *online* and *chatroom* and check students understand *mixed-sex* (girls and boys).
- Give them a maximum of three minutes to read the messages and answer the question.
- Tell them not to worry about unknown vocabulary because they will study this in exercise 3b.
- Ask students to compare with a partner before you check answers with the class. (Note: some messages say they are 'for' single-sex schools – this makes them 'against' mixed-sex schools.)

Message 1: for mixed-sex schools; Message 2: against mixed-sex schools; Message 3: against mixed-sex schools; Message 4: neither for nor against; Message 5: for mixed-sex schools ('I don't think there is any question that mixed schools are better.' = there is no doubt mixed-sex schools are better.)

3b Tell students to read the context carefully to try to guess the nouns.

- If necessary, students should check in their dictionaries.
- In feedback, check students' pronunciation of the four nouns.
- Check students understand *dog eat dog situation* in Message 5 (very competitive, the strongest wins).

1 statistics; **2** curriculum; **3** truancy; **4** bullying

3c Read through the questions as a class and check students understand *proof* (evidence) and *cater for* (provide something for someone).

- Give students three to four minutes to read the messages again and answer the questions.
- Ask students to compare with a partner before you check answers with the class.

1 Emily; **2** Hans; **3** Jane; **4** Martin; **5** Bill

4 Give students three to four minutes to think about their answers and reread the messages if necessary.

- Put them into pairs or small groups to discuss the opinions.
- Tell them to say why they agree/disagree and to ask each other questions if necessary.
- For feedback, ask a few pairs/groups which opinions they agreed with and why.

There are more opinions in the messages than those included in exercise 3c. Students could quickly read the messages again to find additional opinions to discuss in their pairs/small groups.

SPEAKING

5 Ask students to read the statements (1–8) and to ask you for help with any unknown vocabulary.

- Summarise statement 7 (if students get good exam results, their teacher will be paid more).
- Give students five minutes to think about their opinions.
- Then put them into groups of three or four and give them 10–15 minutes to discuss the statements.
- Emphasise that students should try to agree on each statement and to convince others that they are right. Stress that students do not need to agree with each statement but they must all share the same opinion by the end of the discussion. This may mean that they all disagree with a statement.
- While they are speaking, monitor to note mistakes they make with the verb/noun combinations from exercise 2a and any of the other vocabulary introduced in this lesson.
- When they have finished, ask a few groups to tell you the statements they agreed or disagreed with.
- Finally, correct the most common mistakes you noted earlier.

WRITING

6 Give students 10–15 minutes to write their message.

- Move round the room, pointing out mistakes and giving help with vocabulary.
- Take the messages in for marking, paying particular attention to the use of vocabulary in this lesson.

HOMEWORK OPTIONS

Students do the exercises on page 53 of the Workbook.

If you have access to a blog programme, ask students to post their message electronically. Then ask them to read each others' messages and respond. In this way, students will get practise writing online messages.

8.2 MONTESSORI

IN THIS LESSON

Lesson topic and staging

This lesson looks at different teaching methods. Students listen to a university student talking about his chemistry teacher and then focus on a set of vocabulary from the listening. Students then discuss and write about their own favourite/worst teacher. Next, students read a text on Maria Montessori and her approaches to teaching which contextualises the grammar for this lesson: defining relative clauses. Students do a series of activities to explore and practise these clauses, and finally use them in a word definition guessing game.

Objectives

By the end of the lesson, students should have:

- practised extracting specific information and language items from a reading and a listening text
- extended their range of vocabulary in the context of teaching methods
- written a short profile describing their favourite/worst teacher
- revised/extended their knowledge of defining relative clauses and used these in a speaking activity

Timings

If short of time and students have a good understanding of the reading text, you could drop exercise 4c on page 82.

A possible lesson break would be after exercise 5 on page 72 or exercise 8b on page 83.

WARM-UP

This activity encourages students to think about teaching methods and teaching aids they prefer when learning English.

- Write the following on the board:
  - Pictures
  - The whiteboard/blackboard/Interactive Whiteboard (as appropriate to your classroom)
  - Coursebook
  - Dictionary
  - Grammar reference
  - Other students
  - Teacher
- Put students into pairs or small groups and ask them to rank the items in the list depending on how important they are in learning English (1 = most important).
- Tell them to give reasons and to agree/disagree with each other if necessary.
- When they have finished, ask a few pairs/groups for their rankings and reasons.

LISTENING AND SPEAKING

1a Set the activity and play the track without pausing.

- Check answers with the class.

> He says the teacher was good (but they actually didn't like him).

1b Read through the adjectives with the class and check they understand *easy-going* (relaxed, friendly), *strict* (expecting people to obey rules) and *punctual* (arrive at the correct time, not late).

- Give students one minute to tick any adjectives they can remember from their first listening in exercise 1a.
- Then play the track again without pausing.
- Ask students to compare with a partner before you check answers with the class.

> The following adjectives should be ticked: strict, punctual, formal, well-prepared, interesting. (Answers are bold in the audioscript below.)

> **Audioscript and answers to Exercise 1:**
> **Track 2.5**
> We had a teacher called Mr Rojas and he taught us chemistry. He was an excellent teacher, but we couldn't say that we actually liked him. He wasn't friendly, or easy-going – the opposite in fact. He was different from the teachers we normally liked. In fact, he often criticised us. He treated us all equally – well, criticised all of us equally. He didn't treat us like unique individuals so it was funny that we all respected him. He was very **strict**, and always **punctual** – and I don't think he was ever late, and neither were we! He gave us lots of tests and lots of homework, and his **formal** approach to teaching seemed to work. He explained things very clearly and was very good at answering all our questions. He was always very **well-prepared** and his lessons were always **interesting**. He always varied things, changed the pace of the lesson, and used different methods to teach us. The chemistry laboratory was a strange environment to be in but we all enjoyed the classes. In the end, we all passed the chemistry exam and chemistry became my favourite subject on the curriculum.

2 Give students five minutes to find the meanings of the words and then compare with a partner.

- Go through answers with the class.
- Ask students to repeat each word so you can check their pronunciation.

  For further practice, ask students to do exercises V1 5 and V2 6 on page 149 in the Language reference.

3 Remind students of the listening in exercises 1a and 1b and ask if they like this kind of teacher.

- Give them one minute to think about how they could use the vocabulary in exercises 1b and 2 to describe their favourite/worst teacher at school.
- Then put them into pairs and tell them to give as much information as possible and ask each other questions if necessary.
- When they have finished, ask a few students if they would like the teacher their partner described.
- Tell students to read the audioscript on page 176.
- Give them 10–15 minutes to write their profile, and move round the room pointing out mistakes and helping with extra vocabulary.
- Take the profiles in for marking, paying particular attention to the vocabulary from exercises 1b and 2.

When students have written the profiles, post them round the room and ask students to read them all. Then ask the class to vote on the best/worst teacher described.

READING

4a Before students do this activity, focus them on the title and the photos on pages 82-83, and ask if they know or can guess anything about Maria Montessori

Read the text before the lesson so you can confirm the information that students give you.

- Tell students to read the summary before they read the text.
- Students can use their dictionaries to check *pioneered* and *deprived* from the summary.
- Ask them to compare their corrected summaries with a partner before you check with the class.

If possible, reproduce the summary, so that the whole class can see it (maybe using an Interactive Whiteboard or an overhead projector). As you go through the answers, correct the summary.

> Maria Montessori pioneered a new teaching method after she graduated as a ~~nurse~~ **doctor** in 1896 and taught deprived children. She tried to use everyday objects in the class so the children could develop social skills with each other and learn to be ~~competitive~~ **cooperative**. She taught children to experiment and to ~~depend on the teacher~~ **become independent**.

4b Give students one minute to see if they can remember what the dates refer to.

- Then give them two minutes to read the text again to find the dates they can't remember.
- Ask them to compare with a partner before you check answers with the class.

> **a** 1870: Maria Montessori was born; **b** 1896: she graduated from medical school; **c** 1912: she wrote *The Montessori Method*; **d** 1936: she wrote *The Secret of Childhood*; **e** 1952: she died

4c Tell students to read the questions before they read the text again.

- Check students understand *cabinets* (cupboards).
- Give them five minutes to answer the questions.
- Ask them to compare with a partner before you check answers with the class.

> **1** They control the pace, topic and lessons (instead of the teacher or the rest of the class).
> **2** So that they would learn by self-teaching and self-correction.
> **3** The furniture is light so the children can move it around (arrange it as they wish). The cabinets are low, so the children can reach them.
> **4** Children develop a social life based on cooperation rather than competition. They like to work together because the environment offers a range of activities.

5 Lead in by asking students if they would like to learn using the Montessori Method or if they would send their children to a Montessori school.

- Then put students into pairs or small groups to discuss the question.
- Tell students to give reasons for their answers and to agree/disagree if necessary.

> Answers depend on students' own opinions.

To extend this activity, put students in pairs or small groups and ask them to compare the teacher they talked about in exercise 3 with the methods described in the text on Maria Montessori. In feedback, ask students if their school was similar or very different from a Montessori school.

GRAMMAR: defining relative clauses

Ask students to read the example and tell you what a defining relative clause does in a sentence (it identifies or defines things). Then ask students what *who* is called in this example (a relative pronoun).

6a Ask students which words in the list are relative pronouns and which are relative adverbs (relative pronouns: *who, that, which, whose*; relative adverbs: *where, when*).

- Give students a maximum of one minute to find and underline the pronouns and adverbs in the text.
- When you go through the answers, tell students to underline the whole sentence for each pronoun/adverb. This will help them in exercise 6b.

If possible, reproduce the Maria Montessori text, so that the whole class can see it (maybe using an Interactive Whiteboard or an overhead projector). As you go through the answers, underline the pronouns, the adverbs and their clauses.

6b Tell students to read the sentences they underlined in exercise 6a to help them with this activity.

- Ask students to compare with a partner before you check answers with the class and refer students to the examples in the text.

> people: who, that; things or ideas: that, which; people + possessions/ideas: whose; places: where; time: when

For a full explanation, ask students to read G1 on page 148 of the Language reference.

7 This activity practises defining relative clauses but also introduces/revises education vocabulary.

- Tell students to match the sentence halves before they join them using the relative pronouns/adverbs.
- Go through the answers and notes in brackets below with the class.

> 1 b A professor in a British university is someone **who/that** has the highest rank of the teachers in a department. 2 d A university is an institution **where** (or **in which**) students study for degrees and academic research is done. 3 c A thesis is a long piece of writing **which/that** you do as part of a university degree. 4 f A seminar is a class at university/college **where** (or **in which**) the teacher and students discuss a particular topic. 5 e An academic is someone **who/that** teaches and does research in a college or university. 6 a A vacation is a period of the year **when** universities or colleges are officially closed. (Note: In the UK, a university can give degrees. A college teaches for degrees, but they are given by a university.)

8a Tell students to read the first part of the example and ask them if *many things* and *the things* is the subject or object of the sentence (object).

- Then tell them to read the second part of the example with the defining relative clause.
- Finally, elicit the correct rule.

> We can leave out the relative pronoun if it is the *object* of the relative clause.

For a full explanation, ask students to look at G1 on page 148 in the Language reference.

8b Students work individually while you monitor to point out mistakes.

- Refer students to page 148 in the Language reference for help.
- Ask students to compare with a partner before you check answers with the class.

Sentences 3 and 4 are more difficult than the others. In feedback, re-write the sentences on the boards as below:

3 You can phone (some) university tutors if you have a problem.

4 I go to a very good university.

Then draw a circle round the subjects (*you* and *I*) and the objects (*university tutors* and *university*). This will help students see that the pronouns in sentences 3 and 4 refer to the object and so can be omitted.

> 1 *who* cannot be omitted; 2 *that* can be omitted; 3 *who* can be omitted; 4 *which* can be omitted 5 *who* cannot be omitted

For extra practice, ask students to do exercises G1 1 and 2 on page 149 of the Language reference.

9a Read through the introduction with the class (see Background information below) and ask students if there are any similar television or radio games in their countries.

- Then read the three definitions and check students understand *stable* (a place for keeping horses) and *cell* (a very small unit that makes up all living things).
- Play the track without pausing and then put students into pairs to discuss which definition they think is correct.
- Check answers with the class.

'Call my bluff' was a popular radio and TV quiz in the UK. It ran from 1963–2003.

> 1 an instrument which is used to measure electric currents

Track 2.6

Quizmaster, Barry, Felicity, Keira, Michael, Anna, Frank

Q: Team A, now it's your turn, and the next word is ammeter. Barry, would you like to start with Definition 1?

B: Erm … yes, OK. Ammeter. An ammeter is what it says – it's a meter, and we use the meter for measuring electricity, electric current actually. So, it's an instrument which is used to measure electric currents.

Q: Felicity – Definition 2, please.

Fe: Well, Barry's completely wrong – it's nothing to do with electricity. An ammeter is a tiny little animal, so I suppose the word is related to 'ant'. This animal is so small that it only has one cell – we can't see it. So, an ammeter is a very small creature that only has one cell.

Q: Thank you, Felicity. Now, Keira, Definition 3.

K: Felicity is sooo wrong! Barry is almost correct – an ammeter is a machine, a meter in fact, but it isn't a machine that measures electric current. It's a meter that measures temperature – but only in stables. It's important that horses have the correct temperature, so we need a special machine, and that's it. An ammeter is a machine which is used to measure the temperature in a stable.

Q: OK. Now, over to you, Team B. Is an ammeter a meter that is used to measure electric current, a creature that has only one cell, or a machine that measures temperature in a stable? Do you want to start, Michael?

continued…

M: Mmm, I suppose so. Well, I think Felicity is wrong – an ammeter isn't an animal. It must have something to do with measuring, because of the word *meter*. I don't think Felicity really believed her definition anyway. I think the correct definition is Barry's – a meter for measuring electricity. Anna, what do you think?
A: I agree with you, Michael. Barry really seemed confident, and it has to be a meter. So, yes, Barry's right.
M: Do you agree, Frank?
Fr: I don't know. I think it could be Keira's definition – a meter for measuring temperature. But I think I'm going to go for Barry, too.
Q: So you all agree that the correct definition is number 1 – an instrument which is used to measure electricity?
M: Yes.
Q: Team A, who had the correct definition?
B: They're right – it's me – Definition 1!
Q: Well done, Team B – that's six points to you as you all agreed. So, on to the next word ...

9b Make sure both the A/B groups invent the two definitions for *all* their words before they play the game.

- Give students plenty of time to write their definitions.
- Monitor to correct the use of relative clauses.
- Students then follow the instructions on pages 159 (As) and 163 (Bs) in the Coursebook. (Note: the instructions for B students on page 163 of the Coursebook tell students to listen to A's definitions [stage 1] before they invent definitions for their own words [stage 2]. To avoid long pauses in the game, follow the procedure above.)

If you don't have enough students for groups of six, make smaller groups, but with at least two As and two Bs in each team.

If you are short of time, choose only two or three words from the lists for students to define.

HOMEWORK OPTIONS

Students do the exercises on pages 54–55 of the Workbook.

Students do exercises G1 1 and 2 on page 149 of the Language reference.

Students write another profile as in exercise 3 on page 82. If they wrote about a favourite teacher, they should write about their worst teacher and vice versa.

8.3 IS UNIVERSITY WORTH IT?

IN THIS LESSON

Lesson topic and staging

This lesson looks at the pros and cons of going to university. Students read an article on the issue of paying university fees. The article contextualises the grammar focus for this lesson: non-defining relative clauses. Students explore the form of this grammar and then practise using it in writing and speaking activities. Next, students listen to four people talking about university and finally do an extended speaking activity to compare information on education in different countries.

Objectives

By the end of the lesson, students should have:

- practised reading a text to extract specific information and language items
- practised listening to a text to extract specific information
- learned more about and practised using non-defining relative clauses
- participated effectively in extended speaking practice

Timings

If short of time and students are already confident using non-defining relative clauses, you could drop exercise 6 on page 85 and set it for homework

A possible lesson break would be after exercise 7b on page 85.

WARM-UP

This activity asks students to think about the best/worst things about going to university.

- Write the following on the board:
  - Learning new things
  - Taking exams
  - Making friends
  - Not earning money for three or four years
  - Studying hard
- Put students into pairs or small groups and tell them to rank the items in the list from the best (number 1) to the worst (number 5) aspect of going to university.
- Tell them to give reasons and to agree/disagree with each other if necessary.
- When they have finished, ask a few pairs/groups for their rankings and reasons.

READING

1a Focus students on the title of this UK-based article and ask if they pay university fees in their country.

- Explain that in the recent past, university education was free in the UK but now students have to pay.
- Give pairs three minutes to write their list of reasons then one minute to read and compare with the article.

Students can use the Warm-up activity for a few ideas.

> Answers depend on students' own ideas.

1b Tell students to read the extracts before they read the article again and fill the gaps.

- When you go through the answers, check students understand *virtually* (almost) and *proposed* (suggested).
- Ask students to compare with a partner before you check answers with the class.

> **1** c; **2** a; **3** e; **4** b; **5** d

2 Ask students to compare the reasons they find with a partner before you check answers with the class.

> Reasons for not going to university: you have to pay university fees; you will pay higher taxes after university (because you earn more money); you get into debt; you may have to depend on your parents for financial support; you can't be sure you'll get a good job (because there are a lot of graduates).

3 Groups should have a maximum of four students to give everyone a chance to speak.

- Allow five to ten minutes for the discussion.
- In feedback, get a few ideas from one or two groups.

GRAMMAR: non-defining relative clauses

Remind students of defining relative clauses and tell them they are now going to look at non-defining relative clauses.

4 Tell students to read the rules (1–3) before they look at the highlighted examples.

- Put them in pairs to discuss their answers.
- In feedback, refer to the highlighted examples to support the answers given below.

> **1** have; **2** do not; **3** extra

- Read through the Grammar tip with the class and answer any questions students have.

Take this opportunity to tell students that when using a non-defining relative clause in speaking, we normally pause at each comma. Give a model by reading one of the examples given in the Grammar tip.

For a full explanation, ask students to read G2 on page 148 of the Language reference.

5 Students work individually and then compare answers in pairs.

- When you go through the answers, check students understand *honorary degree* (you are given this because you have achieved a lot of important things in society, you don't study for it) and *set out* (presented).

> **1** Oxford University, which has been the target of government attacks, will not give the Prime Minister an honorary degree.; **2** John F Kennedy went to Harvard University, which is the oldest institution of higher education in the United States.; **3** Jean-Jacques Rousseau, who was born in 1712, set out his views on education in his book *Emile*.; **4** The Kumon method for teaching maths was developed by Toru Kumon, who graduated from Osaka University.; **5** Oxford's Bodleian library, which is one of the oldest libraries in Europe, was originally founded in 1320.; **6** Heidelberg University, which was founded in 1386, has its own student prison.

i Oxford University in the UK had its beginnings in the 12th century and is the oldest university in the English-speaking world.

John F Kennedy (1917–1963): 35th President of the United States from 1961 to his assassination in 1963.

Jean-Jacques Rousseau (1712–1778): Swiss philosopher who influenced the French Revolution.

Kumon method: A method where students work individually at their own pace through different levels of Maths. In 2007, there were about four million students using the method in more than 43 countries.

Heidelberg University is in Germany.

6 Go through the example with the class to show how the two sentences have been combined.

- Students then do the activity as per the Coursebook.
- Monitor to point out mistakes but encourage students to look at G2 on page 148 in the Language reference if they need help.
- When you check answers, write the sentences on the board or ask students to do so.

> **1** American universities, which have attracted the world's best students for over 50 years, are now facing a lot of competition.; **2** Last month I went back to Oxford, where I studied history.; **3** Annie Costello, whose opinions have always been highly regarded, became President of the NUS earlier this year.; **4** The University of Manchester, which has over 36,000 students, is the biggest university in the UK. *OR* The biggest university in the UK is the University of Manchester, where there are over 36,000 students.; **5** Aristotle, who studied under Plato, wrote books on many subjects.; **6** Hilary studied politics at Harvard, where she has just been offered a professorship.

i NUS: The National Union of Students in the UK.

Aristotle (384–322 BC) and Plato (428/427 to 348/347 BC): Greek philosophers who still influence European thinking today.

7a Give students a maximum of three minutes to discuss the photos and then elicit one or two ideas about each.

- Divide the pairs into A and B and go through the instructions on pages 159 and 163.
- Give students five minutes to match the pairs of facts but tell them not to worry if they can't do them all or match the facts to a university because you will tell them the answers later.
- Go through the matched pairs and the name of the university in the answers under exercise 7b but don't read out the full sentences.

7b Go through the example on page 85 to show how the two sentences have been combined.

- Give students 10–15 minutes to do the activity as per the Coursebook.
- Monitor to point out mistakes but encourage students to help each other and refer to G2 on page 148 of the Language reference.
- When you check answers, write the sentences on the board or ask students to do so.
- Finally, ask students the most interesting piece of information they learned.

(Note: the clauses can be reversed in all the answers below, e.g. Heidelberg University, which is one of the most famous universities in Germany, was established in 1386.); **1** Heidelberg University, which was established in 1386, is one of the most famous universities in Germany.; **2** Cambridge University, which was founded in 1209, is well-known for producing famous scientists and mathematicians.; **3** Moscow State University, which is situated in the south-west of Moscow, is the oldest and largest university in Russia.; **4** Yale University, which was founded in 1701, is a private university in Connecticut (USA).; **5** Tokyo University, which is best known for its faculties of law and literature, has produced many Japanese politicians.

LISTENING AND SPEAKING

8 Tell students to read the questions before you play the track.

- Pause the track after each speaker to give students a chance to choose the correct answer.
- Finally, ask students to compare with a partner before you check answers with the class.

1 Speaker 2; **2** Speaker 1; **3** Speaker 4; **4** Speaker 3

Track 2.7

1

I'm an American, and I can tell you, a college degree in the US puts you way ahead of people who don't have one. If you want to work in cities like Boston, New York or San Francisco, your starting salary will be much higher

continued...

than guys who don't have a degree, and you certainly need a good salary to afford an apartment in those cities. I think I'll get about $50,000 as a starting salary once I graduate, and I'll get a lot of fringe benefits too, like life insurance and a retirement plan.

2

I'm from Argentina and everyone I talked to said 'go to university' – careers advisers, teachers, family, friends. Why did I listen to them? I've got massive debts now, and no chance of getting a good job. For the last five years, I've been in a dead-end job, with no security, no prospects, and low pay. Most of my friends left school at 16 and they're doing really well now. They got promoted while I slaved away to get a degree, and it isn't worth the paper it's written on. Of course I feel bitter.

3

I did my degree at Cambridge University – it was a three-year course. I don't like the idea that you study for a degree for what it gets you later in life. You should go to university because you're really interested in the subject you choose. I don't think my degree helped me to get a job. OK, it may have given me an edge over non-graduates for getting interviews, I suppose. But I really enjoyed studying French literature, and don't regret it at all. When I left, I applied for lots of jobs, and I think employers liked the fact that I was confident and had good people skills. I'm now a computer programmer, nothing to do with literature.

4

I graduated in 2006, when Germany hosted the World Cup. I did enjoy my time at university, and maybe that's the problem. I did well at school, so it was logical to go to university. I guess I just enjoyed myself too much. Without the discipline of school, I didn't study as hard as I should, so I only just got a degree. A lot of my friends got jobs straight from school and are now doing really well. There are a lot of unemployed graduates around these days. I don't regret my time at university – I learned quite a lot about people, and I did a lot of sport. I'm not sure it really helped my career though.

9a Tell students they are going to find out more information about three of the countries from the listening text in exercise 8, and one other country.

- Make sure each student only looks at the information provided for them.
- While students are taking notes, move round the room to help with vocabulary.

9b Give each student two to four minutes to talk about the country they read about.

- When all four students have spoken, tell them to answer the questions as a whole group.

HOMEWORK OPTIONS

Students do the exercises on pages 56–57 of the Workbook.

Students write a paragraph to compare the system in their country to the one they read about in exercise 9b.

8.4 SCENARIO: TROUBLE AT LAKESIDE

IN THIS LESSON

Lesson topic and staging

This lesson focuses on problem-solving. Students are introduced to the scenario of a college which has experienced a fall in student numbers because of various problems. They then read an email describing some of these problems and listen to a conversation about others. Students then extract the KEY LANGUAGE of discussing possibilities and options from the listening. Finally, the TASK asks students to work together to solve the problems the college is having.

Objectives

By the end of the lesson, students should have:

- extracted specific information from a reading text
- extracted specific information and language items from a listening text
- learned useful phrases for discussing possibilities and options
- used this language in a 'real-life' situation to solve a problem
- participated effectively in extended speaking practice

Common European Framework

Students can use language effectively to discuss possibilities and options to solve a problem.

Timings

If short of time, you could drop exercise 2 on page 86. However, make sure you elicit a range of problems in exercise 1, question 2 and that you set the context clearly before students do exercise 3a on page 87.

A possible lesson break would be either after exercise 2 on page 86 or exercise 3c on page 87.

WARM-UP

- Put student into pairs and tell them they are going to study at a private language school.
- Ask them to discuss and then list the four most important things they would look for when deciding which school to go to (e.g. state-of-the-art computers, experienced teaching staff).
- When they have finished, ask each pair to read their list to the class.
- The class then discusses the different lists and agrees as a class the four most important things.

SITUATION

1 Focus students on the photos and the prospectus title (Lakeside College) on pages 86–87 and ask them where they think this college is.

- Tell students to read the questions before they read the situation and the prospectus extract.
- Then put them in pairs to discuss their answers.
- In feedback, check students understand *spacious* (a lot of space), *well-equipped* (modern equipment), *well-stocked* (a lot of something, e.g. books), and *state-of-the-art* (very modern).
- Finally, ask students what problems Lakeside College has (falling student numbers, many complaints from students).

> Answers depend on students' own opinions and ideas.

2 Read through the introduction with the class.

- Tell students to read the questions before they read the email.
- Then put them in pairs to discuss their answers.
- Get answers from a few pairs.
- In feedback, ask students if any of the issues the representatives have would also be important to them, or if they have ever experienced these problems.

> Answers depend on students' own opinions and ideas.

When you get answers for question 3, ask students what Marie Laforêt should *do* next and try to elicit 'have a meeting with the student representatives'. This will then lead in to exercise 3a.

KEY LANGUAGE: discussing possibilities and options

3a Introduce the context of the meeting and give students 30 seconds to read the notes.

- Explain that Eva (a woman) and Koichi (a man) are the student representatives.
- Play the track without pausing and then give students a few minutes to complete the gaps.
- Tell students not to simply write the words exactly as heard, but to use only two or three words in each gap.
- Ask them to compare with a partner before you check answers with the class.

> **1** parties; **2** noise; **3** room parties; **4** party per; **5** (a) room; **6** Koichi; **7** student union (SU)

Don't let students spend too long trying to use only one or two words in each gap. It's more important that they understand the track than have exactly the right number of words in their notes.

3b Tell students to read the expressions before you play the track again.

- Ask them to compare with a partner before you check answers with the class.
- Tell students they can find these expressions on page 148 in the Language reference.

3, 1, 5, 7, 6, 2, 4 (Answers are bold in the audioscript.)

Audioscript and answers to Exercise 3b: Track 2.8

Marie, Eva, Koichi

M: OK, I accept what you're saying about the library and the equipment, and some of the staff. I'll raise those issues with the Board of Governors. Now, you want to discuss late-night parties in the Halls of Residence, right?

E: Yes, they're a problem. A lot of students have complained about them. There seem to be more and more parties in people's rooms these days, and they're really noisy, you know, loud music, everyone talking at the top of their voices, dancing. They go often go on for hours, and nobody else can do any work. That's the problem.

M: Mmm, that's not fair, is it? A lot of students study in the evenings in their room. They need some peace and quiet.

E/K: Exactly/Right.

M: Let's see, **1 there are several ways to deal with this.** Erm, we could agree to ban parties in rooms, or we could only allow parties after the exams … what do you think, Koichi?

K: Well, **2 the good thing is that it's fair to everyone, but the bad thing is that it wouldn't be very popular**. I mean, everyone likes parties, don't they? It's part of our education.

E: Could I make a suggestion, Marie?

M: Sure, go ahead.

E: **3 Supposing we let each floor of the hall have one party each semester**. That'd reduce the number of parties a lot.

M: Maybe, but there would still be quite a lot of noise when each floor had their party. No, to be honest, I don't think that's the right thing to do. **4 Let's see, what other things can we do?**

K: I've got an idea. **5 How about letting the students book a room in the main building** for parties? You could charge a small fee, and tell them that they have to book, say, four weeks in advance. I think most people would accept that.

M: **6 Yes, good idea. That's the best solution**, I think. Happy with that idea, Eva?

E: Yeah, I think so. You have to do something about the parties, it can't go on.

continued…

M: OK, **7 so … the next thing to do is for me to talk to everyone**. How about if I attend your next student union meeting? I could explain the proposal there.

E/K: Fine/Great.

M: OK then, we seem to have solved that one. Now, there was also the issue of … *[fade]*

For extra practice, ask students to do exercise KL 4 on page 149 of the Language reference.

3c Go through the *headings only* in the OTHER USEFUL PHRASES box and check students understand *options* (different things you can choose from).

- Give students three minutes to match each expression to the headings. Then tell them to look at the KEY LANGUAGE list in the Language reference on page 148 to check their answers.
- Go through the phrases in the OTHER USEFUL PHRASES box with the class.

Thinking about possibilities: There are several ways to deal with this; Talking about options: The good thing is … the bad thing is; Making suggestions: How about letting …, Supposing we let …; Changing your approach: Let's see, what other things can we do?; Making a decision: That's the best solution; Deciding what to do next: So, the next thing to do is …

Take this opportunity to model the expressions and check students' pronunciation. To save time, only ask students to repeat the phrases you think they will have problems with.

TASK: problem-solving

4a Give students five minutes for this activity.

- Make sure each student reads a different problem on page 168.
- Tell them to ask you if they need help with vocabulary.

The maximum number of students in each group is five. If you have fewer students, tell them to each choose one problem on page 168 and ignore the others.

4b Allow 20 minutes for this activity.

- Ask the Chair to decide who speaks first, second and so on.
- Tell students to describe the problem before they discuss how to solve it.
- Tell one student in each group to note the solution the group decides for each problem.
- Remind students to use the KEY LANGUAGE and OTHER USEFUL PHRASES in their discussion and monitor to note common mistakes with this language.

4c You could either ask one student from each group to present all the problems and solutions or a different student to present each problem.

- Tell the other groups to ask questions if necessary.
- Monitor to note common mistakes with the KEY LANGUAGE or OTHER USEFUL PHRASES.

5 Briefly remind the class of each problem before they decide on the best solution they heard in exercise 4c.

- Finally, correct some of the mistakes you noted in exercises 4b and 4c above.

HOMEWORK OPTIONS

Students do the exercises on page 58 of the Workbook.

Students do exercise KL 4 on page 149 of the language reference.

Students take the role of a member of the Board of Governors from exercise 4 and write an email to the college principal describing the solutions they decided for each problem. (Note: not all the KEY LANGUAGE and OTHER USEFUL PHRASES are appropriate to written texts and you may want to tell students which phrases to use in their email.)

8.5 STUDY AND WRITING SKILLS

IN THIS LESSON

Lesson topic and staging

This lesson focuses on two reading strategies (skimming and scanning) and the skills of writing a formal letter. Students discuss when they might use the two reading strategies, then practise them by reading a text on Lifelong Learning. Next, students scan a formal letter for specific points and focus on the conventions of formal letter writing. Students then listen to a man discussing the information he needs about a Summer School course. Finally, students write a formal letter asking for information about the course.

Objectives

By the end of the lesson, students should have:

- learned about and used skimming and scanning as reading strategies
- extracted specific information and language items from a reading and a listening text
- learned (more) about the conventions of formal letter writing
- written a formal letter asking for information about a course

Common European Framework

Students can write a formal letter and extract general and specific information from a reading text.

Timings

If short of time, you could drop exercise 3 on page 88 because the main aim of skimming and scanning is achieved in exercises 2a and 2b. Alternatively, ask students to write the letter in exercise 7b individually for homework and do exercises 7c and 7d in the next lesson. Or, ask students to write their final draft individually at home.

A possible lesson break would be after exercise 3 on page 88.

WARM-UP

- Elicit different things people read (including those they just 'dip into' to find specific information) and write them on the board. Include the following: magazines; newspapers; telephone directories; novels; coursebooks; emails.
- Tell students to find two other students who read/use each of these things regularly by asking 'Do you read x?'.

- Tell them to ask follow-up questions such as 'What kind of novels do you like?', 'What do you use instead of a telephone directory?'

STUDY SKILLS: reading strategies

1 Lead in by asking students if they read all texts in the same way and elicit some differences (e.g. more quickly, slowly, etc.).
- Ask students to read the introductory information and then give them three minutes to answer the questions.
- Put students in pairs to compare answers.
- Go through the answers and the notes in brackets with the class.

> **1** scanning (because you look for the name of a person you already know); **2** scanning (because you look for the name of a village you already know); **3** skimming (because you go through the pages quickly until you see a picture or a title that indicates you will find the article interesting); **4** scanning (because you look for the name of a team you already know); **5** scanning (because you look for the title you already know or a key word e.g. horror, thriller, comedy)

2a Skimming
- Tell students to read the questions and that it isn't necessary to read any detail to answer them.
- Give them a maximum of 15 seconds to answer the questions.
- Elicit answers from the class.

> **1** maybe a leaflet or a magazine; **2** learning/ education at any age and throughout life; **3** Answer depends on students' own opinions.

2b Scanning
- Tell the students to read the questions and ask them what clues they will look for when scanning for the answers (e.g. question 2 will be a number).
- Give them one to two minutes to read the text and answer the questions.
- Check answers with the class, but don't teach the phrase 'you can teach an old dog new tricks' in the final line of the text because this is included in exercise 3.

Tell students to underline the answers in the text rather than make notes.

> **1** 'Learning is not a product of schooling, but the lifelong attempt to acquire it'; 'Learning prepares us for change'; 'You can't teach an old dog new tricks.' **2** 2004 = 44%; 2000 = 40%; **3** Because you can do it in many places (at home, at work, etc.) not just through formal channels.

3 Give students five minutes to discuss the questions.
- Check answers with the class.
- Finally, ask students if they think skimming and scanning are useful strategies and why.

> **1** Students' own ideas; **2** Students' own ideas, accept any reasonable answers; **3** It's more difficult to change/learn new things when you're older.

WRITING SKILLS: a formal letter

4a Tell students to read the questions and then give them two minutes to read the letter and decide their answers.
- Ask them to compare with a partner before you check answers with the class.
- Finally, ask students the function of the letter (to give information about a course) and if they would like to attend a course like this.

> **1** c; **2** b; **3** b; **4** b

4b Letter conventions
- Tell students to look at the letter in exercise 4a to help them decide if the statements are true or false.

> **1** True; **2** False (it goes top left, next to your address); **3** False (you should begin the letter *Dear Mr/Mrs/Ms/Miss* + surname/family name); **4** False (in UK English, if you begin a letter *Dear* + name, you end it *Yours sincerely*. If you begin the letter *Dear Sir/Madam*, you end it *Yours faithfully*); **5** True; **6** False (you should use full forms e.g. *I am* and *we are*, and formal language: see Lesson 6.5 on page 67.)

5 Ask students who the letter in exercise 4a was sent to (the name is top left in the text).
- Read through the introduction to exercise 5 with the class.
- Ask students to predict a few things Manfred might need to know.
- Play the track without pausing.
- Ask students to compare with a partner and if necessary, play the track again.
- Check answers with the class.

> **1** what sort of people attend the course; **2** accommodation; **3** how to pay; **4** how the course is organised; **5** is there a certificate?; **6** are there any examinations? (Answers are bold in the audioscript on the following page.)

Audioscript and answers to Exercise 5: Track 2.9

Manfred, Louise

M: That was a nice letter Jane Goodman sent me, Louise. I'd like to attend the course – it sounds interesting.

L: Yeah, I read the brochure. I must say, I liked the topics they're covering. Professor Dawson's good. I've seen him give lectures in London – he's well worth seeing. I saw his book in a store the other day – you know, it looked really interesting. Why don't you get it before the course begins?

M: Good idea, I'll do that. But Louise, there are some points in the letter I'm not clear about.

L: Oh yes?

M: Well, for one thing, I'd like to know **what sort of people attend the course**. I mean, are they teachers, or students, young or old? And where do they come from, mainly? I don't want to spend the time with a group of people from Germany. I'd prefer an international group, so I can practise my English.

L: Mmm, I can understand that. Why don't you check? Also, have you thought about **accommodation**? I noticed there was a bit about home-stay possibilities in the brochure, but not much else. What about accommodation in halls of residence? They're often cheaper and a lot better than hotels.

M: OK, I'll check that out too when I write to Jane Goodman. You know, I couldn't see anything about **methods of payment** for the course. The prices were all there, but nothing about how to pay. I'd like to pay by cheque if possible, when I arrive. I hope they accept that.

L: I'm sure they will. Another thing – when you write, why don't you find out **how the course will be organised**? I mean, what sort of methods will they use? Will it just be lectures, or will you have to make presentations, individually or in groups? And, erm, will there be a lot of discussion, videos, cassettes, that sort of thing? I don't think you can get as much from just lectures.

M: Good point. One other thing – do you think I'll get a **certificate** or something if I complete the course? That'd be useful. And **are there any examinations**? Oral or in writing? Actually, there are a lot of questions I need to ask.

6 Students do the activity as per the Coursebook.

- Tell students they will be able to use these or similar phrases in exercise 7b.

Beginning the letter: Thank you for your letter + verb-*ing* (enquiring). Ending the letter: We look forward to seeing you at the beginning of the course; If you need any further information, please don't hesitate to contact me. Offering information: I am pleased to tell you that ...,

7a Give students ten minutes to decide how many paragraphs to write and which point should go where.

7b Before students begin, remind them of the letter layout in exercise 4a, the conventions in exercise 4b and the phrases in exercise 6.

- Give students 20 minutes to write their draft and tell them to use their dictionaries or ask you for extra vocabulary.
- While they are working, monitor to point out mistakes but encourage students to self-correct.

For more examples of formal written language, tell students to look at Lesson 6.5 on page 67.

7c Remind students of the proofreading and editing skills in Lesson 7.5 on page 78.

- Allow ten minutes for students to read and make notes on each other's letters.
- Put the pairs together and give them five minutes to comment on the letters.

7d Give students ten minutes to write their final draft.

- Take the letters in for marking, paying particular attention to organisation, formal conventions and the phrases they have seen in this lesson.

HOMEWORK OPTIONS

Students do the exercises on page 58 of the Workbook.

Students individually write the first draft from exercise 7b or the final draft from exercise 7c.

Engineering

9

9.1 FROM ENGINES TO ENGINEERS

IN THIS LESSON

Lesson topic and staging

This lesson looks at engineering and at women in this field. Students read about promoting engineering to women and focus on vocabulary in the text (e.g. *civil engineering*). Next, students listen to a female engineer talking about her experiences. This leads to a focus on word combinations (e.g. *test a prototype*) which students then practise using. Next, students discuss some of the greatest achievements in engineering and finally write a paragraph about one of these.

Objectives

By the end of the lesson, students should have:

- extracted specific information and language items from a reading and a listening text
- expanded their range of word combinations in the context of engineering
- discussed the greatest achievements in the field of engineering
- written about a great achievement in engineering

Timings

If short of time, you could cut the number of categories in exercise 6 on page 91.

A possible lesson break would be after exercise 2c or 5b on page 91.

WARM-UP

- Write the following list of buildings and countries on the board:

1 the pyramids	a) Spain
2 Museo Guggenheim	b) Russia
3 the Golden Gate Bridge	c) Peru
4 Hermitage Museum	d) the USA
5 the Petronas Twin Towers	e) Egypt
6 Machu Pichu	f) Malaysia

- Students match the building to the country and the first to finish shouts 'stop!'
- Give students one point for each building matched correctly and one extra point if they can name the city. (Note: there is a Guggenheim Museum in New York, but the one in the list above is in Spain – hence the Spanish 'Museo'.)

1 e Cairo; **2** a Bilbao; **3** d San Francisco; **4** b St. Petersburg; **5** f Kuala Lumpur; **6** c no city

Gordon L Clegg quote:

This quote means that you need engineers do the practical work while others do the 'academic' work. It implies that engineers are superior to others because their work is more 'real'.

READING

1 To lead in, focus students on the photo on page 90 and ask them what it is.

- Ask students who designs/builds a bridge like this and elicit *architect, engineer*, etc.).
- Read the quote with the class and elicit its meaning (see above).
- Students then do the activity as per the Coursebook.

Answers depend on students' own knowledge and ideas.

2a Tell students they don't need to read details to answer these questions.

- Give them 15 seconds to skim the text and answer the questions.
- Go through answers with the class.

The text is probably a leaflet or an informational ad in a magazine. It's aimed at women (the title and the photo tell you this).

Before students do this activity, you could remind them of the skimming strategy from lesson 8.5.

2b Give students five minutes for this activity.

- Tell students to read the headings before they read the text.
- Tell them to compare with a partner before you check answers with the class.
- Finally, ask the class if they now have more understanding of what an engineer does and/or if the women in the class would consider being an engineer.

1 a; **2** b; **3** d; **4** e; **5** c

2c Check students understand *field [of engineering]* (area, type).

- Ask students to underline the fields of engineering mentioned in paragraph 4.
- Give them three minutes to match the inventions to the fields.
- When you go through the answers, elicit/give the meanings of problem words (e.g. *pacemaker*).

1 roads – civil engineering; 2 aircraft – aerospace engineering; 3 a washing machine – mechanical engineering; 4 microchips – computer engineering; 5 heart pacemaker – biomedical engineering

LISTENING

3a Read through the introduction with the class and check they understand *high position* (important job).

- Set the question and the play the track without pausing.
- Go through the answer with the class. In feedback, don't teach difficult language from the text because this will give students the answers to exercise 3b.

Aerospace engineering (but she *studied* mechanical engineering at university).

3b Tell students to read the statements before you play the track again.

- Give students a few minutes to correct the statements and compare with a partner.
- If necessary, play the track again.
- Go through answers with the class and check any difficult vocabulary (e.g. *lab, feasibility*).

1 She started her career in a test lab (laboratory) for aeroplanes; **2** She worked on commercial planes; **3** She *might* spend time doing tests but she *probably* spends most time managing projects; **4** She likes the challenge of finding solutions to problems, engineering is fun, exciting and satisfying. (Information for each answer is bold in the audioscript below.)

If students find this listening difficult, pause the track at the points shown in the audioscript below and give them time to note their answer.

To help students with this activity, you could tell them that 'scanning' (studied in lesson 8.5) is not only for reading texts but can also be used for listening. Then ask them what key words they could listen for (e.g. statement 3: listen for *at present* or something similar (*now, currently, these days*, etc.).

Audioscript and answers to Exercise 3b:
Track 2.10
Interviewer, Lindsey

I: For our next guest on 'A Woman's World', I'd like to welcome to the programme Lindsey Barone, head of engineering at Swift Aerospace – a very good example of a woman in a man's world.
L: Good morning, everyone
I: Lindsey you're an engineer, but why did you become one? What got you interested?

continued…

L: Well, from a young age I was always interested in how things work. I chose engineering as a career because I wanted to make things better. Engineering isn't just about testing theories and building models. It's about designing new products and finding new uses for old products. I want to improve the way the world works.
I: Mmm, interesting. And could you tell me a bit about your training?
L: Well, I studied engineering at university. I was the only woman in the mechanical engineering department!
I: So, how was that?
L: Well at first I felt a bit uncomfortable, but after a while it didn't bother me. People got used to me and I was treated like anyone else. In fact sometimes it was a bit of an advantage because people liked to have me in their team!
I: You're head of engineering now. How did you get to where you are today?
L: Well, **1 I started in a test lab for aeroplanes**. I did stress and fatigue tests there. Basically, I broke things! Doing that sort of research is very important as it tells you what loads the structures can carry. [PAUSE] Then I went into aeroplane design. **2 I worked on all areas of commercial planes** before moving into project management in the aircraft industry. [PAUSE]
I: Could you tell me a bit more about what you do now?
L: Sure. **3 These days I mainly work in project management. I take ideas for projects and investigate their feasibility** – that means I see if the projects are possible. Next, I develop the objectives and estimate the cost of the project. Then I help the people working on the project to meet their deadlines. I have to make sure projects come in on budget and on schedule. [PAUSE]
I: Now you're head of department and I guess in charge of a lot of men. How do you find that?
L: Well, it wasn't too easy at first. I had to prove myself. When they could see that I had good practical experience and ability, everything was fine.
I: I suppose that's true of anyone who's in charge. OK, Lindsey, finally – what's the best thing about being an engineer?
L: That's an easy one to answer. **4 I love the challenge of finding solutions to problems. I hope that what I do improves people's lives. For me, engineering is fun, exciting and satisfying**. So let's have more women in engineering in the future!
I: Thanks very much, Lindsey. Now, our next guest is someone who … *[fade]*

4 Allow ten minutes for this activity.

- Encourage students to give reasons for their opinions and to agree/disagree with each other.
- In feedback, ask two or three pairs for their ideas.

Answers depend on students' own opinions and ideas.

VOCABULARY: word combinations

5a Tell students some of these combinations are from the listening in exercise 3a and 3b.

- Tell them to use their dictionaries to find the meanings and information about combinations.
- Point out that some verbs match with more than one noun (numbers 3, 5 and 7).
- Ask students to compare with a partner before you check answers with the class.

1 h; **2** c; **3** f or a; **4** g; **5** a or f; **6** b; **7** e or g; **8** d

5b Tell students they will need to change the tense of some verbs to fit the gaps.

- Ask students to compare with a partner before you check answers with the class.

1 do/safety tests; **2** made/breakthrough; **3** found/solution; **4** build, test/model (Note: there is more than one possible answer here. However, *test* is more likely than *build*.); **5** test/theory; **6** do/research; **7** solve/problem; **8** meet/deadlines

For extra practise, ask students to do exercise V1 5 on page 151 of the Language reference.

SPEAKING

6 Read through the list with the class and check they understand *jet airliner* (quickly draw a propeller plane on the board and cross out the propellers, OR draw a jet engine*), thermometer* (to test someone's temperature, mime putting a thermometer in your mouth), *laser surgery* (medical surgery and operations using an intense beam of light, e.g. helping people with eye problems) and *Panama canal* (see background information). Tell students they should add one more achievement *with their partner*.

- While they are speaking, monitor to note common mistakes with the vocabulary from this lesson.
- In feedback, get ideas from two or three pairs.
- Finally, correct some of the mistakes you noted earlier.

Answers depend on students' own ideas and opinions.

(i) Panama Canal: A canal connecting the Pacific and Atlantic Oceans through Panama, Central America

To extend this activity, when students have decided the greatest achievement in each category, put the pairs together and tell them to persuade each other that their answer is better. (If you are short of time, cut the number of categories.)

WRITING

7 If possible, get students to do some research on the engineering achievement they choose, perhaps using the Internet.

- Give students ten minutes to make notes (or longer if they are researching the topic on the Internet).
- Then give them at least 15 minutes to write a first draft of their paragraph and monitor to point out mistakes they make.
- Finally, give students 15 minutes to write the final draft, incorporating the mistakes you pointed out earlier.
- Take the paragraphs in for marking, paying particular attention to the vocabulary taught in this lesson.

HOMEWORK OPTIONS

Students do the exercises on page 60 of the Workbook.

Students do exercise V1 5 on page 151 of the language reference.

Students read the leaflet on page 90 again and write an email to an engineering company asking for more information about a career in engineering. In the email, they should say what aspects they are interested in (e.g. solving problems and finding solutions) and what kind of engineering they would like to do (e.g. transport, medicine).

9.2 SURVIVAL ENGINEERING

IN THIS LESSON

Lesson topic and staging

This lesson looks at how engineering can make people safe. Students read an article about the possibility of asteroids hitting the Earth. They then focus on language contained in the text: vocabulary and the use of the passive. Next, students do a series of activities to explore the form and use of passives in different tenses and use these to complete an email. Finally, students use the passive forms in a speaking activity.

Objectives

By the end of the lesson, students should have:

- practised extracting specific information and language items from a reading text
- extended their range of vocabulary in the context of possible threats to Earth
- revised/extended their knowledge of the passive in different tenses
- practised using passives in an extended speaking activity

Timings

If short of time, you could drop exercise 3 on page 93 and set it as homework. Alternatively, cut exercise 1 on page 92 and begin the reading activities with exercise 2a. However, make sure you provide a lead in to the topic.

A possible lesson break would be after exercise 3 on page 93.

WARM-UP

This activity introduces students to the context of threats to Earth.

- On the board, write *threats to Earth* and check students understand the phrase (dangers that might destroy or harm the Earth).
- Put students in pairs and tell them to write as many threats as they can think of in five minutes. If necessary, give an example, e.g. *poverty*.
- When they have finished, write their ideas on the board. Elicit or give *asteroids from space* (or something similar) and use this as a lead in to exercise 1.

READING

1 Focus students on the photos on page 92, ask them what is happening and elicit/give *asteroid* and *collide*.

- Give students a maximum of two minutes to do this activity and tell them to guess if necessary.
- Tell them to ask you for help with vocabulary or to use their dictionaries.
- When students have checked their answers, ask them which statement they found most surprising.

Answers are on page 168 of the Coursebook.

2a Focus students on the title and ask if anyone knows how it might be possible to stop an asteroid colliding with Earth.

- Tell students to read the list (1–6) and compare with the ideas they had in the previous stage.
- Check students understand *rockets* (quickly draw one on the board), and *reflect* (e.g. in a mirror).
- Elicit/remind students what 'scanning' is (see lesson 8.5, exercise 1 on page 88).
- Ask students what key words they could look for in the text (e.g. *mirror*, *nuclear*, etc.).
- Give students three minutes to scan the text and answer the question.
- Go through answers with the class.

Scientists think numbers 1 and 4 are possible ways of preventing asteroids hitting the Earth.

2b Give students three to five minutes for this activity.

- Explain to students that the introduction (beginning with the words 'Most scientists agree ....') is Paragraph 1.
- Tell students not to worry about vocabulary because they will study this in exercise 3.
- Ask them to compare with a partner before you check answers with the class.
- Finally, ask students the most frightening/surprising/interesting thing they read.

1 para. 3; **2** para. 4; **3** para. 2; **4** para. 3; **5** para. 5; **6** para. 2

3 When students have found all the words, ask them to compare with a partner.

- Go through the answers and tell students that *deflected* in answer 1 is the past participle of *deflect*. (Note: *deflected* will be used as a lead in to exercise 4a below.)

1 deflect [para. 4,] deflected [para. 5]; **2** meteor [para. 1], meteorite [para. 2]; asteroid [para. 1]; comet [para. 3] (see background information below); **3** collision [para. 2]; **4** a threat, b impact, c devastation

(i) An *asteroid* is a rocky body in space. A *meteor* is the name for an asteroid that enters the Earth's atmosphere, and which you can see burning. A *meteorite* is the name for a meteor that survives the atmosphere and hits the Earth. A *comet* is a body, made up mostly of dust and gases, that orbits the sun and occasionally has a 'tail' of light.

GRAMMAR: the passive

4a Remind students of *deflected* in question 1, exercise 3 and tell them to find it in the article.

- Write *can be deflected* on the board and elicit/give the passive structure (*be* + past participle), labelling the relevant part of the sentence. Tell students not to worry about *can* at this stage.
- Tell students that *be* can be in different tenses.
- Give students three minutes to find and underline other examples of the passive. (Make sure they underline the full forms (as in the answers below.)
- Elicit examples from the class and write them on the board.

An alternative to writing on the board: reproduce the article so the whole class can see it (maybe using an Interactive Whiteboard or an overhead projector). As you elicit the examples, underline them in the article.

para. 2: has been struck; was first seen; para. 3: have been found; it is estimated, have not yet been discovered, hasn't been surveyed; para. 4: has just been set up by, will be used, proposed by (see Warning); para. 5: have already been announced, can be deflected, will be used, is expected to

! ... *methods proposed by engineers* is passive. The full form is *methods which are/were/have been proposed by engineers*. This is a defining relative clause that has been removed because we can understand it from the rest of the sentence. You can't match it to one of the tenses in exercise 4b because you don't know which tense it is. If you think this will confuse students, omit the example from this exercise.

4b If students find this activity hard, tell them to look at G1 in the Language reference on page 150 for help.

- Go through the answers and label the tense on each example you wrote on the board in exercise 4a.
- Go through the notes in brackets below and underline the adverbs on the board. Students will need to know the position of adverbs to do exercise 7a.
- Finally, read through the GRAMMAR TIP with the class.

a it is estimated, is expected to; **b** was first seen (Note: the adverb [underlined] goes after *be*.); **c** has been struck, have been found, have not yet been discovered, hasn't been surveyed, has just been set up by, have already been announced (Note: the adverbs [underlined] go after *have* and *have not*.); **d** will be used; **e** can be deflected (Note: the negative is made by using *not* after the modal e.g. *cannot be deflected*.); **f** have not yet been discovered, hasn't been surveyed (Note: in other passive tenses that don't use *have*, *be* becomes negative, e.g. *it is not expected to.)*

4c Elicit/give the meaning of *agent* (the person or thing that does the action) before eliciting the answer to this question from the class.

by

5a Put student in pairs to discuss the question.

- Elicit the answer from the class.

The agent is not important. The passive is used to emphasise the 500 NEOs because they are more important than the agent.

! Students may say that the agent is known because we can guess that it is 'scientists' mentioned earlier in the paragraph. Tell students we aren't sure *exactly* who the agent is.

5b Give students five minutes to find other examples and then compare their answers with a partner.

! The first answer (para. 2: *The rock* ...) is also used in exercise 6 as an example of starting a sentence with information that is already known. It can be interpreted in both ways. If you think this will confuse students, omit it from the answers below.

para. 2: The rock, 2001 YB5, was first seen in December; para. 3: It is estimated, hasn't yet been surveyed; para. 4: will be used; para. 5: can in fact be deflected, is expected

6 Students do the activity as per the Coursebook.

A very clear example of this use of the passive is on page 150 of the Language reference. The example begins with the words *20 scientists are* ...

para. 5: ... an asteroid named Apophis, which is expected to make its ...

Before students do the practice activities beginning with exercise 7, tell them to read G1 in the Language reference on page 150.

7a Tell students to read the email quickly and tell you if it's good or bad news (bad news).

- Elicit or remind students of the form of the present perfect active and passive.
- Give students a maximum of ten minutes to complete the gaps.
- Monitor to point out mistakes and encourage students to refer to the Language reference and the information in exercises 4–6 above.
- Tell students to compare with a partner before you go through answers with the class.

1 has invested; **2** have finally been completed; **3** have been shown; **4** has happened; **5** has been suspended; **6** has not been approved; **7** has not been published; **8** has asked; **9** has arranged; **10** have all invested

7b Students do the activity as per the Coursebook.

was not followed; were not checked; was deleted from (all past simple passive)

SPEAKING

8a Read through the instructions, then tell students to look at the table and read the instructions on page 168.

- Do one example with the class (e.g. 'The Taj Mahal was built in around 1640.').
- Tell students to use their dictionaries to check the meaning of verbs.
- Give students a time-check after eight minutes to tell them they have only two minutes left.
- Monitor to correct use of the passive, tenses and prepositions, but don't correct factual mistakes because these will be discussed in exercise 8b.

8b If pairs have different answers, ask them to try to decide which is correct.

- Go through answers with the class.

If possible, reproduce the answers below so the whole class can see them (maybe using an Interactive Whiteboard or an overhead projector).

> **1** The Taj Mahal was built in around 1640; **2** The ballpoint pen was invented by Laszlo Jose Biro; **3** Nokia Mobile phones are made/ manufactured in Finland; **4** Diamonds are mined in South Africa; **5** The first computer was developed by Alan Turing; **6** The World Wide Web was invented by Tim Berners-Lee; **7** The motor company Fiat was set up/founded by Gianni Agnelli in 1899; **8** The telephone was invented and developed by Alexander Bell; **9** Microsoft was founded by Bill Gates; **10** The X-ray tube was refined by William Coolidge; **11** The Nobel Prize of Physics was awarded to Guglielmo Marconi in 1909; **12** Tea is grown in Sri Lanka; **13** Toyota cars are manufactured/made in Japan; **14** The first steam ship was built in the 18th century; **15** The first motor car was made by Carl Benz in 1884.

8c Tell students to choose one student in their group to rewrite the sentences they can remember.

- Stop them after ten minutes.
- Ask each group to read out their sentences and give one point for each correct answer.

HOMEWORK OPTIONS

Students do the exercises on pages 61–62 of the Workbook.

Students do exercises G1 1 and 2 on page 151 of the Language reference.

Students research one of the items in the table on page 168 and write a paragraph saying who invented it, who developed it, where it was developed, what it is used for, etc.

9.3 SUPERSTRUCTURES

IN THIS LESSON

Lesson topic and staging

This lesson looks at large man-made structures. Students discuss large structures they know about, then read a short text about a transatlantic tunnel and focus on the grammar for this lesson: articles. Students do activities to first revise, then use articles. Students then read two more texts about superstructures and compare these with the text at the beginning of the lesson. Finally, students discuss what superstructure they would like to design and why.

Objectives

By the end of the lesson, students should have:

- practised reading texts to extract specific information and language items
- revised and practised using articles (*a*, *an*, *the* or no article)
- discussed, listened to and responded to ideas about superstructures they know and would like to design

Timings

If short of time and your students can use articles with confidence, you could drop exercise 4 on page 94.

A possible lesson break would be either after exercise 4 on page 94 or exercise 5c on page 95.

WARM-UP

This activity uses *the* when used with superlatives and introduces the topic of superstructures.

- Write the following on the board and check students understand *religious building* (e.g. mosque, church, temple):
  1 The tallest building
  2 The longest river
  3 The highest mountain
  4 The biggest religious building
  5 The busiest international airport
- Put students into small groups and tell them to answer as many questions as possible.
- Give students one point for each correct answer.
- The groups with the most correct answers wins.

> **1** the CN Tower in Toronto, Canada – 553.3m (when the Burj Dubai is finished it will be the tallest building – 808m); **2** The Nile – 6690km; **3** Mount Everest – 8848m above sea level; **4** St Peter's in The Vatican, Rome, Italy; **5** Heathrow, London, UK – 61,348,317 international passengers in 2006

SPEAKING

1 Give students a maximum of ten minutes to discuss the questions.
- Elicit ideas from two or three pairs.

Answers depend on students' own experience and ideas.

If students can't remember the name of a structure, ask them where it is and what its function is. If possible, get the name from other students in the class or give it yourself.

GRAMMAR: articles

2 Focus students on the photo and the title and check they understand *transatlantic* (across the Atlantic Ocean).
- Ask students if they believe such a tunnel is possible.
- Give students 30 seconds to read the text and compare answers with a partner.
- To follow up, ask students if they think it is possible now they've read the article.

Answers depend on students' own ideas.

In feedback, to prepare students for exercise 3, check they understand *magnetically* (demonstrate a magnet attracting and repelling using your hands); *giant* (enormous); *anchors* (draw one on the board) and *decade* (ten years).

3 Ask students to tell you the articles (*a*, *an*, *the* and no article).
- Tell them to read the rules and then find the examples in the text.
- Ask students to compare with a partner before you go through the answers and the notes in brackets.

Take this opportunity to remind students of the pronunciation of articles. *a/an/the* are generally weak /ə/, /ən/, /ðə/. *The* is pronounced /ðɪ/ before a vowel sound (e.g. *the anchors*). Also, remind students that we use *a* before a consonant (e.g. *a magnetically raised train*) and *an* before a vowel (e.g. *an anchor*).

Students may ask why *the* is pronounced /ðə/ before *the United States*. This is because *u* in *United* is pronounced as a consonant.

1 a train; **2** the train, the anchors, the tunnel; **3** the United States, the United Kingdom (Note: countries beginning with *United* always use *the*. Most cities do not use *the* – see 10 below.); **4** the Atlantic Ocean, the Gulf Stream; **5** the largest, the most expensive; **6** the world; **7** the sea (i.e. the water in the Atlantic Ocean); **8** decades; **9** engineers, giant anchors; **10** New York, London

For a full explanation, ask students to read G2 on page 150 in the Language reference.

4 Tell students this text is about Dubai and elicit some information about the city.
- Give students 15 seconds to read the text (without filling the gaps) to see if any of the information they gave you is mentioned.
- Students then work alone to complete the gaps, then compare answers with a partner.
- Go through answers with the class and ask them to give you a reason for the use of the article.
- In feedback, check students are pronouncing the articles correctly (see Tip above).

1 the; **2** no article; **3** the; **4** no article; **5** the; **6** the; **7** the; **8** the; **9** the; **10** the; **11** the; **12** a; **13** a; **14** no article; **15** a; **16** the

READING

5a Focus students on the photos and titles on page 95 and ask them what they think the superstructure is and why it might be needed.
- Give students one minute to read the two articles on page 95 and see if their predictions were correct.
- Then focus students on the table and check they understand *width* (noun of wide).
- Give students a maximum of four minutes to read the three texts and complete the information.
- Ask students to compare their answers with a partner.
- When you go through the answers, check students understand *trillion* (one million million in common English use) and *football pitches* (where you play football).

To make exercise 5a and b more communicative, put students into groups of three and ask each to read one text and answer as many questions as possible. Then tell students to exchange information by asking each other questions.

	Tunnel	Sky City	Ski Dubai
height		1,000 m	85 m
width		400 m at the base	80 m
cost	about $12 trillion		$272 million
length	nearly 5,000 km		
area covered		8 km² floor area	about three football pitches

You could remind students of 'scanning' and ask what key words they will look for when they read.

5b Ask students to compare with a partner before you check answers with the class.

> **1** the magnetically raised train (Text 1); **2** Sky City 1000; **3** 54 minutes; **4** up to eight km deep; **5** 35,000 residents and 100,000 workers; **6** up to 70; **7** –8° c; **8** 6,000 metric tons

5c Put students into pairs to try to answer the question without reading the texts again.

- Then ask them to read the texts to check their answers and to find other problems. Students can use their dictionaries if necessary.
- When you go through the answers, elicit the meaning of *currents*, *earthquake* and *avalanche* or ask them to use their dictionaries.

> Transatlantic tunnel: [some of] the Atlantic's strongest currents (including part of the Gulf Stream); Sky City 1000: Tokyo has a major problem with overcrowding and a lack of green space / danger if there was a fire in the building / some people would be scared to live in such a tall building / Japan's earthquake problem; Ski Dubai: the possibility of avalanches

If you used the Task adjustment above, ask students to tell each other about the problems in their text.

SPEAKING

6a Give students 20 minutes to discuss their structure and write notes on the categories (size, location, etc.).

- While they are working, move round the room to help with extra vocabulary if necessary.

6b Emphasise that the sketch does not need to be detailed.

- When you put groups together, tell them to ask questions about each other's designs.

To extend this activity, post students' sketches around the room. Tell one student in each group to stand next to their sketch (this person can change later). Tell the rest of the class to look at all the sketches and ask questions. Students can use their notes from exercise 6a to answer the questions. When all the students have seen the sketches, put them back into groups of three to decide which is the best. Finally, the class votes on the best design.

HOMEWORK OPTIONS

Students do the exercises on pages 63–64 of the Workbook.

Students do practice activity G2 3 on page 151 in the Language reference.

Students use the notes they made in exercise 6a to write a short description of their design. Take these in for marking, paying particular attention to the use of articles.

9.4 SCENARIO: THE SKY-HIGH PROJECT

IN THIS LESSON

Lesson topic and staging

This lesson focuses on discussing options and making decisions. Students are introduced to the scenario of a big national project to inspire people and attract foreigners. Students listen to a TV news extract about the project and then to two engineers discussing the benefits. This is followed by a third listening which contextualises the KEY LANGUAGE: discussing options and making decisions. Finally, the TASK asks students to discuss various options for the project and to make decisions.

Objectives

By the end of the lesson, students should have:

- extracted specific information and language items from three listening texts
- learned useful phrases for discussing options and making decisions
- used this language in a 'real-life' situation to assess a project
- participated effectively in extended speaking practice

Common European Framework

Students can use language effectively to discuss options, make decisions and assess a project.

Timings

It is better not to cut any of the exercises from this lesson. However, if you are short of time, you could drop exercise 5 on page 97, but make sure you introduce the KEY LANGUAGE as students need this for the TASK.

A possible lesson break would be after exercise 4 on page 96.

WARM-UP

This activity introduces the context for the lesson and allows you to elicit/teach vocabulary for exercise 3.

- Put students into small groups and ask each person to choose one of the photos on pages 96–97.
- Ask students to describe their photo to the others in the group but not to tell them which one it is.
- The other students guess which picture is being described.
- Finally, use the photos to elicit *overpopulated, polluted, homeless people* and *hurricane*.

SITUATION

1 Give students one minute to read the situation and then put them in pairs to discuss the question.

- Get a few ideas from the class.

2a Set the context and tell students to read the questions before you play the track.

- Go through answers with the class.
- To follow up, ask students if their first impressions of the project are good or bad (and why.)

> **1** a vertical city **2** because it will be tallest city in the world and a tourist attraction

Students read about a similar city in lesson 9.3, page 95 (Sky City 1000). You could tell students to look again at this text to give them more idea of what the project may be like.

2b Play the track again while students note down the answers.

> Type of project: building the tallest city in the world; Height: more than 1,500m; Width: 500m at the base; Number of people living in the city: about 40,000; Number of people working in the city: more than 100,000; Facilities in the city: apartments, a hotel, an international conference centre, offices, food outlets, entertainment and leisure facilities, green spaces, fountains, parks and gardens; Future action by the Minister: contact engineering departments in universities (to invite discussion). (Information giving these answers is bold in the audioscript below.)

For 'Facilities in the city' students have to write a lot. You could pause the track after this section to give students time to write. Alternatively, write the facilities (see the audioscript below) on the board and add a few others (e.g. cinema, airport, train station, school). Ask students to copy all the words from the board and then circle the ones they hear when they listen to the track.

> **Audioscript and answers to Exercise 2b:**
> **Track 2.11**
> Some exciting news now from the Minister of the Environment, Susan Lau, which should please all the engineers in our country.
> The Government has announced that it is considering the possibility of **building the tallest city in the world** – a vertical city located just on the edge of our capital, which would bring new life to the city, as well as boosting tourism. It will be **over 1,500 meters high** – at least that's the idea – with **a width of about 500 meters at its base**. The idea is that about **40,000 people will live there**, and over **100,000 will work in the city** during the day. The vertical city, which will be called the Sky-High Project, will have **apartments, a hotel, an international conference centre, offices, food outlets, entertainment and leisure facilities**. And just like any other city, there'll be **green spaces, fountains, parks and gardens**.
> At the moment, it's just an idea, but an exciting one – it would really put the country on the map, no doubt about that. The Minister plans to **contact engineering departments in universities** and invite new angles and discussion of the idea.

3 Give students a maximum of ten minutes to read the facts and discuss the questions.

- Ask two or three pairs to tell the class their ideas.

If you used the Warm-up activity, you will already have taught some of this vocabulary. If not, as a lead-in at the beginning of this activity, focus students on the photos on pages 96–97 and use them to teach problem vocabulary.

> Answers depend on students' own ideas and opinions. Accept any reasonable answers.

4 Read through the introduction with the class and set the task.

- Ask students to check their answers with their partner before they compare them with the ideas they had in exercise 3.
- Go through answers with the class and check any problem vocabulary (e.g. *commute*, *resources*).
- Finally, ask students if their impressions of the project are more positive or more negative than they were after exercise 2b.

> great publicity for the country; attract a lot of tourists; help with the over-population problem; help with the crime problem; much less stress for working people; don't have to commute long distances; plenty of jobs; fewer traffic jams; good way of using the land; puts a lot of people into a small space; efficient use of resources. (Information giving these answers is bold in the audioscript below.)

> **Audioscript and answers to Exercise 4:**
> **Track 2.12**
> A: Hey, did you see on the news last night about the vertical city? What do you think about it?
> B: I think the idea's really good – building the tallest city in the world. It'd be **great publicity for the country**, everyone would talk about it, and it'd **attract a lot of tourists**.
> A: I agree – it's the best idea the government's had for a long time. It'd **help with the over-population problem, and might help with the crime problem** in that area. You could have lots of closed-circuit TVs on all the floors – that'd cut down crime.
> B: Yeah, I think so. And it'd be **good too for working people – much less stress**, probably, as they **wouldn't have to commute long distances** to get to work. There'd be **plenty of jobs** in the new city, wouldn't there?
>
> *continued…*

A: I suppose so. And **fewer traffic jams** as well because people wouldn't have to drive to work. They could walk there or take some kind of internal transport.
B: Yeah, true. There's another benefit, come to think of it – **it's a very good way of using the land in the city**. It's **putting a lot of people in a small space**. And that's an **efficient use of resources**.
A: Yes, good point.
B: So, let's hope the Ski-High Project gets off the ground.
A: Well, depends on a lot of things, I think. Will it be popular with the public? And if it is, will it be feasible?

KEY LANGUAGE: discussing options, making decisions

5 Set the activity and tell students to read the conversations (1–4) before you play the track.

- Play the track, pausing after each conversation to give students time to write.
- Ask students to compare their answers with a partner and if necessary, play the track again.
- Tell students to look at the KEY LANGUAGE on page 150 of the Language reference.
- Finally, go through answers with the class.

Track 2.13

1
A: What do you think about the present name, the Sky-High Project? It's easy to remember.
B: I'm not too sure about that. Another possibility is Tower City. It's short and easy to pronounce. [PAUSE]

2
A: I think Hope is a good name for the city. It'll give accommodation for a lot of poor and homeless people.
B: That's a possible solution. [PAUSE]

3
A: Tower City? Yes, I think that's the best name. Why don't we suggest it to the Minister?
B: Yes, let's do that. It's the best solution, I think. [PAUSE]

4
A: We all agree then. We'll call it Sky-High City.
B: OK, let's put the name in our report to the Minister.

For extra practice, ask students to do exercise KL 4 on page 151 of the Language reference.

TASK: assessing a project

6a Remind students of listening exercise 2b on page 96 and elicit Susan Lau's future action (contact engineering departments in universities to invite discussion).

- Read through the introduction with the class.
- Put students into groups of three or four to choose their five questions.
- Go through the OTHER USEFUL PHRASES box with the class and remind them of the KEY LANGUAGE from exercise 5. Tell them to use these phrases in their discussion.
- Ask students to take brief notes to use later in exercise 6b.
- While they are speaking, monitor to note common mistakes when using the KEY LANGUAGE and OTHER USEFUL PHRASES, but don't correct these until the end of exercise 6b below.

6b Students can use the notes they made in exercise 6a to present their decisions and reasons.

- Encourage them to tell each other if they disagree with the decisions and why.
- Finally, correct some of the mistakes you noted in exercise 6a above.

There is a possibility that one or two students in each original group (formed in 6a) will do all the speaking in activity 6b. To avoid this, instead of asking students to speak to each other as a group, divide them into pairs (i.e. one student from each of two different groups formed in 6a). Then follow the procedure for exercise 6b.

6c Check students understand *feasible* (realistic and possible).

- Get as many different opinions as possible and then ask students to vote.

If you have a large class, put students into two or three groups and ask them to discuss the question in 6c. When they have finished, ask the class to vote.

HOMEWORK OPTIONS

Students do the exercises on page 65 of the Workbook.

Students extra practice exercise KL 4 on page 151 of the Language reference.

Students write an email to Susan Lau describing the decisions they made in exercise 6a and giving their reasons. When marking, pay particular attention to use of the passive and articles. (Note: students can't use the KEY LANGUAGE here.)

9.5 STUDY AND WRITING SKILLS

IN THIS LESSON

Lesson topic and staging

This lesson focuses on ways to prepare to give a talk and then on describing a process in writing. Students listen to an expert giving advice on preparing a talk and decide which information is most useful. They then focus on linking words from the listening, and use these and the advice they heard earlier to give a talk. Next, students read a text on making aircraft and revise the use of the passive. They then order the stages of making and launching a motorbike before using these ideas to write an article to describe the process.

Objectives

By the end of the lesson, students should have:

- learned about strategies for preparing and giving a talk
- extracted specific information and language items from a reading and a listening text
- extended their range of linking words
- revised one use of the passive (studied in lesson 9.2)
- written an article describing a process

Common European Framework

Students can write an article to describe a process.

Timings

If short of time, you could set exercise 11 for homework. Alternatively, drop exercise 8a and 8b on page 98, but make sure you reintroduce use the text on page 99 as a model for students' own writing and check they understand *simulation*, *prototype* and *authorise*.

A possible lesson break would be after exercise 7 on page 98.

WARM-UP

This activity introduces students to the topic of processes.

- Write the following on the board:
  - Put it in the oven to bake.
  - Wait for it to bake.
  - Put the cake mixture in a baking tin.
  - Take it out of the oven.
  - Weigh the ingredients (eggs, butter, etc.).
  - Mix the ingredients.
  - Let it cool down.
  - Eat it.
  - Put the ingredients in a bowl.
- Tell students these are the stages in baking a cake and check they understand *bake* (cook a cake).
- Tell students to put the process in order.
- The first student to finish says 'stop'.
- The winner is the student with the most stages in the correct order.

STUDY SKILLS: preparing for a talk

1 Explain that *giving a talk* means talking to a group of people (e.g. giving a presentation).
- Put students in pairs to discuss these questions.
- Ask three or four students for their answers.

2 Read through the introduction with the class and elicit one example (e.g. *ordering your ideas*).
- Then put students into pairs to discuss other main points they think Lisa Martin will make.
- Get ideas from the class and write them on the board (for use in exercise 4 later).

3a Set the activity and play the track.
- Elicit answers from the class.

> Answers depend on students' own opinions.

3b Ask students to read sentences 1–8 and fill in any gaps they can.
- Play the track again, pausing where indicated in the audioscript to give students time to write, and give students a few minutes afterwards to finish writing.
- Tell students that for answer 7 there is a lot of possible information: explain that they only have to write one idea.
- Ask students to compare with a partner before you check answers with the class.
- Finally, check students understand *essential* (the most important), *software* (a computer programme), and *Powerpoint* (software by Microsoft).

> **1** needs and interests; **2** into sections; **3** essential points; **4** notes on cards; **5** such as Powerpoint; **6** attract the attention; **7** Students write one of the following answers: a famous quotation, an amazing statistic, a question, a joke, a short story; **8** a strong impact. (Information giving the answers is bold in the audioscript below.)

> **Audioscript and answers to Exercise 3b: Track 2.14**
> ... So, when you give any talk, you need to plan it carefully. First of all, think about your audience – who they are, what they know about the subject and what they expect from you. You want to **1 match your presentation to the needs and interests of your audience**. [PAUSE]
> *continued...*

The next stage is to think about how you will structure your talk, how you'll organise it. A good way is to **2 divide your talk into sections**, and tell your audience what the sections are. [PAUSE] For example, you may say, 'I've divided my talk into three parts', then introduce each section with words like *firstly*, *secondly*, *finally* – that's a common way of giving the plan, the map of your talk.
Following that, prepare your material by dividing it into **3 essential points** you want to make, and extra points that you'll make if you have time. [PAUSE] Of course, think carefully about what your overall message will be. Most people use notes when giving a talk. One way is to give each section of your talk a heading, then put the headings on **4 small cards**. [PAUSE] You may like to add a few words to each heading to remind you of what you want to say. Then, number the cards in the order you present your points. Cards will give you confidence, and help you structure your talk.
Next, you'll need some kind of visual aid. If you have **5 to give a very formal talk, you'll probably use software such as Powerpoint.** [PAUSE] But for less formal talks, posters or diagrams may be enough. A word of warning – don't over-use computers. People come to listen to you, not to look at computer screens all the time.
Also, think about the beginning of your talk very carefully; You need to think of a **6 'hook' – that's something to attract the attention of the audience.** [PAUSE] Some people use **7 a famous quotation or an amazing statistic, or ask the audience a question. A lot of presenters like to start with a joke, or tell a short story, maybe something from their experience.** [PAUSE]
Finally, you need to end strongly. Prepare some sentences which will really impress the audience, and make **8 a strong impact** on them. It's good to end the talk with a bang, so say something that will stay in the audience's mind after they've left you.

4 Refer students to the ideas you wrote on the board in exercise 2 to help them answer the first question.

- Give students two minutes to think of other ideas to add.
- Put them in pairs to compare and then get a few ideas from the class.

Write the most useful ideas on the board so that students can refer to them when preparing their own talk.

5 Linkers

- Do one example with the class (e.g. *First of all*).
- Give students a maximum of four minutes to underline the other examples.
- Go through answers with the class and write the phrases on the board for easy reference.

Make sure your board is clearly organised with advice in one area and linking words in another.

First of all; The next stage is to (+ infinitive); Following that; Next; Also; Finally. (Answers are underlined in the audioscript above.)

6a Give students two minutes to choose their topic and ask a few students which they have chosen.

- Then give students ten minutes to prepare their ideas, using points 1–5 as a guide.
- Tell students to make notes and not to write full sentences.
- Emphasise students are not to prepare the talk itself at this stage, but just prepare some ideas.

6b Allow a maximum of ten minutes for this activity.

- Emphasise that student aren't giving the talk yet: they are explaining how they will give the talk and getting feedback on each other's ideas.
- Encourage students to give reasons for the choices they've made and to ask each other questions.

Groups should have a maximum of four students to give all students time to speak and ask questions.

7 Give students 15–20 minutes to prepare their talks.

- Move round the room providing vocabulary and other help if necessary.
- Refer students to the items you wrote on the board in exercises 2 and 5, and the advice in exercise 3b.
- While students are giving their talks, note their use of linking phrases, organisation, 'hooks' and memorable sentences.
- When all the students have finished, comment on their talks using the notes you made above.

If you have a large class, divide the students into three or four smaller groups so that there is more than one talk being given at the same time. This will save time.

WRITING SKILLS: describing a process

8a Focus students on the title and photo with the text on page 99.

- Ask them what they think the first and last stages are in making an aircraft.
- Get a few ideas from the class.
- Tell students to read the questions before they read the text.
- Ask them to compare with a partner before you check answers with the class.
- Finally, ask them if they guessed the first and last stages correctly.

> **1** a to produce the designs used for the initial simulations; b to test some parts of the aircraft; c to test a small number of aircraft and make sure government requirements are met; **2** a certificate from the government agency

8b Tell students to find the words in the text and read the sentence around them before choosing the answer.

> **1** a; **2** b; **3** b

9 Using the passive
- First, ask students if they can remember uses of the passive they studied in lesson 9.2 and get examples.
- Then tell students to read the introduction and examples.
- Give them one minute to find two examples in the text.
- Get answers from the class.

> The designs are produced; (the designs) are then used; a limited number of aircraft are produced (the prototypes); a certificate is issued (by the government agency)

10 Focus students on the photo of the motorbike on page 99 and explain they are going to write about the process of producing and launching a new one.
- Before they read the notes, ask students what they think would be the first and the last stage in production.
- Give them five minutes to read the notes and order the stages.
- Ask them to compare with a partner before you check answers with the class.
- Finally, ask students if they guessed the first and last stages correctly.

> **1** Plan the new motorbike and do the first designs. (Design team); **2** Build the first prototype with the help of engineers. (R&D department); **3** The prototype is tested on special roads. Check if there are any problems and if any changes are necessary.; **4** Changes are made to the prototype and the design is modified. (R&D department); **5** Do further tests, then make more modifications and changes to the engine.; **6** Contact journalists and invite them to test drive the new motorbike.; **7** Results of the test drive are recorded and the journalists prepare articles about the new bike.; **8** Show the new motorbike at trade exhibitions all over the world; **9** Mass-produce the new motorbike. Launch an international marketing campaign.

11 Read through the instructions with the class.
- Give students 20–30 minutes to write their articles.
- While they are writing, move round the room pointing out mistakes with the passive and linking words, and helping with extra vocabulary if necessary.
- Ask students to swap their articles with a partner and comment on each other's work.
- If necessary, students then write a second draft.
- Take the articles in for marking, paying particular attention to passives and linkers.

HOMEWORK OPTIONS

Students do the exercises on page 66 of the Workbook.

Students write the article in exercise 11, if not done in class time.

Review

UNITS 7–9

GRAMMAR

1a Remind or elicit from students that we use *might/could be* if we're not sure, *must* if we're personally sure something is true and *can't* if we're personally sure something isn't true.

- Tell students all the photos are parts of *one* object.
- Give students three minutes to discuss.

1b Tell students to look at the photo on page 168 and if they're still not sure, to use the language from exercise 1a to make more guesses.

- Tell students they will read what the object is in exercise 2.

2 Tell students to read the article quickly to find out what the object in exercise 1a and 1b is.

- Elicit the answer from the class and check they understand what a *hot tub* is (a bath of warm water for people to relax in – usually outdoors).
- Then ask students to fill the gaps and compare their answers with a partner.
- Go through answers with the class.

> **1** might; **2** a; **3** can; **4** is; **5** the; **6** was; **7** has; **8** whose; **9** should; **10** can't; **11** have; **12** be

VOCABULARY

3 Focus students on the title and ask what a *dam* is (a wall to control the movement of water in a river – normally creating a lake). Then ask if students know anything about the Three Gorges Dam in China.

- Ask students to read the text quickly to find out information about the dam.
- Then tell students to fill the gaps.
- Ask students to compare with a partner before you check answers with the class.

> **1** engineering; **2** developed; **3** production; **4** innovation; **5** produced; **6** manufacturing; **7** users

4 Check students understand *e-tutor* (a tutor who teaches electronically and via the Internet.)

- Tell students to read the text quickly and decide if the student is doing well or badly (she's mainly doing well).
- Students then do the activity as per the Coursebook.

> **1** made; **2** Taking; **3** got; **4** handed; **5** do; **6** failed; **7** retake; **8** revising; **9** go; **10** get

5 Read through the instructions with the class and emphasise they are writing a report on themselves *as if they were you*.

- Tell students to use exercise 4 as a model and give them 10–15 minutes to write the report.
- Take the reports in and respond to the comments they make as well as correcting their language.

💡 Because this is more than half-way through the Coursebook, you could take this opportunity to give formal feedback to the students in your class. If possible arrange some one-to-one tutorials with your students and use their reports from exercise 5 as guide for discussing their progress. Alternatively, use the reports as the basis for writing your own report for them on their progress.

KEY LANGUAGE

6 It isn't necessary for students to write the sentences they make.

- Monitor while students are speaking and note mistakes they make with the phrases.
- When they have finished, get a few ideas from the class.
- Correct some of the mistakes you noted earlier.

7 Tell students to read the statements before you play the track.

> **1** True; **2** False (We have a number of options ...); **3** False (... when the passenger in front moves the seat back the TV screen part stays where it is.) **4** False (... takes up less room ...); **5** True; **6** False (Supposing we made it look more stylish or different ..., We need to ask the designers what they can do about it.)

8a Tell students that the dialogue is the same as in exercise 7.

- When they have finished, ask student to compare answers with a partner. Don't confirm answers until after exercise 8b.

> **1** e; **2** h; **3** a; **4** b; **5** g; **6** d; **7** f; **8** i; **9** c

8b Play the track without pausing and then go through answers with the class or ask them to look at the audioscript on page 178.

Track 2.15

A: OK. Thank you all for coming. We have a number of options but I'd like us to look at this one in particular. There are several features I really like. For example, when the passenger in front moves the seat back the TV screen part stays where it is. The good thing about this is that the passenger feels they have more space. This is especially interesting because in reality the seat takes up less room than normal seats. What do you think about it?

B: I'm sure it's good but it looks very similar to any other airline seat.

A: Supposing we made it look more stylish or different so passengers feel they are sitting in something completely new – would that help?

B: Yes, that's a possible solution. And it would appeal to low-fare airlines with lots of economy class passengers. But the other bad thing is that the head rest doesn't move – sometimes you want to change the position without moving the whole seat. We need to ask the designers what they can do about it.

A: Yes, let's do that.

LANGUAGE CHECK

9 Tell students to try all the sentences before they look at the page in the Coursebook to check.

Words that should be deleted are: **1** don't; **2** to; **3** to; **4** that; **5** it; **6** us; **7** be; **8** be; **9** has; **10** the

LOOK BACK

10 The aim of this activity is to remind students of areas they looked at in units 7–9. This will help reinforce any language or skills they had difficulties with or were particularly good at.

Build words into verbs, nouns and adjectives: 7.1, exercise 3; design new products: 7.2, exercise 8; practise grammar for making deductions: 7.3, exercise 5; read about the single-sex schools debate: 8.1, exercises 3a, 3b and 3c; which type of relative clause needs commas: 8.3, exercise 4; write a formal letter: 8.5, exercise 7a, 7b, 7c, and 7d; listen to a female engineer: 9.1; exercise 3a and 3b; find out about asteroids: 9.2, exercise 1, **2** and 2b

If students have problems remembering these exercises, you could put them into small groups to remind each other (as appropriate) of the vocabulary learned, the content of the text, the topic they talked about.

To extend the activity, ask students to choose one of the exercises and write a test for other students. This could be a list of questions, a true/false, a gapfill, etc.

Trends

10.1 IT'S THE NEW THING

IN THIS LESSON

Lesson topic and staging

This lesson looks at trends and how they develop. Students discuss trends in their countries. Then, they read a text about how trends develop. The reading contextualises the vocabulary focus for this lesson: phrasal verbs. Students do a series of activities to focus on the meaning of these verbs, practise using them and then explore their stress patterns. Finally, students write about a recent trend in their country.

Objectives

By the end of the lesson, students should have:

- discussed trends in their countries
- extracted specific information and language items from a reading text
- expanded their range of phrasal verbs in the context of trends
- written about a recent trend in their country

Timings

If short of time, you could cut the number of listed trends in exercise 1a on page 102. Alternatively, set writing exercise 7 for homework.

A possible lesson break would be after exercise 3 on page 102.

WARM-UP

This activity introduces and personalises the topic of trends and fashions.

- Write the following on the board: I like to follow trends and be fashionable. / I don't care about following trends or fashion.
- Give students one minute to think about which sentence is true for them (it may be a combination of both).
- Put them into small groups to discuss the statements and give reasons for their answers.
- Finally, ask how many students thought the first/ second statement was more true for them.

Frank Capra quote:

This quote means that you are a much more fashionable person if you start trends yourself.

(i) Frank Capra (1897–1991): An Italian-American film director. He made a number of extremely popular films in the 1930s and 1940s. His most famous films are *It's a Wonderful Life* and *Mr. Smith Goes to Washington*.

Photo on page 102: This shows people wearing 3D (three dimensional) glasses to watch a film. This was a trend in the 1950s and 1960s and made the action 'come out of' the screen.

SPEAKING

1a Focus students on the photo on page 102 and ask them what it shows (see Background information above).

- Elicit/give *trend* and explain that a trend can be connected to fashion or it can be something that most people do (e.g. a trend in a country for most young people to go to university).
- Tell students to read the list of trends and use their dictionaries for problem vocabulary.
- Then put students into pairs to discuss the questions.

> Answers depend on students' own opinions and ideas.

If you have a mono-national class and students don't know the answer to question 2, tell them to guess. Alternatively, advise them not to do this question.

To extend this activity, if you have a multi-national class, tell students not to discuss question 2 with their partner. When they have finished discussing the other three questions, tell students to move round the room asking as many others as possible to find out which are trends in their countries.

1b Give students a maximum of five minutes to do this activity.

- Get ideas from two or three pairs.
- To follow up, ask students which trends in exercises 1a and 1b they follow/have followed.

See the tip under exercise 1a above.

READING

2a Remind students what 'skimming' is and elicit they don't need to read details to answer these questions.

- Give students a maximum of one minute to do this activity.

- Go through answers with the class and explain that a *tipping point* is the moment something changes from one thing to another.

> **1** a; **2** the image of the front cover of the book, the references to 'In his book', 'In his new work', the text in the final paragraph, especially 'Overall, Gladwell's book is a thought-provoking read ...', 'he writes in a clear style ...'

(!) If your students don't know the word *review*, it's better to teach it when you go through the answers. If you teach it before the activity, you will tell them the answer to question 1.

2b Tell students to read the sentences before they read the text.

- Check students understand *not given* (the information isn't in the text) and *imitate* (try to be like someone else).
- Then allow five minutes for the activity.
- Tell students to compare with a partner before you check answers with the class.

> **1** True (he's Canadian); **2** True (similar to outbreaks of disease); **3** Not given; **4** False (the people they know come from a variety of ... professional ... circles; **5** Not given; **6** True (they are the first to pick up on new trends); **7** False (people want to imitate salesmen)

(i) Malcolm Gladwell is Canadian and has written a number of books on trends. *The Tipping Point* (published in 2000) was a number 1 bestseller about the ideas that a small change can have unpredicted effects, and the phrase has now become part of the English language.

3 Read through the questions with the class and check students understand *trendsetter* (someone who starts a trend or is the first person to do something that later becomes a trend).

- Give students five minutes for the discussion and encourage them to give reasons for their answers.
- Finally, ask two or three pairs for their ideas.

(tip) If students can't think of any recent trends, tell them to look at the list under exercise 1a for ideas. Alternatively, prepare a list of recent trends in the country where you teach and write these on the board.

VOCABULARY: phrasal verbs (3)

4a Lead in by reminding students of sentence 6 in exercise 2b and show that *pick up on* gave the answer.

- Remind students what a phrasal verb is (verb + preposition with a meaning not obvious from its form).
- Then give students five minutes to do the activity.
- Tell students to read the sentence around each verb to help with the meaning.
- Go through answers and the notes in brackets with the class.

> **1** catch on; **2** take over; **3** keep up with; **4** slow down; **5** die out; **6** find out (followed by *about* something); **7** pick up on; **8** buy into (Note: verbs that can't be separated are: *catch on; buy into; keep up with; die out; pick up on*. Verbs that can be separated are: *find out; take over; slow down* (e.g. *find* something *out* OR *find out [about]* something).

4b Students will need to change the grammar of some verbs to fit the sentences.

- Tell student to try to do this activity without looking at exercise 4a.
- They should then look at exercise 4a to check and to complete the ones they didn't remember.
- Finally, check students understand *revival* in number 4.
- Don't go through answers with the class at this stage. Answers will be given in exercise 5a below.

pronunciation

5a Stress

- Emphasise students only need to mark the stress on the phrasal verb.
- Pause the track after each question to allow students time to check answers and then mark the stress.
- Go through the underlined stress with the class.
- Finally, if necessary, read each sentence to the class to check the grammar of their answers.

(tip) If you think students will find it difficult listening to check answers *and* mark stress at the same time, play the track once to check answers and again to mark the stress.

> **Audioscript and answers to Exercise 4b and 5a: Track 2.16**
>
> 1 What trend do you think will be the next to catch on?
> 2 Do you try to keep up with your friends and neighbours?
> 3 Why do you think trends slow down?
> 4 Which trends that have died out will have a revival, do you think?
> 5 How do you personally find out which trends are becoming popular?
> 6 Which trends have taken over in your country recently?
> 7 Which newspapers and magazines are the first to pick up on new trends in your country?
> 8 Which recent trend are you not going to buy into?

5b Play the first question and ask students what the intonation pattern is.

- Ask students to repeat this question and correct their stress and/or intonation.
- Then play the track, pausing after each question for students to repeat.
- Correct if necessary.

When teaching intonation, don't try to demonstrate the pattern on the whole sentence. Teach only the most important intonation pattern. In these questions, the most important pattern will be at the end.

6 Tell students they need to ask the questions with phrasal verbs NOT the original questions in exercise 4b.

- While students are speaking, monitor to note common mistakes with the grammar of phrasal verbs, stress and intonation.
- Encourage students to give reasons for their answers and to ask follow-up questions.
- In feedback, ask students if they heard about any surprising trends.

Answers depend on students' own opinions and ideas.

WRITING

7 Give students five minutes to choose a trend and write a few notes about it.

- Then give them 15 minutes to write their paragraph.
- Move round the room to help with vocabulary and to point out mistakes.
- Take the paragraphs in for marking, paying particular attention to the use of phrasal verbs.

To extend this activity, when students have finished writing, post the paragraphs round the room. Ask students to read all the paragraphs and then discuss the following in small groups: 1 Were any trends the same as ones in your country/city? 2 Which trends were mostly for young people? 3 Were any trends odd/strange/boring? 4 Which trends have you followed or would you follow?

HOMEWORK OPTIONS

Students do the exercises on page 67 of the Workbook.

Students do exercise 7 or write another similar paragraph.

Students do research in magazines, newspapers, the Internet to find out about current trends in music, fashion, movies, etc. In the next lesson, they tell other students about the trend they found most interesting and why.

10.2 TRENDS IN FASHION

IN THIS LESSON

Lesson topic and staging

This lesson looks at trends and the fashion industry. Students read a text about fashion trends started by films. Then they focus on vocabulary: adjective order (e.g. *a red silk evening dress*). Next, students listen to a conversation in a shop which contextualises the grammar focus: expressions of quantity. Students do a series of activities on the use of this grammar and then practise it. Finally, students discuss trends in fashion and how these affect them.

Objectives

By the end of the lesson, students should have:

- practised extracting specific information and language items from a reading and a listening text
- revised/learned how to order adjectives
- revised/extended their knowledge of expressions of quantity (e.g. *a couple* of, *a little*)

Timings

If short of time, you could drop exercise 8 on page 105 and set it for homework.

A possible lesson break would be after exercise 3 on page 105.

WARM-UP

This activity personalises the topic of trends and fashion.

- Write the following on the board:
  - Buy a fashionable car
  - Buy a house in a fashionable area
  - Buy lots of designer clothes
  - Go on holiday to a fashionable city
- Tell students to choose two things from the list to do/buy.
- Put students into pairs or small groups to compare their decisions and give reasons.
- Finally, find out from the class which were the most popular things to do/buy.

READING

1 Give students a maximum of four minutes to discuss the photos.

- Tell them not to worry if they don't know the answers because they will read about them in exercise 2a.

- To follow up, ask students if they've seen any of these actors' films and if they liked them. (Note: You can confirm information students give you about the actors' names and their films, but don't confirm the trends or students will have no reason to read the text in exercise 2b.)

(i) Uma Thurman (top left): American. She's been in *Dangerous Liaisons, Pulp Fiction, Kill Bill* and others. Audrey Hepburn (bottom left): 1929–1993. Born in the Netherlands. She was in *Roman Holiday, Breakfast at Tiffany's, My Fair Lady* and others. In later life, she was a Goodwill Ambassador for the UN. Marlon Brando (top right): 1924–2004. American. He was in *A Streetcar Named Desire, On the Waterfront, The Godfather* and others. Zhang Ziyi (bottom right): Chinese. Born 1979. She's been in *Crouching Tiger Hidden Dragon, The House of Flying Daggers, Memoirs of a Geisha* and others.

2a Focus students on the title and tell them the article mentions the four actors in the photos.

- Tell them to read the questions and check they understand *look* (a way of dressing or styling your hair), *in terms of* (with reference to) and *accessories* (e.g. hats, shoes, bags).
- Give students three minutes to read the text and answer the questions. (Note: Students may find information mentioned in more paragraphs than the rubric gives. These are noted in brackets in the answers below.)
- Ask them to compare with a partner before you check answers with the class.

a paras. 2 and 3 (and possibly para. 1 – jeans and jacket are simple); **b** para. 1; **c** para. 4; **d** paras. 1, 2, 4 (and possibly para. 3 – the wig); **e** 4

2b Tell students to look at the table before they reread the text.

- Give students a maximum of five minutes to complete the table.
- When you go through answers with the class, check students understand *crisp* (clean, pure).
- Finally, ask students if they have worn or would wear any of the fashions in the table and why/why not?

Paragraph	1	2	3	4
Name of film	The Wild One	Breakfast at Tiffany's	Pulp Fiction	Memoirs of a Geisha
Main star	Marlon Brando	Audrey Hepburn	Uma Thurman	Zhang Ziyi
Year of film	1954	1961	1994	2005
Fashion trend started	black leather motorcycle jacket	simple black dress	crisp white shirt	kimonos and kimono accessories

VOCABULARY: adjective order

3 Elicit Marlon Brando's fashion trend: *black leather motorcycle jacket*.

- Elicit that the words before the noun are adjectives (or behaving like adjectives).
- Ask student what each adjective describes (e.g. black = colour).
- Then tell them to look at the table in exercise 3 to check.
- Give students five minutes to order the sentences and use their dictionary for difficult words.
- Ask them to compare with a partner before you check answers with the class.

1 a white pine dining table; **2** a green plastic garden chair; **3** a red silk evening dress; **4** a black wooden picture frame

LISTENING

4 Briefly discuss this question as a whole class.

Answers depend on students' own opinions.

5 Read through the introduction with the class and check students understand *upmarket* (expensive).

- Tell students to read the advice and check they understand *pressurise* (force people to do something).
- Ask students to compare with a partner before you check answers with the class.
- Finally, ask students if they would like a salesperson who followed this advice.

The following should be ticked: 2, 4. (The information giving these answers is bold in the audioscript below exercise 6a.)

GRAMMAR: expressions of quantity

6a Elicit an expression of quantity from the class (e.g. *a lot of*).

- Tell students to read sentences 1–10, then play the track.
- Ask students to compare with a partner before you check answers with the class.

The answers are underlined in the audioscript below.

If possible, reproduce the audioscript so that all the students can see it (maybe on an Interactive Whiteboard or an overhead projector). When you go through the answers underline them in the text.

Audioscript and answers to Exercise 5 and 6: Track 2.17

Manager, Chloe

M: Hello Chloe, good to see you. We've got 1 a little time before my next meeting, so … how are things going?

continued…

C: Very well, thanks. I've really enjoyed my first week here. I've talked to 2 a lot of the trainees and served 2 a few customers.
M: No problems, I hope?
C: Not really. There were just 3 a couple of customers who were a bit difficult, but they were OK in the end.
M: Good. Let me give you one or two tips while I have the time. First of all, 4 many trainees think they don't need to know anything about the rest of the store, but we've found the best sales staff are not just fashion specialists, **they also find out about the rest of the store so they can help customers when they're looking for other sections**. So don't forget, you'll need to answer questions about other departments, especially cosmetics and jewellery.
C: Right, that's good advice. By the way, I've noticed no one wears any kind of uniform in this department. Most of the assistants seem to be wearing designer labels. Is that your policy then?
M: Yes. We have 5 no rules about uniforms. Staff can wear some of our fashions. You see, you and your colleagues are models for our fashions as well as advisers. We picked up this idea last year in Milan during their fashion show. We visited a few of the top stores in Milan and learned a lot from them.
C: So you travel abroad?
M: Yes. I used to do all the trips on my own with 6 no help but last year I took 6 some of the assistants along with me. It's good training for them.
C: Wow! I didn't realise you did that. No wonder you keep your staff for years!
M: We believe in treating staff well, it's very important. Actually, we need to start thinking about next year's fashion shows – but we've got 7 plenty of ideas and we'll get 7 some information from the organisers soon.
C: Do you have any other tips for me, like, how to approach customers? I don't have a lot of sales experience.
M: I know, but you've got the right personality. Look, the best piece of advice I can give you is to give customers 8 enough time to make up their minds without any pressure. **Give them 9 a lot of attention and 9 plenty of advice but only when they need it.** It's your job to judge the right moment. OK? Never oversell or put too much pressure on a customer. We have 10 enough sales assistants to do the job properly.
C: Thanks very much. That's very helpful.
M: Good, well Chloe, I must be off to my meeting. I've enjoyed chatting to you. Well done, you've had a very good first week.

It's a good idea to briefly check students know the meaning of these quantifiers because the Language reference doesn't give the meaning of them all. Ask students which mean a lot (*plenty of*, *a lot of*, *many*), nothing/zero (*no*), a small number (*a couple of*), the right amount or not too much (*enough*).

6b Ask students to give you an example of a countable and an uncountable noun (e.g. *salesperson/advice*).

- Then give them a maximum of five minutes to complete the table.
- Tell them to use the information in the audioscript on page 179 if they aren't sure.
- Ask students to read G1 in the Language reference on page 152 to check their answers.
- Quickly go through answers with the class.

used with countable nouns	a couple of, a lot of, a few, many, no, plenty of, enough, some
used with uncountable nouns	a little, a lot of, no, plenty of, enough, some

For a full explanation, ask students to read G1 in the Language reference on page 152.

7 Students do the activity as per the Coursebook.

- Go through answers with the class.

1 a few; **2** some; **3** plenty of/a lot of; **4** a lot of; **5** a couple of/a few

8 Focus students on the categories and the table.

- Read the example below the table with the class to show them they need to finish the sentences themselves.
- Give students ten minutes to write as many sentences as possible.
- Move round the room pointing out mistakes with quantifiers but encourage students to self-correct.
- After ten minutes ask students how many sentences they wrote.
- Get a few sentences from the class.

SPEAKING

9 Give students three minutes to think about their answers.

- Put them in groups with a maximum of four so that all students have a chance to speak.
- Allow 10–15 minutes for the discussion.
- Monitor to note common mistakes when using adjective order or expressions of quantity.
- When they have finished, ask students for some factors that affect what we wear.
- Finally, correct some of the mistakes you noted earlier.

HOMEWORK OPTIONS

Students do the exercises on pages 68–69 of the Workbook.

Students do exercise G1 1 on page 153 of the Language reference.

Students write a paragraph about different trends in clothes, hair and accessories they have adopted at different times in their lives (e.g. 'When I was a teenager, I had my hair …, I used to wear'). They should say why they adopted these trends – or, if they have never followed trends, they should say why not and what factors *do* affect their choice of clothes, hair etc. (e.g. climate, job).

10.3 LIVING LONGER

IN THIS LESSON

Lesson topic and staging

This lesson looks at the fact that people in many parts of the world are living longer. Students read an article about living to 100. They then focus on the pronunciation of numbers in the text and practise using these. The article contextualises the grammar for this lesson: infinitives and *-ing* forms. Students do two activities to study which verbs take which form and then practise using them. Finally, students discuss statements about ageing populations.

Objectives

By the end of the lesson, students should have:

- practised reading a text to extract specific information and language items
- revised/learned the pronunciation of different numbers and practised using these
- revised/learned which verbs take the infinitive and/or the *-ing* form (e.g. *enjoy dancing*) and practised them
- learned more about and discussed the issue of ageing populations in modern society

Timings

If short of time, you could drop exercise 4 on page 107.

A possible lesson break would be after exercise 4 on page 107.

WARM-UP

- Focus students on the title of this lesson and then write the following on the board:
  - 1 Living to 100 is a good thing because …
  - 2 Living to 100 is a bad thing because …
- Divide the class into two groups (A and B) and tell As to discuss statement 1 and Bs to discuss statement 2.
- This issue is also discussed in exercise 1 question 5. Don't ask students here if they want to live to 100. Just ask them to discuss the pros and cons.
- Give them five minutes for the discussion, and to list as many reasons as possible.
- Mix As and Bs in pairs or groups of four.
- Tell them to persuade each other that living to 100 is a good or a bad idea.

READING

1 Focus students on the photos on pages 106–107 and ask them what's happening in each.

- Ask students why more older people are doing activities like these in some societies.
- Then explain that students are going to read an article about living to 100.
- Tell them to read questions 1–5 and check they understand *retire* (to stop work because of your age), and *pension* (money paid by government or privately to retired people).
- Allow five minutes for pairs to discuss the questions.
- For question 5, tell students to think about the pros and cons they listed in the Warm-up.

> Answers depend on students' own experience and opinions.

2a Give students a maximum of one minute for this activity.

- To follow up, ask students if families in their country/countries are getting smaller, as is the trend in Europe.

> **1** Because of the decline in infant mortality: fewer children died young due to better healthcare and better food production; **2** They're getting smaller, people are having fewer children.

2b Tell students to read the sentences before they read the text again.

- Allow a maximum of ten minutes for this activity.
- Ask students to compare with a partner before you check answers with the class. (Note: the answer to number 1 is in the second bullet point next to the title.)
- In feedback, check students understand *sharp rise* (a fast and large increase), *dramatically* (very significantly, a lot), and *top out* (stop increasing, become level).

> **1** 2030; **2** the 1950s; **3** 63.0 years; **4** 90; **5** 100; **6** around 2010; **7** 11 to 12 billion

When you check answers, listen to students' pronunciation of the numbers. This will help you decide how much time you need to spend on exercises 3a and 3b below.

pronunciation

3a Put students in pairs to say the numbers and discuss how they are pronounced.

- Ask a student to say each number to the class.
- Play the track for students to compare their pronunciation.
- Pause the track after each number for students to repeat.
- Correct their pronunciation.
- If necessary, play the track again to give more practice.

TRACK 2.18
100 *[a hundred]*, the early 1950s, 46.4, 40%, the year 2000, the year 2010 *[twenty ten]*, 500 million

3b Read the example with the class.

- Give students three minutes to note what each number refers to by looking at exercise 2b and the article.
- Put students into pairs to ask and answer questions.
- While they are working, monitor and note common mistakes when pronouncing the numbers.
- Finally, correct some of the mistakes you noted earlier.

For answers, see exercise 2b and the article.

To extend this activity and to give extra practice: Tell students to write five personally significant numbers on a piece of paper (e.g. the year they were born, the number of people in their country/city). Put students in pairs and tell them to ask each other 'What does xxx refer to?' and to give the answers. Tell them to ask follow-up questions (e.g. 'Is your country's population growing?').

4 Tell students to read the questions and try to answer some before they read the article again.

- Give them five minutes to check their answers and do the questions they couldn't remember.
- Ask them to compare with a partner before you check answers with the class.
- In feedback, check students understand *decline* (become less, get smaller).

1 because of a decline in infant mortality due to improved healthcare and better food production; **2** because of medical advances; **3** because new drugs will be available which will slow down the ageing process; **4** because people prefer to have fewer children and smaller families; **5** because the anti-ageing drugs will start to become more widely available

(!) Students may have problems with question 5 because it is a negative question. You may need to help students when you go through the answers.

GRAMMAR: infinitives and *-ing* forms

5a Elicit an example of an infinitive with *to* (e.g. *to go*) and an *-ing* form (*going*).

- Explain that when one verb follows another, the second verb may use an infinitive with *to*, an *-ing* form, or both.
- Check students understand *enable* in rule a (make it possible to do something).
- Students then do the activity as per the Coursebook.
- Go through the answers and notes in brackets with the class.

a infinitive with *to* (Note: *people* is the object here.); **b** infinitive with *to*; **c** *-ing* form OR infinitive with *to* (Note: there is no difference in meaning here.); **d** *-ing* form

5b Focus students on the table and example answers already given.

- Allow a maximum of ten minutes for this activity.
- Ask students to compare with a partner before you check answers with the class.
- Tell students to read the GRAMMAR TIP.

Tell students to draw a bigger table in their notebooks to give them space to write the answers.

Verbs followed by (object +) infinitive with *to*	Verbs followed by *-ing*	Verbs followed by both forms
want promise manage expect allow decide teach hope	enjoy suggest	start continue like love begin hate advise

(Note: *like/love* + infinitive with *to* is more common in US English.)

For a full explanation, ask students to read G2 in the Language reference on page 152. Pay particular attention to the section about *would*.

6 Students can use their dictionaries to check the verbs not introduced in exercises 5a and 5b (e.g. *gave up*).

- Go through answers with the class.

Students can add any new verbs to the table in exercise 5b as a record.

1 a, b; **2** b, c; **3** a, c; **4** a, b; **5** a, c; **6** a, b

For extra practice, ask students to do exercise G2 3 and 4 on page 153 of the Language reference.

SPEAKING

7a Read through the instructions and statements with the class.

- Check students understand *compulsory* (a rule, you have to do this), *birth rate* (how many children are born), *look after* (take care of), *treats* (how you behave towards someone), *treating illness* (make it better) and *overweight* (fat).
- Give students three minutes to do this activity.

Answers depend on students' own opinions.

7b Allow 10–15 minutes for students to discuss the statements.

- Encourage them to give reasons and ask each other questions if necessary.
- Finally, ask the class which statements they agreed or disagreed with strongly and why.

HOMEWORK OPTIONS

Students do the exercises on pages 70–71 of the Workbook.

Students do exercise G2 3 and 4 on page 153 of the Language reference.

Students write a paragraph on the pros and cons of living to 100.

Students write a letter to the magazine in which the article on page 106 appeared. In the letter, they should explain their opinions on two of the statements in exercise 7a. When you mark the paragraphs, pay particular attention to the use of infinitive with *to/-ing* form.

10.4 SCENARIO: BELLEVIEW

IN THIS LESSON

Lesson topic and staging

This lesson focuses on reading and listening to extract specific information and the language of meetings (e.g. stating the purpose, encouraging others to speak, making a point, summarising, etc.). The scenario is a seaside town that has changed greatly over 30 years. Students read two texts comparing the town now and 30 years ago, and then listen to councillors talking about different problems. Next, students read two texts expressing positive and negative opinions of the town. Students then listen to a councillor talking to residents and focus on the KEY LANGUAGE. Finally, the TASK asks students to hold a meeting to discuss the town's problems.

Objectives

By the end of the lesson, students should have:

- extracted specific information and language items from reading and listening texts
- learned useful phrases for holding a meeting
- used this language in a 'real-life' situation to discuss problems and find solutions
- participated effectively in extended speaking practice

Common European Framework

Students can use language effectively to hold a meeting and solve problems.

Timings

If short of time, you could ask students to only read 'Belleview, UK: today' and to answer question 2 in exercise 1.

A possible lesson break would be after exercise 3b on page 108.

WARM-UP

- Ask students to think about their town/city/country and how it has changed in their lifetime.
- Tell them to write four to five changes.
- Put students into small groups to compare the changes and say how they feel about these.
- For feedback, ask the class if their changes were similar or different to the other students.

SITUATION

1 Focus students on the photo and ask them if this looks a nice place to live.

- Tell students this is a seaside town called Belleview, and they are going to read about it.
- Focus students on the titles of the texts (Belleview, UK; 30 years ago and Belleview, UK; today) and ask how they think the town might have changed.
- Students then do the activity as per the Coursebook.
- In feedback, ask students if they would prefer to live in Belleview today or 30 years ago, and why.

> 1 It's much livelier now, there are more young people, two new universities, English language schools, an airport, many more restaurants and nightclubs; it's also more noisy, not very safe and has its share of social problems; 2 answers depend on students' own ideas

2a Explain that a town council is the local government of a town in the UK and the mayor is the head councillor.

- Tell students to write the three categories on a separate piece of paper so they have room to make notes. Advise them to record answers in note form.
- Play the track and then ask students to compare answers with a partner.
- If necessary, play the track again.
- Go through answers with the class and make sure students have all the information so they can refer to it in exercise 2b.
- Finally, ask students if there is any vocabulary they need help with.

When you check answers, make sure students understand *parking attendants*, *parking ticket* and *parking fine*. This vocabulary is needed for exercise 4a later.

> 1 cars: parking is a problem; number of cars increasing; car owners pay big fines for parking tickets; visitors complain because parking difficult and expensive; 2 beaches: people don't like paying to go on beaches (American idea); feel a beach is public land; 3 young people: bad behaviour getting worse; don't move for older people on pavements; rude on buses; noisy and badly-behaved late at night; bad image for town (Information giving these answers is bold in the audioscript below.)

If you think there is too much for each student to write, put them into groups of three and tell each student to focus on a different category. Students then compare their notes. If you have weaker students, ask them to make notes on 'beaches' because there is less information to process.

Audioscript and answers to Exercise 2a: Track 2.19

Mayor, Councillor 1, Councillor 2

M: Let's talk about the quality of life here. In my opinion, the situation's getting serious. I get letters every day from people complaining about one thing or another. There seems to be a feeling that Belleview isn't a very nice place to live in anymore.

C1: I don't know about that. Older people aren't very happy, but young people enjoy living here. But there are some worrying trends, I must admit – things we need to sort out.

M: Oh yes?

C1: **1 Well, parking, for instance. More and more people have cars** … so, what do we do? We employ an army of parking attendants to put tickets on cars. **Car owners have to pay big fines, they aren't happy, and visitors complain because parking's so difficult and expensive.** I hear car owners are going to demonstrate to draw attention to the problem.

M: Hmm, parking is a huge problem, I agree. An attendant even tried to put a ticket on my car the other day! What else do you think people are unhappy about?

C1: **2 Well, they certainly don't like paying to go on some of our beaches. I think we made a big mistake following the American trend, charging people to use beaches. It's been very unpopular with everyone. People feel the beach is public land, so why should they pay to go on it?**

M: OK, but they don't seem to understand – the money is used to improve the beaches' facilities and keep them clean.

C2: Sorry, could I just say something, please?

M: Of course, go ahead.

C2: I'd like to mention something else which is annoying people – **3 bad behaviour by young people**. It's getting worse every year. You know what I mean. **They stand around on the pavements, and don't get out of the way if older people want to pass. And in the buses, they never offer their seat to women with young children. It's so impolite. And what about late at night! They're so noisy and badly-behaved. People can't stand this kind of behaviour – it creates a really bad image for the town.** We've got to do something about it. The situation's getting out of control.

2b Give students three minutes to discuss this question in pairs and give reasons.

- Get ideas from a few pairs and ask other students if they agree.

> Answers depend on students' own opinions.

3a & **b** Read through the introduction and explain that the letter and email are replies to an article in the local newspaper. (Note: The article referred to here is *not* the article activity in exercise 1.)

- Tell students the email is on the left and the letter on the right.
- Give students a maximum of five minutes to underline the main points.

- Tell them to use their dictionaries or ask you for help with vocabulary.
- Put students into pairs and give them three minutes to swap information.
- Go through answers with the class.
- Finally, ask students if they sympathise more with the email or the letter.

Email main points: doesn't agree with criticisms; Belleview is a great town; a lot to do; good nightlife; good sports facilities; council should sell the aquarium to build a new sports centre
Letter main points: not happy with living in Belleview in recent years; more focus on young people (than older people); not enough places for older people to enjoy themselves; beachfront is now for younger people; town centre noisy and not safe at night; unhappy about rumour that aquarium will be sold

If possible, reproduce the texts so that the whole class can see them (perhaps using an Interactive Whiteboard or an overhead projector). When you go through the answers with the class, ask a student to underline the main points in the text they read.

KEY LANGUAGE: the language of meetings

4a Check students understand *residents* (people who live in an area).

- Tell students to read the questions before you play the track.
- Ask students to compare with a partner before you go through answers with the class.
- Finally, ask students if they think the residents are right to complain.

1 Complaints are: have to wait a long time for a parking permit; parking attendants give too many fines; not enough car parks; **2** Actions agreed: explain the situation to parking attendants; ask council to think about building more car parks. (Information giving these answers is bold in the audioscript under 4b below.)

4b Ask students to read the sentences and try to fill gaps before you play the track.

- Ask students to compare with a partner before you check answers with the class.

1 to discuss; **2** unhappy with; **3** acceptable; **4** look into; **5** could I just; **6** point; **7** comment; **8** sum (Answers are underlined in the audioscript below.)

Tell students that all the phrases are on page 152 in the Language reference.

Audioscript and answers to Exercise 4: Track 2.20
Councillor, Resident 1, Resident 2

C: Good morning everyone. Thanks for coming. We're here 1 to discuss the parking problem in your area. First of all, tell me what the problem is, exactly, and then we'll look at solutions. Yes, Mrs … er, go ahead please.

R1: Thank you, I'm Ingrid Oberman. To be honest, I'm very 2 unhappy with the present situation. **I've been waiting for over a year for a parking permit. I contacted your office and they tell me there's a long queue**, and that I have to wait my turn. It's not fair.

C: Mmm, I understand how you feel – it's a long time to wait, I must say. But you must understand our position. There are more and more cars for the spaces available. Frankly, I'm not sure I can do anything to help.

R1: I don't agree. For one thing, you could tell parking attendants not to issue so many fines. **If you park in the wrong space for just two minutes, a parking attendant rushes up, puts a ticket on your car, and you get a £40 fine**. Ridiculous! It's not 3 acceptable – I'm sure you understand that.

C: Mmm, I see how you feel. Look, I'll 4 look into the matter and talk to the parking department. That might help …

R2: Sorry, 5 could I just say something please.

C: Yes, Mr Ashley, please make your 6 point.

R2: Well, I strongly believe **there are not enough car parks in the town**. Why not build more car parks? If you did that, there'd be more spaces for parking outside our house or apartment. At the moment I'm spending £400 a month to rent a garage. I can't afford to do it much longer.

C: Thank you for your 7 comment. But there's no easy answer. As you know, car parks cost a lot of money, and take time to build. We have other big projects that need finance, and our budget is limited. But I note your suggestion… [*fade*]

C: Well, to 8 sum up, I'll **talk to the parking attendants and explain the situation to them**, that you feel they're doing their job a little too efficiently, and I'll **ask the council to look into the possibility of building more car parks**. Thanks very much everyone. Have a good day.

5 Do the first example as a whole class and then give students five minutes to match the phrases.

- Go through answers with the class and emphasise the functions (e.g. encouraging people to speak).

An easier way to do this activity is to ask students to put each phrase from exercise 4b under the functions in the OTHER USEFUL PHRASES box. Students can then check their answers by looking at the KEY LANGUAGE on page 152 of the Language reference.

TASK: participating in a meeting

6a Ask students to read the introduction and then divide them into three groups (A, B and C) with two or three students in each group. If you have a larger class, you could either put more than three students in some of the groups or form six groups (i.e. two group As, two Bs, two Cs).

- Make sure students only look at their group's information.
- Move round the room to make sure all students understand their information.

6b Put students into new, larger groups so that there are mayor and councillors, younger residents and older residents in each.

- Tell students to use the KEY LANGUAGE and OTHER USEFUL PHRASES in their meeting.
- Give students 20 minutes to discuss the problems and decide on the solution to each.
- While students are speaking, note mistakes they make with the KEY LANGUAGE and OTHER USEFUL PHRASES.
- When they have finished, ask each group which solution they decided on for each problem.
- Finally, correct some of the more common mistakes you note earlier.

If you have more than one group after you have put the groups from 6a together, the mayor and the residents' leaders will not be able to lead *all* the meetings. Tell students that the council representative (either the mayor or the councillor) leads the discussion in each group.

HOMEWORK OPTIONS

Students do the exercises on page 72 of the Workbook.

Students do exercise KL 5 on page 153 of the Language reference.

Students write a summary/the minutes of the meeting in exercise 6b, recording what was agreed.

Students write a short entry in a travel brochure to describe their own city/town/country, or the one they are studying in. They can use the example in the situation on page 108 for ideas.

Students write an email or a letter to their local paper describing how their city/town has changed in the last five to ten years and saying whether they think this is a good or a bad thing. They can use the email and letter on page 108, and points they discussed in the Warm-up activity for ideas.

10.5 STUDY AND WRITING SKILLS

IN THIS LESSON

Lesson topic and staging

This lesson focuses on how to record/learn words and on describing trends in writing. Students read about English vocabulary and discuss ways they record words. Next, students try three ways of recording words clearly. Then students listen to people talking about learning vocabulary and decide which techniques they might use. Students then study words to describe trends. Next, students read a report and consider the order of paragraphs and how to avoid repeating phrases. Finally, students write a short report themselves.

Objectives

By the end of the lesson, students should have:

- learned about methods and techniques for recording and learning vocabulary
- extracted specific information and language items from a reading and a listening text
- extended their range of vocabulary to describe changes and trends
- analysed and written a short report on trends in household types (e.g. married, one person)

Common European Framework

Students can write a report to describe changes and trends.

Timings

If short of time, you could ask students to do exercise 4 at home and decide which method suits them. Then check answers in the following lesson. Alternatively, students write the report in exercise 8 at home.

A possible lesson break would be after exercise 5b on page 111.

WARM-UP

This activity introduces the idea of recording vocabulary clearly.

- Ask the class to look quickly at lesson 10.1 and tell you what area of vocabulary was covered (phrasal verbs).
- Tell them to close their Coursebooks and in pairs try to remember as many verbs as possible.
- If students can't remember them all, tell them to look at their notes (if they have any).
- Ask the class if their notes help them (the answer from many students will be 'No'). Then ask students if they have any particular method for recording or helping them to remember vocabulary, and elicit a few examples.

- Finally, tell students that the first part of this lesson is about recording vocabulary clearly.

STUDY SKILLS: recording and learning vocabulary

1 Students discuss this question in pairs.
- Get a few ideas from the class.

Answers depend on students' own opinions.

2 Ask students if they can guess how many words there are in English and how many they need to learn to understand the majority of things they hear in everyday life in an English-speaking community (2,500 words make up about 80% of everything we say and hear).
- Then give them 30 seconds to read the text and check their predictions.
- Students then do the activity as per the Coursebook.
- Go through the answers with the class and check students understand *active vocabulary* (words you use) and *passive vocabulary* (words you recognise but don't generally use).
- Finally, ask students if they agree that it's easy to communicate generally in English, but more difficult to say exactly what you mean.

1 vocabulary; **2** communicate; **3** grammar; **4** words; **5** active; **6** read

3 Tell students that in order to learn *exactly* what words mean and how they are used, you need to record them clearly.
- Give students a maximum of three minutes to write 1, 2 or 3 in the boxes.
- Then allow at least five minutes for students to compare with a partner.
- Finally, ask students which items (1–8) they will try to do in future.

4 If you did the Warm-up activity, ask students if their vocabulary notes were clear and why/not.
- Then read through the introduction to exercise 4 with the class.
- Students then do the activity as per the Coursebook.
- Tell students to look at Units 8, 9 and 10 in the Coursebook (which cover the topics listed under a) or use a dictionary for help with the meaning of words.
- Go through answers with the class. (Note: the method in c is one of matching words to pictures/symbols. The charts and tables are examples of pictures you could use to help you remember the words *pie chart*, *bar chart* and so on. Method c is not suggesting that pie charts themselves are a good way of recording vocabulary.)

- Finally, ask students which method they will try using in future. Suggest they try a different method the next few times they record vocabulary. This will help them decide which method they find most useful.

a Topic headings

Education	**Engineering**	**Trends**
get a degree revise for exams hand in an essay	build a prototype do safety tests solve a problem	follow fashion go out of fashion start a craze

b Diagrams: Add one word to each empty branch in the clothes circle. Accept any reasonable answers.; **c** Pictures/symbols: **1** pie chart; **2** bar chart; **3** (line) graph; **4** table; **5** flow chart

To help students focus on the benefits of each method (a–c), ask students to stop working after a and quickly discuss with their partner how useful the method was. Then tell them to do b, and repeat this procedure until they have done and talked about all three methods.

When you have checked answers with the class, put students into pairs or small groups and ask them to discuss *additional* methods they use. Finally, get examples from the class and ask students which of these additional methods they would find most useful and might try in the future.

5a Learning vocabulary
- Lead in by asking students if they find it easy or difficult to learn and remember vocabulary.
- Tell students to read the introduction and items a–f.
- Play the track and pause after each speaker to give students time to answer.
- Finally, ask students if they already use any of these methods.

a 2; **b** 6; **c** 1 **d** 5; **e** 3; **f** 4

5b When you get students' answers to this question, ask them why/why not?

TRACK 2.21
1 I like to test myself by putting new vocabulary I want to learn onto cards. I put an example sentence with the word or phrase missing on one side of the card. On the other side I put the word or phrase. I often test myself when I'm on the train.
2 I like to organise new vocabulary under topic areas, for example verbs, nouns and idioms connected to a subject, like crime, so I can concentrate on learning vocabulary on the same theme.
3 I like to have word families in my vocabulary book. I test myself by starting with a verb or noun and then try to remember adverbs or adjectives, and synonyms and opposites.
4 For difficult vocabulary I try to make a link with my own language, so I try to think of a word that sounds the same, and I remember the new word that way.
continued…

> 5 I like to record new vocabulary onto a tape and listen and repeat when I'm driving my car. I think pronunciation is really important.
> 6 I try to note down five new words each day and learn their meaning. What I do is write them on post-it notes and stick them on a board in my office.

WRITING SKILLS: describing a trend

6a Explain that students are going to write a short report on changes and trends, but are first going to look at some useful vocabulary.

- Focus students on the symbols in the table and ask them to guess what each one means.
- Then read through the instructions and do the first example with the class.
- Give students five to ten minutes to complete the table.
- Check answers with the class.

↑	↓	↳	→
increase (verb/ noun) go up (verb) rise (verb/ noun) grow (verb)	drop (verb/ noun) decline (verb/ noun) fall (verb/ noun) decrease (verb/ noun)	level off (verb) stabilise (verb)	remain stable

6b Do the example (number 1) with the class and show how the graph represents the words.

- Give students five to ten minutes to complete the activity.
- Ask them to compare with a partner before you check answers with the class.

> **1** a slow/steady/gradual/significant fall/drop/ decline/decrease; **2** a sharp/significant increase/ rise; **3** a slight increase/rise; **4** a sharp/sudden/ dramatic drop/decline/decrease; **5** a steady drop/ decline/fall/decrease; **6** a steady increase/rise

Students may interpret these graphs in different ways. Demonstrate each one using your hands, e.g. *a sudden fall* = move your hand along flat and suddenly let it drop. Alternatively, give examples, e.g. *a significant fall* = from 100 to 25.

7a Tell students the text is a report about spending on entertainment in different areas.

- Focus students on the bar chart and orientate them by asking a few questions (e.g. 'Which country spent the most/least on music/magazines?').
- Then give students three minutes to do the activity.
- Go through answers with the class.

> **a** 2 ('Overall, ...'); **b** 4 ('We conclude ...); **c** 3 ('For all three ...'); **d** 1 ('This bar chart ...')

7b Avoiding repetition

The aim of this activity is to focus students on avoiding repetition, but also to introduce a further set of phrases they can use in exercise 8.

- Explain that repeating the same vocabulary many times in one text is not 'good style' in English.
- Tell students to try to do this activity without looking in their dictionaries.
- Ask them to compare with a partner and then go through answers with the class.

> results – findings; carried out – commissioned by; study – survey; shows – finds; double – twice as much; greatest increase – largest rise; slight – small; sharp rise – sudden increase; significant decrease – marked fall; fairly constant – relatively stable

8 First, focus students on the chart and check they understand *household* (the people living in a home/ house) and *lone* (single).

- Give students three minutes to discuss the chart with a partner.
- Then give them 20 minutes to write their description.
- Monitor to point out mistakes students make, but encourage them to self-correct.
- Finally, take the work in for marking, paying particular attention to organisation, repetition and the phrases from exercises 6 and 7b.

To encourage proofreading and editing: When students have finished their descriptions, tell them to swap with another student and comment on organisation, repetition and use of phrases from exercise 6 and 7b. Students make corrections if necessary.

HOMEWORK OPTIONS

Students do the exercises on page 73 of the Workbook.

Students do exercises KL 5, V1,2 6 and V2 7 on page 153 of the Language reference. (Note: some of the vocabulary comes from previous lessons.)

Arts and media

11

11.1 TYPES OF MEDIA

IN THIS LESSON

Lesson topic and staging

This lesson looks at media genre. Students think about how often they use various media, then read and listen to some reviews introducing vocabulary describing them. Next, students look at words to describe media genres (e.g. *plot, classic*) and try a method for recording vocabulary from lesson 10.5. Students then discuss their favourite TV programmes, books, etc. and write a review of one of these. Finally, students discuss setting up a museum collection for books, film or recorded music.

Objectives

By the end of the lesson, students should have:

- extracted specific information and language items from reading and listening texts
- expanded their range of vocabulary to describe types of media genres
- written a review
- discussed different types of media genres

Timings

If short of time, you could drop exercise 7 and ask students to write their review for homework.

A possible lesson break would be either after exercise 3b on page 112 or exercise 5c on page 113.

WARM-UP

This activity focuses on music that students like.

- Tell students they are going to a desert island (an island with nothing on it) to live. They can take food, water and three pieces of music.
- Give them three minutes to write down the three pieces of music they'd take with them.
- Then put them into small groups and ask them to tell each other which music they chose and why.
- Encourage them to ask each other questions to get as much information as possible.
- Finally, ask each group if any choices were the same, or if they chose modern or classical music.

Andy Warhol quote:

This quote means that with more and more access to the media, more people will become known to the public – but only for a short time. This idea is something that now seems to be happening with reality TV.

(i) Andy Warhol: 1928–1987. An American artist involved in the Pop Art movement of the 1960s. He is famous for creating paintings of everyday commercial products (e.g. a can of tomato soup), and of celebrities such as Marilyn Monroe and Elizabeth Taylor.

READING AND LISTENING

1a Focus students on the photo on page 112 and ask students if they know who this is and what she's famous for. (The photo shows the French actress Audrey Tautou at a photo call for the film *The Da Vinci Code* at the 2006 Cannes Film Festival.)

- Put students in pairs to discuss how often they use the different media.
- For feedback, ask students which medium they use most.

> Answers depend on students' own experience.

1b Keep students in the same pairs as exercise 1a and give them a maximum of five minutes to do this activity.

- Ask two or three students for their answers.

> Answers depend on students' own experience.

An important aim of exercises 2a, 2b, and 3a is to introduce new vocabulary related to the media. Tell students to keep a record of the new words and expressions they learn because these will be useful when they write a review in exercise 7 on page 113.

2a Give students a maximum of one minute to read the texts and decide the type of media.

- Ask students to compare with a partner before you check answers with the class.

> Review 1: TV [words/phrases that help: series (a collection of programmes on the same or similar topic), sound, filming techniques, narration, documentary]; Review 2: CDs [words/phrases that help: music, two-disc set]; Review 3: computer games [words/phrases that help: graphics (pictures and images), instruction menus (used for telling the player what to do)]

(i) David Attenborough: Born 1926. British nature documentary maker.

Mozart: 1756–1791, Austrian classical composer.

2b Lead in by asking students what symbols reviewers often give to show how much they like something.

- Elicit/give star ratings and tell students to look at the star ratings in the box.
- Give students five minutes to read the texts again and use their dictionaries for unknown vocabulary.
- Ask students to compare with a partner.
- Go through answers with the class and help with any phrases they didn't find in their dictionaries.
- Finally, ask students if they would watch or buy any of the products.

If students need to look in their dictionaries for a lot of the words, allow them five to ten minutes for this activity.

Answers will depend on students' interpretation but the most logical answers are: Review 1: excellent [words/expressions: breathtaking; groundbreaking; superb; masterpiece], Review 2: average or good [words/expressions: high cost might make some people think twice, might still be worth buying], Review 3: terrible or poor [disappointed, just about adequate, impossible to follow, nothing exciting happens, think long and hard before buying this one]

3a & **b** Set the activity and play the track without pausing.

- Ask students to compare with a partner before you check answers with the class.
- Students may find Reviews 5 and 6 more difficult. If necessary, for Reviews 5 and 6 tell students that a *novel* is a book telling a story, and that *viewers* are the people watching a TV programme.
- Help students with any descriptive words or phrases they don't know as this will help them give a star rating in exercise 3b. Alternatively, ask them to look at the audioscript on page 180 and use their dictionaries.

Review 4: radio, likely star rating ****; Review 5: books, likely star rating *; Review 6: TV, likely star rating ***** (Note: this is a TV programme reviewing old films.) (The information giving these answers is bold in the audioscript below.)

Audioscript and answers to Exercise 3: Track 2.22

4

Good morning listeners. Last night, I attended the first live recording of the **new comedy series** *It's a Laugh,* which is **going out on Radio Comedy Channel 1**. It'll be on every Monday evening for six weeks. I'm pleased to report that the series lives up to its name. It's hilarious. Some of the jokes don't always work but overall I really recommend it. You'll enjoy yourselves.

5

Even though you're probably fans of his, I'm sorry to tell you all that **there's no real plot**. It's meant to be a **gripping thriller** but nobody seems to have a reason for doing anything. I couldn't relate to any of the **characters**. This is the worst **novel** I have **read**

continued...

recently. I found the first few **chapters** very heavy going. I know his first novel was excellent but this was a huge disappointment.

6

Good evening, **viewers**. The first of the old films we're discussing tonight is *Dracula,* the 1931 version. It's a classic example of the horror genre and I'm sure it'll keep you on the edge of your seats. It made Bela Lugosi an international star and its dark atmosphere is truly frightening.

i Boris Karloff: 1987–1969. An English actor who made mostly horror films in the USA. His most famous movie is *Frankenstein* (1931) in which he played the monster.

VOCABULARY: media genres

4a Lead in by asking students if they've read or seen the films of the Harry Potter series, if they like hospital dramas, if they listen to the radio, and if they like horror movies.

- Give students 30 seconds to read the four reviews and say if they are positive or negative.
- Then give students five minutes to complete the gaps, using their dictionaries if necessary. If students use their dictionaries, tell them to only find the words in the box and not other words in the text. Other vocabulary is looked at in exercise 4b.
- Go through answers with the class.

1 novel; **2** plot; **3** chapter; **4** episode; **5** series; **6** atmosphere

4b Students do the activity as per the Coursebook.

- Ask students to compare with a partner before you check answers with the class.
- In feedback, elicit/give the meaning of *edge-of-your-seat suspense* by miming and facial expression.
- To follow up, ask students if they've seen *ER* and/or *Psycho* and if they agree with the reviews.

1 gripping; **2** incomparable; **3** moving; **4** groundbreaking; **5** outstanding; **6** hilarious; **7** classic; **8** breathtaking

5a Read through the instructions with the class and show them where *documentary* has been put.

- Give students a maximum of five minutes to complete the mind map.
- Ask them to compare with a partner before you check answers with the class.

radio/TV programmes: documentary, series, hospital drama; types of music/CDs: classical; cinema/books: novel, horror

5b Give students five to ten minutes for this activity.

- Tell students to use their dictionaries to find words they don't know. (Note: some words can go under more than one category.)
- When you go through the answers, check *page-turner* and ask students for examples of some of the genres. Students will discuss which genres they like in exercise 6 so don't spend too much time eliciting their preferences at this stage.

Ask students to work in pairs for this activity so they can teach each other words they don't know. In feedback, draw the mind map on the board and fill in the words or ask students to fill them in.

> radio/TV programmes: sitcom, soap, current affairs programme, crime, animation, reality, science fiction; types of music/CDs: reggae, jazz, folk, country, hip hop, opera, soul; cinema/books: page-turner, crime, animation, autobiography, science fiction

5c Allow five minutes for students to do this activity individually.

- Put them into pairs to compare and teach each other new words.
- Go through answers with the class and add them to the mind map on the board.
- Check the class understands the words added.

> Answers depend on students' own knowledge.

6 Give students two minutes to think about their answers before putting them into groups to discuss.

- Allow 10–15 minutes for the discussion.
- Encourage students to ask each other questions to get as much information as possible.
- In feedback, ask students which was the most popular genre in each category.

Groups should have a maximum of four students so that everyone gets a chance to speak.

WRITING

7 Give students two minutes to decide which genre their review is about and prompt with ideas if necessary.

- Point out to students that the language in the reviews on pages 112–113 is relatively simple and that reviews tend to use a lot of adjectives.
- Allow 15–20 minutes for students to write their reviews.
- Monitor to help with extra vocabulary if necessary.
- Ask students to swap their reviews with a partner and decide if, for example, they would like to read this newspaper or visit this website.
- Finally, take the reviews in for marking, paying attention to the use of vocabulary from this lesson.

To extend this activity, when students have finished their reviews, post them round the room. Ask students to read all the reviews and decide which newspaper or magazine they would like to read, which radio programme they would like to listen to, or which website they would like to visit. To follow up, tell students to read, listen to or visit the newspaper/magazine, the radio programme, or the website and to write another review giving their own opinions.

SPEAKING

8 Read through the situation with the class and check they understand *Arts Council* (a government department that gives money to arts projects) and *grant* (the money they give).

- Divide the class into three groups (A, B and C) and give them ten minutes to prepare their case.
- Tell all the students in each group to make notes.
- While they are working, monitor to help with extra vocabulary if necessary.
- Then form new groups so that there is at least one A, one B and one C student in each group.
- Give students 15–20 minutes to present their case and listen to others.
- Encourage them to ask each other questions to get as much information as possible.
- While students are speaking, monitor and note mistakes when using the vocabulary from this lesson.
- When they have finished, ask the whole class to discuss the merits of each case and then vote on which media will get the grant. (Note: students cannot vote for their own medium.)
- Finally, correct a selection of the mistakes you noted earlier.

HOMEWORK OPTIONS

Students do the exercises on page 74 of the Workbook.

Students do exercises V1,2,3,4 6 and V2,3 7 on page 155 of the Language reference.

Students read, listen to or visit the newspaper/magazine, the radio programme, or the website they read about in exercise 7, and write another review giving their own opinions.

Students write an email to the Arts Council telling them which medium they chose to award the grant to and giving their reasons.

11.2 MEDIA RECLUSES IN THE ARTS

IN THIS LESSON

Lesson topic and staging

This lesson looks at famous recluses in the arts. Students read about three recluses and swap information with others. Next, students study arts-related vocabulary from the texts and then discuss their opinions on recluses and celebrities. The texts contextualise the grammar focus for this lesson: reported speech. Students do a series of activities looking at the form and practise using reported speech. Finally, they use this grammar in a speaking activity.

Objectives

By the end of the lesson, students should have:

- practised extracting specific information and language items from a reading text
- extended their range of vocabulary in the context of the arts
- participated in a speaking practice activity on the topic of celebrities and the works they produce
- revised/extended their knowledge of reported speech and practised using these forms

Timings

If short of time, you could drop exercise 4 on page 115. Alternatively, set exercise 3 on page 115 for homework and check answers in the following lesson.

A possible lesson break would be after exercise 4 on page 115.

WARM-UP

This activity helps you find out if students can use reported speech.

- Ask students to think of one of the following: their favourite book, film, piece of music, TV show, newspaper or magazine. Then tell them to summarise why they like it in one short sentence. (They can take notes to help them remember the sentence if necessary.)
- Ask students to move round the room telling others the book, film, or piece of music, etc. they chose and why they like it.
- When they move on to the next student, they have to report what the previous student said before giving their own information (e.g. First: 'Maria said she …'; Second: 'I like … because …').
- While they are speaking, listen to find out if students are using reported speech.
- Finally, ask students if anyone had the same or similar tastes in books, films, etc.

READING

1 Focus students on the lesson title, article heading and the two photos: can they predict what the article might be about? Do any students know who Syd Barrett was?

- Set the activity and give students a maximum of one minute to read the introduction to check their answer. (Make sure students don't read the text on page 114 at this stage.)
- Elicit the answer from the class.
- To follow up ask students if they can name any famous recluses.

> b (Note: this answer depends on the phrase *decided not to play the media game*, i.e. they do the opposite of most celebrities described in the introduction.)

2a Use the follow up in exercise 1 as a lead in to this activity.

- Ask students to read the questions before they read their text.
- Tell students to use their dictionaries to help them answer question 1, but not to worry about other vocabulary because they will study this in exercise 3.
- Give students five minutes to read their text and answer the questions.
- Don't check answers at this stage because students will swap information in exercise 2b.

2b Give students a maximum of nine minutes to swap information (three minutes for each student).

- Quickly go through answers with the class.

> **1** Syd Barrett: an eccentric genius, content, polite; J.D. Salinger: reclusive, enjoys being with people, friendly; Stanley Kubrick: perfectionist genius, said to be eccentric, reclusive, rude and tactless; **2** Syd Barrett: *Piper at the Gates of Dawn*; J.D. Salinger: *The Catcher in the Rye*; Stanley Kubrick: *2001: A Space Odyssey*; **3** They didn't want to talk to the media, they were reclusive, not a good relationship; **4** Syd Barrett: walked, painted, gardened, said he 'wasted time' ; J.D. Salinger: writes (for himself), travels all over the world; Stanley Kubrick: continued to make films; **5** Answers depend on students' own opinions.

2c Give students two minutes individually to read the questions and decide which questions they can answer.

- Put them back into groups to swap information and complete the questions.
- Finally, go through answers with the class. (Don't ask follow-up questions at this stage because exercise 4 provides a follow-up discussion.)

1 Stanley Kubrick; **2** J.D. Salinger; **3** Stanley Kubrick (and possibly Syd Barrett – a bald, fat man said Syd couldn't talk); **4** Stanley Kubrick; **5** J.D. Salinger; **6** Syd Barrett; **7** Stanley Kubrick; **8** Syd Barrett; **9** Stanley Kubrick; **10** J.D. Salinger

John Lennon: one of the Beatles pop group in the 1960s and early 1970s. Shot by Mark Chapman.

VOCABULARY: words connected with the arts

3 Keep students in the same groups as exercise 2 for this activity.

- Tell students to only find the words from their own text (see brackets after each definition).
- When they have found the words, tell them to swap information with the others in their group.
- Go through answers with the class.

An alternative procedure: Students use all three texts to find the words, but tell them to only look at the paragraphs referred to in the brackets.

1 a hit; **2** a bestseller; **3** a blockbuster; **4** a masterpiece; **5** a household name; **6** a critic; **7** royalties; **8** an epic; **9** a rumour

SPEAKING

4 Put students in the same groups as exercise 2.

- Check they understand *the right to a private life* in question 2 (natural or legal permission to have privacy).
- Allow ten minutes for the discussion.
- Finally, ask each group to tell the class their answer(s) to one of the questions.

When you elicit answers to question 4, write one or two on the board. You will be able to use these as an example in exercise 8.

GRAMMAR: reported speech

5a Lead in by asking students if they can give you an example of reported speech.

- Give students one minute to read the example and note their answer. (Note: students should focus on the part of the sentence in italics.)
- Ask them to compare with a partner before you check answers with the class. In feedback, tell students that *told* is an example of a reporting verb.

While students are thinking about this question, write the example on the board. When you elicit answers, circle the relevant part of the sentences and tell students to do the same in the Coursebook.

The subject changes (*I* = *He*) and the tense changes (*travel* = *travelled*).

5b Read through the example with the class and ask them to underline it in the text.

- Give students a maximum of five minutes to find and underline the other examples.
- Ask students to compare with a partner before you check answers with the class. (Don't highlight the changes made in the examples at this stage. Students will study this in exercise 6a.)

1 Syd told the reporter that he walked a lot.; **2** A bald, fat man [answered the door and] said that Syd couldn't talk.; **3** Syd asked him to leave.; **4** [One of his] professors insisted he was the worst English student in the history of the college.; **5** He told a reporter that he liked to write but that he wrote for himself.; **6** She added that he enjoyed being with people.

6a Students do this activity individually and then compare answers with a partner.

- Go through answers with the class.

1 the verbs change tense (from the tense used in direct speech); **2** told, said, asked, insisted, added; **3** after the reporting verb asked (asked him *to leave*). (Note: we can also use the infinitive with *to* after *told* but in this case *told* means *instructed, requested, ordered*. There is no example of this in the answers to Exercise 5b.) **4** *tell* needs a personal object

6b Read through the introduction with the class.

- Give students a maximum of one minute to answer the question and compare with a partner.
- Elicit answers from the class.

Present simple becomes past simple (5b, numbers 1, 4, 5 and 6); *can* becomes *could* (5b, number 2)

GRAMMAR TIP

Read through the grammar tip with the class and give examples of pronoun change from exercise 5b. Alternatively, use the grammar tip to ask a question ('What changes do we make to pronouns?') and elicit the answer from the class. (Note: there are no changes to adverbs in 5b.)

For a full explanation, ask students to read G1 in the Language reference on page 154.

7 Do the first example with students by writing the direct speech on the board and eliciting changes.

- Give students ten minutes to complete this activity.

- Move round the room pointing out mistakes, but refer students to exercises 5b, 6a, 6b and the Language reference if they need help.
- Ask students to compare with a partner before you check answers with the class.

To make the answers clear, write the direct speech on the board and elicit changes for each sentence.

> **1** The band said (that) they expected their new CD to be a big hit.; **2** He said (that) he was writing a new article today/then/that day.; **3** She said (that) she had just finished writing a new book for her publisher.; **4** He said (that) Val had refused to speak to the reporters yesterday/the day before.; **5** They said (that) they would finish the recording tomorrow/the next day.

For extra practice, ask students to do exercises G1 1 and 2 on page 155 of the Language reference

8 To lead in to this activity, remind students of one of the rumours they discussed in exercise 4 (if you followed the tip, you will have written examples on the board).

- Read through the example in the Coursebook with the class.
- Give students one minute to think of a rumour.
- Tell students to move round the room to speak to as many students as possible.
- After five minutes, tell students to sit down and make quick notes to help them remember.
- Then give students five to ten minutes to write the rumours in reported speech.
- While they are working, monitor to point out mistakes, but refer students to exercises 5b, 6a, 6b and the Language reference if they need help.
- When they have finished, get ideas from four or five students.
- Finally, ask students which was the most interesting rumour they heard.

For another example, ask students who told them one of the rumours in exercise 4 and use this information to change the direct speech into reported speech, e.g. Jill said that Nicole Kidman was having a baby.

HOMEWORK OPTIONS

Students do the exercises on pages 75–76 of the Workbook.

Students do practice exercises G1 1 and 2 on page 155 of the Language reference.

Students note interesting/surprising/funny/sad things that people say to them for the next few days. They then write these in reported speech and tell other students about them in the next lesson(s).

11.3 THE LIFE OF A FOREIGN CORRESPONDENT

IN THIS LESSON

Lesson topic and staging

This lesson looks at foreign correspondents and their jobs. Students listen to a journalist talking about a job interview. This contextualises the grammar focus: reported questions. Students do a series of activities to study the form of reported questions and then practise using them. Next, students read about a British foreign correspondent and then focus on vocabulary in the text. Finally, students use reported questions in a speaking and writing activity.

Objectives

By the end of the lesson, students should have:

- extracted specific information and language items from a listening and a reading text
- revised/learned about the form and use of reported questions
- practised using reported questions in an extended speaking and writing activity

Timings

If short of time, you could drop exercises 7b and 8 on page 117 and set them for homework. If very short of time, you could drop all the READING activities and either set them for homework or do them in another lesson.

A possible lesson break would be after exercise 5 on page 116.

WARM-UP

This activity helps you find out if students can use reported questions.

- At the beginning of the lesson, ask the class a few questions, e.g. 'Did you have a good weekend/ evening/morning? What are you doing after the lesson?'
- Make sure the questions sound as normal as possible and just part of the class routine.
- When you've listened to answers and asked follow-up questions, ask students if they can remember what you asked them.
- Put them in pairs to tell each what they can remember, beginning with the words 'He/she asked us …'.
- Get ideas from the class and listen for their use of reported questions.
- Finally, tell students they will be studying reported questions later in the lesson.

LISTENING

1 Focus students on the three photos at the bottom of page 116 and ask them what job these people are doing (foreign correspondent).

- Go through the introduction and emphasise that in the conversation Richard is talking *about* the interview (not the interview itself).
- Put students into pairs or small groups to discuss the questions.

2a Tell students to read the questions before you play the track.

- Ask students to compare their answers with a partner.
- Check answers with the class.
- Finally, ask students if any of the questions they guessed in exercise 1 were mentioned.

1 Because he enjoys travelling and he wants travelling to be part of his job as a journalist.; 2 He thinks he's got a good chance of getting the job.

2b Give students one minute to read the questions and tick those they can remember.

- Then play the track without pausing.
- Ask students to compare with a partner before you check answers with the class.

(Note: The audioscript is under exercise 4a below.)

The following should be ticked: 1, 2, 4, 5, 6, 7, 8 and 10.

3 Put students into pairs or small groups for this activity.

- In feedback, ask how many students would/wouldn't like the job.

GRAMMAR: reported questions

4a Focus students on the example and ask them to underline the reported question in the audioscript on page 180.

- Then give students three minutes to find and underline the other examples.
- Check answers with the class.

If possible, reproduce the audioscript so that the whole class can see it (perhaps on an Interactive Whiteboard or an overhead projector). Underline the examples with the students.

The numbers before each answer refer to the questions in 2b above. **1** She asked me why I wanted to be a foreign correspondent; **2** … she wanted to know what parts of the world I was interested in; **4** She asked if I spoke any foreign languages; **5** She wanted to know where I'd gone to university;

continued…

6 [she wanted to know] if I'd taken any further qualifications; **7** She also wanted to know what articles I'd written; **8** … she asked me what qualities a journalist needed to be a foreign correspondent; **10** … she asked if I was physically fit. (Answers are bold in the audioscript below.)

Audioscript and answers to Exercise 2:
Track 2.23
Nura, Richard

N: Hi, Richard. How did you get on in the interview? Did it go well?
R: I don't know really. I think so.
N: So … what kind of questions did they ask you?
R: Well, the editor of the newspaper did most of the talking. **1 She asked me why I wanted to be a foreign correspondent**, and obviously I was expecting that. I said that I'd travelled a lot when I was a student, that I enjoyed travelling and that now I was a journalist, I wanted it to be part of my job. Then **2 she wanted to know what parts of the world I was interested in.**
N: Mmm, what did you say?
R: Well, all the Arab countries, and South America. I told her that I also knew Brazil and Argentina well, so they would be interesting to report on.
N: I see. What else did she ask you? Those questions don't sound too difficult.
R: No, they weren't really. Well, the subject of languages came up. **4 She asked if I spoke any foreign languages.**
N: Ha! That was an easy one for you!
R: Yeah, I told her I was bilingual in English and Arabic, and that I spoke Spanish and Portuguese fluently. She seemed pretty impressed.
N: I'm sure she was. Did she offer you the job on the spot?
R: Not quite. **5 She wanted to know where I'd gone to university**, **6 and if I'd taken any further qualifications. 7 She also wanted to know what articles I'd written**, and so on. There was only one difficult question really …
N: Oh yeah?
R: Mmm, **8 she asked me what qualities a journalist needed to be a foreign correspondent**. I wasn't sure how to answer that one.
N: How did you handle it?
R: Well, I said, obviously, I'd never done the job, but I had thought about it. I said that foreign correspondents had to be able to make decisions without waiting for people to tell you what to do. So, they needed to show initiative when they were reporting in a foreign country.
N: I think that's a really good answer. Was she pleased?
R: She seemed to be. Anyway, there were a few more questions, then at the end, **10 she asked if I was physically fit.**
N: Funny question, but I suppose it's important if you travel a lot in your job.

continued…

R: Yes, true. Anyway, I said that I went to the gym three times a week, so I should be.
N: Good answer. Do you think you'll get the job?
R: I've got a good chance, I think, but I wasn't the only candidate. I'll just keep my fingers crossed, and hope for the best.

4b Tell students to look at the examples in the audioscript when answering these questions.

- Ask students to compare answers with a partner.
- When you go through the answers, ask students to give you the relevant example from the audioscript.

1 yes/no questions; **2** doesn't change; **3** statement; **4** often changes tense

For a full explanation, ask students to read G2 on page 154 of the Language reference

5 Allow students ten minutes for this activity.

- Monitor to point out mistakes, but refer students to exercises 2b, 4a, 4b and the Language reference if they need help.
- Ask students to compare with a partner before you check answers with the class.

To help students, tell them to first decide if the question is a *yes/no* or a *wh-* question.

1 They asked me if I was good at reporting.; **2** They asked me if I was able to/could write notes quickly.; **3** They asked me what time I usually started work.; **4** They asked me If I enjoyed working as a reporter.; **5** They asked me what I did when people didn't answer my questions.; **6** They asked me how much time I spent travelling abroad.; **7** They asked me if I ever felt afraid in a crisis.; **8** They asked me what problems I had when I was reporting.

For extra practice, ask students to do exercise G2 4 on page 155 of the Language reference.

READING

6 Put students in pairs or small groups and give them three minutes to discuss the questions.

- Get a few ideas from the class.

Answers depend on students' own opinions and ideas.

7a Ask students if they have ever seen Rageh Omar on the television (he used to report on BBC World and currently works for Al Jazeera English, an international television news channel based in Doha, Qatar).

- Tell students to read the questions (a–e) before they read the extracts.
- Tell students not to worry about problem vocabulary at this stage because they will study it in exercise 8.
- Go through answers with the class.

1 e; **2** d; **3** a; **4** c; **5** b

7b Give students five minutes to read the extracts again and answer the questions.

- Ask them to compare with a partner before you check answers with the class.
- Follow up by asking if students would like to do this job more (or less) than at the beginning of the lesson.

1 para. 5; **2** para. 2; **3** para. 1; **4** para. 1; **5** para. 2; **6** para. 4; **7** para. 3

8 Tell students to look at the sentence around the words to try to guess the meanings.

- If necessary, students can use their dictionaries.
- Ask students to compare with a partner before you check answers with the class.
- Check students' pronunciation of these words.
- Finally, help students with any other words they want to know the meaning of.

1 wangle; **2** traineeship; **3** single out; **4** brought home to; **5** daunted; **6** chutzpah; **7** integrity

SPEAKING AND WRITING

9 Read through the instructions with the class and check they understand *witnessed* (saw something happen).

- Give students one minute to decide their important news event.
- Then give students ten minutes to write questions and prepare notes. Tell them not to look at each other's questions/notes at this stage.
- Allow five to ten minutes for the interview.
- Then give students 15 minutes to write the account.
- Monitor to point out mistakes with reported speech but encourage students to self-correct.
- Finally, ask two or three pairs to read their accounts to the class.
- Take the accounts in for marking, paying particular attention to reported speech.

HOMEWORK OPTIONS

Students do the exercises on pages 77–78 of the Workbook.

Students do practice exercise G2 4 on page 155 of the Language reference.

Students watch/listen to an interview on television/radio, note the questions asked and then write an account. For example, He/she asked if …, and then asked whether … . (Note: it is not important if the original interview is in English or the student's own language.)

11.4 SCENARIO: THE SILVER SCREEN

IN THIS LESSON

Lesson topic and staging

This lesson focuses on the language of comparing and contrasting (e.g. *it's much better than*). Students are introduced to the scenario of a TV broadcaster deciding on a new film to produce. Then, they listen to two executives talking about film-making and focus on the KEY LANGUAGE of comparing and contrasting. Next, students read four proposals for new films and listen to the directors talking about them. Finally, students use this information to discuss which film should be produced.

Objectives

By the end of the lesson, students should have:

- extracted specific information and language items from reading and listening texts
- learned useful phrases for comparing and contrasting
- used this language in a 'real-life' situation to compare and contrast given information and reach a decision
- participated effectively in extended speaking practice

Common European Framework

Students can use language effectively to compare and contrast given information.

Timings

If short of time, you could drop the number of films students discuss by omitting one or two of the written proposals and their corresponding listening texts in exercise 5a.

A possible lesson break would be after exercise 3 on page 118.

WARM-UP

This activity focuses on the topic and vocabulary of film genres introduced earlier in this unit.

- Write the following film genres on the board:
  - Horror
  - Comedy
  - Musical
  - Science fiction
  - Animation
- Tell students to order the film genre from most to least favourite.
- Put them into pairs to compare their lists and give reasons. Monitor to find out if students are using comparative structures in their discussion because this will help you decide if students need reminding in Exercises 6 and 7 on page 119.

SITUATION

1 Focus students on the photos and ask if anyone they know has been involved in making a film. Focus students on the title of this lesson ('The silver screen') and elicit or explain the meaning (it refers to movies and movie making). The 'screen' is the surface that movies are projected onto at the cinema. 'Silver' refers to the silver used in screens in early Hollywood movies.

- Set the question and ask students to discuss their ideas in pairs.
- Get a few ideas from the class and check students understand *raise its profile* (become better known).

> Answers depend on students' own ideas.

2a Set the context and check students understand *direction they want to follow* (the way they want to do things).

- Play the track and then elicit answers from the class.

> No, they disagree on the direction to follow.

2b Ask students to read the list (1–8) and tick the items they can remember from the first listening.

- Then play the track again and tell students to tick the items they didn't remember.

> The following should be ticked: 1, 3, 4, 6, 8. Students might also tick: 5 (something which will really sell around the world).

KEY LANGUAGE: comparing and contrasting

3 Give students a few minutes to try to complete the sentences without listening again.

- Play the track and if necessary pause at the places shown in the audioscript to give students time to write.
- Ask students to compare with a partner before you check answers with the class.
- Finally, tell students the KEY LANGUAGE is listed on page 154 of the Language reference.

> **1** very different from; **2** same as; **3** quite similar to; **4** much better than; **5** less important than; **6** a lot worse (The sentences with these answers are bold in the audioscript below.)

> **Audioscript and answers to Exercises 2 & 3:**
> **Track 2.24**
> *Dan, Bob*
> D: Well Bob, you know I think that this is a great opportunity for the company, but **1 it's very <u>different from</u> the kind of things we've done in the past**. We could make a lot of money, but we could also lose a lot. [PAUSE]
>
> *continued...*

B: Dan – don't worry too much. **2 It's the <u>same as</u> TV really, just everything's bigger**. [PAUSE]
D: I hope you're right. I just want a safe investment, something **3 which is <u>quite similar to</u> the sort of stuff we usually make.** I think some kind of mystery is the sort of thing most people really like. [PAUSE]
B: Now, that's where we disagree again. I think this is a great opportunity to do something very different – you know, a proper big budget film, something which will really sell around the world, and **4 something <u>much better than</u> what we've been doing recently**. You know, those rather sad mini-series about unhappy housewives. I don't think the genre is that important really. It could be action, adventure, or even a musical. It just has to be different! [PAUSE]
D: I see your point Bob, but we need to be sure exactly what we want. What are our main criteria for investing?
B: Well for me it has to be down to the originality of the idea. That's what'll get people interested and help sell it.
D: Yes, I understand that, but I also think the experience of the director is important. They can make or break a film and they make a difference to its sales.
B: True. Actually, **5 I think the director is <u>less important than</u> the location, though**. I think we need plenty of locations around the world so people see places they've been to or would like to visit. So the film becomes aspirational.
D: Mmm, good point, and a variety of locations will help to sell the film in different places. It'll have more international appeal, but if we choose a film like that it'll be more expensive, don't forget. We have to think about cost.
B: Yes, we do, but if we want a big hit, we'll need to spend more.
D: Maybe I'm being too careful, but I don't want to spend millions and find **6 we have something <u>a lot worse</u> than our usual TV series.**
B: Yes, you *are* a careful person Dan. Maybe that's why you're successful. But film-making is always a big risk, whether for TV or cinema.

TASK: choosing a film to produce

4 Read through the instructions with the class.

- Give students eight minutes to read the four 'pitches' and to add information to the chart. (Point out that they can only fill in some areas of the chart: they will learn more from the listening in 5a and b.)
- Monitor to check students are answering the questions correctly and to clarify any difficult vocabulary.
- Don't go through answers with the class at this stage (this will be done after exercise 5b).

Answers for exercise 4 are given (bold) in the chart below exercise 5b.

5a Keep students in the same groups as exercise 4 for this activity.

- Explain that students are going to listen to the four directors of the proposed films in the pitches (1–4) they read in exercise 4.
- Play the track without pausing.
- Ask students to quickly compare answers with the rest of their group before you check answers with the class.

Pitch 1: Extract 4; Pitch 2: Extract 1; Pitch 3: Extract 2; Pitch 4: Extract 3

5b Keep students in the same groups as exercise 4 for this activity.

- Explain that while they listen, students will be able to complete more of the chart in exercise 4.
- Pause the track after each extract to give students time to fill in the rest of the chart.
- Ask students to compare with their group before you check answers with the class.
- If necessary, refer students to the audioscript on page 180 in the Coursebook.

Answers to exercise 5b (and exercise 4, in bold)

	Hands Up	Alien Attack	Exit Strategy	Midnight Sun
Genre	**Romantic comedy**	Science fiction	Thriller	Action/ adventure
Locations	**Very romantic (e.g. Venice, St Petersburg,** Moscow), smart, luxurious hotels, magnificent villas, country houses	Cheap locations, film in the studio	Many locations around the world, USA, Switzerland, Australia and Brazil	Japan and the Philippines
Actors/ cast	**Unknown but real people**	Director will decide	Lead actress = major Hollywood star	Unknown actor (very good-looking and charismatic), unknown actress
Special features	**See Locations;** terrific script, funny situations and clever dialogue	Stunning special effects, exciting visually, hundreds of spaceships flying across the screen	Twists and turns in story, probably a sequel, lead character becomes female James Bond	Choreographed fight scenes, will be done by best choreographers in the business
Ending	Sad (because audiences want something different)	Uncertain (so they can make a sequel)	A big surprise	Happy (so audience with be satisfied)
Budget	**$40-50 million**	$60-80 million max	At least $100-120 million	$50-70 million max

If possible, for exercises 4 and 5b, reproduce the chart so that the whole class can see it (perhaps using an Interactive Whiteboard or an overhead projector). As you go through answers, fill in the chart.

Track 2.25

1

What can I say – who doesn't enjoy this sort of film? Look how successful *Star Wars* was. I know a lot of people in the business and I don't think I'll have problems casting for the film. There are a couple of big stars I might be able to get. I promised not to mention their names until I get finance for the project, but they're very interested. Also, the special feature of the film will be the special effects – they'll be out of this world! *[laughs]* I know it's really important to get a good special effects guy. The top man in Hollywood is Jack O'Brien, and he's a personal friend of mine.

As you know, I've done a few films in my time, some good, some bad. But this one's looking real good to me. I like the script. It's not just an action film – it doesn't just depend on special effects. There's a lot of interest in how the group of survivors work together to save the planet. The ending will be uncertain so we could make a sequel. We won't need to spend money on a lot of locations as we can make the whole film in the studio. The budget will be about $60–80 million, but a lot of that is for the special effects. We'll have hundreds of spaceships flying across the screen.

2

I jumped at the chance to buy this script. It's written by a young writer called Mark Fulton, who's becoming very popular. The script is based on his *first* book – it was a bestseller and it introduces Fulton's main character, Melanie Drake. This is really the special feature – the character of Melanie Drake. She's a great character – beautiful, mysterious and cool – and she always manages to get out of dangerous situations by using her intelligence and charm. She'll make money for you for years to come. I don't know exactly who'll play her yet, but it'll be one of the biggest female stars in Hollywood. I know the budget is big, probably about $100–120 million, but as well as a big star, there'll be locations all over the world – the USA, Switzerland, Australia and Brazil. There'll be a lot of twists and turns in the story and the ending will be a big surprise. I realise we could easily go over budget if we're not careful. But the return on your money could be fantastic. Remember, if you don't back me, you may regret it for the rest of your lives.

3

The simple stories are always the best in this business. The film will appeal to people all over the world. Asian filmgoers love this type of film, and now cinema fans in other countries are becoming really interested. People nowadays want films to have a good story line, a real hero and heroine – someone they can admire. I have in mind a young, unknown actor who wants to play the main role. He's very good-looking and charismatic – I think he'll become an international star, like Bruce Lee. The leading female role will also be played by an unknown actress. The fight scenes are of course the special feature – one lasts over ten minutes. They will be choreographed by the best in the business. Almost all of the action will take place in Japan and the Philippines. There won't be a lot of dialogue in the film, so it'll be easy to dub, and distribute worldwide. It's a very moral story with a happy ending, so audiences will go away satisfied.

continued…

The budget will be about $50–70 million. I've made this sort of film before, when I worked in Hong Kong.

4

I really hope you'll support this project, I'm confident it'll make a lot of money for all of us. We've got a top camera crew who'll do most of the filming. The special feature is the terrific script. Very well written, funny situations and clever dialogue. Everyone who's read it thinks it's great. The action takes place mainly in Venice – it's such a romantic location – and also Moscow. We'll use unknown actors for the main parts because we need real twins. We'll save money here, so a lot of the money will go on finding really good locations for the big scenes – you know, smart, luxurious hotels, magnificent villas and country houses, and so on. The sets will look fantastic – audiences love that sort of thing. The budget will need to be between $40 and $50 million. The ending will be sad because there are too many films with happy endings these days. I think audiences want something different. I know this'll be my first full-length film, and I'm really excited about it. I just know it'll make my reputation and lead to other big projects.

6 Ask students to look again at the topics in listening exercise 2b and elicit if they think any of these are more important than others when choosing which film to produce. Explain *criteria* by telling students that the items in the list in exercise 2b are all ideas for helping you decide which film to make, i.e. criteria.

- Then give students three minutes to add criteria to exercise 2b.
- Go through the OTHER USEFUL PHRASES box on page 119 and remind students of the KEY LANGUAGE.
- Put students into groups of three or four and give them 15 minutes for the discussion. Tell them to use the criteria listed in exercise 2b and the criteria they added earlier in this activity to help them make a decision.
- Monitor to note mistakes they make with the KEY LANGUAGE and OTHER USEFUL PHRASES.

7 Ask each group which film they chose and their reasons.

- Encourage other groups to disagree if necessary.
- Vote on the final decision.
- Finally, go through any mistakes you noted earlier.

HOMEWORK OPTIONS

Students do the exercises on page 79 of the Workbook.

Students do exercise KL 5 and V1,2,3,4 6 on page 155 of the Language reference.

Students write a letter to the director of the film they chose to produce in either Exercise 6 or 7. They should give the reasons for their choice.

11.5 STUDY AND WRITING SKILLS

IN THIS LESSON

Lesson topic and staging

This lesson focuses on delivering a talk and writing a report in the context of organising a street festival. Students discuss how to deliver a talk effectively, then look at and listen to mistakes people often make. Next, students listen to and practise delivering a sample talk. They deliver a talk from notes provided, before preparing and delivering one of their own. Students then focus on writing a report. They read a sample report and look at how to make generalisations. Finally, students write a report based on the talk they gave earlier.

Objectives

By the end of the lesson, students should have:

- discussed advice on how to give a talk and delivered one of their own
- extracted specific information and language items from a reading and a listening text
- learned how to make generalisations in English when writing a report and written one of their own

Common European Framework

Students can write a report using language to make generalisations.

Timings

If short of time, you could set exercise 8 for homework.

A possible lesson break would be after exercise 5 on page 120.

WARM-UP

This activity introduces the topic of festivals and events.

- Put students into small groups and give them three minutes to name as many famous festivals as they can.
- Elicit the lists to the board and give one point for each festival. Give another point to any student who can give two pieces of information about a festival.

STUDY SKILLS: delivering a talk

1a Check students understand *talk* as a noun.

- Allow pairs five minutes to discuss the statements.

1b Allow five minutes for this activity.

- Get ideas from the class and make sure students give their reasons.
- Try to reach agreement on which pieces of advice are generally not a good idea.

> Answers depend on students' opinions but *generally* statements 5, 6, 10 are not good. Statement 10 depends on how many questions you think is good (a very large number is not good). Statement 3 is a good idea but not necessarily at the beginning of the talk and not if you can't tell jokes well. Statement 4: you don't need to speak in a loud voice but your voice should be clear.

2 Lead in by focusing students on the photo on page 121 and elicit *festival*. Explain that the talk students will hear is about a festival.

- Ask the class what kind of mistakes people make when giving a talk.
- Set the activity and ask students to read the four descriptions.
- Play the track and then get answers from the class.
- Finally, ask students if they are guilty of any of these mistakes if they give a talk.

> **1** the rambler; **2** the gabbler; **3** the mumbler; **4** the 'no plan' presenter

Track 2.26

1

Good morning, everyone. I want to talk about our plans for the music and dance festival in September. It was a pity about the rain last year, wasn't it? It rained so much and people got really fed up. Only a few people attended each day and the festival was a total disaster. We were all so disappointed – the sponsors weren't very happy, I can tell you. OK, let me get back to the subject. We plan this year to invite local dance groups and musicians as well as performers from abroad. I've divided my talk into three parts, so first, I'll tell you what arrangement we've made regarding bookings … *[fade]*

2

Hi everyone, I'm going to talk about our plans for the music and dance festival in September. I'm sorry, I'm a bit nervous, but I'll do my best to tell you how we're going to arrange things. My talk is divided into three parts. First, I'll talk about how the performers make bookings – in other words, how much they have to pay – where they can get forms, and so on. Then I'll talk about how we're advertising the festival, finally, I'll explain why this will be a very good festival for you to sponsor. If you have any questions, please interrupt me at any time. Is that all right everyone? *[fade]*

3

Good morning, everyone. It's nice to see you all. Thank you for giving up your time to listen to me.

I'm going to talk to you about our plans for the music and dance festival in September. Let me tell you about how I'd like to organise my talk. First, I want to talk about our booking system, where performers can get the application forms, what the entrance fee is, and so on. After that I'll talk about how we'll advertise the festival, and finally, I'll explain why you should sponsor the festival. *[fade]*

continued…

4
Hi everyone, well, I'd like to talk about our music and dance festival which takes place in September. I was thinking of telling you about the overseas performers we've invited, but maybe I'll do that later on. How about this? Why don't you ask me some questions and I'll try to answer them. *(SILENCE)*. Oh right, OK then, as you don't seem to have any questions, let me think about some points I can cover. Well ... you're probably interested to know how the dancers and singers can apply for the festival. OK, we've produced an application form, erm ... they put down some details about themselves and enclose the fee ... *(fade)*

3 Explain that students are going to practise delivering the beginning of the talk from exercise 2.

- Play the track and ask the class why it is well-delivered (see exercise 2 above).
- Give students one minute to read the transcript quietly (but not silently) to themselves.
- Then put them into pairs and tell one student to deliver while the other listens, then vice versa.
- After each delivery, tell the listener to make comments on their partner's performance.
- Finally, ask if anyone would like to deliver the talk to the rest of the class.

Track 2.27
Good morning, everyone. Thank you for coming to my talk. I'm going to tell you about our plans for the music and dance festival in September. I've divided my talk into three parts. I'll start by telling you about the kind of performers we're trying to attract and I'll mention some well-known people who'll attend the festival. Next, I'll discuss how we're advertising the event – what plans we have for that. I know that's of interest to you. Finally, I'll explain why this will be the ideal festival for you to sponsor. I'll be pleased to answer any questions at the end of my talk. Is that OK, everyone? Good. Right, let me tell you about the performers we hope to ... *(fade)*

People are normally very nervous about giving a talk in public. Don't force anyone to give a talk in open class. Exercises 3, 4 and 5 use pairs or small groups to make students feel more secure. Encourage them by giving lots of praise, don't correct too much and make your comments general rather than specific.

4 Give students three minutes to read their notes.

- Then put students into A/B pairs to deliver/listen to the talks and ask each other questions.
- While they are speaking, monitor to note good points and mistakes (rambling, mumbling, etc.).
- Finally, go through the good points you noted earlier and then some of the mistakes.

5 Give students one minute to decide on their festival and prompt with ideas and vocabulary if necessary.

- Then give 10–15 minutes for students to prepare.
- While they are delivering the talks, monitor to note good points and mistakes (rambling, mumbling, etc.)
- Finally, go through the good points you noted earlier, and then some of the mistakes.

WRITING SKILLS: a report

6a Ask students to read the headings and then give them two minutes to read and match.

- Go through answers with the class.

1 E; **2** B; **3** C; **4** F; **5** D; **6** A

6b Allow a maximum of three minutes for this activity.

- Get a few ideas from the class.

1 over 50,000 people attended, the weather was [mostly] good, performers were excellent and well received by the public, acts for children were popular, performers started and finished on time, music and dance routines of Ethiopian group, on the whole people satisfied with food and service, gave great pleasure to many people, brought together different cultural communities, generally sponsors pleased with the organisation; **2** reduce crowds at popular events, more signs, more variety of food, programmes of daily events, accommodations for mothers with young children, more security staff, advertise the event earlier

7 Making generalisations

- Read the introduction and examples with the class.
- Give students two minutes to find other examples.
- Elicit answers and write them on the board.

People attending were mainly families, people of all ages, a large number from, the majority were singers ..., a wide variety of, almost all of ..., perhaps the highlight of, there were many, on the whole, some people, a large number of people, in general, most of them

8 Give students 20 minutes to plan and write their reports.

- Monitor to help with vocabulary and to point out mistakes.
- When they have finished, ask them to swap with another student and ask if they would like to go to the festival they read about.
- Finally, take the reports in for marking, paying attention to the use of generalisations.

HOMEWORK OPTIONS

Students do the exercises on page 80 of the Workbook.

12 Crime

12.1 REAL CRIMES?

IN THIS LESSON

Lesson topic and staging

This lesson looks at crimes and how serious we think they are. Students discuss different crimes and their levels of seriousness. They then read a text about a crime and then do a series of activities to focus on vocabulary contained in the text. Then students discuss issues arising from the text. Finally, students write a letter to a newspaper giving their opinions on the crime.

Objectives

By the end of the lesson, students should have:

- discussed the levels of seriousness of different types of crime
- extracted specific information and language items from a reading text
- expanded their range of vocabulary in the context of crime
- written a letter to a newspaper giving their opinions on a crime

Timings

If short of time, you could drop exercises 3b and/or 4 on page 123, but make sure you teach the meaning of the three items of vocabulary in exercise 4. Alternatively, set writing exercise 7 for homework.

A possible lesson break would be after exercise 4 on page 123.

WARM-UP

This activity introduces the topic of anti-social behaviour and how students feel about it.

- Write the following on the board:
  - Someone stole your wallet.
  - A family member lied to you.
  - A close friend borrowed money from you and didn't return it.
  - A friend read your diary.
  - You were asked to leave the class because you are always late.
- Tell students to think about how they would feel about each statement.
- Then ask them to move round the class and speak to other students to find someone who feels the same.
- Finally, ask a few students how they felt about each statement and if any others felt the same.

Woody Allen quote:

This amusing quote is based on the English phrase 'crime never pays' (i.e. you will be punished for what you do). *Pays* does not necessarily mean *money* but does mean *benefits someone*. The quote contradicts the phrase by pretending crime is a 'real' job and saying that it's a good choice for a career.

SPEAKING

1a Lead in by focusing students on the photo on page 122 and ask them what is happening.

- Then ask the class if they think this is a 'serious' crime.
- Set the activity and give students two minutes individually to decide their opinions on the activities and check vocabulary in their dictionaries.
- Put them into groups of three or four and allow ten minutes for the discussion.
- Get a few ideas from one or two groups.

1b Give students three minutes individually to decide their three additional activities.

- Move round the room to help with vocabulary if necessary.
- Then put students into the groups from exercise 1a and allow ten minutes for the discussion.
- Get a few ideas from each group and ask the class if they agree.

To extend this activity, elicit five examples of 'quite serious crimes' from exercise 1a and write them on the board. Ask students to order them from most to least serious. Students should agree/disagree with each other and give reasons. Finally, ask each group for their order and ask the rest of the class if they agree.

READING

2 Tell students to read the introduction and then elicit an example of *things teenagers do* that are against the law (e.g. under-age driving).

- Put students into pairs and give them three minutes to discuss their ideas.
- Get a few ideas from two or three pairs.

3a Focus students on the title of the report and check they understand *cyber* (relating to messages and information on the Internet).

- Tell students to read the questions before they read the text.
- Tell them not to worry about unknown vocabulary because this will be studied in exercises 5a and 5b.
- Ask students to compare with a partner before you check answers with the class. At this stage, don't ask students how serious the crime was because they will discuss this in exercise 6.
- In feedback, check students understand *sick of the sight of* (looking at something makes you feel ill, normally because you've had too much of it), *random* (not ordered or organised) and *donated* (gave something to a charity).

1 £1,600 ($2,000) of chocolate; **2** Dublin, Republic of Ireland; **3** by placing an order on the Internet and giving a random credit card number; **4** an American company; **5** an Argentinean man; **6** four days; **7** Some chocolate was eaten by the boy, some chocolate was recovered by the police and the family and donated to a children's charity in Dublin, the boy wasn't charged, he's sick of chocolate.

3b The aim of this activity is to introduce the words *distressed*, *dumbfounded* and *remorseful*.

- Give students three minutes to reread the text and answer the questions, and to use their dictionaries if necessary.
- Check answers with the class and ask which words gave them the answers.
- Finally, check students can pronounce the three words.

1 a (distressed); **2** b (dumbfounded); **3** a (remorseful)

4 Give students a few minutes to think about their experiences. If students don't want to talk about their own experiences, they can talk about someone they know or have heard about.

- Then give pairs five minutes to describe their experiences.
- Encourage students to ask each other questions to get as much information as possible.
- If your students know each other well, you could ask them for the most surprising/amusing/frightening experience they heard about. If you think this would be too personal, ask students if anyone would like to tell the whole class about one of their experiences, but don't push them to do so.

VOCABULARY: crime, technology and money

5a Go through the examples with the class and ask them to underline these words in the text.

- If necessary, tell students to use their dictionaries for the other words they find. (Note: the columns headed 'Technology' and 'Money/business' are not checked in exercise 5b. Give students the meaning of any words they don't know in these columns or ask them to use their dictionaries.)
- Ask students to compare with a partner before you check answers with the class.

To make feedback clear, draw the table on the board and fill in the words as you elicit them.

Crime/law	Technology	Money/ business
criminal (noun); case (noun); legal (adjective); police (noun); fraud squad (noun); investigating (verb); fraud (noun); witnessed (verb); evidence (noun); juvenile (noun); charged (verb); false pretences (adjective/ noun); offender (noun)	surf (verb) cyber (adjective) Internet (noun) computer (noun) Net (noun)	credit card (noun) ordering (verb) home deliveries (noun) order form (noun) placed an order (verb) goods (noun) order (noun) suppliers (noun)

5b Ask students to compare with a partner before you check answers with the class.

- Most words in the 'Crime/law' column are checked in exercise 5b. However, you will need to teach *fraud squad* and *false pretences*.

1 case; **2** legal; **3** fraud; **4** investigate; **5** witness; **6** evidence; **7** juvenile; **8** charge; **9** criminal/ offender

6 Give students two minutes to think about the questions.

- Put them into small groups and allow a maximum of ten minutes for the discussion. (Note: If you are going to use the Task extension below, tell students not to discuss question 2.)
- While students are speaking, note common mistakes they make with the vocabulary from exercise 5.
- Get a few ideas from two or three groups.
- Finally, correct mistakes you noted earlier.

To extend this activity, instead of discussing question 2 during exercise 6, use it as a role play. Put students into groups of four and tell them to choose one person each. Each student must choose a different person. Then give them ten minutes to explain to each other what they would do. Tell students to ask each other questions and to give their opinions on what other students say they would do.

WRITING

7 Explain that 'the newspaper' is the one in which the report on page 123 appeared.

- Tell students to read the beginning and ending of the letter.
- Give them five minutes to make notes on what to write.
- Move round the room to provide vocabulary if necessary.
- Then give students 15–20 minutes to write their letters.
- When they have finished, ask them to swap with a partner for proofreading.
- Then give them three minutes to make any changes to their letters.
- Finally, take the letters in for marking, paying particular attention to organisation of ideas and the vocabulary from exercise 5.

Alternatively, when students have made final changes to their letters, post them round the walls. Ask students to read all the letters to find out if they and other students share similar opinions.

HOMEWORK OPTIONS

Students do the exercises on page 81 of the Workbook.

Students write a letter giving their opinions of one of the activities in exercise 1a on page 122.

Students research other cyber crimes (perhaps using the Internet) and then report back to the class on their findings.

12.2 THE CAUSES OF CRIME

IN THIS LESSON

Lesson topic and staging

This lesson looks at different causes of crime. Students listen to three criminals talking about their crimes. Then, they read a text about different theories on the causes of crime and decide which theory might explain the crimes they heard earlier. Next, students look at word combinations from the reading text and practise using these. Then students focus on the third conditional from the earlier listening text. Students do activities focusing on the meaning, form and use of the third conditional. Finally, students discuss issues related to crime and criminals.

Objectives

By the end of the lesson, students should have:

- practised extracting specific information and language items from a listening and a reading text
- extended their range of word combinations (e.g. *criminal + behaviour*)
- revised/extended their knowledge of the third conditional and practised using this form
- discussed topical statements about crime in an extended speaking practice.

Timings

If short of time, you could drop exercise 8 on page 125 and set it for homework. Alternatively, cut the number of discussion items in exercise 9.

A possible lesson break would be after exercise 5b on page 125.

WARM-UP

This activity revises the first and second conditionals in preparation for the third conditional introduced in this lesson.

- Write the following on the board:
  - Find a lot of money in the street
  - Be famous
  - Go out this weekend
  - Learn to speak English very well
- Tell students to make up complete sentences using the phrases above, the words *if* or *when* and the first of second conditional. If necessary, elicit the use and structure of each form. (Note: students can choose either conditional form depending on how likely they think this event will be.)

- Then put students into small groups and ask them to compare their sentences. Tell students to ask each other questions to get more information if necessary.
- While students are discussing, monitor to point out mistakes and provide vocabulary if necessary.

LISTENING

1 Give students one minute to think about their answers and then put them in pairs to compare.

- Get a few answers from the class and write the reasons students give for the crimes on the board.

Answers depend on students' own knowledge.

If your class all come from the same country, you could elicit three recent and/or famous crimes and write them on the board.

2a Remind students of the reasons they gave in exercise 1 and ask them to copy the list you wrote on the board.

- Play the track without pausing and tell students to tick the items from the list if they are mentioned.
- Elicit answers from the class and tick the reasons on the board.

Answers depend on items in the list on the board.

2b Give students one or two minutes to complete parts of the table from memory.

- Then play the track again, pausing after each speaker to give students time to write.
- Ask students to compare with a partner before you check answers with the class.
- To follow up, ask students if they sympathise with any of the criminals and why.

If possible, reproduce the table so what the whole class can see it (perhaps on an Interactive Whiteboard or on an overhead projector). When you go through answers, write them in the table.

	1 Carlos	2 Frank	3 Gina
1 Crime?	Hit someone in a club, attacked a policeman	Organised a robbery at the airport, gold worth over £10 million	Stealing from shops, houses, and cash machines
2 Age of criminal?		51	21
3 Reason for crime?	He lost his temper – hadn't learned to control it as a child, like his dad, a violent man	Easy way to make a living, he enjoyed planning big robberies	Poor background, no money, no job
4 Plans for future?	Keep out of trouble, settle down, lead a normal life	Retire to a villa in Spain	Move out of the area and start a new life (maybe get some qualifications)

Track 2.28

1

It's no surprise I'm in prison. I'm just like my dad. He was a big man, and he had a very quick temper. He was violent at home, always hitting me and my mum, and he was violent outside the home, always picking arguments and fighting with people, so he was in and out of prison all the time. I'm the same. That's why I'm in jail at the moment. Me and some mates, we went to a club, someone said something I didn't like and I hit him. Really hard, so he was badly injured. The police came and took me off to the station. In the corridor of the police station, I did something really stupid. I lost my temper with a police officer and attacked him. I'm sorry now, of course. If I had learned to control my temper when I was a kid, I wouldn't have hit the police officer. You just can't do that. In prison, I attend a class on how to control your anger. I'm learning a lot from the instructor and the other people in the class. I think it'll be useful when I come out of prison, I'll be able to control my temper better. Actually, all I want to do now is keep out of trouble, settle down and lead a normal life.

2

The newspapers called me 'Mr Big'. I liked that, but I didn't like the sentence I got, 20 years in prison. I didn't expect to be caught. You see, I plan crimes, but I don't actually commit them. I get other people to do that. I know I'm very intelligent – everyone says so. If I had wanted to, I could have become a top businessman or maybe a lawyer. But early on, I decided to follow a life of crime. It was an easy way to make money. And later, I started planning really big robberies. That's what I really enjoyed. I organised some big robberies, and we made lots of money. But then I planned a robbery at the airport – gold bullion, worth over £10 million. Unfortunately, my team of robbers made a mistake. They stayed at the airport too long. If they had done the job more quickly, they would have left in time, and the police wouldn't have caught them. One of my gang gave my name to the police and I was arrested. I'm 51 now. When I get out of prison, I'll buy a villa in Spain and retire there. Plenty of my friends are already over there.

3

My parents didn't have much money but they were good to me. We lived in a poor area in Glasgow. A lot of people were unemployed and the crime rate was high. When I was about eight years old, I joined a gang of girls and we used to go shoplifting – you know, stealing things from shops and stores. It was great fun, until we got caught. I'll never forget my mum's face when the police officer came to our door. Then when I was a teenager, I started stealing from houses and when they caught me, I was sent to Reform School – that's where they put young people who commit crimes. When I came out, I couldn't get a job and I was unemployed for over a year. So what choice did I have? If I hadn't been unemployed, I wouldn't have started robbing cash machines. I was sent to prison for two years. I'm 21 now, and I don't want to go back to prison. I think I've been so unlucky in my life. If I had lived in a different area, I wouldn't have become a criminal. And, I might have tried harder if I hadn't been unemployed. So, my life would have been totally different. I would have studied at night school if I had found a good job, and got some qualifications. Anyway, now I'm going to move out of the area and make a new start somewhere else.

READING

3a Lead in by asking students which (if any) of the criminals in the listening they sympathise with and why (see follow up in exercise 2b procedure above).

- Set the activity and give students two minutes to read and match.
- Check answers with the class.

> Genetic causes: 1 Carlos; Environment: 3 Gina; Choice: 2 Frank

3b Tell students to read the statements and check they understand *anti-social* (bad behaviour in society and with people) and *tend* (this usually happens).

- Give students two minutes to read and match.
- Ask them to compare with a partner before you check answers with the class.

If you have a fairly strong class, students can match the statements without reading the text again. To encourage them to read the text, ask students for examples.

> **1** genetic causes; **2** choice; **3** environment; **4** genetic causes; **5** genetic causes; **6** choice

4 Put students into pairs/small groups to discuss the question.

- Get a few ideas from the class.

To help students with this discussion, remind them of the crimes they talked about in exercise 1 and tell them to decide which cause (genetic, environment, choice) was the reason for these crimes.

VOCABULARY: word combinations

5a Students can use their dictionaries to check any unknown words in this activity.

- Ask them to compare with a partner before you check answers with the class. (Note: in question 1 *influence* can also be combined with *behaviour* but the exercise is focusing on noun/adjective + behaviour combinations. If students ask about *influence*, tell them that you need to add an object [e.g. *influence their behaviour*].)
- Check students can pronounce *vicious*.

The quote in the reading text following *a vicious circle* gives a good example of this phrase.

> **1** criminal, human, good, bad, anti-social; **2** long; **3** genetic; **4** close; **5** career; **6** vicious

5b Students do this activity individually and then compare with a partner.

- Check answers with the class.
- To follow up, ask a few students who they have a close relationship with, what there is a long tradition of in their country, and if they've made a career decision yet.

(!) The use of *criminal* and *anti-social behaviour* will often depend on the context, i.e. anti-social behaviour in one society may well be criminal in another.

> **1** criminal behaviour; **2** close relationships; **3** long tradition; **4** anti-social behaviour; **5** career decision

For extra practice, ask students to do exercise V1,2 4 on page 157 of the Language reference. (Note: this exercise includes vocabulary from lesson 12.1.)

GRAMMAR: third conditional

6a Explain that the examples all come from the listening texts students heard in exercise 2 (underlined, along with other examples, in the audioscript above).

- Give students three minutes to answer the questions.
- Ask them to compare with a partner before you check answers with the class.
- Finally, ask students to read the summarising information at the end of this activity.

To reinforce the context, ask students to underline the examples in the audioscript on page 181. Students can then look at the situation around the examples to help them answer the questions in this activity.

> **1 a** no, **b** no; **2 a** no, **b** no; **3 a** no, **b** no, **4 a** yes, **b** no

6b Give students three minutes to fill the gaps in the rule.

- While they are working, write example 1 from exercise 6a on the board.
- Check answers with the class and underline the relevant part of the example on the board.
- Finally, elicit the negative of *had done* (*hadn't done*) and the pronunciation of contracted *would(n't) have*, *could(n't) have* and *might have*. Tell students that we normally say *might not have* with a contracted *not have*.

> The third conditional is *if* + past <u>participle</u>, + *would(n't)* <u>*have*</u> + <u>past</u> participle. We can also use <u>*could*</u> or *might* in the main clause.

For a full explanation, ask students to read G1 on page 156 of the Language reference.

7 Students do this activity individually.

- Monitor to point out mistakes but refer them to exercise 6 and the Language reference if they need help.
- Ask students to compare with a partner before you check answers with the class.

1 had planned, would/might/could have succeeded; **2** had acted, would/could/might have prevented **3** hadn't driven, wouldn't have/might not have had **4** wouldn't/might not/couldn't have increased, had been **5** wouldn't/might not/couldn't have caught, hadn't left

8 To give students guidance, ask them to read the example and the *if* clauses (2–4) *before* they think about how their lives could have been different.
- Tell students to ask you if they need extra vocabulary.
- Monitor to point out mistakes with the third conditional, but encourage students to self-correct by referring to exercises 6 and 7, and the Language reference.
- When students have finished their sentences, put them into pairs to compare.
- Encourage students to ask each other questions to get as much information as possible.
- While students are speaking, monitor to note mistakes with the pronunciation of contractions.
- In feedback, ask students the most interesting/surprising thing they heard.
- Finally, correct the most common mistakes with the pronunciation of contractions.

For further practice, ask students to do exercise G1 1 on page 157 of the Language reference.

SPEAKING

9 Read through the statements with the class and check they understand *greedy* (want a lot of everything), *crime doesn't pay* (see explanation on page 160 of the quote on page 122 of the Coursebook) and *petty* (not serious, unimportant).
- Give students a few minutes to think about their opinions.
- Then put them into groups to discuss the statements.
- Encourage them to give reasons for their answers and to agree/disagree as necessary.
- Finally, ask each group which statements they agreed with and why.
- In feedback, encourage students to challenge other groups' ideas.

HOMEWORK OPTIONS

Students do the exercises on pages 82–83 of the Workbook.

Students do exercise G1 1 and/or V1,2 4 on page 157 of the Language reference.

Students choose one of the statements from exercise 9 and write a paragraph saying why they agree/disagree.

12.3 THE BIG DIG

IN THIS LESSON

Lesson topic and staging

This lesson looks at major crimes and how they were committed. Students learn a set of words in the context of people in crime. They then read two crime reports and swap information with another student. Next, students listen to people talking about a robbery which contextualises the grammar focus: modals (past deduction). Students do a series of activities on the meaning and form of this grammar and then practise using it. Finally, students do a group speaking activity to solve a crime.

Objectives

By the end of the lesson, students should have:
- extended their range of vocabulary in the context of crime
- extracted specific information and language items from a listening and a reading text
- revised/learned about the form and use of modal perfects (e.g. *should have* + past participle)
- engaged in an extended speaking activity to solve a crime

Timings

If short of time, in exercises 2 and 3, ask all students to read only the text on page 126 rather than different texts.

A possible lesson break would be either after exercise 4 or 5 on page 126.

WARM-UP

This activity helps you find out what vocabulary related to crime students already know.
- On separate parts of the board, write *people involved in crime* and *crimes* and draw a circle round each.
- Put students into pairs or small groups and give them three minutes to think of as many words or phrases in each category as possible.
- Elicit answers and write them on the board around either *people involved in crime* or *crimes*. Make sure the whole class understands all the words elicited.
- Finally, tell students they are going to extend their vocabulary in exercise 1.

VOCABULARY: people in crime

1a This activity gives vocabulary that students need for exercise 2 below.

- Focus students on the photo on page 127 and ask who the people are (policemen, investigators, etc.).
- Tell students they are going to learn words for people in crime. Students can also use their dictionaries.
- Ask students to compare with a partner.
- Go through the answers with the class.

> **1** captor, thief; bank robber, suspect; **2** hostage; **3** lawyer (UK English), attorney (US English), prosecutor; **4** robbery, kidnapping

1b Students can use their dictionaries for help with this activity.

- Elicit answers from the class.
- Finally, ask students which crimes *getaway* and *ransom* are often connected with (bank robbery and kidnapping).

> The three extra words (fingerprints, getaway, ransom) are connected with crimes.

READING

2a Focus students on the photo on page 127 and ask them what the 'hole' is probably for.

- Elicit *tunnel* and *dig*, and any guesses about the tunnel's use.
- Explain that students are going to read two different texts.
- Tell them to read the questions (1–6) first and to only read the text given to them. Tell students to note their answers but not to write whole sentences.
- Monitor to check students have answered the questions correctly and help with additional vocabulary they need (e.g. *retrieved, recovered, safe and sound, drain*).
- Don't check answers in open class because students will exchange information in exercise 2b.

2b Give students a maximum of eight minutes to swap information using the notes they made in exercise 2a.

- Check answers with the class.

> Bank Robbers Tunnel Their Way to Millions
> **1** Fortaleza Central Bank, Brazil, South America; **2** 260 feet long, connecting a house to the bank, thieves put in electric lights, air conditioning, wooden floors; **3** $68 million; **4** money; **5** about $8 million; **6** they've recovered about $8 million, arrested eight people, they know that one suspect was kidnapped and killed, they suspect some suspects might be involved in other tunnelling bank robberies in Uruguay and Argentina (Cordoba), they believe one suspect is Moises Teixeira da Silva
>
> *continued…*
>
> The Big Dig
> **1** a bank in Buenos Aires, Argentina; **2** a hole in the bank's basement wall covered with a locked iron lid, the tunnel joined a drain that emptied into the Plata River; **3** estimated $25-$70 million; **4** about $200,000 bank cash, more than 140 safe-deposit boxes and their contents (money, property); **5** none (or not given); **6** they found 19 hostages safe and sound , they found the hole and the tunnel

3 When students have ordered the events, ask them to tell their partner.

- Encourage students to ask questions to get as much information as possible.
- Go through answers with the class and check they understand *stormed the building*.
- Follow up by asking students which crime is more amazing.

Use these crimes to help elicit *spectacular* (which students need for exercise 4 below).

> Student A: **1** c; **2** d; **3** f; **4** e; **5** g; **6** b; **7** a (Note: 6 and 7 may be reversed. It is not clear in the report.)
> Student B: **1** b; **2** c; **3** a; **4** e; **5** d; **6** g; **7** f

4 Encourage students to describe the robberies in as much detail as possible.

LISTENING

5 This listening provides examples of modal perfects for exercise 6a.

- Read through the introduction and tell students this is a true story.
- Ask students to read the questions and check they understand *reward* (money given by the police or others, generally for information), and *tracing* (following clues to find stolen money).
- Play the track and if necessary, pause after each speaker to give students time to answer.
- Ask students to compare with a partner before you check answers with the class.

> **a** 1; **b** 8; **c** 2; **d** 7; **e** 4; **f** 3; **g** 6; **h** 5

Track 2.29

1
They took so much money that everyone in this country and in Europe will be aware of it, and they might have wanted to use the money in Europe.

2
They shouldn't have stolen such a large amount of money. Someone found a huge bag of cash the other day and the first thing they thought was, 'Could it have come from that Tonbridge job?'

continued…

3
Basically, they can't have planned it properly. They should have involved fewer people. And you know, the more people involved, the greater the chance a friend or relative will tell the police. Mind you – some friend.
4
The £2 million reward might have got some informers and other criminals interested. The culture of not informing on other criminals no longer exists. People will do anything to get their hands on that much money.
5
Banks have become much better at tracking bank notes, so there is a possibility that they might have traced some of the cash.
6
The police think someone with inside knowledge could have been involved – someone who works there – and if so that person will be the most likely one to offer up information when they are questioned by the police. They won't be used to police questioning and they could be the weakest link.
7
The security people must have been very careless. The robbers could have been caught easily if the security people were doing their jobs properly.
8
Well in one sense it couldn't have been more successful. They got away with £50 million.

GRAMMAR: modals (past deduction)

6a Emphasise that students must answer *from the speaker's point of view* and if necessary, answer the first question as a whole class.

- Ask students to compare with a partner before you check answers with the class.

The speaker's point of view is essential for the answers to numbers 3 and 7.

1 not sure; **2** yes; **3** no; **4** no; **5** not sure; **6** not sure; **7** yes; **8** yes

6b Elicit/tell students that all the examples in exercise 6a are 'guesses' or 'deductions' the speakers believe.

- Give students five minutes for this activity and ask them to compare answers with a partner.
- Go through answers with the class and emphasise again that these are 'guesses' or 'deductions'. (Note: for meaning d, *must* and *can't* both mean that something is logically certain from the speaker's point of view. *Can't* means the speaker believes something didn't happen, *must* means they are certain it did.)

a 2 ; **b** 4; **c** 1, 5, 6; **d** 3, 7; **e** 8

While students are working, write one of the examples from exercise 6a on the board. In feedback for exercise 6c, highlight the relevant parts.

Modals for present deduction were studied in lesson 7.3 on page 75 in the Coursebook.

6c Elicit the answer from the class and highlight the form on the board (see Tip above).

For a full explanation, ask students to read G2 on page 156 of the Language reference

Check students' pronunciation of the contracted forms *can't've, shouldn't've, should've, must've, might've, could've, couldn't've. Might* is not normally contracted *mightn't've* but as *might not've*. Tell students we don't use double contractions (e.g. *couldn't've*) in writing. Tell students the opposite of *must've* is *can't have*.

7 Remind students that we don't use double contractions (e.g. *couldn't've*) in writing.

- Give students a maximum of ten minutes to write their sentences.
- Monitor to point out mistakes but encourage students to use exercise 6 and the Language reference if they need help.
- Put students into pairs and give them five minutes to discuss their sentences.
- Encourage them to give reasons for their ideas.
- Monitor and note mistakes with perfect modals and the pronunciation of contractions.
- Get a few ideas from two or three pairs.
- Finally, correct the most common mistakes you noted earlier.

SPEAKING

8 The perfect murder

- Read through the instructions with the class and tell students to read the newspaper report.
- Help students with any unknown vocabulary.
- Give each student a letter (A–F) and ask them to read their role card.
- Tell students to use their dictionaries for unknown vocabulary.
- Put students into groups of six and allow 15–20 minutes for the discussion.
- Tell students to use modal perfects when making guesses and deductions.
- Monitor and note mistakes with perfect modals and the pronunciation of contractions.
- When they have finished, ask each group who committed the crime and how.
- Finally, correct the most common mistakes you noted earlier.

HOMEWORK OPTIONS

Students do the exercises on pages 84–85 of the Workbook.

Students use the role cards (A–F) from exercise 8 to write sentences similar to exercise 6a.

12.4 SCENARIO: YOU, THE JURY

IN THIS LESSON

Lesson topic and staging

This lesson focuses on the language of presenting a case and discussing a verdict. Students are introduced to the scenario of a Crown Court in England. They listen to extracts from a court case and focus on the KEY LANGUAGE. Students then read about three court cases and finally use this information and the KEY LANGUAGE in the main TASK to present a case and discuss a verdict.

Objectives

By the end of the lesson, students should have:

- learned useful phrases for presenting a case and discussing a court verdict
- extracted specific information and language items from reading and listening texts
- used the Key language in a 'real-life' situation to present and discuss court cases
- participated effectively in extended speaking practice

Common European Framework

Students can use language effectively to present a case and discuss a verdict.

Timings

If short of time, you could drop one case from exercise 4 so that students discuss only two cases in exercise 5.

A possible lesson break would be after exercise 3b or 4 on page 128.

WARM-UP

This activity introduces the topic of juries in court.

- Write the following on the board:
  - Over 18 years old
  - Well-educated
  - Broad-minded
  - Gets on well with other people
  - Has a lot of different experiences
- Tell students these are possible qualities for a good jury member and check they understand each one. *Broad-minded* means you are tolerant and open to different ideas.
- Ask students to order the qualities from most (1) to least (5) important.
- Put them into pairs to compare the order, and tell them to give reasons and decide on an order they both agree on.
- Put the pairs together in groups of four and repeat the previous stage.
- Repeat the procedure until the whole class has agreed on an order.

SITUATION

1 Tell students they are going to read and hear about a court case.

- Tell them to read the question before they read the situation.
- Students can use their dictionaries to find unknown vocabulary (particularly *prosecution*, *defence*, *jury* and *verdict*).
- Get a few answers from the class.

If your students are all from the same country, this activity can be done as a group discussion. If they are from different countries, put different nationalities in pairs or small groups and ask them discuss the similarities between their countries' systems.

2 Set the context and ask students if they think this is a serious crime.

- Tell students to read the three questions (a–c) and then play the track without pausing.
- Ask students to compare with a partner before you check answers with the class.

> **a** Extract 2; **b** Extract 1; **c** Extract **3** (The audioscript is below exercise 3a.)

KEY LANGUAGE: presenting a case and discussing a verdict

3a Give students three minutes to try to complete the gaps.

- Play the track again and pause after each extract to give students time to write.
- Ask students to compare with a partner before you check answers with the class.
- Tell students the KEY LANGUAGE is listed on page 156 of the Language reference.

> **1** evidence; **2** witnesses; **3** client; **4** case, events; **5** doubt; **6** defendant; **7** ways; **8** believe; **9** certain; **10** clear (Answers are bold in the audioscript below.)

> **Audioscript and answers to Exercise 2 & 3: Track 2.30**
>
> **1**
>
> Members of the Jury, the facts of this case are simple. You have a poor, homeless man who faced a lonely night in a cold station. To keep warm, he went into a bookshop, read a book for a while, and then decided to go out, probably to get a cup of tea. And then he thought, why don't I take a few books with me to have a
>
> *continued...*

look at while I sit on a bench? I'll put them back later when I've finished my tea. **1** The **evidence** clearly shows that the manager of the bookshop acted too quickly. He accused my client of being a thief in front of other customers. **2** I will bring **witnesses** to confirm that he is an honest man who has fallen on hard times. **3** I am sure that you will find my **client** innocent.

2

4 The facts of the **case** are clear. Let me summarise the **events** for you. A homeless man goes into a bookstore early in the evening. He has no money, so he slips three books into the inside pockets of his overcoat, hoping that nobody will see him, then leaves the shop without paying. I suggest to you that this man probably goes into stores quite often to steal books, and then sells them to local second-hand bookshops. He does not deserve your sympathy. He is simply a common thief.

5 There should be no **doubt** in your minds that this man is guilty of theft. A witness will claim that she noticed the man looking around to make sure that no one saw him stealing the books. Unfortunately for him this man forgot that the store has security cameras. **6** I am confident that you will find the **defendant** guilty.

3

J1: **7** You can look at it in two **ways**, I think. Do you believe the witness who said he was definitely stealing the books, or do you believe the man himself? He said he was just borrowing the books for half an hour to read on the bench outside the store. Then he was going to return them. But he didn't get the chance to do it. **8** I **believe** he's innocent because the manager didn't give him a chance to explain before calling the police. He seems an honest person to me. What do the rest of you think?

J2: Mmm, it's a difficult one. On the one hand, he had some good character witnesses, but on the other hand, one witness is sure he was stealing the books. Personally, **9** I'm not **certain** he's guilty because I think he acted on impulse, without really thinking. What does anyone else think?

J3: Well, I've made up my mind. I'm certain he's guilty. He didn't look honest to me. No, he didn't fool me for one minute.

J2: I don't think it's a case of trying to fool us. **10** It's **clear** to me that he's not guilty.

For extra practice, ask students to do exercise KL 3 on page 157 of the Language reference.

3b Give students about three minutes for this activity. (Note: students need to match the sentences in exercise 3a to the person or people who would be likely to say them, not to the person who actually says them in the audioscript above [e.g. sentence 1 could be said by either the prosecution or the defence, although it is actually said by the defence in the audioscript].)

- Check answers with the class.
- Follow up by asking students if they have been or would like to be on a jury and why.

> Numbers refer to the sentences in 3a. **a** 4, 5, 6; **b** 1, 2, 3; **c** 1, 4; d 7, 8, 9, 10

TASK: discussing court cases

4 Tell students to read the six questions before they read the cases.

- Students can use their dictionaries to check unknown vocabulary.
- Ask them to compare with a partner before you check answers with the class.
- To follow up, ask students which case they think is the most serious and why.

> **1** Case three; **2** Case two; **3** Case one; **4** Case two; **5** Case one; **6** Case three

5 Before you put students into their groups, tell them to read the instructions very carefully and ask you if they don't understand.

- Go through the OTHER USEFUL PHRASES box with the class and tell students 'There is no evidence that a crime was committed' can only be used by the defence.
- Put the class into their groups and give each student a letter (A–E).
- For each case:
  - Give the prosecution and defence students about three minutes to reread their case on pages 128–129 and their information on the page given (e.g. A = page 160, B = page 165).
  - Then give the prosecution and defence students a few minutes to look again at the KEY LANGUAGE and OTHER USEFUL PHRASES and think about what they are going to say.
  - At the same time, tell the jurors to reread the relevant case and read their instructions on page 129.
  - Give jurors about five minutes to think of questions they might want to ask.
  - Before jurors discuss the verdict, remind them of the KEY and USEFUL LANGUAGE.
  - While students are speaking, note mistakes they make with the KEY and USEFUL LANGUAGE.
  - At the end of each case, ask the jurors what their verdict is.
- At the end of all three cases, correct some of the mistakes you noted earlier.

Students have to change roles in this activity. For each case, make sure the students are in the correct roles.

HOMEWORK OPTIONS

Students do the exercises on page 86 of the Workbook.

Students do exercise KL 3 on page 157 of the Language reference.

Students write a short newspaper report on the case they gave a verdict for in exercise 5. (Note: not all the KEY and USEFUL LANGUAGE can be used in a written account.)

12.5 STUDY AND WRITING SKILLS

IN THIS LESSON

Lesson topic and staging

This lesson focuses on summarising and writing a narrative using cause and effect. Students read advice on summarising. They then listen to a lecture on home security and discuss the merits of two summaries before listing information included in the lecture and the summaries. Students then listen to a lecture on car security and write a summary. Next, students focus on linking words for cause and effect, and practise using these. They then read a witness statement on an accident and list the causes and effects. Finally, students write a witness statement about another accident.

Objectives

By the end of the lesson, students should have:

- extracted specific information from reading and listening texts
- learned (more) about how to write a good summary and written one of their own
- extended their knowledge of linking words when describing cause and effect
- written a narrative describing cause and effect

Common European Framework

Students can write a summary and a narrative (using cause and effect).

Timings

If short of time, you could set exercise 7 for homework.

A possible lesson break would be after exercise 4b on page 130.

WARM-UP

This activity introduces the idea of summarising.

- Ask students to think of their favourite book/film/TV show.
- Put students into pairs and give them five minutes to tell each other about the book, film or TV show.
- When they have finished, give students a few minutes to summarise from memory what they heard. They should use no more than twenty words. Tell students they have to decide on the most important points to include in their summary because they cannot write more than twenty words.
- Ask students to move round the room and read their summary to others.
- To follow up, ask a few students which of the books, films or TV shows they would like to read or see.

STUDY SKILLS: summarising

1 Lead in by asking students if they found it easy using only twenty words in the Warm-up above.

- Ask students for a few ideas on important things to remember when summarising.
- Set the activity and give students a maximum of two minutes to read the text.
- Check answers with the class.

> Pick out the main points, use your own words, read the original again to make sure you haven't missed any key points, don't write in note form

2a Introduce the activity and check students understand *safety chain* (mime using one) and *burglar alarm* (draw one or mime setting the alarm before you leave the house).

- Play the track and tell students to take short notes while they are listening.
- Ask students to compare notes with a partner before you check with the class.

Write each item (a–e) and the board and make *short* notes under each one as you elicit ideas from the class. Students can use notes on the board to remind them of the lecture content when they do exercise 2b below.

> **a** close windows at the front when you're in the back or the garden, open windows are an opportunity for burglars, use window locks; **b** don't leave notes on the front door saying you're not there; **c** ask visitors who claim they're from the gas company, etc. for ID; **d** allow you to open the door a little and see who's there, nobody can push the door open, many people forget to use their chains; **e** expensive, protects you when you are away, very effective

2b Give students two minutes to read the summaries before you put them in pairs to decide which is better.

- Remind students that notes from the lecture are written on the board and they can use these to check the content of summaries A and B.
- Tell students to list the good points about each summary as they are speaking.
- Finally, ask a few pairs which summary they thought was better and why.
- Don't tell students at this stage which summary you think is better. Students need to decide for themselves.

2c Keep students in the same pairs as exercise 2b. Read through the instructions with the class and emphasise that each student in a pair should read a different summary (either A or B).

- Give students one minute to read their summary and then play the track again without pausing.
- Then give them three minutes to compare and decide if their answer in exercise 2b is still true.
- Ask the class if anyone has changed their mind about the better summary and why.

3 Give students five minutes for this activity to complete the chart and then ask them to check their answers by reading the audioscript on page 182.

- Ask students to compare with a partner before you check answers with the class.
- In feedback, make sure the class realises that Summary A is better. Tell students it's not necessary to include point 4 as this is extra information. It's also fine to use 'the expert' instead of a name.

	Lecture	Summary A	Summary B
1 Gives the name of the speaker.	✓	(✓) the expert	
2 Give the main topic (home security).	✓	✓	✓
3 Gives the order in which the information will be/is presented.	✓	✓	
4 Points out that people don't always use safety chains.	✓		
5 Lists the methods for creating security.	✓	✓	
6 Finishes with a conclusion.	✓	✓	

Track 2.31

Good morning. I'm Police Constable Martin Wilkes and today I am going to talk to you about simple home security. How can we improve security in the home and how can we protect ourselves? In the first part of my talk I'm going to mention simple precautions that don't cost anything. In the second part, I'll talk about devices you can buy to help with home security.

You might think I'm stating the obvious, but in my experience failing to follow these simple steps leads to most security problems. First, always remember to close the doors and windows at the front of your house or apartment when you are at the back of the building or in the garden, especially in warm weather. Leaving your windows open creates a target and an opportunity for burglars. Second, don't leave signs that you are not at home, such as leaving a note on the front door saying you've just gone to the shops and you'll be back soon. Another simple precaution is to ask for identification from any visitors who claim they are from the gas, electricity or water companies.

continued…

Now for the second part of my advice. An easy way of improving security is to buy and fit locks for your windows. Window locks are cheap to buy and easy to fit. A further simple and cheap device is a safety chain. This allows you to open the front door just a little. You can then see who is calling and talk to them. The advantage of the safety chain is that no one can push the door open and come into the house. You mightn't believe it but many people who have safety chains forget to put them on when opening the door to strangers. A more expensive security method is to fit improved locks to all your doors. These locks are difficult to force open so they keep your property safe. An even more expensive method is to fit a burglar alarm for when you're away from home. Alarms are very effective ways of deterring burglars. If you use all these methods you'll find that you can make it very difficult for thieves to burgle your home.

4a Tell students their notes should be short and not to write sentences at this stage.

- Ask students to compare notes with a partner.
- If necessary, play the track again.
- Elicit ideas from the class and write notes on the board as below.

To make this activity easier for students, ask students what information they expect to hear in the lecture *before they listen*. This will help them focus.

Topic: 1 car security (no thieves), 2 your security in car (safety). **Main points:** 1 lock car (even short time), hide valuables (e.g. boot), remove radios, sat nav. etc., use immobilisers, tracking devices, car alarm. 2 lock doors, unlock at high speeds, when stationary – lock doors and close windows, put valuables in back. **Conclusions:** car security = *of* car but also your security *in* car

Track 2.32

Good morning. Today I'm going to talk about two main topics. The first is car security. That means keeping your car secure. The second is security in the car. That means keeping yourself safe and secure in the car.

If you have a car or if you're a passenger in a car there are some simple tips that will help you to protect your goods. The first tip is always to lock the car, even if you're just going to be away from it for a few moments. Secondly, never leave anything valuable where it can be seen, even if the car is locked. If you can't take your valuable goods with you, make sure they are locked in the boot of the car. Radios, DVD players and satellite navigation systems are expensive. Remove them from the car when you park. Nowadays, a lot of drivers use car immobilisers, which prevent thieves from starting the car, and tracking devices that help the police track the position of your stolen car. Finally, if your car is old and doesn't have an alarm, put one in.

Now, let's switch to security in the car – your personal security. The first thing to do is to lock your car doors as soon as you get in. A common trick for thieves is to wait for a driver to get in the car, then to open the passenger door and steal a bag on the passenger seat, for example. But

continued…

there is one point to always remember – release the locks when travelling at high speed. This helps you get out of the car quickly in case of an accident.
My next point concerns protecting yourself when you are stationary. If you see any crowds or if someone on the street shouts at you, lock all the doors and close all the windows. This is a simple precaution to prevent theft from the car. My mother once nearly had her bag snatched as she sat in the car at some traffic lights on a busy street. Fortunately, she was very quick-thinking and managed to hold the thief's fingers, bending them backwards and forcing him to drop the bag in the car. She then closed the windows, checked that the doors were locked and drove away. She was lucky. But unless you follow my advice you mightn't be so lucky. Of course, you shouldn't really leave your bag or briefcase in the front with you – it's much safer in the back, with the doors locked.
Finally, worse than this is carjacking – someone jumping in at traffic lights and stealing your car with you in it. This is less likely to happen if your doors are locked.
So, remember, car security is not only the security *of* your car and of things in it, but also your security *in* the car. Follow my advice and stay safe. Thank you.

4b Give students 15–20 minutes to write their summaries.

- Move round the class to give advice if necessary.
- Ask students to swap summaries and comment on each other's work.
- Take the summaries in for marking, paying attention to the number of main points mentioned, clarity and organisation.

WRITING SKILLS: a narrative using cause and effect

5a Linkers

- Explain that students are going to write a witness statement (the story of what happened for the police) about an accident.
- Ask students for linking words they have studied in other units in the Coursebook (e.g. *In conclusion, Firstly, On the one hand*).
- Tell students that 1–4 are causes and a)–d) are effects.
- Give students two minutes to match the sentences.
- Check answers with the class and tell them to underline the word or phrase that links the sentences (*As a result, so, The result was, Consequently*).
- Tell students that *so* normally continues as one sentence and that *As a result* and *Consequently* are followed by a comma.

1 d; 2 b; 3 a; 4 c

5b Read through the example with the class and elicit a couple of other suggestions.

- Tell students to read the causes (2–6) and note what the result might be.
- If students have problems thinking of results, provide some ideas.
- Students then write sentences describing the results.
- Monitor to point out mistakes and encourage students to self-correct using the examples in exercise 5a.
- Ask students to compare with a partner before you elicit a few answers from the class.

Answers depend on students' own ideas.

6 Tell students the witness statement is about a road accident between a bike and a Mercedes car.

- Ask them to predict what might have happened.
- Students then read the statement and list the causes and effects.
- Check answers with the class and highlight the linking phrases (underlined in the answers below).

Cause	Effect
1 I was late for work	due to heavy traffic
2 Mercedes passed very close at speed.	This caused me to lose my balance.
3 I lost my balance.	Which then resulted in me falling off the bicycle.
4 I fell off the bicycle.	As a result, I injured my ankle.
5 The driver was scared	so he reversed and drove away.

7 Narrative using cause and effect

- Give the students four minutes to read the notes and look at the map.
- Put them into pairs and tell them to describe the events together.
- Then give students 20 minutes to write the witness statement.
- Monitor to point out mistakes with linking words/phrases.
- Finally, take the statements in for marking, paying attention to the use of cause, effect and linking words/phrases.

HOMEWORK OPTIONS

Students do the exercises on page 87 of the Workbook.

Students write a paragraph describing a true situation (an accident, something amusing, etc.) using cause, effect and linking words.

Students find a magazine/newspaper article they are interested in and write a summary.

Review

UNITS 10–12

GRAMMAR

1a Before students read the articles, tell them that all three are about criminals and crimes.

> 1 c; 2 b; 3 a

1b Tell students to match the sentences to the articles and write the number of the article in the space provided after each sentence.

- Go through answers with the class.
- Then tell students to choose the correct verb in each sentence.
- Ask students to compare with a partner before you check answers with the class.

> **1** Article 3, could have got; **2** Article 1, 'd paid; **3** Article 3, can't; **4** Article 3, have; **5** Article 2 (and possibly 3), had; **6** Article 2, would; **7** Article 2, must; **8** Article 1, 'd gone

2 Tell students to check the direct speech in the articles to help them write these reported speech sentences.

- Monitor to point out mistakes students make with reported speech and refer them to G1 on page 154 of the Language reference for help.
- Ask students to compare with a partner before you check answers with the class.
- Finally, ask students which article they thought was the strangest/funniest.

> **1** was; **2** hadn't; **3** if he could go; **4** didn't know who; **5** were still looking for

VOCABULARY

3 First, ask students to read the TV guide and tell you which programmes they would like to watch and why.

- Students then do the activity as per the Coursebook.

> **1** a; **2** a; **3** b; **4** b; **5** b; **6** b; **7** d; **8** a

KEY LANGUAGE

4 Focus students on the photo and ask where the people are and what they probably do.

- Tell students to read the instructions in this activity to check their answers to the question above.
- Ask students to read the two questions and then play the track.
- Ask students to compare with a partner before you check answers with the class.

> **1** appearance wasn't good, bad paintings, uncomfortable seats; **2** in a completely new building, nearer the lecture rooms

5a Give students five minutes to complete the gaps before they compare answers with a partner.

- Monitor to see which items students find particularly difficult but don't correct them.
- Don't confirm answers with the class until after exercise 5b.

5b Play the track, pausing after the items students found difficult in 5a to give them time to write.

- Go through answers with the class or ask them to look at the audioscript on page 183.

> **1** discuss; **2** clear; **3** unhappy; **4** comments; **5** different; **6** say; **7** something; **8** ways

Track 2.33

A: OK. Thank you all for coming. We're here to discuss the new space the university has given us for a coffee bar. Firstly, I'd like to say that it's clear to me that the new area is much better than what we had before so I'd like us to be positive about it.

B: I agree. I was very unhappy with the appearance of the old coffee bar. It had lots of bad paintings on the wall and really uncomfortable seats. I think this new area could be a much nicer place to relax.

A: Thank you for your comments – I think we'd all agree with you. This is very different from the old recreation area. For a start, the room is in a completely new building and nearer the lecture rooms.

C: Sorry, could I just say something please? I think the university could give us something much better than this area. After all, we pay fees …

A: I understand that but you can look at it in two ways. Yes, it's not perfect, but it's better than what we had.

LANGUAGE CHECK

6 Tell students to try all the sentences before they look at the page in the Coursebook to check.

> **1** of; **2** of; **3** to; **4** at; **5** about; **6** off; **7** to; **8** me; **9** if; **10** have

LOOK BACK

7 The aim of this activity is to remind students of areas they looked at in units 10–12. This will help reinforce any language or skills they had difficulties with or were particularly good at.

> the order of adjectives: 10.2, exercise 3; take part in a meeting: 10.4, exercise 6b; write a review: 11.1, exercise 7; read about a recluse: 11.2, exercises 2a, 2b and 2c; listen to a journalist taking about an interview: 11.3, exercises 2a and 2b; words for different types of criminals: 12.3, exercise 1a; solve a crime: 12.3, exercise 8; summarise a lecture: 12.5, exercises 4a and 4b

If students have problems remembering these exercises, you could put them into small groups to remind each other (as appropriate) of the vocabulary learned, the content of the text, the topic they talked about.

To extend the activity, ask students to choose one of the exercises and write a test for other students. This could be a list of questions, a true/false, a gapfill, etc.

Extra practice key

Unit 1

G1 1
1 Is; **2** Do; **3** Does; **4** does; **5** Have/done; **6** are; **7** May [*or* Can]; **8** was; **9** did; **10** has/taken [*or* Did/take]
G2 2
2 Who designed the test?; **3** What does Oprah Winfrey own?; **4** Who married Joe DiMaggio?; **5** How many languages is he able to speak?; **6** What is your favourite time of the year?; **7** What is the reason you're leaving?
G3,4 3
1 do/study; **2** work; **3** prefer; **4** depends; **5** 'm working; **6** 're setting up; **7** do/know; **8** get; **9** 'm getting
KL 4
1 b; **2** e; **3** d; **4** a; **5** f (Extra phrase c)
V1 5
1 adventurous; **2** cautious; **3** energetic; **4** moody; **5** reliable; **6** thoughtful; **7** open-minded; **8** self-confident
V2 6
1 antisocial; **2** bicycle; **3** discomfort; **4** misunderstand; **5** monorail; **6** overshadowed; **7** redefine; **8** outperform; **9** ex-president; **10** underrated
V2 7
1 bicycle; **2** misunderstand; **3** underrated; **4** outperformed; **5** monorail

Unit 2

G1 1
1 was; **2** led; **3** crossed; **4** stopped; **5** had; **6** ran; **7** started; **8** flew; **9** completed
G2 3
1 Have you **ever** been to France?; **2** I've **already** told you that – don't ask me again.; **3** Bill and Martin have **never** seen it so let's watch it now.; **4** Haven't you finished it **yet**?; **5** Have you **already** finished your lunch?; **6** Why haven't you **ever** told me?; **7** I haven't had time to speak to her **yet**.; **8** Has he **ever** been late for class?
G3 4
1 've climbed; **2** Have/ridden; **3** did/die; **4** Did/have; **5** 's just announced; **6** raised; **7** 've never lived; **8** met; **9** have/had; **10** 've visited
KL 5
1 On the one hand it's cold.; **2** On the other hand it's beautiful.; **3** There are arguments for and against.; **4** Another disadvantage is that it's expensive.; **5** It'd be a good idea to ask other people.; **6** I think we should see what they say.
V1 6
1 travel; **2** abroad; **3** journey; **4** trip; **5** destination; **6** package holiday
V2 7
1 b; **2** d; **3** g; **4** e; **5** a; **6** f; **7** c
V3 8
1 around; **2** out; **3** on ; **4** off; **5** to; **6** back

Unit 3

G1 1
1 for; **2** For; **3** since; **4** Since; **5** for
G1 2
1 has/since; **2** been; **3** long/you; **4** haven't; **5** teaching/for; **6** hasn't; **7** having; **8** watching
G2 3
1 prepared; **2** been packing; **3** been waiting; **4** been driving; **5** written; **6** seen; **7** been; **8** been working
KL 4
1 in; **2** about; **3** on; **4** up; **5** into; **6** to
KL 5
1 Just one last question.; **2** I'm glad you asked me that.; **3** That's a very good question.; **4** Let me just think about that for a moment.; **5** I thought you might ask me that.
V1 6
1 glamorous; **2** stressful; **3** flexible; **4** rewarding; **5** challenging
V2 7
1 g; **2** c; **3** a; **4** f; **5** d; **6** b; **7** e
V3 8
1 time; **2** work; **3** time; **4** work; **5** time

Unit 4

G1 1
1 'll look; **2** 're meeting; **3** 're going to get [*or* 're getting] ; **4** 'm doing; **5** 're going to offer; **6** 'll probably go; **7** will be; **8** 'll stay
G2 2
1 If you revise, you'll pass your exams.; **2** We should ask your teacher for the correct answer when we see him.; **3** The world might only have one or two languages in the future unless we protect them.; **4** I won't go unless you go.; **5** If there isn't lots of traffic, I'll be there at about 5 p.m.; **6** When the class ends, we'll go for coffee.; **7** Unless I'm busy, I'll give you a call.; **8** If you don't have much money, you should stay in.
KL 3
1 sure; **2** think; **3** cause; **4** worth; **5** like
V1 4
1 accent; **2** foreign; **3** bilingual; **4** dialect; **5** native; **6** grammar
V2 5
1 down; **2** behind; **3** up; **4** by; **5** on; **6** up; **7** with
V3,4 6
1 allow; **2** die; **3** disastrous; **4** disappearance; **5** extinction; **6** let

Unit 5

G1 1
1 advertised [*or* could advertise]; **2** would [*or* might] happen; **3** 'd give; **4** were; **5** asked; **6** wouldn't know; **7** Could/give; **8** could reach
G2 3
1 less important; **2** big; **3** more complex; **4** fastest; **5** cheaper; **6** highest; **7** as; **8** more
G2 4
1 much better; **2** a little; **3** as interesting; **4** much more; **5** the least
KL 5
1 e; **2** f; **3** b; **4** d; **5** c; **6** a; **7** g
V1 6
1 endorse; **2** eye-catching; **3** sponsorship; **4** catchy; **5** logo; **6** slogan; **7** exotic
V2,3 7
1e advertising manager; **2i** TV commercial; **3j** vast sums; **4d** mail order; **5h** product placement; **6f** interactive website; **7a** fast food; **8g** junk food; **9b** persuasive message; **10c** word-of-mouth

Unit 6

G1 1
1 was studying; **2** worked; **3** was checking; **4** called; **5** were searching; **6** was; **7** was living; **8** was wearing; **9** were planning; **10** kept
G2 2
1 c; **2** a; **3** e; **4** b; **5** d
G1,2 3
1 had seen; **2** 'd applied; **3** was trying; **4** had invested; **5** gave; **6** had already done; **7** was working; **8** had had; **9** went; **10** was looking
KL 5
1 would; **2** placing; **3** afraid; **4** paid; **5** check; **6** feel; **7** sounds
V1 6
1 staff; **2** customer; **3** invest; **4** profit; **5** partner; **6** price; **7** taxes; **8** wholesaler
V2 7
1 go bankrupt; **2** launch a company; **3** launch/introduce a product; **4** make a profit; **5** negotiate a contract

Unit 7

G1 1
1 Sorry but I can't help you with this.; **2** We should make it stronger.; **3** Can you come with us tonight?; **4** You don't have to ask for his permission.; **5** I can use steel in this design.; **6** You shouldn't bother him until after lunch.; **7** Keep that wood. It could/might be useful later.; **8** You have to/must use recyclable products because of the new law.
G2 2
1 b; **2** c; **3** a; **4** f; **5** d; **6** e
G1,2 3
1 don't have to; **2** shouldn't; **3** must; **4** have to; **5** can't; **6** can; **7** must; **8** could

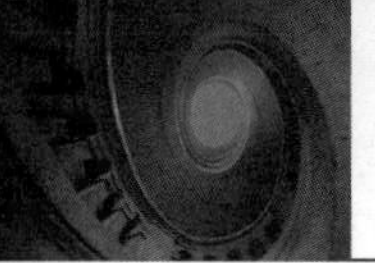

Extra practice key

KL 4
1 several; 2 made; 3 appeal; 4 value; 5 looks; 6 aimed; 7 points
V1,2 5
1 traditional; 2 designer; 3 user; 4 innovative; 5 artistic; 6 scientific; 7 manufacturer; 8 futuristic; 9 functional; 10 engineer
V3 6
1 consumerism; 2 efficiency; 3 industrialisation; 4 streamlining; 5 modernity; 6 optimism

Unit 8

G1 1
1 –; 2 where; 3 whose; 4 –; 5 –; 6 –; 7 who [*or* that]; 8 whose
G1 2
1 The school where I studied gets good results.; 2 The people who live next door are friendly.; 3 The girl who works at the library was at the meeting.; 4 This is the station where I met John.; 5 The idea which you suggested yesterday is a good one. ; 6 The band whose CD I bought last week are playing here tonight.
G2 3
1 Maria Montessori**,** who was an Italian educationalist, developed the Montessori method.; 2 This course, **which** is run by Professor Jones, is my favourite.; 3 His theory, **which** is really nothing new, says we learn best by 'doing'.; 4 The University, which was founded in 1803**,** is the most famous in our country.; 5 The Prime Minister, who ~~he~~ was a student at this university, is going to make a visit here next month.; 6 The manager of Westtown Bank, who we spoke to ~~her~~ yesterday, gave us the wrong information.; 7 I gave the book to my friend John, **who** always likes to try new authors.; 8 They want to knock down King's Hospital, where I was born ~~in~~.
KL 4
1 ways/deal; 2 How about; 3 good thing; 4 best solution; 5 next/do
V1 5
1 hand in; 2 graduate; 3 exams; 4 approach ; 5 criticise ; 6 unique
V2 6
1 compulsory education; 2 continuous assessment; 3 primary school; 4 higher education; 5 corporate training; 6 distance learning

Unit 9

G1 1
1 The shuttle is flown into space.; 2 The tests were done yesterday.; 3 The new brand has been launched.; 4 Our questions haven't been answered.; 5 The new plane was built in Seattle.; 6 Tennis can be played in the morning.; 7 A new environmental policy has been announced by the President.; 8 The rockets are fired from mission control.
G1 2
2 It was announced **by the Prime Minister** today that he would resign within the week.; 3 It is the third time that the Earth has been hit **by an asteroid** in recent years.; 4 The bridge was first built ~~by people~~ in the 1920s.; 5The emergency meeting was organised **by our managing director**.; 6 The criminal was sent to prison ~~by the judge~~ for three years.
G2 3
1 an; 2 –; 3 a; 4 the; 5 –; 6 a; 7 –; 8 the; 9 the; 10 –/the
KL 4
1 e; 2 c; 3 a; 4 d; 5 b
V1 5
1 made; 2 doing; 3 do; 4 built; 5 test; 6 found; 7 solved; 8 meet
V2,3 6
1 a; 2 a; 3 c; 4 b; 5 c; 6 b

Unit 10

G1 1
1 a couple; 2 enough; 3 A few; 4 plenty of; 5 Some; 6 None; 7 A lot
G1 2
1 A few **of** my old friends …; 2 Plenty **of** people …; 3 Can I talk to you about something for **a** couple of minutes?; 4 Give him **a** little more time …; 5 There are **a** lot of students …; 6 None **of** the people in my family …
G2 3
1 e; 2 a; 3 f; 4 b; 5 d; 6 c
G2 4
1 to live; 2 to cancel; 3 watching; 4 to play; 5 helping; 6 driving; 7 to come; 8 taking; 9 to see

KL 5
1 point; 2 matter; 3 say; 4 comment; 5 here; 6 sum; 7 acceptable; 8 unhappy
V1,2 6
1 into; 2 out; 3 down; 4 up; 5 on; 6 on; 7 out; 8 over; 9 up; 10 off
V2 7
1 dramatic; 2 stable; 3 steady; 4 rise; 5 slight; 6 declined

Unit 11

G1 1
1 She said she travelled 50 miles a day.; 2 He told us that he didn't want to talk about it.; 3 He said he had called three times.; 4 My father told me to go home.; 5 Jemma said that Mel was going to Australia.; 6 The tour guide said they had lived there from 1863 to 1899.; 7 She said she was leaving.; 8 The teacher told the class to stop talking.
G1 2
1 would; 2 had spoken; 3 wasn't available; 4 was/trying; 5 could; 6 had spoken; 7 had said; 8 could; 9 couldn't; 10 to try calling
G2 3
1 Thierry asked me if I had seen you.; 2 Your boss wanted to know if you were late.; 3 They asked me why I didn't take the job.; 4 She wanted to know why you hadn't called.; 5 Your parents asked me where you were.
G2 4
1 The shop assistant asked if she could help me (him/her).; 2 The receptionist wanted to know why I (he/she) was there.; 3 The tourist asked if I (he/she) lived in London.; 4 The policeman wanted to know if this was my (his/her) car.
KL 5
1 b; 2 e; 3 d; 4 c; 5 f; 6 a
V1,2,3,4 6
1 plot; 2 dub; 3 series; 4 hilarious; 5 moving; 6 documentary; 7 special; 8 characters
V2,3 7
MUSIC: folk, reggae, hiphop, soul; BOOKS: chapter, novel, page turner, autobiography; TV PROGRAMMES: documentary, reality, sitcom, soap, episode

Unit 12

G1 1
1 If Dmitry **had** asked me to help, I would have.; 2 If he hadn't left so much evidence, the police wouldn't **have** caught him.; 3 I might have become a solicitor if I **had** worked harder at school.; 4 If you'd ~~had~~ listened to me, you wouldn't have taken the job.; 5 Sorry, but if the plane ~~would~~ had left on time, I wouldn't have been so late!; 6 You **could** have come if you had wanted to.; 7 We wouldn't have missed the deadline if everyone had ~~been~~ done what they promised.; 8 If I hadn't ~~have~~ heard the news, I wouldn't have known.
G2 2
1 The thief must have smashed the lock.; 2 The car owner might have forgotten where he parked the car.; 3 They can't have been home because the lights weren't on.; 4 They might have left a message on your voicemail.; 5 The kids must have been really hungry because they ate everything.; 6 They can't have got in from the back because there isn't a door there.; 7 They shouldn't have taken the book without asking me.; 8 They can't have planned the project properly because it went completely wrong.; 9 We should have taken out insurance when we went on holiday.
KL 3
1 evidence + shows; 2 facts + case; 3 find + client; 4 doubt + minds; 5 you + defendant; 6 look + ways; 7 certain + guilty; 8 believe + innocent
V1,2 4
1 g; 2 f; 3 e; 4 d ; 5 a; 6 b; 7 c
V1,3 5
1 kidnapping; 2 suspect; 3 getaway; 4 lawyer; 5 investigate; 6 witness; 7 fingerprints

List of photocopiable worksheets

1 A	Questions, questions	Individual, then whole class	Question forms and personality vocabulary
1 B	Prefix dominoes	Pair/group work	Prefixes and vocabulary practice
2 A	Going on a journey	Pair/group work	Phrasal verbs
2 B	Who's been to China?	Individual, then whole class	Present perfect, past simple, with time expressions and adverbs
3 A	Match the preposition	Pair/group work	Job advertisement vocabulary and dependent prepositions
3 B	Business and people	Pair work	Present perfect simple and continuous, work-related vocabulary
4 A	Subjects, skills and hobbies	Pair/group work	Phrasal verbs
4 B	Mall and cinema: town site or country site?	Pair/group work	Future forms, first conditional and language for accepting/rejecting ideas
5 A	What would you do if …?	Pair/group work	Second conditional in a personalised context
5 B	Who will buy …?	Pair/group work	Comparatives, superlatives, and language for giving a presentation
6 A	Business words pelmanism	Pair/group work	Business word collocations
6 B	Who stole the money?	Group work	Past continuous and past perfect
7 A	Build a word	Group work	Common word building endings
7 B	Where am I going?	Pair work	Modal verbs
8 A	What's my word?	Group work	Defining relative clauses
8 B	A true story	Pair/group work	Non-defining relative clauses
9 A	It's a race …	Pair/group work	Articles
9 B	Knock it down	Pair/group work	Passive forms using different tenses
10 A	A black silk evening dress …	Pair/group work	Adjective order using clothes vocabulary
10 B	Infinitive or *-ing*?	Individual, then pairs	Infinitive and *-ing* forms after selected verbs
11 A	Media word search	Individual/pair work	Media (descriptive) vocabulary
11 B	'Why did filming stop today?'	Individual/pair work	Reported speech in the context of movies
12 A	People in crime	Pair work	Reinforcement of crime vocabulary
12 B	Crime trends comparison	Individual/pair work	Modal perfects in the context of crimes; interpreting statistics from a chart

1a Questions, questions (use after Lesson 1.2)

Aims: to provide further practice of question forms (different tenses) and personality vocabulary; to give students the opportunity to find out more about other students in the class

Grouping: individual then whole class

Procedure:

- Give each student a copy of the worksheet and ask them to write some notes in the second column. Make sure they only write notes and not full sentences.
- Tell students they are going to ask the other students in the class about the notes they made. Give them a few minutes to think about the questions and help them form the questions if necessary.
- Then ask students to move around the room and ask their questions of as many other students as possible. Encourage them to ask follow-up questions to get more information.
- When they have finished, ask one or two students to tell the whole class some of the information they found out.

(Note: The vocabulary in the final section of this questionnaire is taken from Lesson 1.1: Vocabulary: personality adjectives exercises 2 and 3 on page 6 of the Coursebook. Students can use more than one of these adjectives when they complete the final section.)

1b Prefix dominoes (use after Lesson 1.3)

Aim: to provide further practice of the prefixes *ex-*, *re, mis, under, over bi, anti, mono, out, semi, dis* and vocabulary from exercises 3a and b, 4a and b

Grouping: pairs or groups of three

Procedure:

- Provide one set of cards for each pair (or group of three).
- Divide the cards equally among the students in each pair/group and ask them to put their pile of cards face down.
- Explain the activity: students have to make new words, each time matching a prefix on a domino with one of the words.
- One student turns over the top card from their pile and puts it on the desk where everyone in their pair or group can see it.
- The next student turns over the top card in their pile and puts it next to the first card if it makes a word.
- The cards can be put in front of or after the card(s) already on the desk. If a student can't make a word, they put their card at the bottom of their pile and the next student takes a turn.
- If a student thinks a word is incorrect, they can challenge the other student. If necessary, the teacher decides.
- The first student to use all their cards wins the game. If it is not possible for ANY student to use all their cards, the student who has used the most cards wins the game.

(Note: *dislike* is not included in the cards.

Note: Students may make words that are not included in exercises 3a and b, 4a and b in the Coursebook, e.g. *under + perform, re + cycle, out + do*. If this happens, they should use their dictionaries to confirm the word is correct or ask the teacher.)

2a Going on a journey (use after Lesson 2.2)

Aims: to provide further practice of the phrasal verbs *look around, set out, stop off, get to, get back, carry on*; to encourage students to use this limited number of verbs as often as possible in a real context

Grouping: pairs or groups of three

Procedure:

- Go through the instructions with the class and check they understand *sightseeing* (visiting and looking at different tourist attractions).
- Make sure they only write one or two words when answering sentences and that they write them in a random order in the circles.
- Put students into pairs or groups and tell them to ask questions about the notes their partner wrote in the circles. For example, *July 30th* – 'Is this the date you set out on your last holiday?'
- Tell students to ask follow-up questions when they can (e.g. 'Why couldn't you look around X? Why did you have to set out so early?').
- When they have finished, ask one or two students to tell the rest of the group something interesting they found out (this will probably be connected to places their partner(s) look around).

2b Who's been to China? (use after Lesson 2.3)

Aim: to provide further practice of present perfect and past simple, with time expressions and adverbs

Grouping: individual, then whole class

Procedure:

- Give each student a copy of the chart from the worksheet and ask them to read the text in the chart. Explain that they are going to do a role play, and will ask questions to find out about each other's 'characters'.
- Explain that, before the role play, they need to make questions from the phrases in the first column of the chart. Elicit the first two questions ('Where were you born? Have you ever lived in other countries?').
- Give students, individually, about five minutes to decide on the rest of the questions. Help them if necessary and check they understand the vocabulary (e.g. *abroad*) and that they are using the time expressions and adverbs accurately.

- Then give students a role-play card each and explain that this is their character. Give them a minute to read the information and help with any unknown vocabulary if necessary. Tell students that 'this country' in the role cards refers to the country in which they're studying this course.
- Ask the students to move around the room asking questions to as many others as possible. (Stress that they need to answer as their character, not as themselves.) When they find someone who has done one of the things in the first column, they write the name in the second column. Tell them they need to ask follow-up questions to get as much information as possible.
- When they have finished, ask 'Who's been to China?'.

3a Match the preposition (use after Lesson 3.1)

Aim: to practise job advertisement vocabulary and dependent prepositions

Grouping: pairs or groups of four

(Note: The vocabulary cards include four additional items of job-related vocabulary + prepositions from the advertisements on page 27 in the Coursebook: *prepared to*; *opportunity for; expected to*; *assistant to*. These were not practised in exercise 5 on page 27. If students can't remember these items, ask them to check in the advertisements at the end of the game.)

Procedure:

- Give each pair or group a set of vocabulary and preposition cards. Put the two sets of cards in separate piles face down between the students.
- One student turns over the top card from one pile (they can choose which pile).
- The next student turns over the top card from the other pile.
- If the cards are a pair (e.g. *looking* + *for*), the first student to say 'correct' wins the pair.
- If the cards are not a pair, students put both cards at the bottom of their piles.
- Repeat until all the cards are gone. The student with the most cards wins.

(Note: if there are no matches after 12 tries, mix the cards and start again.)

3b Business and people (use after Lesson 3.4)

Aim: to provide further practice of the present perfect simple and continuous, and work-related vocabulary

Grouping: pairs

Procedure:

- Tell students they are going to do a magazine interview.
- Divide the class into journalists and business people.
- Give students the appropriate section of the worksheet and ask them to read the instructions. (Note: the business people should *not* write full sentences.)
- Encourage journalists to use the present perfect in their questions, and business people to remember as much work-related vocabulary as possible.
- When they are ready, put students into pairs (journalist/business person) for the interview. Remind business people they may need to use present perfect in some of their answers.
- If time, change roles and repeat the procedure above.

4a Subjects, skills and hobbies (use after Lesson 4.1)

Aims: to provide further practice of the phrasal verbs *let down, fall behind, pick up, get by, catch on, take up, keep up with*; to encourage students to use this limited number of verbs as often as possible in a real context

Grouping: pairs or groups of three

Procedure:

- Go through the instructions with the group and check they understand *skill* and *hobby* by eliciting examples of each.
- Make sure they only write one or two words when answering sentences and that they write them in a random order in the boxes.
- Put students into pairs or groups and tell them to ask questions about the notes their partner wrote in the boxes. For example, *Maths* – 'Is this a subject at school that you picked up easily or you fell behind in?'
- Tell students to ask follow-up questions when they can (e.g. 'Why did you find Maths difficult? Why do you think you would pick up x quickly?').
- When they have finished, ask one or two students to tell the rest of the group something interesting they found out.

4b Mall and cinema: town site or country site? (use after Lesson 4.4)

Aim: to provide further practice of future forms, first conditional, and language for accepting and rejecting ideas

Grouping: groups of four (or pairs)

Procedure:

- Go through the scenario with students and check they understand *committee* (group of people to make a decision) and *site* (a place where something will be built).
- Go through the descriptions of the two sites and check students understand *destroyed* (completely changed, removed) and *make room* (give enough area/space for another building).

- Give out the role cards. This activity will work better with groups of four but, if you have put students in pairs, give one student a 'haven't decided' card and the other either a town site or a country site card. Ask students to read their cards and check they understand *mall* (a big building with a lot of different shops), *multi-screen cinema* (a big building with a lot of small cinema screens), and *in favour of* (you think this is a good idea).
- Tell students to make some notes on the different points and questions.
- Ask students to discuss the problem and decide where the mall, the cinema and the car park will be built. Encourage them to use future forms and the first conditional structure (see the Coursebook pages 40 and 43) and the Key Language on page 45 of the Coursebook).
- When they have finished, ask each group to say where they will build the new complex and why. To extend the activity, encourage the groups to questions one another's decisions.

5a What would you do if ...? (use after Lesson 5.2)

Aim: to provide further practice of the second conditional in a personalised context

Grouping: pairs or groups (maximum of four students in each group)

Procedure:

- Give each student a worksheet and ask them to tick one of the answers to the questions: a), b) or c). Stress that they should be honest and ask them to think about the reasons for their answers. If necessary, check students understand *responsible for* (it's your job/in your job description), *resign* (leave your job), *force yourself to eat it* (eat it even though it's difficult and you hate it), and *burgled* (someone steals things from your house).
- Elicit that the situations are all unreal situations in the present or future. Then elicit a second conditional sentence for the first situation, e.g. 'If I was responsible for advertising this drink, I'd resign from my job'.
- Put students in pairs or groups and ask them to compare their answers BUT NOT to show one another their worksheets. Encourage them to ask follow-up questions and give their opinions, if possible using the second conditional, e.g. 'If you did that, you'd get a bad reference from your boss.', 'If you said the drink was bad for children, you'd lose your job immediately.', etc.
- When they have finished, ask one or two pairs/groups which answers were the most popular and why.

5b Who will buy ...? (use after Lesson 5.4)

Aim: to provide further practice of language for comparisons and the Key and Useful Language in the Scenario section of Unit 5

Grouping: pairs or groups (maximum of four students in each group)

Procedure:

- Give one worksheet to each student and allow a few minutes for them to read the information individually.
- Put students into pairs or groups. Go through the instructions and ask students to use the language for comparisons they saw on page 53 of the Coursebook.
- When they have decided who will probably buy the car, give them about ten minutes to make notes for the presentation.
- Ask one or two students from each group to give their presentation to the rest of the class.

6a Business words pelmanism (use after Lesson 6.3)

Aim: to test students understanding of and reinforce business word collocations

Grouping: pairs or groups (maximum of four students in each group)

Procedure:

- Cut up the cards, mix them together and place them face down and separate from each other on the table/floor in front of each pair or group of students.
- One student turns over two cards and if they are a match (e.g. *make/a profit*), they keep the cards. They then turn over two more cards and repeat.
- If the cards are not a match, the student replaces them, face down, in the exact positions they were in before.
- The next student then tries to make a match in the same way (trying to remember where the cards that form combinations are).
- Repeat this procedure until all the cards are gone.
- The student with the most cards wins the game.

6b Who stole the money? (use after lesson 6.3)

Aim: to provide further practice of the past continuous and past perfect

Grouping: groups of four

Procedure:

- Put students into groups of four and give them the situation sheet and one role card each (make sure that each student has a different role card).
- Ask students to read the situation and their role card.
- If necessary, remind students of past perfect '(What had you done by...?') and past continuous ('What were you doing at...?') questions.
- Then tell them to take it in turns and ask questions to the person indicated on their role card. All the students in the group need to listen to the answers, but only the person asking the question needs to make notes.

- When all the students have asked and answered the questions, tell them to decide who probably took the money. If necessary, students can remind each other of the answers they heard by referring to their notes. Alternatively, students can ask some of the questions again.

Answer: Anna probably stole the money because she was the only person alone in the office (at three o'clock, reading files).

7a Build a word (use after Lesson 7.1)

Aim: to provide reinforcement and encourage memorisation of common word building endings

Grouping: groups of three to six

Procedure:

- Provide one set of cards for each group. Cut the cards up, mix them together and give five cards to each student in each group. Put the remaining cards in a pile face down on the table in front of each group of students.
- Explain the activity: The students have to make sets of words or word-building endings. They need three words/word-building endings to make a set (e.g. *produce/-r/-t* OR *produce/-t/-tive* OR *produce/-r/-tive*).
- Students take it in turns to either pick up the top card from the pile or take one card (without seeing what is written on it) from another student. If they pick up a card from the table, they must put one of their cards at the bottom of the pile. If they take a card from another student, they must give one of their cards to that student. They must never have more than five cards in their hand.
- When a student has made a set, they put it on the table in front of them and explain any letters they need to change in the word to attach the suffix (e.g. *produce – productive*).
- This student then takes three cards from the pile (so that they still have five cards in their hand).
- The game stops when all the cards in the pile are finished.
- The winner is the student with the most sets.

7b Where am I going? (use after Lesson 7.3)

Aim: to provide further practice of modal verbs

Grouping: pairs

Procedure:

- Give each student two cards each (a country and a city) and tell them not to show the cards to each other.
- Explain that it's the student's birthday and their partner is taking them for a surprise holiday. They have to listen to the clues and try to guess where they're going.
- Students take it in turns to read out the clues on their card. After each clue, their partner has to try and guess where they're going ('It might be London. It can't be Singapore because it's never cold there. It must be in Europe because of the climate.' etc.).
- If they guess *before the sixth clue*, they win the card but if they need all six clues, they don't win the card.
- The second student then reads the clues on one of their cards and the first students tries to guess the destination.
- The procedure is repeated until all the cards have been used.
- The winner is the student with the most cards.

8a What's my word? (use after Lesson 8.2)

Aim: to provide further practice of defining relative clauses and education-related vocabulary

Grouping: groups of four

Procedure:

- Cut up the cards and put one set face down on the table in front of each group of students.
- Put students in pairs in their groups (i.e. if you have a group of four, there will be two pairs).
- Tell one student to pick up the top card and describe it to his/her partner (e.g. 'It's a place where you have lessons'). The partner has to guess the word (e.g. *classroom*). If they guess the word correctly, the pair keeps the card. If the first student doesn't know the word, they put it at the bottom on the pile and take the next one. They must describe as many words as possible in one minute. They cannot use the word itself in the description.
- After one minute, the second pair says 'stop' and then follow the same procedure above.
- Repeat the procedure until students have guessed all the words. The winners are the pair with the most cards.

8b A true story (use after Lesson 8. 3)

Aim: to provide further practice of non-defining relative clauses

Groupings: pairs or groups (maximum of four)

Procedure:

- Tell students they are going to read a true story. Cut up the story cards and give one set to each pair/group. Tell them to read the cards and decide the correct order for the story. Help with vocabulary if necessary.

D, B, G, E, H, F, A, C

- Then give each group a set of additional information cards. Students have to decide where this information goes in the story and make non-defining relative clauses. They need to discuss (using language for possibilities and options) and decide what changes should be made to the text to fit in the non-defining relative clauses.

This is a true story that happened to me when I was a child at school. I was about 12 years old at the time and I'd been going to this school for about two years.

continued…

One morning in December, **which I remember was a very cold month that year,** I arrived at the school earlier than usual to play football in the playground. As always I was with my friend, Jamie, **who/whom I had known since I was five years old,** However, after about 15 minutes we were so cold we couldn't feel our fingers. So, we decided to go into the school buildings**, which were new and well-heated,** to try to keep warm.
As we were walking towards the main doors, Jamie suddenly said 'Did you see that?'. 'See what?', I asked. 'A face at the window', Jamie said, 'a man's face'. I told him it was probably the caretaker, but Jamie insisted he'd never seen the man before.
We went into the school and walked to our classroom. But as we entered the room, we heard a loud knocking sound. The sound came from the ceiling**, where birds sometimes lived**. 'It's the birds', I said. 'Not in December', Jamie replied.
We told the teacher what we'd heard, but for the rest of the day we heard nothing more and forgot all about the man and the noise. When the school bell rang**, which it did every day at three o'clock,** we packed our books away and went home.
The next day at eight o'clock**, when we usually arrived at school,** we saw there were police cars outside. One of the police officers**, who was standing in front of the doors,** said that the school was closed and told us to go home.
When we got to my house, my father told us what had happened. The police**, who had been called to the school by the caretaker,** had found a man living in the new ceiling**, which had been built about a year before**.
Later we found out that he had moved into the space between the new ceiling and the original one about two months before. He'd made himself a home**, where he had a bed, some books and a reading light,** but had always been very quiet until that cold day we went to play football.

9a It's a race … (use after Lesson 9.3)

Aim: to provide further practice and reinforcement of *a*, *an*, *the*, or no article

Grouping: pairs or groups of four (two pairs in a group of four)

Procedure:

- Give each student (or pair) one sentence card. Make sure that each student in a pair (or pair in a group of four) has a different sentence card.
- Cut up the article cards and put them on the table, face up, in front of the students.
- Students have to decide if each sentence on their card needs *a*, *an*, *the*, or no article. They then take the article they need from the table. Tell students that they must be as fast as possible because there aren't enough article cards for all the gaps on both the cards – it's a race.
- When all the article cards have been used, they give their sentence card to another student/pair to check. If they have used an article where they shouldn't, they must give that article to the other student/pair.
- The student or pair with the most article cards at the end is the winner.

9b Knock it down (use after Lesson 9.2)

Aim: to provide further practice of passive forms using different tenses

Grouping: pairs and groups of four

Procedure:

- Go through the scenario with students and remind them that we often use the passive in formal presentations.
- Put students into pairs and give one information card to each pair.
- Give them about 20 minutes to write their presentation. Move around the room to help with vocabulary and check they are using passive forms (e.g.e 'Foxley House has been used as a Young People's Centre since 1965'; 'The report will be produced by the end of this year', etc.).
- Put the pairs in groups of four (two pairs in each group) and tell them to give their presentations.

(Note: Encourage students to use some of the Key and Useful Language from Unit 8 [page 87] and Unit 9 [page 97] in the Coursebook.)

- After the presentations, ask students to discuss the advantages of disadvantages of demolishing the two buildings and to decide which one should be demolished.

10a A black silk evening dress … (use after Lesson 10.2)

Aim: to provide further practice and reinforcement of adjective order using clothes vocabulary

Grouping: pairs or groups of four (two pairs in a group)

Procedure:

- Give each student or pair of students a large sheet of paper (or ask them to turn to a blank page in their note books) and ask them to write 'A' ten times down the left hand margin.
- Mix up the word cards and put them face up on the table in front of the students.
- Individual students have to take one card at a time to make phrases using a colour, a material, a function/class, and a noun. For example, *A green, cotton sun hat*. However, all students can take cards at the same time and do not need to take turns.
- The cards must be placed on the piece of paper next to each 'A' with all the words in the correct order.
  - They can only have one card in their hand at a time and if they decide not to use it, they must return it to the table for other students to use.
  - They must finish one phrase before beginning the next (so they can't take all the 'colour' words at once).

  - They can move cards from one phrase to another when they have more than one phrase.
  - All the phrases must have a realistic meaning (e.g. *a brown leather summer dress* is unlikely because leather is too hot for the summer).
- If students don't know a particular word, they can ask you or look it up in their dictionary.
- The game finishes when all the cards have been used, so students have to be fast.
- Ask students to check each other's phrases for correct word order and for meaning.
- The winner is the student/pair of students with the most correct phrases.

(Note: Remind students that *rain* + *coat* is normally written as one word.)

10b Infinitive or *-ing*? (use after Lesson 10.3)

Aim: to provide further practice and reinforcement of infinitive and *-ing* forms after the verbs *enable, advise, want, hope, expect, allow, begin, continue, enjoy, hate, manage, teach, promise* and *decide*

Grouping: individually, and then pairs

Procedure:

- Give one worksheet to each student and tell them they must think of activities rather than 'things' to finish the sentences (e.g. 'At the weekend, I enjoy going …' etc.).
- Give students ten minutes to complete the sentences. Walk round the room to check that students are using the correct form (either infinitive with *to*, or *-ing*).
- When they have finished, ask students to give their worksheet to a partner.
- Students read their partner's sentences and choose six to ask more questions about. Tell students *not* to write the questions they want to ask.
- Put students into pairs to ask/answer the questions.
- When they have finished, ask students the most interesting/surprising/strangest thing they heard.

11a Media word search (use after Lesson 11.1)

(Note: This activity will also be useful revision of vocabulary immediately before Lesson 11.4 exercise 6 on page 119 of the Coursebook.)

Aim: to provide reinforcement of media (descriptive) vocabulary

Vocabulary in this activity is:

atmosphere	plot	sitcom
gripping	electrifying	moving
hilarious	breathtaking	science fiction
outstanding		

Grouping: individual or pairs

Procedure:

- Give each student a copy of the word square and tell them there are ten words hidden in the square. They should search both across and down. All the words come from the vocabulary exercises on page 113 of the Coursebook.
- Give students plenty of time to find the ten words before giving them the answer square.

11b 'Why did filming stop today?' (use after Lesson 11.3)

Aim: to provide further practice of reported speech in the context of movies

Grouping: individual and pairs

(Note: If you have a class smaller than ten, leave out some of the characters, e.g. the composer or assistant director. If you have a large class, give the same character to more than one student.)

Procedure:

- Explain that all the students are working on a new movie. There was a problem at the studio today and filming stopped early. No-one knows what the problem is, but everyone wants to know.
- Give one role card to each student. Explain that this is their 'character' and what they have to say about why filming stopped. Help with any difficult vocabulary.
- Give each student a notes sheet. Students then move around the room and ask other students their role, and then ask 'Why did filming stop today?'. Students make notes (not full sentences) next to each character's title on the notes sheet.
- As they get information they can pass it to other students by asking/answering 'What did the Director say?', 'What did the Leading Actor say?', etc. They have to answer this question using reported speech.
- When they have all the information, put students into pairs to write a report for the studio. Write the verbs *said, told, asked* and *added* on the board. They should use reported speech and reported questions, with the verbs from the board, when they write their reports

12a People in crime (use after Lesson 12.3)

Aim: to provide further reinforcement of crime vocabulary

Grouping: pairs

Procedure:

- If necessary, ask students to look through the vocabulary in Lesson 12.3 exercise 1a again.
- Put the definition cards in a pile face down on the table in front of each pair of students.
- One student picks up a card and reads it to the other student. If the other student guesses the word, they keep the card. If they don't know the word, the card is put at the bottom of the pile.
- Students take it in turns to read/guess until all the cards have been used. The winning student/pair is the one with the most cards.
- Then ask each student to choose one of the '*people in crime*' words (i.e. not *getaway, fingerprints* or *robbery*) but not to tell anyone else their word.

- Students take it in turns to ask yes/no questions to guess which 'person in crime' the other students are (e.g. 'Are you a criminal? Do you commit crimes in a bank? Do you work in a court?' etc.).

A word to describe when money is stolen from a bank	A robbery
A person whose job it is to represent/defend a suspect in court	A lawyer
The marks the police look for at a crime scene. These marks are made with the fingers	Fingerprints
A person who argues in a court the reasons why a suspect is guilty	A prosecutor
A person who steals things from another person or place	A thief
A person who steals money from a bank	A bank robber
A word to describe when criminals drive off very quickly in a car	A getaway
Taking someone by force and asking other people to give money to give them back	Kidnapping
Someone the police believe has committed a crime, but they are not completely sure yet	A suspect
When a criminal has taken someone by force, a word to describe the money they ask for	A ransom
A person a criminal takes as a prisoner in order to get money or to stop police catching them	A hostage
A person whose job it is to represent/defend a criminal in an American court	An attorney

12b Crime trends comparison (use after Lesson 12. 3)

Aims: to provide further practice of modal perfects in the context of crimes; to practise interpreting statistics from a chart

Grouping: individual and pairs

Procedure:

- Give the Crime trends section to each student and go through the instructions with them.

1 House burglary; **2** Mugging

- Ask students to suggest some reasons why the crime levels changed between 1999 and 2001. Encourage them to use the modal perfect in their answers if possible.
- Put students into pairs and give each student an information card (each partner in a pair must have a different information card).
- Explain that part A of the card has the possible reasons for the change in levels of two crimes from the pie charts. Give them five minutes to write sentences using the modal perfect to express these reasons (e.g. 'Banks might have used/installed more security cameras in 2001.', 'More muggers might have assaulted their victims.').
- Explain that part B of the card has their opinions on the two crimes their partner has written about. Tell them to listen to their partner and when they hear their partner mention the ideas in part B, they should give their opinion (e.g. Student 1: 'Street lighting might not have been very good in 2001.'; Student 2: 'No, street lighting must have been good (because the government gave a lot of money to street lighting).'

QUESTIONS, QUESTIONS

	My notes
In my free time I …	
The kind of place I usually go for my holidays	
Where I went for my holiday last year	
An interesting country or place I've been to	
Something adventurous I've done (or a friend has done)	
Where I'm working or studying at the moment	
Something fun I did last month	
Something I hated doing when I was a child	
A good book I've read or a good movie I've seen recently	
I'm generally a self-confident / generous / ambitious / easy-going / quiet / talkative / strong-willed person	

PREFIX DOMINOES

mono	anti	out	bi	over	under	mis	re	ex-
run	used	behave	rated	president	define	boss	understand	confident
out	re	bi	under	mis	ex-	dis	over	semi
social	circle	do	rail	perform	comfort	cycle	shadowed	lingual
semi	over	dis	ex-	mis	under	bi	re	out
run	used	behave	rated	president	define	boss	understand	confident
ex-	re	mis	under	over	bi	out	anti	mono
social	circle	do	rail	perform	comfort	cycle	shadowed	lingual

A GOING ON A JOURNEY

Write short answers to the following sentences about a holiday you had or a journey you did in the past (one or two words is enough). Write your answers in any circle below, but not in the same order as the questions. Try to give as many answers as possible.

- The day/date/month you set out on the holiday/journey
- The name of the place you set out from
- The day/date/month you got to your destination
- The name of a town you stopped off in while travelling from one place to another
- Somewhere you wanted to stop off in for longer but couldn't
- The reason why you couldn't stop off, but had to carry on with your journey
- Somewhere you really enjoyed looking around
- Somewhere you didn't enjoy looking around
- Somewhere you wanted to look around but couldn't
- The earliest time you had to set out to go sightseeing
- The latest time you got back to your hotel after sightseeing
- The day/date/month you got back to your own country/city

WHO'S BEEN TO CHINA

Find some who:	Name(s)
Wasn't born in this country	
Has lived in other countries	
Arrived in this country recently	
Hasn't travelled much for years	
Travelled a lot when they were a child	
Has lived in this country for less than five years	
Studied abroad	
Bought a ticket recently to travel abroad	
Has worked in another country	
Has visited more than four countries	
Has never been outside Europe	
Has never travelled alone	

ROLE CARDS

You were born in Bangkok, Thailand in 1978. Your parents worked for international schools in many different countries, so all your life you've lived abroad. Some of the countries you've lived in are: China, Indonesia, Vietnam and Australia. You came back to this country to go to university in 1997 and you've lived here since then. You haven't been anywhere for a few years because you travelled so much when you were a child.

When you were a child, your parents took you and your sister abroad for your holidays every summer. The best place you visited was the USA because you've always loved American music. When you were 17, you moved to the USA to study at university, and you've lived and worked there ever since. Some of states you've lived in are New York, California and Texas. You came back to this country last week, but just to visit your parents.

You were born in this country and have lived here all of your early life, but always wanted to experience different cultures. In 1999, you got a job with an international travel agency and moved to Mexico City to manage a very busy office there. While you were living in Mexico, you visited a lot of different South American countries: Brazil, Argentina, Peru, Bolivia and Colombia. Brazil was your favourite.

You are on a long holiday – one year of travelling alone around the world. You left your home country six months ago and have been in this country since last month to study English. On your travels, you've visited Egypt, Morocco, Tunisia, Spain, Italy, Austria, Hungary and Poland. Your favourite country was Egypt because you loved the history and the beautiful weather. Last week you bought a ticket to your next destination – China.

Your father was a famous explorer and when you were a child you travelled all over the world with him, experiencing different countries and cultures. You can't remember how many countries you've already visited. You came to this country four years ago to study and it's the country you love more than any other. You've haven't decided where you want to go next, but at the moment you're very happy here.

For the last ten years, you've been to a different country for your holidays: France, Spain, Italy, Greece, Poland, the Czech Republic, Germany, Norway, and last year you went to Romania. You've always travelled with your friends because you really don't live travelling alone. You've never been outside of Europe but would love to go to Asia. You've wanted to go to China since you were a small child – such an interesting culture!

Card set 1: job advertisement vocabulary

looking	experience	depend	responsible
knowledge	fluency	report	prospects
prepared	opportunity	expected	assistant

Card set 2: dependent prepositions

of	for	in	on
in	to	for	for
to	to	for	to

BUSINESS AND PEOPLE

<table>
<tr><td colspan="2">You are a famous and successful business person. You are going to be interviewed for a magazine called Business and People. The magazine has a monthly section on the lives of successful business people from around the world. Use the ideas below to write short notes about your work and life to prepare for the interview. Do not write full sentences.</td></tr>
<tr><td><u>Your career</u>
How many companies worked for?
Name of present company?
How long with present company?
Position at present company? How long?</td><td><u>Challenges, success and failure</u>
The most difficult job/task you've done?
The biggest challenge you've faced?
Mistakes you've made?
Something you haven't done but would like to?
Advice to young business people?</td></tr>
<tr><td colspan="2">The skills that make you so successful?</td></tr>
<tr><td><u>Your working day</u>
What time do you get up?
You often work from home. Why? How long?
Your work-life balance? Good/bad? Why?</td><td><u>Your work around the world</u>
Living in which country now? How long?
How many countries before this one?
Your favourite country? Why?</td></tr>
<tr><td>You've received many business awards
How many? What for?</td><td>You do charity work
Your present charity? How long?
How many charities?</td></tr>
<tr><td>You're married. Who to? How long?</td><td>Your interests. What are they? How long?</td></tr>
</table>

<table>
<tr><td colspan="2">You are a journalist working for a magazine called Business and People. The magazine has a monthly section on the work and lives of successful business people from around the world. You are going to interview one of them. Use the ideas below to write some questions to ask the business person.</td></tr>
<tr><td><u>His/her career</u>
How many companies worked for?
Name of present company?
How long with present company?
Position at present company? How long?
His/her most difficult job? Why?</td><td><u>Challenges, success and failure</u>
The biggest challenge he/she's faced?
Mistakes made?
Something he/she hasn't done but would like to?
Advice to young business people?</td></tr>
<tr><td colspan="2">The skills that make him/her so successful?</td></tr>
<tr><td colspan="2"><u>His/her work around the world</u>
Living in which country now? How long?
How many countries before this one?</td></tr>
<tr><td>Business awards? How many? What for?</td><td>Charity work? How long?
How many charities?</td></tr>
<tr><td>Married? Who to? How long?</td><td>His/her interests? How long?</td></tr>
</table>

SUBJECTS, SKILLS AND HOBBIES

Write short answers to the following sentences about subjects you studied at school and skills you've learned, or would like to learn. Write your answers in any circle below but not in the same order as the sentences. Try to answer as many as possible.

- A skill or a subject you picked up easily in the past
- A skill or subject you think you could pick up easily in the future
- A subject you found difficult at school and where your lack of understanding let you down
- A subject at school you got by in but weren't very good or very bad
- A subject at school you fell behind in
- What you did to try to keep up with the subject above
- A way of teaching that helps you catch on when a subject is difficult
- A hobby or a subject you would like to take up in the future

4B MALL AND CINEMA: TOWN SITE OR COUNTRY SITE?

SCENARIO

The local government of Newton is going to build a new shopping mall, a multi-screen cinema and a big car park. You are all residents of Newton and are members of a committee to advise the local government on where the new mall and cinema complex will be built. There are two possible sites for the new buildings; both have their advantages and disadvantages.

The town site

The first site is in the centre of town where a public park will be destroyed to make room for the new buildings. There is a school, a lot of houses, some local shops and a very busy road near the site.

The country site

The second site is outside the town where fields and woods will be destroyed to make room. People go for walks in the woods at weekends. The fields are used to grow vegetables for the local shops in the town. There are no houses, shops, schools and only a small road nearby.

ROLE CARDS

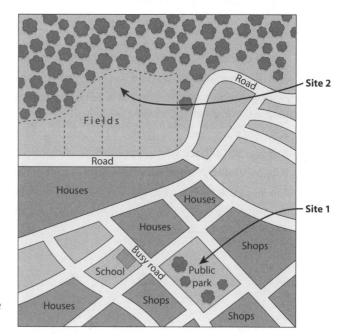

You are a local resident. You have children at the school near the town site and use the park and the local shops. You also use the woods at weekends and like the locally grown vegetables. You **haven't decided** if you are more in favour of the town or the country site. Think about the following:

- more traffic in the town/country (what problems will this cause?)
- the town site is close to the school (what problems will this cause?)
- you and your children use the park in the town *and* the woods in the country
- will local shops close if everyone drives to the country site for their shopping?
- the country site is less convenient (what problems will this cause?)
- any other problems with the town or the country site?

You are the director of the new shopping mall and multi-screen cinema. Your company will make a lot of money from the new constructions. You **haven't decided** if you are more in favour of the town or the country site. Think about the following:

- the town site is close to the school (what problems will this cause?)
- if the country site is approved, people will have to travel away from local shops to go to there (what problems will this cause?)
- is it cheaper to build in the town or the country?
- both sites will attract people from other towns (is this better for the country site or the town site?)
- how will residents feel about losing the woods and the fields outside town?
- any other problems with the town or the country site?

You are a local shopkeeper selling vegetables grown in the nearby fields. You are more **in favour of the town site**. Think about the following:

- people will have to travel away from your shop to go to the country site (what problems will this cause?)
- the car park at the new mall (why is this a good thing for you?)
- the town site is convenient for local residents (is this good for you?)
- competition from the new mall (is this a problem for you?)
- people from other towns will come to the new mall and cinema (why is this good for you?)
- any other problems with the country site?

You are a local government representative and want the shopping mall and multi-screen cinema built because of the taxes the government will be able to collect from the new business. You are **in favour of the country site** because the building work will be easier and cheaper there. Think about the following:

- how will the building work at the town site affect local residents?
- will the traffic be a problem?
- how will residents feel about losing the park in their town?
- the school is near the town site (why is this a problem?)
- will competition in the town make local shops close?
- any other problems with the town site?

WHAT WOULD YOU DO IF ...?

Answer the questions below honestly and then compare your answers with other students in your group.

1 You're responsible for advertising a new children's fruit drink which you know isn't very good for them because it has lots of added sugar. In the advertisement, would you:

a) say it's good for children because of all the fruit it contains?

b) say it might be bad for children because it has lots of sugar, but promote it as a fun, party drink?

c) resign from your advertising job because you can't advertise such a product?

2 You're applying for a job you really want and you know you can do well. However, you don't have all the necessary experience: Would you:

a) lie about your experience on the application form *and* at the interview?

b) tell the truth on the application form *and* at the interview?

c) lie on the application form but tell the truth when you go for an interview?

3 A homeless person asks you for money on the street, but you only have a little change which you need for your bus fare. Would you:

a) say you don't have any change?

b) say you will come back later and give him some change (but not return)?

c) give him the change you have?

4 You're at your friend's house for dinner and you hate the food. Would you tell your friend:

a) that you don't like the food?

b) that you're really sorry, but you're not very hungry, and not finish the food?

c) that the food is lovely and force yourself to eat it with a smile on your face?

5 Your friend has just given you tickets for a really big football match. You love football more than anything else. But the match is on Monday afternoon and you also have a very important meeting at work that day. Would you:

a) phone work, lie to your boss that you're sick, and go to the match?

b) take a day's holiday from work to go to the match, even though you know your boss will be furious?

c) give the tickets to someone else?

6 You are looking after a friend's house while she is on holiday. Two days before she returns, the house is burgled. Would you:

a) call her immediately and tell her?

b) wait two days, until she comes to pick up the house key from you, and then tell her?

c) call another friend and ask them to tell her?

WHO WILL BUY ...?

You are advertising executives and you are doing some market research to decide the kind of person who is going to buy the following product:

A new and expensive 'green' car which is environmentally friendly, uses 'green' fuel and can run on electricity for short distances. It is also luxurious, well-designed – *and* fast. It is ideal for someone who likes driving or has to drive a lot for their job, but who also has an eye for design. The car is big enough for a family, but sporty enough for single people who like a bit of adventure.

Below is the information you have received on four people with different ages, salary levels, etc. With the other executives in your group, compare the information and discuss who will probably buy the car. Give reasons.

When you have decided who will probably buy the car, give a short presentation to the other groups of executives.

Name:	Andrew
Age:	46
Salary:	150,000 Euros
Average work hours per week:	45
Andrew says:	'I'm really interested in politics. I'm very worried about the environment and what's happening to our countryside. I hate driving, but I have to have a car because I live five miles from the nearest shop!'

Name:	Petra
Age:	32
Yearly salary:	100,000 Euros
Average work hours per week:	60
Petra says:	'I work long hours and have to drive a lot to and from different clients. I try to spend all my spare time with my kids – I've got three. When I'm too busy, my husband picks them up from school and does the shopping.'

Name:	Paul
Age:	25
Salary:	40,000 Euros
Average work hours per week:	55
Paul says:	'I'm working a lot at the moment so I can earn more in the future. I have to travel a long way by train to my job – I hate it! I'm about to become a father and I'm really excited – but I do worry about what the world will be like for her (or him!) in the future.'

Name:	Simona
Age:	55
Salary:	300,000 Euros
Average work hours per week:	70
Simona says:	'Okay, I work hard and earn a lot, but I'm single so I spend a lot on myself – on clothes, going out, holidays, beautiful flat in the centre of town. I love driving and need a car to go with my fashionable image – that's important to me.'

make	a contract
make	a profit
make	a product
make	bankrupt
found	a company
go	into business
run	a company
introduce	a product
go	bankrupt
launch	a company
launch	a product
negotiate	a contract
go	into business

WHO STOLE THE MONEY?

SITUATION SHEET

You work for a small company. There are four employees (Anna, Peter, Jane and Simon) and only two rooms (a meeting room and an office). Yesterday, some money was stolen from the office and today you need to find out who probably took it.

ROLE CARDS

ANNA			
09.00	11.00	12.00	15.00
• Meet new client with Peter in meeting room • Go to shop with Peter to buy coffee	• Write report in office	• Lunch with Jane in the office	• Read files in office
Ask Simon: What he'd done before three o'clock What he was doing at midday What he was doing at three o'clock		Notes:	

PETER			
09.00	11.00	12.00	15.00
• Meet new client with Anna in meeting room • Go to shop with Anna to buy coffee	• Email clients in office	• Lunch with client in meeting room	• Talk with Simon in meeting room
Ask Jane: What she'd done before three o'clock What she was doing at midday What she was doing at three o'clock		Notes:	

JANE			
09.00	11.00	12.00	15.00
• Edit report in office • Go to chemist to buy medicine	• Talk with Simon in meeting room	• Lunch with Anna in the office	• Left work at 14.30 because feeling ill
Ask Peter: What he'd done before three o'clock What he was doing at midday What he was doing at three o'clock		Notes:	

SIMON			
09.00	11.00	12.00	15.00
• Email clients in office • Go to dentist	• Meet with Jane in meeting room	• Lunch with brother in restaurant	• Meet with Peter in meeting room
Ask Anna: What she'd done before three o'clock What she was doing at midday What she was doing at three o'clock		Notes:	

PEARSON Longman

design	-er	design
-ed	-tist	science
-tific	manufacture	-er
-ing	produce	-r
-tion	-tive	engineer
engineer	-ing	use
-r	use	-able
develop	-er	-ment
-ing	innovate	-or
-tion	-tive	invent
-or	-tion	-tive
-ist	art	-istic

WHERE AM I GOING?

A COUNTRY

1 It's a very dry country in most parts.
2 It's very hot in the north but cooler in winter in the south.
3 It has a small population.
4 But it's a very, very large country.
5 One of the cities has a famous bridge and opera house.
6 There are a lot of animals you can't find naturally anywhere else in the world.

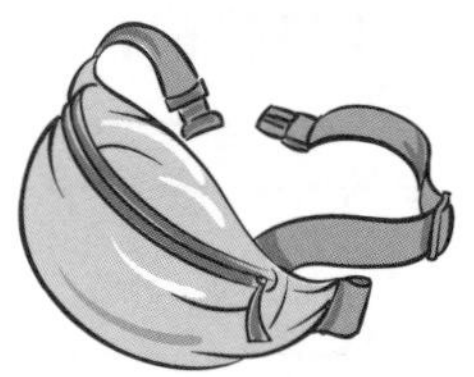

A CITY

1 It's hot and humid in the summer and cold with snow in the winter.
2 It's by the sea.
3 It's got lots of tall buildings.
4 The streets are very long and very straight.
5 There's a very well-known statue.
6 English is the first language.

A COUNTRY

1 This is an enormous country.
2 It's cold in the north with mountains, and hot in the south.
3 It's made up of many different provinces or states.
4 The people speak many different languages but there's only one official language.
5 It has many factories and produces things the whole world uses.
6 The population is more than one billion.

A CITY

1 It's warm in the summer and cold in the winter.
2 It's inland (not by the sea).
3 It's on a river.
4 The people love their food and their fashion.
5 There's a very famous tower.
6 The people speak French.

classroom	homework	vacation
professor	seminar	teacher
degree	break	thesis
lesson	languages	book
Science	Mathematics	sports
brochure	exam	essay
degree	certificate	e-learning
head teacher	black/whiteboard	correspondence course
postgraduate	library	IT room
tutor	History	Geography
pass	fail	university

A TRUE STORY

STORY CARDS

A: When we got to my house, my father told us what had happened. The police had found a man living in the new ceiling.

B: One morning in December, I arrived at the school earlier than usual to play football in the playground. As always I was with my friend, Jamie. However, after about 15 minutes we were so cold we couldn't feel our fingers. So, we decided to go into the school buildings to try to keep warm.

C: Later we found out that he had moved into the space between the new ceiling and the original one about two months before. He'd made himself a home, but had always been very quiet until that cold day we went to play football.

D: This is a true story that happened to me when I was a child at school. I was about 12 years old at the time and I'd been going to this school for about two years.

E: We went into the school and walked to our classroom. But as we entered the room, we heard a loud knocking sound. The sound came from the ceiling. 'It's the birds', I said. 'Not in December', Jamie replied.

F: The next day at eight o'clock we saw there were police cars outside. One of the police officers said that the school was closed and told us to go home.

G: As we were walking towards the main doors, Jamie suddenly said 'Did you see that?'. 'See what?', I asked. 'A face at the window', Jamie said, 'a man's face'. I told him it was probably the caretaker, but Jamie insisted he'd never seen the man before.

H: We told the teacher what we'd heard, but for the rest of the day we heard nothing more and forgot all about the man and the noise. When the school bell rang, we packed our books away and went home.

ADDITIONAL INFORMATION CARDS

it rang every day at three o'clock	she was standing in front of the doors
I'd known him since I was five years old	the time we usually arrived at school
birds sometimes lived there	they had been called to the school by the caretaker
it had been built about a year before	they were new and well-heated
I remember it was a very cold month that year	he had a bed, some books and a reading light there

SENTENCE CARDS

1 I've lived in _______ UK all my life.

2 This is _______ best movie I've ever seen.

3 How long have you lived in _______ Paris?

4 _______ pen is something you should never be without.

5 _______ Pacific is _______ biggest ocean in the world.

6 _______ children don't often enjoy _______ homework.

7 I've always had _______ nice car. I bought _______ car I'm driving now last year.

8 _______ Mona Lisa is _______ very famous painting.

9 _______ evening at the movies is always enjoyable.

10 _______ homework I did last night was really difficult.

---

1 I've lived in _______ China all my life.

2 This is _______ most boring book I've ever read.

3 How long have you lived in _______ USA?

4 _______ pens are something you should never be without.

5 _______ Himalayas are _____ tallest mountains in the world.

6 _______ people all over _______ world are travelling more and more each year.

7 Why do you want _______ new car? _______ one you have now is okay.

8 _______ Taj Mahal is probably _______ most beautiful building in _______ India.

9 That was _______ interesting film, wasn't it?

10 Did you like _______ coffee I gave you _______ last week?

ARTICLE CARDS

the	the	the	the	the	the	the	the
the	the	the	the	a	a	an	an

SCENARIO

You are on a committee drawing up plans for a new park in your home town. To make way for the park, one of two important local buildings will have to be demolished (knocked down).

You have been asked to give a presentation to other members of the committee to present facts about one of the two buildings. Use the information and the verbs on the card your teacher gives you to prepare your presentation.

After you have given your presentation and heard the other members' talk about their building, discuss which of the two buildings should be demolished.

Information card 1: Foxley House

Designer: Harold Fitzgerald (famous and important architect)
Builder: Unknown
Date: 1835
Changes to building: Another (3rd) floor (1906), swimming pool (1933), new stairs (1990)
Past uses: Davies' family home (bought 1835, sold 1955, empty 1955–1964), Young People's Centre (bought 1965)
Present uses: Young People's Centre (sports facilities, café, meeting rooms)
Future uses: Possibly a nursing home for old people
Condition: Bad (storm damage 1997)
Report on demolition: Ready end of this year

Use passive forms and the following verbs in your presentation:

- Design
- Buy
- Add
- Live in
- Leave empty
- Need (repair)
- Build
- Sell
- Replace (stairs)
- Use
- Damage
- Produce (report)

Information card 2: Channing Theatre

Designer: Susan Smith (important, modern architect)
Builder: James Townsend (famous local builder)
Date: 1967
Changes to building: New windows (1989), air-conditioning (1992), two meeting rooms (1993)
Past uses: Theatre (internationally famous), conferences, meetings
Present uses: Conferences, meetings, private parties
Future uses: Possibly a cinema or a theatre, maybe a Young People's Centre (café, meeting rooms, TV room)
Condition Bad (fire damage to part of building 2005)
Report on demolition: Ready end of this year

Use passive forms and the following verbs in your presentation:

- Design
- Buy
- Add
- Live in
- Leave empty
- Need (repair)
- Build
- Sell
- Replace (stairs)
- Use
- Damage
- Produce (report)

brown	leather	walking	boot
black	plastic	rain	coat
white	fur	winter	jacket
red	silk	summer	jacket
green	cotton	sun	hat
blue	silk	evening	dress
white	cotton	sun	hat
red	cotton	baseball	cap
black	woollen	business	suit
blue	woollen	school	uniform

10B INFINITIVE OR *-ING*? (USE AFTER LESSON 10.3)

Finish the following sentences in a way that is true for you:

1 My English studies will enable me ....

....

2 My parents always advised me ....

....

3 I've always wanted ....

....

4 Next year, I hope ....

....

5 Next year, I expect ....

....

6 My parents never allowed me ....

....

7 Last year, I began ....

....

8 Next year, I'll continue ....

....

9 At the weekend, I enjoy ....

....

10 I've always hated ....

....

11 When I was a child, I was taught ....

....

12 I've recently decided ....

....

Now swap this worksheet with a partner and read their answers. Choose *six* sentences and think of some questions to ask your partner to get more information. Don't write your questions.

Ask your partner your questions and answer the questions they ask you.

MEDIA WORD SEARCH

Y	J	F	B	J	J	X	A	G	N	L	K	D	S	H	V	H
V	N	P	U	S	D	A	T	M	N	G	H	O	P	P	P	V
A	B	S	L	I	H	N	M	O	V	I	N	G	L	M	C	D
U	R	I	P	T	M	C	O	A	S	F	G	J	O	B	L	C
L	E	K	B	C	A	E	S	U	Y	L	P	W	T	W	U	C
A	A	P	W	O	U	N	P	L	M	N	B	H	U	Y	T	F
P	T	K	J	M	U	I	H	T	V	F	R	Y	K	S	S	F
C	H	A	R	A	C	T	E	R	S	C	K	T	B	K	T	M
F	T	K	L	H	F	N	R	D	H	H	J	K	G	F	A	B
V	A	H	C	J	L	A	E	D	G	I	Y	O	R	M	N	S
D	K	P	R	T	E	W	N	C	R	L	G	D	I	J	D	M
G	I	I	L	F	D	S	H	G	T	A	H	F	P	K	I	N
M	N	J	M	C	C	A	T	U	P	R	J	G	P	L	N	B
B	G	M	I	E	L	E	C	T	R	I	F	Y	I	N	G	V
A	T	E	J	T	I	O	A	T	I	O	R	S	N	G	B	C
P	R	D	N	G	J	P	W	F	K	U	B	D	G	M	R	L
L	E	C	B	B	N	P	E	G	M	S	N	F	J	A	E	O
O	W	S	C	I	E	N	C	E	F	I	C	T	I	O	N	I

ANSWERS

Y	J	F	B	J	J	X	**A**	G	N	L	K	D	S	H	V	H
V	N	P	U	**S**	D	A	**T**	M	N	G	H	O	**P**	P	P	V
A	**B**	S	L	**I**	H	N	**M**	**O**	**V**	**I**	**N**	**G**	**L**	M	C	D
U	**R**	I	P	**T**	M	C	**O**	A	S	F	G	J	**O**	B	L	C
L	**E**	K	B	**C**	A	E	**S**	U	Y	L	P	W	**T**	W	**U**	C
A	**A**	P	W	**O**	U	N	**P**	L	M	N	B	H	U	Y	**T**	F
P	**T**	K	J	**M**	U	I	**H**	T	V	F	R	Y	K	S	**S**	F
C	H	A	R	A	C	T	**E**	R	S	C	K	T	B	K	**T**	M
F	**T**	K	L	H	F	N	**R**	D	H	**H**	J	K	**G**	F	**A**	B
V	**A**	H	C	J	L	A	**E**	D	G	**I**	Y	O	**R**	M	**N**	S
D	**K**	P	R	T	E	W	N	C	R	**L**	G	D	**I**	J	**D**	M
G	**I**	I	L	F	D	S	H	G	T	**A**	H	F	**P**	K	**I**	N
M	**N**	J	M	C	C	A	T	U	P	**R**	J	G	**P**	L	**N**	B
B	**G**	M	I	**E**	**L**	**E**	**C**	**T**	**R**	**I**	**F**	**Y**	**I**	**N**	**G**	V
A	T	E	J	T	I	O	A	T	I	**O**	R	S	**N**	G	B	C
P	R	D	N	G	J	P	W	F	K	**U**	B	D	**G**	M	R	L
L	E	C	B	B	N	P	E	G	M	**S**	N	F	J	A	E	O
O	W	**S**	**C**	**I**	**E**	**N**	**C**	**E**	**F**	**I**	**C**	**T**	**I**	**O**	**N**	I

'WHY DID FILMING STOP TODAY?'

ROLE CARDS

You are the Director:	'The Leading Actor is like a child and he just walked out. He won't let me direct.'
You are the Leading Actor:	'The Director isn't any good. She tries to make me look stupid. And I had to leave to meet my friend for dinner.'
You are the Supporting Actor:	'I can't work with the Leading Actor. He's like a child. I think I should be the lead.'
You are the Producer	'There are problems with the Director and the Leading Actor. They hate each other.'
You are the Screenplay Writer:	'The Leading Actor doesn't like the words I gave him to say. So, I'm writing another screenplay.'
You are the Financier:	'I'm not sure. Do you know why? I know we don't have any money for another day's filming.'
You are the Casting Agent:	'I didn't choose the right Leading Actor for the Director. I'll have to find another actor.'
You are the music Composer:	'I don't know why filming stopped. Can you tell me?'
You are the Camera Person:	'I'm not sure. But I think here's been a problem between the Producer and the Director.'
You are the Assistant Director:	'I don't know. I'm trying to find out why. Maybe the Casting Agent made a mistake choosing the actors.'

NOTES SHEET

Director	
Leading Actor	
Supporting Actor	
Producer	
Screenplay Writer	
Financier	
Casting Agent	
Composer	
Camera Person	
Assistant Director	

A word to describe when money is stolen from a bank	A person whose job it is to represent/defend a suspect in court
The marks the police look for at a crime scene. These marks are made with the fingers	A person who argues in a court the reasons why a suspect is guilty
A person who steals things from another person or place	A person who steals money from a bank
A word to describe when criminals drive off very quickly in a car	Taking someone by force and asking other people to give money to give them back
Someone the police believe has committed a crime but they are not completely sure yet	When a criminal has taken someone by force, a word to describe the money they ask for
A person a criminal takes as a prisoner in order to get money or to stop police catching them	A person whose job it is to represent/defend a criminal in an American court

CRIME TRENDS COMPARISON

CRIME TRENDS

Look at the pie charts below showing crime trends in a particular region of the UK in 1999 and 2001. Discuss the questions below the charts.

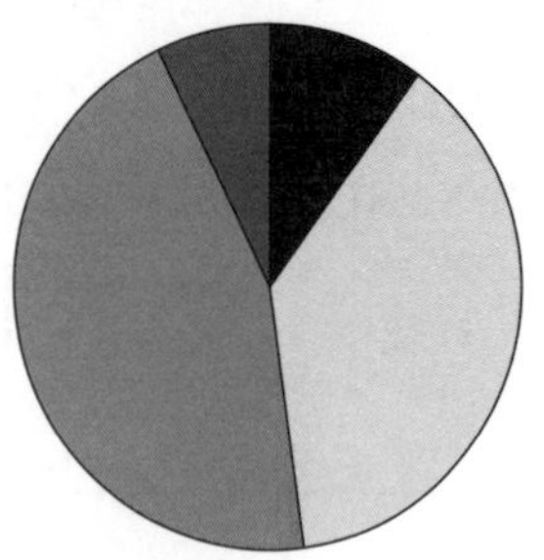

1999 – % of total crimes reported
- bank robbery – 10%
- mugging – 38%
- house burglary – 45%
- assault – 7%

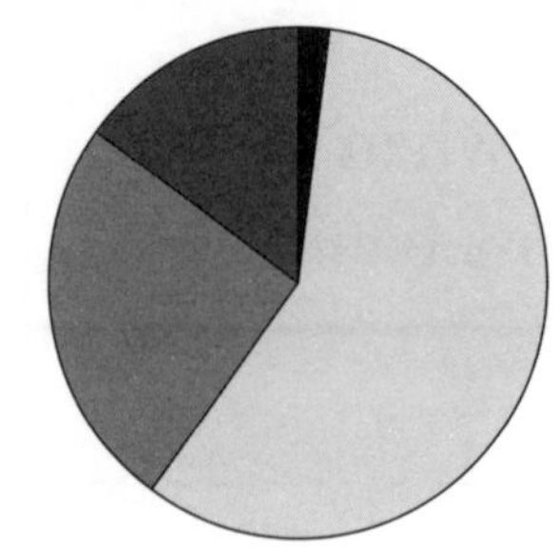

2001 – % of total crimes reported
- bank robbery – 2%
- mugging – 58%
- house burglary – 25%
- assault – 15%

 bank robbery  mugging  house burglary  assault

Questions

1 Which crime fell the most?

2 Which crime increased the most?

Information card 1	
A: You have seen the figures for reported crime in 1999 and 2001. You have some ideas about why the figures have changed. Use the information below to write your ideas.	
Bank robbery	– maybe more security cameras in 2001 – maybe more police in the streets around banks in 2001 – maybe the police caught the robbers
House burglary	– maybe more alarms on people's houses, better locks on doors and window – maybe more police walking the streets at night
B: You are going to listen to your partner's ideas about mugging and assault. Interrupt your partner and give your opinion when necessary.	
Mugging	• Burglars began mugging – NOT POSSIBLE (because you know they're different people) • Street lighting not good – NO, YOU'RE SURE IT WAS GOOD (because government gave a lot of money to street lighting)
Assault	• More police on streets – YES, YOU'RE SURE (because government gave more money for police in 2000)

Information card 2	
A: You have seen the figures for reported crime in 1999 and 2001. You have some ideas about why the figures have changed. Use the information below to write your ideas.	
Mugging	– maybe burglars stopped burgling houses and began mugging people – maybe people carried more mobile phones, money, etc. in 2001 – maybe street lighting not as good at night in 2001
Assault	– maybe more muggings = more assault in 2001 – maybe victims fight muggers more in 2001 – maybe more police on the streets
B: You are going to listen to your partner's ideas about bank robbery and house burglary. Interrupt your partner and give your opinion when necessary.	
Bank robbery	• More security cameras – YES, YOU'RE SURE (because you saw more videos produced in 2001) • Police caught the robbers – NOT POSSIBLE (because there weren't more robbers in prison at the end of 2001)
House burglary	• More alarms, better locks – YES, YOU'RE SURE (because there was a TV advertisement about security in 2000)